Criminal procedure
in magistrates' courts

Criminal procedure in magistrates' courts

A. P. Carr, MA (Cantab)
Barrister, Deputy Clerk
to the Peterborough Justices

London
Butterworths
1983

England	Butterworth & Co (Publishers) Ltd, 88 Kingsway, LONDON WC2B 6AB
Australia	Butterworths Pty Ltd, SYDNEY, MELBOURNE, BRISBANE, ADELAIDE and PERTH
Canada	Butterworth & Co (Canada) Ltd, TORONTO Butterworth & Co (Western Canada) Ltd, VANCOUVER
New Zealand	Butterworths of New Zealand Ltd, WELLINGTON
Singapore	Butterworth & Co (Asia) Pte Ltd, SINGAPORE
South Africa	Butterworth Publishers (Pty) Ltd, DURBAN
USA	Mason Publishing Co, ST PAUL, Minnesota Butterworth Legal Publishers, SEATTLE, Washington; BOSTON, Massachusetts; and AUSTIN, Texas D & S Publishers, CLEARWATER, Florida

Carr, A. P.
Criminal procedure in magistrates' courts.
1. Procedure (Law)—England 2. Courts—England
3. Police magistrates—England
I. Title
344.205'12 KD7309

ISBN 0-406-01067-6

Typeset by Phoenix Photosetting, Chatham
Printed by Mackays of Chatham Ltd

Preface

The law of criminal procedure was, until comparatively recently, a neglected subject. The main works on the subject: *Archbold's Criminal Pleading and Practice*, and *Stone's Justices' Manual* are comprehensive and excellent in themselves but perhaps somewhat forbidding to the person coming fresh to the subject. Criminal procedure as it is taught for professional qualifications has a heavy emphasis on the superior courts: the Crown Court, the High Court and the Court of Appeal. However, for the newly-qualified solicitor or barrister the most pressing problem will be how to acquaint himself with procedure in the magistrates' court. The vast bulk of all criminal litigation is conducted in the magistrates' courts and the procedural problems which can be encountered there can be no less difficult than in the Crown Court.

The aim of this book is to present, in narrative form, a description of procedure in the magistrates' court when dealing with criminal cases. The narrative form has been adopted because it is less difficult for the person unfamiliar with the subject to follow the various steps in the procedure. Nevertheless, no apology is made for the number of footnotes in the text since, as every advocate knows or soon will know, it is no use putting forward a proposition without some authority to support it. The footnotes provide some authority for most propositions in the text and for this purpose recourse has been made to authorities reported only in the *Criminal Law Review* where no better authority exists. Where the view put forward is merely that of the author, this has been made clear so that the reader may accept or reject it as he wishes. The intention is that the reader should be able to obtain an intelligent understanding of the broad outlines of the subject with an insight into some of the practical problems to be encountered, and that he should be encouraged to progress to a further study of the subject in the pages of *Stone's Justices' Manual*.

I would like to acknowledge the considerable contribution which has been made to this book by John Spencer, Fellow of Selwyn College Cambridge. His encouragement and perceptive criticism have helped immeasurably in shaping some of the arguments in this book. I would also especially wish to thank Syd Taylor without whose wizardry with the typewriter and sharp eye the publisher's task would have been much more difficult.

I would wish to express my appreciation to Messrs Hutchinson & Co for permission to reproduce from their publication *Keeping The Peace* and also the Home Office for permission to reproduce the extract from *Sentence of the Court* in chapter 14.

The law is stated generally as it was on 1 October 1983, and therefore includes the provisions of the Criminal Justice Act 1982 and the Mental Health Act 1983, except those sections which have not been brought into effect at the time of writing. These are noted in the text where appropriate.

The difficulties of the writer were compounded by the chequered history of the Police and Criminal Evidence Bill. At the time that chapter 2 was written it was still not clear whether the Bill would become law, and of course the subsequent General Election caused it to lapse. It is expected that the Bill will be reintroduced in October, but in view of the stormy passage of the previous Bill it is not yet certain what form the new Bill will take.

Finally, the Lord Chancellor's Department is in the course of preparing draft regulations to enable further provisions of the Legal Aid Act 1982 to be implemented and a brief description of these proposals is contained in an Appendix to this book.

A. P. Carr

Peterborough
September 1983

Contents

Table of Cases

Cases are listed under the name of the accused whenever the usual method of citation would cause them to be preceded by "R v" indicating that the prosecution was undertaken by the Crown. Page references printed in bold type indicate that a Practice Direction has been set out in full.

PAGE

Table of Statutes

References in this Table to *Statutes* are to Halsbury's Statutes of England (Third Edition) showing the volume and page at which the annotated text of the Act will be found. Page references printed in bold type indicate where a section is set out in part or in full.

Chapter 1

Preliminary matters

The purpose of this chapter is to describe briefly the organisational background to magistrates' courts and general matters concerning the hearing of a summary case. It is almost inevitable that a chapter such as this will include a collection of matters which are more conveniently dealt with in isolation from the general description of the criminal process and therefore, like many introductions, there is no harm in leaving it alone until the rest of the book has been digested.

The magistrates and their courts

THE COMMISSION OF THE PEACE[1]

A magistrate derives his judicial authority from his name being included on the commission of the peace. The Sovereign acting through the Lord Chancellor[2] decides who shall be placed on the commission and to help him in his selection he will act on the recommendations of various Advisory Committees. The identity of members of a Committee is secret except for the secretary to the Committee. The names of candidates for appointment are forwarded by the interested parties to a clerk to the justices who sends them to the secretary to the Advisory Committee.

There is a commission of the peace for each county, each of the London commission areas and the City of London.[3] Therefore in any one county all the magistrates would be on the same commission.

Within a county or London commission area (but not the City of London)[4] there may be several petty sessional divisions which are the smaller administrative parts of the whole commission area.[5] To be appointed to a commission, a magistrate must reside in the commission

1 The law on the appointment and organisation of magistrates and their courts is to be found in the Justices of the Peace Act 1979 (referred to in the notes as JPA 1979).

2 JPA 1979, s 6. In Merseyside, Greater Manchester and Lancashire it is the Chancellor of the Duchy of Lancaster who is responsible for appointments.

3 JPA 1979, ss 1–3.

4 Ibid, s 42.

5 Ibid, s 4.

area or within 15 miles of the boundary[6] and he must retire on reaching 70 years of age.[7] When he is appointed he will be assigned to one of the petty sessional divisions in his commission area and will normally fulfil his judicial functions for that division, although he does have legal authority to act in any part of his commission area.

STIPENDIARY MAGISTRATES

Most magistrates' courts are composed of a bench of lay justices, but there is power under the Justices of the Peace Act 1979 for the Crown to appoint professionally qualified salaried magistrates, known as stipendiary magistrates outside London and metropolitan stipendiary magistrates in London. These magistrates must be barristers or solicitors of not less than seven years' standing and they are by virtue of their office a justice of the peace for the commission area for which they are appointed (or in London, for each of the London commission areas and for the counties of Essex, Hertfordshire, Kent and Surrey). In a petty sessions court the most important distinction between a stipendiary magistrate and a lay bench is that the stipendiary will usually sit on his own to determine cases (both trials and guilty pleas) with the exception of granting or transferring a licence.[8]

Although the Act provides for the appointment of up to 40 stipendiary and 60 metropolitan stipendiary magistrates, full use has not yet been made of these powers and so for the advocate outside London, advocacy before a stipendiary is still very much the exception.

PROTECTION OF JUSTICES[9]

A defendant may appeal against the decision of the magistrates but he may also wish to sue them for damages. In considering whether such an action will lie a distinction may be drawn between acts done by the magistrates within their jurisdiction and acts done in excess or out of their jurisdiction. An example of an act done within their jurisdiction might be where a bench hears an application for a remand in custody by the police and grants the application without allowing the accused to be heard. This would be an improper course of action by the bench but in remanding the accused in custody they would not be acting outside their jurisdiction; they would be exercising their jurisdiction in an improper way. On the other hand the magistrates might exceed their jurisdiction by, for example, hearing and determining an information laid after the time limit had expired.

6 Ibid, s 7.
7 Ibid, s 8.
8 Cf JPA 1979, ss 13–16 for stipendiaries outside London and ss 31–34 for metropolitan stipendiary magistrates.
9 JPA 1979, Part V.

The Justices of the Peace Act 1979[10] provides that if a cause of action exists it shall be a tort on the case and if the act complained of is done within the jurisdiction the plaintiff must allege malice or absence of reasonable and probable cause. If the magistrates are alleged to have acted in excess or outside of their jurisdiction, these allegations of ill-will are not necessary.[11] An example perhaps of an act in excess of jurisdiction might be the issuing of a warrant of commitment for a fine which had already been paid.

However, the Act leaves it open whether there is a right to sue the justices at all. In the latest authority on the matter[12] Lord Denning (together with Ormrod LJ) took the view that no right of action lay against justices who were acting within their jurisdiction and that section 44 of the Justices of the Peace Act 1979 was not really necessary as the common law had developed since its progenitor, the Justices Protection Act 1848 had been enacted so that justices had immunity (even if they had in fact acted with malice). The defendant's remedy was by way of appeal which, especially in view of legal aid, was more readily available today. For gross abuse the justice could be removed from office.

Where the allegation concerned an act done in excess of or outside the jurisdiction it was felt that the justice should not be held liable if he does his work in the honest belief that it is within his jurisdiction.

> What he does may be outside his jurisdiction – in fact or in law – but so long as he honestly believes it to be within his jurisdiction, he should not be liable.[13]

Although this may be the legal position, a magistrates' courts committee may consider an application for compensation in an appropriate case, more in the way of an ex gratia payment.

Apart from the provisions mentioned above, Part V of the Act also makes special provisions for immunity in certain situations. If a justice were to be sued he could insist on trial in the High Court[14] and where he has become involved in litigation he may be (and must be where he had acted reasonably) indemnified by the magistrates' courts committee.[15]

PETTY SESSIONAL DIVISIONS

The commission area will have been divided into petty sessional divisions and all the magistrates for a division will constitute the 'bench' for that division. From their number they will elect a chairman

10 S 44.
11 JPA 1979, s 45.
12 *Sirros v Moore* [1975] QB 118, [1974] 3 All ER 776.
13 Ibid, p. 136 and p. 785.
14 JPA 1979, s 51.
15 Ibid, s 53.

and a number of deputy chairmen[16] and amongst their other duties they will appoint their representatives to the magistrates' courts committee.

Each petty sessional division consists of a bench of magistrates assigned to sit in that particular division of the commission area. It will have at least one court house where it will conduct its business on a regular basis. In addition the justices may appoint a place to be an 'occasional court house'[17] but their powers are limited when they are sitting in such a court house.[18] In addition to the court house the magistrates' courts committee will have provided the bench with administrative staff and a clerk to the justices.

THE MAGISTRATES' COURTS COMMITTEE

Each commission area will have its magistrates' courts committee[19] composed almost entirely of justices from the petty sessional divisions in its commission area.[20] The functions of this Committee are inter alia to provide the equipment and the accommodation for the various magistrates' courts and to appoint the justices' clerks and their staff. The funding to do this comes 20% from the local authority and 80% from the Home Office.

THE CLERK TO THE JUSTICES

The clerk to the justices has an administrative and a legal function. The volume of work passing through a magistrates' court can be quite considerable. Not only is there the criminal work to consider, but also there is the work derived from the justices' jurisdiction over licensing matters and their domestic jurisdiction, including, of course, the collecting and payment of money under maintenance orders. To cope with the enormous amount of paper work which is created, the clerk to the justices may well have a large administrative staff. One administrative official who is of direct importance to an advocate is the person responsible for the listing of the cases to appear in a court on a given day. In the larger courts there may be a member of staff whose main function is to ensure that there are enough courts scheduled for a particular day to cope with the case load. Furthermore, he will have to ensure that there is neither too much nor too little work in each court.

16 Ibid, s 17 and the Justices of the Peace (Size and Chairmanship of the Bench) Rules 1964.

17 Magistrates' Courts Act 1980 (referred to in the notes as MCA 1980), s 147.

18 To 14 days' imprisonment or a £1 fine. All the justices' business may be conducted in a petty sessional court house but the range of business in an occasional court house is limited (MCA 1980, s 121(3)).

19 Unless there is a composite committee for two areas.

20 JPA 1979, s 20 and the Magistrates' Courts Committee (Constitution) Rules 1973.

If a solicitor who is representing a client who has pleaded not guilty to a charge and whose case has been scheduled to last half a day in court, finds that for some genuine reason the case cannot proceed on that day he should inform the court and the other party as soon as possible. If this is done in time it may be possible to reprogramme the court, and therefore the court may have little objection to an adjournment, but if the solicitor simply turns up on the appointed day and, without warning, informs the court that he is not ready to proceed he will meet with a very icy reception indeed and the court might be inclined to let the case proceed in any event. Every solicitor should, therefore, always be at pains to help the court listing by providing reliable estimates of the length of time required for a not guilty hearing or by giving plenty of advance notice that there will be a request for an adjournment of an otherwise lengthy matter.

The other aspect of the justices' clerk's duties is to provide his magistrates with legal advice. The justices do receive some basic training in law and procedural matters but they naturally rely heavily on their clerk for his legal advice. The clerk to the justices is appointed by the magistrates' courts committee and must be a barrister or solicitor of not less than five years' standing.[1] In any court but the smallest, a justices' clerk could not expect to sit in every petty sessional court for the magistrates to ask him for his advice, and although in theory a bench of magistrates could sit without a clerk, in practice this would never happen. Accordingly, the justices' clerk will have a deputy clerk and perhaps several assistants who are qualified to sit in court and advise the magistrates on the law. These assistants (known as court clerks) must themselves be either barristers or solicitors, or be qualified in accordance with the Justices' Clerks (Qualification of Assistants) Rules 1979. Even if a bench is being advised by a court clerk they may still ask the clerk to the justices to attend on them and advise them on a particular case.[2]

Proceedings in the court room

A summary trial or committal proceedings must generally be held in open court[3] before two or three magistrates for a trial,[4] or one or more magistrates for committal proceedings.[5] In front of the bench will be the court clerk and in front of him the prosecutor and the defence solicitor.

1 JPA 1979, s 26.
2 Ibid, s 28(2).
3 MCA 1980, s 121(4).
4 Ibid, s 121(1).
5 Ibid, s 4(1).

THE BENCH

There must be at least two and in practice not more than three magistrates to hear an information.[6] The justices are lay persons and there is the need to ensure that their outside activities do not compromise a fair hearing. Accordingly, justices may be disqualified from sitting in certain cases. There are several principles for deciding whether a magistrate should adjudicate on a particular case.[7]

(a) By statute a justice who is a member of a local authority cannot sit on a case involving that local authority as a litigant.[8]
(b) A justice cannot sit on a case in which he has a pecuniary interest.[9]
(c) A justice should not sit if a reasonable onlooker would conclude that there was a reasonable likelihood of bias[10] (note it is the impression of bias that is created, not whether there was in fact actual bias in the case, which disqualifies the magistrate).

In practice the situations which are common are where the justice is a member of a local council which is involved in a case, or where a justice knows a witness or defendant personally. Magistrates are usually punctilious in declaring an interest. If they have any doubt they will declare their interest to the parties who may well decide that, unless the justice is disqualified by statute, or has a pecuniary interest, they wish to proceed.

A problem may also be posed by the justice who knows that the accused has previous convictions. If a magistrate has sat on remand proceedings in a case and for the purpose of making the decision whether the remand should be in custody or on bail he has been informed of the defendant's previous convictions, he is then disqualified from sitting on the summary trial of an information.[11] In smaller courts in particular, the situation often arises where the bench know a particular defendant not as a personal friend but because they have seen him on many previous occasions before the court, in fact he is a 'regular'. In law there is no rule against a justice sitting on such a case as this[12] (in fact if there was such a prohibition in a small court with a regular clientele the judicial system would soon be paralysed),

6 The Justices of the Peace (Size and Chairmanship of Bench) Rules 1964. The maximum number is seven.
7 See generally R. D. S. Stevens *Bias and Impartiality in Magistrates' Courts* (Barry Rose).
8 See JPA 1979, s 64.
9 *Metropolitan Properties v Lannon* [1969] 1 QB 577, [1968] 3 All ER 304.
10 *R v Altrincham Justices, ex p Pennington* [1975] QB 549, [1975] 2 All ER 78 (where a justice was disqualified because he was a member of the complainant education authority) and *R v Abingdon Justices, ex p Cousins* [1965] Crim LR 43, DC where the chairman of the bench was the defendant's headmaster who had previously written an adverse report on him, and so the conviction was quashed.
11 MCA 1980, s 42
12 *R v Metropolitan Stipendiary Magistrate, ex p Gallagher* (1972) 136 JP Jo 80.

although of course if such frequent meetings between a particular bench of magistrates and a defendant can be avoided, so much the better. In an extension of this principle it is not improper for a bench to hear several not guilty hearings concerning the same individual one after the other although this should be avoided if possible.[13]

When the bench of lay magistrates is sitting in a court, one of their number will be the chairman of that bench (though he is not necessarily the chairman or a deputy chairman of the bench as a whole) and all remarks made by the bench will be made through him. The other magistrates should remain silent except when consulting with their chairman. The advocate will address the bench either collectively as 'your worships' or the chairman alone as 'Sir' or 'M'am'.

THE CLERK

In front of them the justices will have their clerk. His main duty is to advise the magistrates on any points of law which occur in the course of the hearing. From the following chapters in this book it will become apparent that procedure in the magistrates' court is not only complicated, but can also demand that a certain amount of speaking be done by the court itself: the defendant will have the charge read to him, the election whether to be tried summarily or on indictment with a warning about committal for sentence will have to be given in the case of an either way offence, and, especially with an unrepresented accused, there may well have to be a large amount of dialogue between the court and the defendant, prosecutor and witnesses. Although a large part of procedure in magistrates' courts is regulated by the Magistrates' Courts Rules 1981 the justices have an inherent power to regulate their own procedure in court and consequently the allocation of the speaking roles between the bench and their clerk will vary from bench to bench, depending on the confidence of the magistrates and the usual practice adopted in their courts. Nevertheless, the clerk is in a sensitive position because he is there in an advisory capacity and there is a danger that he might assume a too dominant role in the proceedings. It must be clear at all times that it is the magistrates who are making the decisions and not the clerk.

The role of the clerk is partly defined by statute:

Justices of the Peace Act 1979, section 28

(3) It is hereby declared that the functions of a justices' clerk include the giving to the justices to whom he is clerk or any of them, at the request of the justices or justice, of advice about law, practice or procedure on questions arising in connection with the discharge of their or his functions, including questions arising when the clerk is not personally attending on

13 *R v Sandwich Justices, ex p Berry* (1981) 74 Cr App Rep 132 and see also *R v Liverpool City Justices, ex p Topping* [1983] 1 All ER 490, [1983] 1 WLR 119.

the justices or justice, and that the clerk may, at any time when he thinks he should do so, bring to the attention of the justices or justice any point of law, practice or procedure that is or may be involved in any question so arising.

In this subsection the reference to the functions of justices or a justice is a reference to any of their or his functions as justices or a justice of the peace, other than functions as a judge of the Crown Court.

(4) The enactment of subsection (3) above shall not be taken as defining or in any respect limiting the powers and duties belonging to a justices' clerk or the matters on which justices may obtain assistance from their clerk.

and further guidance is contained in Practice Directions in 1953 and 1981[14] the latter of which is given in full below:

Practice Direction

1. A justices' clerk is responsible to the justices for the performance of any of the functions set out below by any member of his staff acting as court clerk and may be called in to advise the justices even when he is not personally sitting with the justices as clerk to the court.

2. It shall be the responsibility of the justices' clerk to advise the justices as follows: (a) on questions of law or of mixed law and fact; (b) as to matters of practice and procedure.

3. If it appears to him necessary to do so, or he is so requested by the justices, the justices' clerk has the responsibility to (a) refresh the justices' memory as to any matter of evidence and to draw attention to any issues involved in the matters before the court, (b) advise the justices generally on the range of penalties which the law allows them to impose and on any guidance relevant to the choice of penalty provided by the law, the decisions of the superior courts or other authorities. If no request for advice has been made by the justices, the justices' clerk shall discharge his responsibility in the presence of the parties.

4. The way in which the justices' clerk should perform his functions should be stated as follows. (a) The justices are entitled to the advice of their clerk when they retire in order that the clerk may fulfil his responsibility outlined above. (b) Some justices may prefer to take their own notes of evidence. There is, however, no obligation on them to do so. Whether they do so or not, there is nothing to prevent them from enlisting the aid of their clerk and his notes if they are in any doubts as to the evidence which has been given. (c) If the justices wish to consult their clerk solely about the evidence or his notes of it, this should ordinarily, and certainly in simple cases, be done in open court. The object is to avoid any suspicion that the clerk has been involved in deciding issues of fact.

5. For the reasons stated in the *Practice Direction* of 15th January 1954, [1954] 1 All ER 230, [1954] 1 WLR 213, which remains in full force and effect, in domestic proceedings it is more likely than not that the justices will wish to consult their clerk. In particular, where rules of court require the reasons for their decision to be drawn up in consultation with the clerk, they will need to receive his advice for this purpose.

14 [1981] 2 All ER 831, [1981] 1 WLR 1163.

6. This Practice Direction is issued with the concurrence of the President of the Family Division.

2nd July 1981. LANE CJ.

In the magistrates' courts procedure may of necessity have to be less formal than in the Crown Court and so the clerk may have to intervene to assist the course of justice when dealing with an unrepresented defendant. But he should not intervene to act as an advocate assisting one party against another, he is there to assist the bench by ensuring that both parties present their case properly and to clear up any ambiguities.[15] It is also quite clear that he may interrupt the proceedings if necessary to draw the magistrates' attention to a matter of law, and indeed where a point involving the admissibility of evidence is concerned, he may have to be very alert. However, although he is the justices' legal adviser, he may not himself decide points of law although it is accepted that the magistrates would normally follow his advice and would indeed be very unwise not to do so.[16] There has been one extension of the justices' clerk's duties concerning the regulating of the course of evidence in that in a trial involving an unrepresented defendant where he is in danger of losing his shield under section 1(f) of the Criminal Evidence Act 1898 because of the manner of his questioning prosecution witnesses, the clerk should ask the magistrates to retire and together with the prosecutor he should explain to the defendant that he is running the risk of having his previous convictions made known to the magistrates.[17]

The cases on the subject of the role of the clerk can perhaps be divided into two categories each with the common theme that the justices' clerk should not appear to be influencing the magistrates in their decision. The first category concerns the clerk who is seen to misbehave in court by, for example, passing a note to the bench pointing out evidence prejudicial to the accused,[18] but most cases concern the second category, where there is no direct evidence of any improper conduct by the clerk but an impression is gained by an onlooker that he is influencing their decision. This raises the vexed question of whether the clerk should retire with the magistrates. In the light of the Practice Direction and the reported cases there are two desiderata for the clerk:

(a) only advise on the law;
(b) give advice in open court.

As every justices' clerk will know, however, this is often (and usually) impossible. The clerk should certainly only advise on the law

15 *Simms v Moore* [1970] 2 QB 327, [1970] 3 All ER 1.
16 *Jones v Nicks* [1977] RTR 72.
17 *R v Weston-Super-Mare Justices, ex p Townsend* [1968] 3 All ER 225, (1968) 132 JP 526.
18 *R v Stafford Borough Justices, ex p Ross* [1962] 1 All ER 540, [1962] 1 WLR 456.

but very often it is not possible to give a short statement of legal principle because the advice will be inextricably bound up with the facts found by the magistrates. Furthermore, in order to make their findings of fact, the magistrates may well require advice on the law of evidence whether they appreciate this or not. Accordingly, the clerk will need to be present in the retiring room to offer his advice at various stages of the magistrates' discussion. In addition, as any advocate will be aware, the law of sentencing has seen a tremendous growth in the past few years. To pass a sentence of imprisonment, for example, requires the bench to traverse a veritable minefield of complex legal considerations for which it is essential that the clerk should give his advice, and it is submitted that this advice can only be given in the retiring room in order to avoid an unseemly debate on the various sentencing options open to the court in front of the accused himself. Even general considerations of sentencing practice may call for advice from the clerk – for example what is the average penalty for the particular offence with which the bench is concerned or what guidelines on sentencing have been given by the superior courts.

The law at present is that the clerk may only enter the retiring room if requested to do so[19] and otherwise must remain in court and give his advice in open court. But if he is invited into the retiring room, he should remain there only for as long as necessary which, in complicated cases, may be for the whole of the retirement period. It is submitted that in all cases, even where he has been invited into the retiring room, the clerk should inform the advocates at least, of the advice he has given on a pure matter of law so that if he is wrong he may be corrected, or if there is a dispute the parties will be able to appeal as they will know the basis on which the magistrates reached their decision.

THE COURT ROOM

There are no regulations governing the size and layout of a court room and they may range in size from a vast hall to a small room the size of a domestic lounge. The size of the court room does have some importance, however, in that court proceedings are generally held in open court, that is to say that members of the general public have a right to be admitted.[20] The major statutory exceptions to this are where the court is sitting as a juvenile court[1] (or is hearing domestic proceedings) or is sitting as examining justices and where the ends of justice would not be served by sitting in open court.[2]

19 Cf *R v East Kerrier Justices, ex p Mundy* [1952] 2 QB 719, [1952] 2 All ER 144, nor should he retire with the justices as a matter of course. *R v Southampton Justices, ex p Atherton* [1974] Crim LR 108, (1973) 137 JP 571, DC.
20 MCA 1980, s 121(4).
1 Children and Young Persons Act 1933, s 47.
2 MCA 1980, s 4. Note also the restrictions on publishing the names of the complainant and defendant in rape cases by virtue of the Sexual Offences (Amendment) Act 1976, and the restriction on publishing the names of children under s 39 of the Children and Young Persons Act 1933.

The general principle is that the parties (and members of the public) should be able to see and hear what is going on.[3] For this purpose the court room should be provided with an adequate number of seats having regard to the facilities available. However, every court has the inherent right to exclude the public if this is necessary for the administration of justice.[4] For example, the court can exclude troublemakers by force if need be[5] (or perhaps even long-winded advocates).[6] The public may even be excluded if their presence would hinder or prevent a witness from giving evidence.[7] But because of the necessity for justice to be seen to be done, the circumstances are rare when the court would need to sit in camera and if such an application is made, although it may be made in the absence of the public, the justices must announce their decision in open court.[8]

Photographs
Although the magistrates may be sitting in open court it is an offence to take a photograph or sketch of proceedings in a court room.[9]

Tape recorders
It is a contempt of court to use a tape recorder (other than for the purpose of making an official transcript) in a court without the leave of the court.[10] Guidelines for the decision whether to grant leave were given in a *Practice Direction*[11] which may be summarised thus:

(a) has the applicant a reasonable need to use the tape recorder?
(b) is there a risk of a recording being used to brief witnesses?
(c) what is the possibility of distracting proceedings, or distracting or worrying witnesses?

The advocates

RIGHTS OF AUDIENCE

The magistrates have a discretion to allow anyone to appear in their court as an advocate even if he is not the informant or the defendant, nor is there any limit on that discretion. The discretion is not confined

3 *R v Denbigh Justices, ex p Williams* [1974] QB 759, [1974] 2 All ER 1052.
4 *R v Denbigh Justices; Scott v Scott* [1913] AC 417.
5 *R v Butt* (1957) 41 Cr App Rep 82.
6 *The Times* 21 January 1899.
7 *Moosbrugger v Moosbrugger* (1913) 109 LJ 744.
8 *R v Ealing Justices, ex p Weafer* [1982] Crim LR 182; *R v Reigate JJ, ex p Argus Newspapers* [1983] Crim LR 564.
9 Criminal Justice Act 1925, s 41.
10 Contempt of Court Act 1981, s 9. (but it is not a contempt of court which can be *dealt* with by a magistrates' court).
11 [1982] Crim LR 253.

to cases where it is a strict necessity for another person to represent a party to the proceedings, but it is a proper exercise of the discretion whenever it would secure or promote convenience and expedition and efficiency in the administration of justice.[12] On the other hand a party is entitled to be represented by a barrister or solicitor. The position is therefore that a person has a right to be represented by a barrister or solicitor but he may only be represented by another lay person if the court exercises its discretion in his favour.[13]

THE PROSECUTOR

Who is the prosecutor?

The simple answer to this question would be to say that it is the informant. Most prosecutions are brought by the police and to any observer of the magistrates' court for a particular district it would appear that the chief constable or one of his senior officers was a very busy man because he would appear to be the informant in every case. In practice, a constable who detected an offence would forward a report of the case to his superior officer, such as an inspector, who would decide whether a prosecution would be initiated. This superior officer would in effect become the informant in the case although even here the chief constable may have appointed just one officer to act as the informant in all cases. Although his name would appear on all the informations and summonses it is recognised that he is acting on behalf of the chief constable and the police force under his control, therefore if he were to die the proceedings would still carry on.[14]

Once the police have received information which would lead them to suspect that a crime has been committed they have a discretion whether to institute formal proceedings but they must examine the merits of each case and they are not entitled to have a blanket policy of not prosecuting a particular category of offence.[15]

Private prosecutors

There is nothing to prevent any person laying an information and becoming a prosecutor but in general most 'private prosecutions' are conducted by large government institutions such as the Department of Health and Social Security or local authorities. Private individuals rarely institute proceedings and this is not surprising because to institute a private prosecution requires some legal knowledge and can

12 *O'Toole v Scott* [1965] AC 939, [1965] 2 All ER 240 and *Simms v Moore* [1970] 2 QB 327, [1970] 3 All ER 1.

13 See *Simms v Moore* [1970] 2 QB 327, [1970] 3 All ER 1; for a discussion on the 'McKenzie friend' see C. T. Latham (1974) 138 JP 428.

14 *Hawkins v Bepey* [1980] 1 All ER 797, 144 JP 203.

15 See *R v Metropolitan Police Comr, ex p Blackburn* [1968] 1 All ER 763, [1968] 2 WLR 893.

be very expensive, especially if it is unsuccessful. Most people are content to have the police do their prosecuting for them. If the police do not consider a case worth prosecuting, an individual will not often take the risk himself.[16] In addition, the private prosecutor may find his prosecution in a more serious case taken over by the Director of Public Prosecutions with the sole intention of aborting the proceedings.

THE ATTORNEY-GENERAL AND THE DIRECTOR OF PUBLIC PROSECUTIONS

The Attorney-General is the senior law officer of the Crown and the Director of Public Prosecutions is a senior official appointed by the Home Secretary.

The Attorney-General is a political appointee and amongst his functions is to give or withhold his consent to prosecutions under certain enactments, usually matters which may be politically delicate such as offences contrary to section 8 of the Official Secrets Act 1911, section 1(2) of the Public Order Act 1936 and section 6 of the Race Relations Act 1965.[17]

The Director of Public Prosecutions is not a political appointment and his powers and duties are set out in the Prosecution of Offences Act 1979. His duties include prosecuting prescribed classes of cases in all the various criminal courts, including cases which appear to him to be of importance or difficulty.[18] In this way a degree of uniformity of approach can be achieved in the handling of serious offences.

The chief constable in a particular police area must notify the Director of Public Prosecutions (commonly referred to as the DPP) where there appears to him to be a prima facie case for proceeding in certain very serious matters, notably:

(a) cases of murder or abortion;
(b) where the chief constable thinks the advice of the DPP is desirable;
(c) where the consent of the Attorney-General, Solicitor-General or DPP is required before a prosecution can be initiated; and
(d) in addition the DPP has specified further serious matters about which he would wish to be consulted.[19]

A situation that can be overlooked in the magistrates' court is the

16 An exception to this is the offence of common assault (s 42 of the Offences Against the Person Act 1861) where people involved in a dispute with neighbours very often initiate proceedings themselves (with the frequent result being a binding over of all parties). The provisions of s 42 virtually ensure that the proceedings are a private prosecution.

17 See *Archbold* (41st edn) para 1–117.

18 Prosecution of Offences Act 1979, ss 2 and 3 and Prosecution of Offences Regulations 1978. The DPP may even intervene purely for the purpose of aborting the proceedings; cf *Raymond v A-G* [1982] Crim LR 826.

19 Listed in the footnote to reg 6 of the Prosecution of Offences Regulations 1978 in volume III of *Stone's*.

requirement in section 30(4) of the Theft Act 1968 that the consent of the DPP is required before a prosecution can be initiated for certain offences committed by one spouse against another.[20]

> Proceedings shall not be instituted against a person for any offence of stealing or doing unlawful damage to property which at the time of the offence belongs to that person's wife or husband, or for any attempt, incitement or conspiracy to commit such an offence, unless the proceedings are instituted by or with the consent of the Director of Public Prosecutions:
>
> Provided that –
>
> (a) this subsection shall not apply to proceedings against a person for an offence –
>
> (i) if that person is charged with committing the offence jointly with the wife or husband; or
>
> (ii) if by virtue of any judicial decree or order (wherever made) that person and the wife or husband are at the time of the offence under no obligation to cohabit.

If for any reason the requisite consent of either the Attorney-General or the DPP has not been obtained, any subsequent proceedings will be a nullity.[1] It would cause a considerable obstacle to the apprehension of criminals if the police had to wait until they had the required consent before they could arrest an accused or ask for a warrant, and so section 6 of the Prosecution of Offences Act 1979 provides that the requirement for consent does not preclude an arrest or remand for an offence before the consent is obtained.

Withdrawal of proceedings

Where a prosecution for any offence (even a purely summary one) is wholly withdrawn or is not proceeded with within a reasonable time and there is some ground for suspecting that there is no satisfactory reason for this, the clerk of the court is under a duty to notify this to the DPP.[2]

Companies

As every lawyer will know a company has a distinct personality of its own. Nevertheless it will still need an individual to come along to court to speak on its behalf.

20 See *Smith on Theft* (4th edn) paras 461–465 and *Woodley v Woodley* [1978] Crim LR 629 (consent not required when there was a matrimonial injunction in force requiring the husband not to enter the wife's house).

1 *R v Angel* [1968] 2 All ER 607, [1968] 1 WLR 669.

2 Prosecution of Offences Regulations 1978, r 9.

Statutory representative

Generally for proceedings in the magistrates' court a company will appoint a statutory representative under the provisions of section 33(6) of the Criminal Justice Act 1925 and Schedule 3, paragraph 8 to the Magistrates' Courts Act 1980. His appointment need not be under the seal of the corporation and a statement authorising the representative to act for the company signed by the managing director or any person having the management of the affairs of the company will be sufficient.

The statutory representative may:

(a) make a statement before examining justices in answer to the charge;
(b) consent to summary trial where appropriate; or
(c) enter a plea of guilty or not guilty on behalf of the company;

but in the interests of justice the court may allow the representative to mitigate on behalf of the company and will not usually confine him to the powers provided for in the Criminal Justice Act 1925.

Appearance by barrister or solicitor[3]

A company, like any other individual, may be represented by a barrister or solicitor who would not be under the same restrictions as the statutory representative and could therefore present the company's case more fully.

Lay representative

The discussion of the positions of statutory representatives and advocates is based on the law as it is generally understood but since the cases of *O'Toole v Scott*[4] and *Simms v Moore*[5] it will appear that the court has a discretion to allow anyone to appear for a company. Nevertheless the court would of course be concerned that the person before them has the authority of the company to represent them and that he is acting within the scope of that authority.

Representative for Magistrates' Courts Act procedure

A plea of guilty by letter under the procedure in section 12 of the Magistrates' Courts Act 1980 may be entered by a letter signed by a director or secretary of the company; there is no need for a formal statutory representative to be appointed.[6]

MODE OF TRIAL

Mode of trial proceedings for an either way offence are applicable equally to a defendant corporation as to an individual, but there are some important differences.

3 MCA 1980, s 122.
4 [1965] AC 939, [1965] 2 All ER 240.
5 [1970] 2 QB 327, [1970] 3 All ER 1.
6 MCA 1980, Sch 3, para 4.

A company cannot be committed for sentence under section 38 of the Magistrates' Courts Act 1980[7] and the justices must bear this in mind when considering mode of trial. If the bench decides that summary trial is appropriate, the representative would be asked whether the company consents to summary trial but if the company has neglected to send a representative the magistrates may proceed to summary trial without the company's consent (provided of course the defendant company has had adequate notice of the hearing). If the company is jointly charged with an individual for an either way offence however, the magistrates cannot proceed to summary trial without the consent of them both.

SERVICE OF NOTICES AND SUMMONSES

For the purpose of the service of these documents they may be served at the registered office of the company.[8]

SENTENCING

For obvious reasons the only sentences applicable to a corporation are a fine, compensation, or discharges. In road traffic cases which carry endorsement and disqualification the company may be fined but as it has no licence it cannot receive an endorsement or disqualification.

Interpreters

Where an accused is ignorant of the English language so that he is unable to follow the proceedings, the evidence at the trial must be translated for him.[9] There can be no derogation from this and it is up to the court to ensure that he understands the proceedings. Of course, if the accused, although he is a foreigner, does understand all or part of the proceedings, there need be no translation of the part of the proceedings that he does understand. If the solicitor has a client who does not understand English and he is unable to obtain an interpreter the police may have a list of interpreters who are available for court work.

An interpreter who is imployed in court will usually take a special interpreter's oath that he will translate matters to the best of his skill and understanding. The costs of using an interpreter can be ordered by the court to be paid out of central funds whether the offence is

7 Ibid, Sch 3, para 5.
8 R 99 (3) and (4) of the Magistrates' Courts Rules 1981.
9 See generally *R v Lee Kun* [1916] 1 KB 337.

indictable or purely summary and whether the accused is convicted or acquitted.[10]

Disturbances in court

In the day-to-day business of any magistrates' court it is inevitable that there will be cases of disturbance in court.

DISTURBANCE BY MEMBERS OF THE PUBLIC

Where a spectator causes a disturbance in court, the simplest remedy is usually for the offender to be ordered out of the court room and, if necessary, removed by a police officer or usher. If the disorderly behaviour is so bad that it amounts to a breach of the peace the offender may be bound over to keep the peace and if he does not acknowledge that he is bound over, he can be committed to prison for up to six months.[11]

An alternative remedy to the bind over is now available to magistrates under section 12 of the Contempt of Court Act 1981.

> 12(1) A magistrates' court has jurisdiction under this section to deal with any person who –
>
> (a) wilfully insults the justice or justices, any witness before or officer of the court, during his or their sitting or attendance in court or in going to or returning from the court; or
>
> (b) wilfully interrupts the proceedings of the court or otherwise misbehaves in court.
>
> (2) In any such case the court may order any officer of the court, or any constable, to take the offender into custody and detain him until the rising of the court; and the court may, if it thinks fit, commit the offender to custody for a specified period not exceeding one month or impose on him a fine not exceeding £500 or both.[12]
>
> (3)–(5) omitted.

If a person is committed for contempt, he will be committed to prison for a specified period of up to one month (or if he is aged 17–20 inclusive, to detention under section 9 of the Criminal Justice Act 1982).

It will be appreciated that the power to commit for contempt is a very great one and because of its summary nature there is a risk of abuse. Accordingly, the bench shall think carefully before invoking the procedure:[13] merely ejecting the culprit from court may be sufficient,

10 Administration of Justice Act 1973, s 17.
11 *Scott v Scott* [1913] AC 417, 29 TLR 520. *R v Denbigh Justices, ex p Williams* [1974] QB 759, [1974] 2 All ER 1052.
12 There is a limit of £50 for children and £200 for young persons.
13 See generally *Balogh v Crown Court at St Albans* [1974] 3 All ER 283, 138 JP 703.

but if proceedings for contempt are initiated the better course of action would be to detain the offender until the end of the court business when tempers may have cooled. The period of detention already suffered by then, and an apology, may suffice.

When considering a contempt the court must be satisfied beyond a reasonable doubt that the contempt took place and make it plain to the offender what the conduct is that is complained of. However, the vast majority of contempt proceedings will be concerned with behaviour in the face of the court and so there would usually be little difficulty about proof. If the court is satisfied that the offender was wilfully (ie intentionally) in contempt of court it may commit him, but once the offender is committed to custody the magistrates may revoke the committal of their own motion or on representations made to them by the offender to purge his contempt.

The offender who has been ordered to pay a fine or committed to custody may appeal against the fine or committal (but not the finding of fact on which it was based) to the Crown Court.[14] Legal aid will be available to a person in contempt proceedings.[15]

THE DISORDERLY DEFENDANT

In addition to the action outlined above, the court can continue the proceedings in the absence of the accused. Committal proceedings can be heard in the absence of the accused by virtue of section 4(4) of the Magistrates' Courts Act 1980 and so can mode of trial proceedings (section 18(3)). A trial of an information can also take place without the accused being present (section 11(1)). By virtue of section 122 of the Magistrates' Courts Act 1980, except in situations where the attendance of the accused is expressly required, he will be deemed not to be absent if he is represented by a solicitor or barrister. Apart from the examples quoted above, ie committal proceedings and mode of trial etc, the accused must also be present before a custodial sentence is imposed[16] and for sentences such as probation or community service he must consent to the making of an order. A disqualification from driving may be ordered in the absence of an accused but only where he has been given notice of the court's proposal to disqualify him.[17]

Process in Scotland and other parts of the United Kingdom

Problems can arise today especially in view of the increased mobility of

14 Contempt of Court Act 1981, s 12(5).
15 When s 13 of the Contempt of Court Act is brought into force.
16 MCA 1980, s 11(3).
17 Ibid, s 11(4).

the population, where an individual leaves the jurisdiction of an English court and travels to Scotland or Northern Ireland. Here is a brief description of the provisions governing the procedure for serving process and enforcing court orders between the various jurisdictions.

WARRANTS AND SUMMONSES

A warrant of arrest for a person charged with an offence issued in England and to be executed in Scotland or Northern Ireland may be executed there in the same way as a Scottish or Northern Irish warrant would be executed in its own country.[18] Where the offender has gone to the Isle of Man or the Channel Islands, the procedure under the Indictable Offences Act 1848 has to be used. This procedure involves the English court issuing the warrant and sending it to the appropriate court together with a declaration that the signature of the justice signing the warrant is authentic. The 'foreign' court will then indorse the warrant (or 'back' it) and it will then be executed.[19]

A summons issued in England for an offence may be served in Scotland or Northern Ireland in the same way as it could in England[20] (eg by post) and in the Isle of Man or Channel Islands by 'backing' it in the same way as a warrant.[1]

Where a warrant is issued for execution in Scotland or Northern Ireland but it is not for an offence, the warrant must be 'backed' in the same way as a warrant for an offence in the Channel Islands and there is a similar procedure for summonses.[2]

SENTENCES

Suspended sentences

If the defendant commits an offence punishable with imprisonment in Scotland he will be in breach of his suspended sentence[3] and a certificate signed by or on behalf of the Lord Advocate is evidence of the fact that the offence is punishable with imprisonment in Scotland.[4]

Community service

By virtue of the amendments made to the Powers of Criminal Courts

18 Criminal Law Act 1977, s 38.
19 Indictable Offences Act 1848, s 13 and cf MCA 1980, s 126.
20 Criminal Law Act 1977, s 39.
1 Summary Jurisdiction (Process) Act 1881.
2 Although warrants of commitment for non-payment of a fine are not warrants issued in respect of an offence they may be executed in Scotland and Northern Ireland without backing by virtue of ss 38A and 38B of the Criminal Law Act 1977 (as inserted by s 52 of the Criminal Justice Act 1982).
3 Powers of Criminal Courts Act 1973, s 22 (does not apply to offences committed in Northern Ireland).
4 Powers of Criminal Courts Act 1973, s 52.

Act 1973 by Schedule 13 to the Criminal Justice Act 1982 an English court may make a community service order where the defendant will reside in Scotland or Northern Ireland. (The minimum age being 17 for Northern Ireland.) The court in Scotland or Northern Ireland will then deal with any amendment or breach of the order.

Probation

The court can make a probation order where the defendant will reside in Scotland[5] even to the extent of imposing a condition of residence in Scotland.[6] If the offender breaches the order whilst in Scotland either the Scottish court can deal with him for the breach or commit him in custody or release him on bail until he can appear in the English court.[7]

Fines

There is power for the court imposing a fine to make a transfer of fine order to Scotland[8] or where a warrant of commitment has been issued for non payment of a fine it may be executed (without 'backing') in Scotland or Northern Ireland.[9]

The Republic of Ireland and elsewhere

The foregoing provisions do not apply to the Republic of Ireland but there is a separate code contained in the Backing of Warrants (Republic of Ireland) Act 1965. If the offender is outside the British Isles, process issued by an English court is inapplicable and resort would have to be made to extradition proceedings if these are available.

5 Powers of Criminal Courts Act 1973, s 10.
6 *R v Saunders* [1980] QB 72, [1979] 2 All ER 267.
7 Powers of Criminal Courts Act 1973, s 10.
8 MCA 1980, s 90.
9 See 2, p 19, above.

Chapter 2

Arrest and the investigation of offences

This chapter is concerned with matters preliminary to the instituting of court proceedings, and in one sense it is peripheral to the main subject of this book. Nevertheless it is important that some discussion is devoted to these matters, because they can affect the later stages of the criminal process, especially where the admissibility of evidence is concerned. Accordingly, it is proposed to mention in outline the arrest of an accused, the police powers of search, the questioning of the accused and the preliminary gathering of evidence.

The arrest of a suspected person

D steals a bottle of whisky from a shop and runs off down the road. The shopkeeper may shout 'Stop, thief!' One might hope that the thief, stricken with remorse, would immediately stop and return and then surrender himself to the police, but one would probably hope in vain. In reality the only way in which D would go to the police station would be if he were physically compelled to do so, ie if he were arrested. On the other hand, contrast this with the case of the motorist parked on a double yellow line. If he were arrested and dragged down to the police station by an officious traffic warden, this would generally be considered to be a deplorable state of affairs. Therefore a distinction has to be drawn between the offences which can justify such an interference with the liberty of the individual, and those lesser offences where such an intrusion would be unwarranted.

Three situations have to be distinguished: offences where the accused may be arrested forthwith, where the accused can only be arrested with the prior written authorisation of a magistrate (a warrant of arrest) and those offences for which the accused can never be arrested.

(a) OFFENCES WHICH CARRY A POWER OF ARREST WITHOUT WARRANT

At common law

There is a power of arrest given to both a private citizen and a police officer to arrest a person committing a breach of the peace, or where a breach has already occurred and a renewal is feared or where it is honestly believed on reasonable grounds that a breach of the peace will be committed.[1]

General statutory power of arrest. A general power of arrest is given by section 2 of the Criminal Law Act 1967. This section applies to offences or attempts to commit offences where either the sentence is fixed by law (eg murder), or the maximum penalty on indictment is five years' imprisonment or more. These are termed 'arrestable offences'.

Where the offence concerned is an arrestable offence (eg theft, as the maximum penalty on indictment is ten years' imprisonment), the precise scope of the power of arrest depends on whether the arrestor is a private individual or a police constable.

Where an arrestable offence is actually taking place or has been committed, the private citizen has a power of arrest because either he or a constable may arrest the person responsible or the person reasonably believed to be responsible. But where an arrestable offence is suspected but has not in fact taken place, only a constable has power to arrest the suspected culprit and then only if his suspicion was reasonable.[2] Similarly, where an accused is about to commit an arrestable offence or is reasonably believed to be about to commit such an offence, again only the constable has a power to arrest him.

The powers of arrest given to a private individual are generally speaking limited to the situation where the accused is caught red-handed, whereas the constable's powers are extended to cover the subsequent investigation and tracing of the offender.

The result of this is that the private individual takes a risk if he arrests an offender because if it later turns out that an offence was not committed, he may be liable to be sued for damages for false imprisonment.[3]

Specific statutory power of arrest. If there is neither a common law power of arrest nor a power of arrest under section 2(6) of the Criminal Law Act 1967, the statute which creates the offence may give a power of arrest. For example, a power of arrest is given to a constable who reasonably suspects a person of committing an offence under section 5 of the Public Order Act 1936, by section 7(3) of that Act. But where a statute does give a power of arrest the terms of that power must be carefully studied as the terms of the power may be more limited than under section 2(6) of the Criminal Law Act 1967.[4]

1 *R v Howell* [1981] 3 All ER 383, 73 Cr App Rep 31.

2 A constable's reasonable belief may be based on information given to him by another: *R v Francis* [1972] Crim LR 549, and for a discussion on reasonable belief see *Dumbell v Roberts* [1944] 1 All ER 326, and *Shaaban Bin Hussien v Chong Fook Kam* [1969] 3 All ER 1626, referred to in a series of articles by K. Devlin 'Arrest and Detention' (1971) 135 JP passim.

3 As in *Walters v W. H. Smith & Son* [1914] 1 KB 595.

4 See *Wills v Bowley* [1982] Crim LR 580, HL for the power of arrest under s 28 of the Town Police Clauses Act 1847 and the words 'found committing' and see also G.

(b) WARRANTS OF ARREST

The three previous categories have been concerned with the power to arrest the accused forthwith. Although there are a large number of statutory powers of arrest, there will be some offences where a power of arrest is not available under these provisions. In this case the police cannot arrest the accused forthwith but must receive a written authorisation from a magistrate to arrest the accused. This is called a warrant and is obtained by laying an information before a justice of the peace; however, a warrant is not available for all offences, and further discussion on this point will be found in chapter 3.

(c) OFFENCES FOR WHICH THERE IS NO POWER OF ARREST

As a warrant would not be available for such an offence as parking on a double yellow line, a constable could not arrest the offending motorist. He might ask the accused for his name and address and if this were forthcoming, he could then lay an information before a magistrate and obtain a summons ordering the accused to attend court. If the accused declined to give his name and address, the constable would have to follow him until he could obtain sufficient details of the accused's identity in order to lay an information, for example by using his personal radio to check the registration number of the car on the Police National Computer.[5]

ENTRY TO EFFECT AN ARREST

Even if the constable has the power to arrest the accused under one of the provisions mentioned above, he may have yet another problem in that the accused may have left the street where the offence was committed and secreted himself on private premises. It might be presumed, quite reasonably it is submitted, that if Parliament has given authority for the liberty of a person to be restrained by the power of arrest, it would follow that there would be the power to pursue the accused to effect his arrest. Whilst this is true for the common law power where a breach of the peace is involved[6] or where the power of arrest is for an arrestable offence under section 2(6) of the Criminal Law Act 1967,[7] where the power is given by a specific statute there is no

Williams 'The Interpretation of Statutory Powers of Arrest without Warrant' [1958] Crim LR 73 and 154. Naturally, if there is no statutory power of arrest available, the constable may only use the common law power of arrest if a breach of the peace is feared. Cf *Wershof v Metropolitan Police Comr* [1978] 3 All ER 540, 68 Cr App Rep 82.

5 Note the provisions of ss 161–168 of the Road Traffic Act 1972 requiring a person to provide information as to identity and in particular s 164 which provides a power of arrest for certain offences where evidence of identity is not given.

6 *McGowan v Chief Constable of Kingston upon Hull* [1968] Crim LR 34, DC.

7 *Swales v Cox* [1981] 1 All ER 1115, [1981] 2 WLR 814.

power of entry unless it is specifically conferred by the relevant Act.[8] For example, under the Street Offences Act 1959 there is a power of arrest but no power of entry to effect the arrest.[9] If the constable is in possession of a warrant of arrest, he cannot use the warrant of arrest as authority to enter although he may instead rely on a search warrant or, if the offence is an arrestable offence, he could rely on section 2 of the Criminal Law Act 1967. The possession of a warrant would be grounds for 'reasonable suspicion' under that section.

Where there is no power of entry the police have an implied permission to enter premises for lawful purposes just like any other citizen[10] but if that licence is revoked by, for example, the accused telling them to leave the premises, they must leave after having been given reasonable time to effect their withdrawal.[11]

PROCEDURE ON ARREST

When an accused is arrested there is no special formula of words which must be used[12] but it is important that he should know he is under arrest[13] and furthermore he should know the reason for his arrest.[14] When arresting an accused under whatever authority, the person making the arrest can only use such force as is reasonably necessary[15] and where the arrest is being carried out under the authority of a warrant the constable, although he need not have the warrant on his person at the time, must show it to the accused on demand as soon as reasonably practicable.[16]

The power to search

In the process of gathering evidence in a criminal investigation the police may wish to search either an accused person or certain premises. The power to do this is derived partly from the common law and partly from statute.

8 *Clowser v Chaplin, Finnegan v Sandiford* [1981] 2 All ER 267, [1981] 1 WLR 837.
9 *R v McKenzie and Davis* [1979] Crim LR 164 (Bristol Crown Court).
10 *Robson v Hallett* [1967] 2 QB 939, [1967] 2 All ER 407, and a wife can give permission to enter in her capacity as occupier of the premises: see *R v Thornley* [1981] Crim LR 637.
11 *Davis v Lisle* [1936] 2 KB 434, [1936] 2 All ER 213. For a discussion on whether certain Anglo Saxon words revoked an implied licence to enter cf *Snook v Mannion* (1982) Times, 19 March.
12 *R v Inwood* [1973] 2 All ER 645, [1973] 1 WLR 647.
13 If the accused is deaf the constable must communicate to the accused the reason for his arrest in some alternative way and do what a reasonable man would do in the circumstances: *Wheatley v Lodge* [1971] 1 All ER 173, [1971] 1 WLR 29.
14 *Christie v Leachinsky* [1947] AC 573, [1947] 1 All ER 567.
15 Criminal Law Act 1967, s 3.
16 MCA 1980, s 125.

SEARCH OF THE PERSON OF THE ACCUSED

At common law an arrested person can be searched when there are reasonable grounds for believing that he has on him material evidence concerning the offence with which he is charged,[17] or that he has a weapon which he might use to cause himself or another injury, or an implement to effect his escape.[18]

Some statutes in addition authorise a search, eg section 23 of the Misuse of Drugs Act 1971 (unlawful possession of a controlled drug) and in this example the power of search may be used even though the defendant has not been arrested.

SEARCH OF PREMISES

The police may wish to enter and search premises in order to obtain evidence to detect an offender or to strengthen the case against a person already arrested. The question of the power of search of premises involves consideration of two matters: how do the police lawfully enter the premises? and second, having searched the premises, what items may they retain for use as evidence?

THE POWER OF ENTRY

The police may enter premises either because they have a right to be there since they are already exercising a power of entry to effect an arrest, or because they have specific written authority to enter and search premises under a search warrant, or they may simply have been invited onto the premises by the occupier.

Entry to secure an arrest

Where the accused has been arrested the police may search the premises on which they found him and retain any articles which are material evidence against him on the charge for which he has been arrested and, by analogy with search warrants, for other offences in which he is implicated.[19]

The question then arises: What if in the course of the search the police find evidence of an offence committed not by the arrested person but by a third party? According to Horridge J in *Elias v Pasmore*[20] the

17 *Dillon v O'Brien and Davis* (1887) 20 LR Ir 300, 16 Cox CC 245.

18 The modern authority on this is *Lindley v Rutter* [1981] QB 128, [1980] 3 WLR 660. See also *D. J. Stephens 'Search and Seizure of Chattels'* [1970] Crim LR 79 and 139.

19 *Dillon v O'Brien* (1887) 20 LR Ir 300, 16 Cox CC 245. See also *Jeffrey v Black* [1978] 1 QB 490, [1978] 1 All ER 555, where a search of the accused's home was unlawful where he had been arrested elsewhere (although perhaps the search may not have been unlawful if the items searched for (cannabis) bore a close relationship to the offence for which he was arrested (theft)).

20 [1934] 2 KB 164.

police may seize articles which are in fact evidence of a crime committed by anyone, so that the unlawful seizure would be justified if the articles were evidence used subsequently to convict a third party of an offence. However, this case (frequently subjected to criticism) must be considered in the light of the later case of *R v Waterfield and Lynn*[1] which decided that in the absence of a search warrant a constable had no *duty* to detain property on the ground that it could be used in evidence where no person had been charged and *Ghani v Jones*[2] where the *power* to detain property where no person was charged was strictly limited.

Search warrants

The situation may arise where the police cannot effect an entry to arrest the accused because either he is not there or he has already been arrested.[3] The police cannot enter premises under a general right to detect and investigate crime[4] nor in this situation can they enter under the power to effect an arrest. Unless they are invited to enter by the occupants of the premises, they must seek the written authorisation of a justice of the peace or other specified person. For example, by virtue of section 26(2) of the Theft Act 1968 a police superintendent or officer of superior rank may authorise in writing a constable to search premises for stolen goods if the occupant has been convicted of handling or other offences of dishonesty punishable with imprisonment within the five years preceding the application, or if a person who has been in occupation within the previous 12 months has been convicted of handling within the five-year period.

This authorisation is known as a search warrant. Even a justice of the peace does not have a blanket power to issue a search warrant, his authority must come from common law or statute.[5] At common law there was only a power to issue a search warrant to search for stolen goods but this power has been extended by numerous statutes and in fact the common law power to search for stolen goods has been made redundant by the power of a justice of the peace to issue a warrant under section 26(1) of the Theft Act 1968.

One interesting aspect of this piecemeal growth of the power to issue is that there are a warrant gaps in the power, the most glaring example being the lack of authority to issue a search warrant in the case of murder which is referred to below.

1 [1964] 1 QB 164, [1963] 3 All ER 659.
2 [1970] 1 QB 693, [1969] 3 All ER 1700.
3 As in *McLorie v Oxford* [1982] 2 QB 1290, [1982] 3 All ER 480. But see *Jeffrey v Black* [1978] 1QB 490, [1978] 1 All ER 555.
4 *Entinck v Carrington* (1765) 19 State Tr 1029.
5 Some statutes, eg s 2(5) of the Public Order Act 1936, restrict the issue of a warrant to a High Court judge.

Where there is a power for a magistrate to issue a search warrant, the police must lay an information before him in the same way as an information for a warrant of arrest. The magistrate has to balance the desirability of detecting and apprehending criminals against the invasion of a citizen's home and privacy, and he would wish to satisfy himself of the reliability of the information on which the application is based and the character of the occupants (eg are they innocent parties who would be amenable to a police request for permission to enter and take the suspect articles).

The hearing before the magistrate would be ex parte, that is, in the absence of the accused or the occupier of the premises.

Having satisfied himself on these points, the magistrate would issue the warrant. The warrant would usually give the power to search and seize[6] the articles specified in the warrant if the statute authorising the warrant requires this. Although the warrant may be issued under a particular statute, eg section 6 of the Criminal Damage Act 1971, the constable may seize articles other than those named on the warrant. In *Chic Fashions (West Wales) Ltd v Jones*[7] a search warrant for stolen goods was deemed not only to cover the goods specified in the warrant but also any goods reasonably believed to be stolen goods and to be material evidence of theft or receiving by the accused or anyone associated with him. In *Ghani v Jones*[8] Lord Denning extended his own principle in *Chic Fashions* to include other serious offences committed by the accused or a person associated with him. Thus in *Garfinkel v Metropolitan Police Comr*[9] where a warrant to search for explosives was issued under the Explosive Substances Act 1883, evidence implicating the accused in a conspiracy to pervert the course of justice was lawfully seized by the police.[10]

Where a warrant is issued, the local police in default of any other powers can only act on the authority of the warrant. Thus if the warrant, owing to an error, authorises the search of Flat 45 instead of Flat 30 the police cannot search Flat 30 on that warrant.[11] Apart from the general discussion of the scope of warrants mentioned above, the scope of a warrant under a particular statute depends on the wording of the statute, thus a warrant under section 3(1) of the Obscene

6 The one term implies the other *McLorie v Oxford* [1982] 3 All ER 480, [1982] 3 WLR 423.

7 [1968] 2 QB 299, [1968] 2 All ER 229. See now s 26(3) of the Theft Act 1968.

8 [1970] 1 QB 693, [1969] 3 All ER 1700.

9 [1972] Crim LR 44.

10 But it is submitted that, contra *Elias v Pasmore* [1934] 2 KB 164, the police cannot seize goods that have no criminal connection with the accused. The Court of Appeal in *Ghani v Jones* specified that the seizure of the articles must be lawful at the time of the seizure, ie that they are evidence implicating the accused in some way, the seizure cannot be justified ex post facto by its use as evidence against an unconnected third party.

11 *R v Atkinson* [1976] Crim LR 307.

Publications Act 1959 allows the search to be made within a period of 14 days but does not allow more than one search on the warrant.[12] A search warrant may authorise the search of a solicitor's office for documents belonging to the client as any privilege involved would be that of the client who would not be exempt from the effects of a search warrant.[13]

Entry by invitation

A power of entry is only needed where the police wish to enter premises without the consent of the occupier and so it can happen that the police are invited to come in by the defendant and he is then interviewed during which time he may produce items of evidence, or the police may observe articles in the room which may appear suspicious to them. Do the police have power to seize and retain them where no arrest has taken place? If the police are told to leave the premises before they seize the articles, then it is submitted that the seizure will be unlawful because by then (subject to being allowed a reasonable time to leave) they will have become trespassers, but where the goods have already been handed to them they will be able to retain them in spite of the wishes of the occupier where the following criteria are fulfilled:[14]

(a) The police officers must have reasonable grounds for believing that a serious offence has been committed – so serious that it is of the first importance that the offenders should be caught and brought to justice.
(b) The police officers must have reasonable grounds for believing that the article in question is either the fruit of the crime or is the instrument by which the crime was committed or is material evidence to prove the commission of the crime.
(c) The police officers must have reasonable grounds to believe that the person in possession of it has himself committed the crime, or is implicated in it, or is accessory to it, or at any rate his refusal must be quite unreasonable.
(d) The police must not keep the article, nor prevent its removal, for any longer than is reasonably necessary to complete their investigations or preserve it for evidence. If a copy will suffice, it should be made and the original returned. As soon as the case is over, or it is decided not to go on with it, the article should be returned.

From this it can be seen that there are omissions in the law. The most often cited example is the investigation of murder referred to in

12 *R v Adams* [1980] QB 575, [1980] 1 All ER 473.
13 *R v Peterborough Justices, ex p Hicks* [1978] 1 All ER 225, [1977] 1 WLR 1371; *Frank Truman (Export) Ltd v Metropolitan Police Comr* [1977] QB 952, [1977] 3 All ER 431.
14 *Ghani v Jones* [1970] 1 QB 693, [1969] 3 All ER 1700.

Ghani v Jones by Lord Denning, where there is no power to issue a search warrant and, therefore, unless the police are actually arresting an accused they may not enter premises to search for a body unless they are invited to do so by the occupier. The problem was also highlighted in *McLorie v Oxford*.[15]

X was charged with attempted murder by driving a motor car at the victim (X was subsequently convicted of grievous bodily harm). The police arrested X at the house of his father but they did not seize the car which was the instrument of the crime. Later the police returned to seize the car but were refused entry. The police then entered as trespassers and whilst seizing the car were assaulted by D. His conviction of police assault was set aside as the police were not acting in the execution of their duty since they had no power to enter the premises as they had neither a warrant nor were they entering to effect an arrest (the accused X already having been arrested) nor had they any permission to enter. The only remedy suggested by the court to the police in this situation was nominally to 'seize' the vehicle when effecting the arrest and then return later for the item 'seized'.

The police interviewing of suspects

In the usual case before the magistrates' court where the defendant pleads not guilty, the crucial evidence against him will be the evidence of the police officer relating what the accused said to the police when he was interviewed. It is because of the importance of this evidence and the possibility that what appears to be conclusive evidence may be unreliable, that the procedure for interviewing suspects is subject to regulation. This regulation is provided by guidelines laid down by the judges of the Queen's Bench Division, known as the Judges' Rules.

The rules set out the manner in which the judges expect the police and other similar authorities to conduct their investigations. The rules can be summarised as follows:

(a) When the police are making general inquiries they may question any person whom they consider may be able to help them (Rule I).

(b) When they have some evidence[16] which leads them to suspect a particular individual they may continue to ask him questions but before they do so they must caution him (Rule II) 'You are not obliged to say anything unless you wish to do so but what you say may be put into writing and given in evidence.'

(c) The third stage is reached when the police have enough evidence to go

15 [1982] 3 All ER 480, [1982] 3 WLR 423.

16 Ie evidence capable of being presented to a court, *R v Osborne* [1973] 1 QB 678, [1973] 1 All ER 649. Thus it may be reasonable to arrest an accused on hearsay evidence which would be insufficient to charge him. Cf *Glinski v McIvor* [1962] AC 726 and L. James (1978) 142 JP 325.

beyond suspicion and actually charge the suspect (or inform him he is to be prosecuted if a summons is contemplated) (Rule III). As soon as the police have enough evidence the accused must be charged (paragraph (d) of the preamble to the Rules) and having been charged he must be cautioned again whereupon the police cannot ask him any further questions except in exceptional circumstances in Rule III (b), eg to clear up ambiguities.

VOLUNTARY STATEMENTS

During the course of questioning by the police the accused may wish to make a written statement setting out his case. The way in which this statement is to be taken is prescribed in Rule IV and in the Administrative Directions appended to the Rules.[17]

THE JUDGES' RULES IN THE POLICE STATION

Paragraph (a) of the preamble to the rules refers to the duty of the citizen to help a police constable to discover and apprehend offenders but it should also be remembered that a person is generally under no obligation to reply to a police officer's questions.[18]

In practice the accused would be asked questions at the scene of the crime or at his home until the obligation to caution under Rule II arose and then he would be arrested and taken to the police station for further interview until sufficient evidence was obtained for him to be charged. If the police are not in a position to arrest him, the accused may only be 'invited' to the police station to 'assist with inquiries';[19] he cannot be compelled to go to the police station nor remain there.[20]

When at the police station (or indeed anywhere else), the interview

17 A voluntary statement containing admissions will be evidence at the trial of the accused under an exception to the hearsay rule, but a purely exculpatory statement would be generally inadmissible as being a self serving statement, ie only repeating what the defendant was saying in the witness box, eg *R v Thompson* [1975] Crim LR 34.

Where there is a mixture of admissions and exculpatory statements the entire statement would be admitted for the court to consider it as a whole, the exculpatory statements would reflect on the attitude of the defendant at the time he made them, but of course the weight of any denials would be diminished where there had been a lapse of time during which the accused could compose himself and prepare a statement. On this subject generally see *R v Duncan* (1981) 73 Cr App Rep 359, [1981] Crim LR 560 and the commentary there and at [1979] Crim LR 428 by D. W. Elliott and J. N. Wakefield.

18 Except for certain statutory exceptions, eg s 168(2) of the Road Traffic Act 1972 (duty of owner of vehicle to provide information concerning the driver of a vehicle when an offence was committed) and s 2 of the Official Secrets Act 1920.

19 See the strictures on the use of these words by Lawton LJ in *R v Lemsatef* [1977] 2 All ER 835, [1977] 1 WLR 812.

20 Para (b) of the preamble to the Rules.

must be conducted in accordance with the Administrative Directions which particularly emphasise the need to record the occasions when the 'cautions' were administered and statements taken, with any pauses or refreshments taken. The time when the accused was charged should be noted and a written copy of the charge sheet should have been handed to him.

The provision which has caused problems is that in paragraph 7 of the Administrative Directions; in particular the allowing of the defendant to make a telephone call and consult his solicitor. By statute[1]

> Where any person has been arrested and is being held in custody in a police station or other premises, he shall be entitled to have intimation of his arrest and of the place where he is being held sent to one person reasonably named by him without delay or, where some delay is necessary in the interests of the investigation or prevention of crime or the apprehension of offenders, with no more delay than is so necessary.

This affords a right to inform a person reasonably named by the accused, such as his solicitor, forthwith unless the interests of the investigation or the prevention of crime or apprehension of offenders dictate otherwise, and in paragraph 7 of the Administrative Directions the defendant should be allowed to speak to his solicitor 'provided that no hindrance is reasonably likely to be caused to the processes of investigation or the administration of justice' eg where the interview is being conducted in the early hours of the morning and it would be unreasonable to delay matters until normal office hours when the accused's solicitor would be available.

After having informed the accused orally of his rights and having displayed the notices to this effect as prescribed by paragraph 7(b) of the Administrative Directions, the police have no obligation to inform the accused before each interview that he may telephone his solicitor but if he asks for his solicitor the police will have to consider this request.[2] It must be a great temptation to them to deny the solicitor access to his client on the ground that he will advise his client to say nothing, although this is not a legal ground for refusing access.[3]

SANCTIONS FOR BREACH OF THE RULES

The provisions mentioned above, including section 62 of the Criminal Law Act 1977, do not carry any sanction of law for non-compliance but that is not to say they are without effect for a sanction is contained in paragraph (3) of the preamble to the rules. At the trial of the accused the magistrates when considering any confession that he had made to the police, would have to be satisfied that it was made voluntarily before it was admitted in evidence. An admission not made voluntarily is inadmissible.

1 Criminal Law Act 1977, s 62.
2 *R v King* [1978] Crim LR 632 (1st instance); on appeal [1980] Crim LR 40.
3 See *R v Lemsatef* [1977] 2 All ER 835, [1977] 1 WLR 812.

Paragraph (e) provides:

> . . . (I)t is a fundamental condition of the admissibility in evidence against any person, equally of any oral answer given by that person to a question put by a police officer and of any statement made by that person, that it shall have been voluntary, in the sense that it has not been obtained from him by fear of prejudice or hope of advantage, exercised or held out by a person in authority, or by oppression.

Arguments concerning the admissibility of confessions under this part of the Judges' Rules centre on whether there was an actual threat or inducement (eg a promise of bail is the classic example) and if there was, did the threat or inducement come from a 'person in authority'. A catalogue of examples will be found in the section of *Stone's* dealing with evidence and confessions.

The other limb of the paragraph is whether the accused was oppressed into making the confession by, for example, lack of sleep or refreshment and reference should be made to *R v Prager*.[4]

If the essential test of the admissibility of a statement by the accused is its voluntary nature, a statement obtained in flagrant breach of the Judges' Rules might be less likely to be accepted as being voluntary but not necessarily so, thus where an accused was improperly denied the right to see a solicitor the subsequent admission was still held to be voluntary and therefore admissible.[5]

However, even where the statement was voluntary and thus prima facie admissible, the court may still have a discretion to exclude it if it was unfairly obtained by a trick or other reprehensible conduct.[6] This would be extremely problematic for the magistrates' court and it would be very difficult for the magistrates to decide first that an admission was voluntary (and thus *probably* true) and then exclude it with the result that the accused would probably be acquitted.

The whole question of the admissibility of confessions poses severe practical problems in the magistrates' court. In the Crown Court the issue of admissibility is determined at a 'trial within a trial' in the absence of the jury. In the magistrates' court it is the magistrates themselves who determine the admissibility of the confession. The Judges' Rules pose the question: is the confession voluntary, not is it true? It would be a feat of mental gymnastics for a bench to decide (a) a confession was true but (b) that the confession was not made voluntarily and was thus inadmissible, and consequently dismiss it from their minds when considering their verdict in the case. At one

4 [1972] 1 All ER 1114, [1972] 1 WLR 260. This case is the usual starting point for a discussion on statements obtained by oppression. Cf also *R v Gowan* [1982] Crim LR 821 for further comments on the nature of oppression.

5 See *R v Elliot* [1977] Crim LR 551 and commentary thereon.

6 This is an exception to the general rule in *R v Sang* [1980] AC 402, [1979] 2 All ER 1222 limiting the discretion to exclude unfairly obtained evidence.

time, the magistrates might even hold a 'trial within a trial' before themselves but now it is held that this procedure is inappropriate. The question of admissibility should be decided as one of the matters in the general course of the trial, ie the justices should hear the evidence and attach to it what weight they think fit, or even disregard it altogether if it is appropriate.[7]

Bringing the arrested person before the court

After the accused has been arrested he should be brought before a magistrate without delay unless that delay is necessary or reasonable.[8] Where the accused has been arrested on a warrant the police will already have had to lay an information before a justice of the peace and their investigations will have been at least substantially completed, accordingly the police will have only to comply with the terms of the warrant which in the case of a warrant without bail will be to arrest him and forthwith deliver him to the court from custody.

In the situation where the police have exercised a power of arrest without warrant they may find themselves in difficulty. Section 43 of the Magistrates' Courts Act 1980 provides that where an arrested person is brought to a police station and he is not to be brought before a magistrates' court within 24 hours, a senior officer or officer in charge of the police station must inquire into the case and unless the offence is in his view a serious one, the accused must be granted bail either to return to the police station (if inquiries have not been completed), or to appear at the appropriate magistrates' court.

Where the offence is a serious one and the accused is not bailed, or is not brought before the court within 24 hours, he must be brought before a magistrates' court 'as soon as reasonably practicable' which means in effect no more than about 48 hours.[9]

For this reason the police may wish to delay charging the accused, preferring him to be 'helping them with their inquiries' without having been arrested so that he does not have to be produced before the court until their inquiries are completed and so that they may continue asking him questions which would otherwise be precluded by Rule III of the Judges' Rules after a charge has been preferred.

When a client comes to a solicitor having been charged with an

7 *SJF (an infant) v Chief Constable of Kent, ex parte Margate Juvenile Court* (1982) Times, 17 June.

8 *Dallison v Caffery* [1965] 1 QB 348, [1964] 2 All ER 610 and see also *McCarrick v Oxford* [1982] Crim LR 750.

9 *R v Hudson* (1980) 72 Cr App Rep 163, [1981] Crim LR 107; *R v Holmes, ex p Sherman* [1981] 2 All ER 612, 145 JP 337, but this is not a rigid rule: *R v Nycander* (1982) Times, 9 December.

offence he will have been given a charge sheet[10] and will have been bailed to court under section 43(1) of the Magistrates' Courts Act 1980, or if he has not been charged yet, he may be bailed to return to the police station under section 43(3) of the Act. In either event failure to surrender to the bail would be an offence under the Bail Act 1976.

Other procedures for obtaining evidence

Mention has already been made of the procedure for interviewing the accused and there are three other procedures which should be mentioned in so far as they affect the magistrates' court.

EVIDENCE OF IDENTITY[11]

Although this is not a textbook on evidence, the question of the identity of the culprit can pose some acute procedural problems. In the general run of cases the accused will be pleading not guilty on the basis that he did the act complained of but did not have the requisite mens rea, eg the screwdriver in his shopping bag was not paid for because he was unaware that it had fallen off the shelf and into his bag, or in the case of a charge of assault the defendant might maintain that he acted in self-defence. In effect, the accused is admitting that he is the person the police are looking for but that his acts have an innocent explanation. Where identity is in issue, the normal method of proof by calling witnesses to court and identifying the accused by pointing him out at the hearing would act unfairly because the witnesses would be heavily influenced by the presence of the accused in the dock and all fingers would, as it were, point at the defendant. Therefore the witnesses should normally identify the accused at an identification parade held under strict conditions prescribed by the Home Office Circular 109/78 reproduced in Volume I of *Stone's*.

An identification parade is no use, however, unless there is a suspect available. If there is as yet no suspect, then the witnesses may be asked to look at selections of photographs which are designed to be as fair as possible so that, for instance, the witness should be shown at least 12 photographs of a similar type. Guidance on the use of photographs is set out in the Home Office Circular already referred to.

Once a suspect has been identified from photographs, the other witnesses should not be shown photographs, but all the witnesses should attend an identity parade at which the suspect is present. At the accused's trial, if identity remains in issue then evidence can be given of the identity parade and, if the nature of the defence demands it,

10 See para 6 of the Administrative Directions.
11 The leading authority on this is *R v Turnbull* [1977] QB 224, [1976] 3 All ER 549.

evidence of the photographs, but caution always has to be exercised with the use of photographs because of the natural suspicion of the bench that the photographs are 'mug shots' of convicted criminals and that the defendant may fall into that category.

It would only be in exceptional cases that the prosecution would be allowed to identify the accused in court for the first time where identity was in dispute, such as the situation where the accused refused to take part in an identification parade.[12]

FINGERPRINT ORDERS

Under the provisions of section 49 of the Magistrates' Courts Act 1980, a police officer not below the rank of inspector may ask the court for an order that the fingerprints be taken of a defendant who is not less than 14 years of age and is either in custody or is charged with an offence punishable with imprisonment. It is too late to make the application if the defendant is convicted, but whether conviction means the finding of guilt or the sentencing of the accused is not clear.[13] If the order is made, the prints must always be taken at the court house if the accused is on bail,[14] or if he is in custody, they may be taken at the place to which he is committed. If the accused is acquitted or discharged in committal proceedings, the fingerprints obtained must be destroyed.

Unfortunately there is no authoritative guidance on how the magistrates should exercise their discretion.[15] It cannot be sufficient that the police need the fingerprints for their records as this would be sufficient to justify an order in every case. The grounds of an application, it is submitted, must relate to the investigation of the offence before the court, eg to eliminate other suspects or to confirm the identity of the accused, or to implicate him in other unsolved offences. Furthermore, the gravity of the offence must be taken into account as it would be unusual to take fingerprints in a breathalyser case without some suspicion that the accused is implicated in a more serious matter.

APPLICATIONS UNDER THE BANKERS' BOOKS EVIDENCE ACT 1879

A final matter which is worth mentioning is when an application is made to the court for an order to inspect and take copies of the defendant's (or a third party's[16]) bank account under section 7 of the

12 Eg *R v John* [1973] Crim LR 113.

13 See (1979) 143 JP Jo 281.

14 *R v Jones (Yvonne)* [1978] 3 All ER 1098.

15 A judicial discretion: *George v Coombe* [1978] Crim LR 47. See J. Richman (1977) 141 JP Jo 196 and also (1973) 137 JP Jo 180.

16 Great care should be exercised before ordering the inspection of an account of a third party. The account, although in name that of a third party, should either be de facto that of the party to the proceedings or an account over which he exercises control (cf the cases referred to in *Stone's*). Recent cases have been concerned with

Bankers' Books Evidence Act 1879. The criteria by which the justices should make their decision were set out in *Williams v Summerfield*.[17]

(a) The justices should warn themselves of the importance of the step which they are taking in making such an order as it is a serious infringement of the liberty of the subject.
(b) Is there any other evidence in the possession of the prosecution to support the charge?
(c) Is the application merely a 'fishing expedition' in the hope of finding some evidence on which to hang the charge?
(d) The order should not be an instrument of oppression.
(e) If the justices are in serious doubt they may leave the matter to be determined by a High Court judge.

If the justices decide to make an order they should limit the disclosure to the period strictly relevant to the charge. An application would not have to be dismissed because the accused says that he intends to plead guilty as he could quite easily change his mind.[18]

Although the application may be made ex parte the better practice is to give notice to the defendant[19] and more particularly to a third party where the application is to inspect his account insofar as it is admissible in evidence against the accused.

orders concerning the spouse of an accused where an order was allowed even where the spouse could not be compelled by the ordinary rules of evidence to testify against the party to the proceedings, *R v Andover Justices, ex p Rhodes* [1980] Crim LR 644, but in the 'relative' cases as in the cases where inspection of a third party account is ordered, notice should be given to all concerned. Cf *R v Grossman* (1981) 73 Cr App Rep 302, [1981] Crim LR 396.

17 [1972] 2 QB 512, [1972] 2 All ER 1334.

18 *Owen v Sambrook* [1981] Crim LR 329, and see (1981) 145 JP Jo 108.

19 *R v Marlborough St Metropolitan Stipendiary Magistrate, ex p Simpson* (1980) 70 Cr App Rep 291, [1980] Crim LR 305.

Chapter 3

Information, summons and warrant

Introductory

When a crime has been detected the first stage in the criminal process is for the police to gather evidence to enable them to identify the culprit. This may be a very quick operation where the defendant is caught in the act of committing the offence, or it may take months or even years of patient detective work. Once the police have identified the person against whom they feel they have sufficient evidence to present a case, then they may initiate criminal proceedings.

In the previous chapter it was seen how the action to be taken by the police is governed by whether the offence concerned is an arrestable or non-arrestable offence. In the case of an arrestable offence the police may apprehend the defendant and keep him in their custody until he is brought before the magistrates' court. Alternatively, they may bail the accused to appear at court, that is, inform him of a date and time to appear at a specified magistrates' court with the sanction that failure to appear on the appropriate occasion itself carries a legal penalty.

For a non-arrestable offence, the police may only gather their evidence until they have sufficient to implicate the accused, but at no time can they forcibly detain him to bring him before the court.

Therefore an accused person suspected of an offence may find himself in one of these three situations:

(i) Arrested and brought to court in custody.
(ii) Arrested and bailed by the police to attend court.
(iii) Summoned to court.

This chapter concerns itself with the next stage of the process, the initiation of the criminal procedure before the magistrates' court.

Securing the attendance of the accused at court

If the accused is in the custody of the police after his arrest there is no problem about ensuring his attendance at court because, as described in the previous chapter, the police will produce him from custody.

If the accused has been bailed by the police to attend court, then if he does not answer to his bail, the court may issue a warrant for his arrest under section 7 of the Bail Act 1976.

This chapter is mainly concerned with the third situation where the police have not arrested the accused and so cannot physically produce him in person or bail him to attend court. In this situation, they will have to apply to the court for process to bring the accused to court.

The information[1]

LAYING AN INFORMATION

The process to secure the attendance of an accused is started by the laying of an information before a justice of the peace.[2] An information is a formal accusation against an individual that he has committed an offence (and it is the formal 'charge' on which he will be tried in court, the equivalent of the indictment for a trial at the Crown Court). When the accusation has been made, the magistrate may decide to issue a summons to the accused instructing him to attend court on a particular date to answer the accusation, or he may if the information has been substantiated on oath, issue a warrant for the accused's arrest, the warrant being either backed for bail or without bail.

Suppose for example that a witness is in the Acme supermarket in Borchester and he sees a man steal a screwdriver from a display. He follows the thief outside and sees X who is a justice of the peace. The witness is too frightened of the thief to arrest him and so he says to X 'I have just seen John Doe steal a screwdriver from the Acme supermarket, Borchester, which is an offence contrary to section one of the Theft Act 1968'. The witness has just laid an oral information before a magistrate.

An alternative method of laying an information is to put the accusation in writing and deliver it to a magistrates' court either personally or by post.[3]

The third method of laying an information is to put the allegation into writing and substantiate it by a statement made on oath which may be annexed to the information in the form of a deposition.

The actual method used to lay the information is important because it may determine the action which can subsequently be taken. In practice a purely oral information is rare (except where alternative or additional matters are introduced at a trial) because the court will

1 MCA 1980, ss 1–3, 123, 124 and 127.

2 Or justices' clerk (Justices' Clerks Rules 1970, except the laying of an information on oath).

3 In which case the information will be deemed to have been laid when it is received by an authorised official of the justices' clerk's office. *R v Manchester Stipendiary Magistrate, ex p Hill* [1982] Crim LR 755.

require a written record of the offence alleged. Usually all informations are made in writing. Informations substantiated on oath are also not too common because as will be seen, the purpose of substantiating an information on oath is to obtain a warrant for the accused's arrest. In the majority of such cases the police will have had a power of arrest for the original offence and will have exercised this option already.[4]

Accordingly it is proposed next to look at the way in which a written information should be prepared.

THE FORM OF AN INFORMATION[5]

A suggested form of an information is to be found in the Magistrates' Courts (Forms) Rules 1981, Form 1, but courts often adopt their own versions of this whilst complying with the various prescribed requirements for an information.

Here is an example of an information:

Borchester Magistrates' Court

CODE: 1234

DATE: 1st April 1983.
THE INFORMATION OF: P.C. 99 Dixon Rutland Constabulary
WHO (ON OATH) states
THAT John Doe of 10 Gas Street, Borchester, did on the 30th March 1983 at Borchester in the County of Rutland steal one screwdriver belonging to the Acme Supermarket P.L.C.
Contrary to section one of the Theft Act 1968.

Taken (and sworn) before me

John Worthy
Justice of the Peace.

A closer examination of the information will reveal several factors which must be borne in mind when laying an information.

(a) THE PROSECUTOR

The vast majority of informations are laid by the police and they usually have some senior officer authorised by the chief constable to be the informant in all their cases. But a private individual of course may be an informant, or the information may be laid for him by counsel or a solicitor or someone authorised by him.[6]

The general rule is that anyone may start a prosecution and thus lay

4 Note the expression is 'substantiated' on oath. Accordingly, the information may be laid and then substantiated any time thereafter in order to obtain a warrant.
5 Magistrates' Courts Rules 1981, rr. 4, 12 and 100.
6 Ibid, r 4(1)

an information, but for certain offences which may be either politically sensitive or otherwise out of the ordinary, the consent of one of the law officers of the Crown will be required. These offences are discussed in chapter 1, above.

(b) THE DATE OF THE OFFENCE

Generally speaking there is no time limit for taking proceedings for an indictable offence on indictment but no information may be tried by a magistrates' court where the information was laid more than six months from the date of the offence.[7] This means in effect that an information laid outside the six-month time limit would be worthless where a purely summary offence were concerned, and where the offence was triable either way and summary trial was decided upon, the information could not be proceeded with.

There are of course exceptions to the general rule covering time limits, and so the matter of time limits should always be considered. Exceptions to the general rule for summary offences are to be found in the various offences against the social security legislation (one-year limit) and those offences specified in the Road Traffic Act 1972, section 180 (where the time limit is specified as being within six months of the date when the prosecutor had sufficient knowledge of the offence, with an overall limit of three years from the date of the offence) and proceedings to which the Vehicles (Excise) Act 1971, section 30 applies.

(c) THE PLACE WHERE THE OFFENCE WAS COMMITTED

The power to issue process on an information depends also on the magistrates having territorial jurisdiction. The circumstances in which the magistrate has jurisdiction to issue process are set out in section 1(2) of the Magistrates' Courts Act 1980:

> (2) A justice of the peace for an area to which this section applies may issue a summons or warrant under this section –
>
> (a) if the offence was committed or is suspected to have been committed within the area, or
>
> (b) if it appears to the justice necessary or expedient, with a view to the better administration of justice, that the person charged should be tried jointly with, or in the same place as, some other person who is charged with an offence, and who is in custody, or is being or is to be proceeded against, within the area, or
>
> (c) if the person charged resides or is, or is believed to reside or be, within the area, or
>
> (d) if under any enactment a magistrates' court for the area has jurisdiction to try the offence, or

7 MCA 1980, s 127. where an information is laid alleging an offence to have taken place between two dates, one outside the time limit, evidence can only be given of activities within the time limit.

(e) if the offence was committed outside England and Wales, and, where it is an offence exclusively punishable on summary conviction, if a magistrates' court for the area would have jurisdiction to try the offence if the offender were before it.

The 'area' referred to means the commission area for which the magistrate is appointed, ie a county outside London, or within London, a London Commission Area or the City of London.[8] The power to issue process under (c) above is limited by section 1(5) because for a summary offence a summons cannot be issued only on the basis that the accused resides in the particular commission area (and has committed the offence elsewhere) although a warrant may be issued to secure the accused's attendance at a court which would have the jurisdiction to try him. However, as will be seen, the power to issue a warrant is subject to limitations such as the information having to be laid on oath.

The scope of the power to issue process is extended by (d) above which allows the magistrate to issue process whenever it has jurisdiction to *deal* with an offence. The jurisdiction to *deal* with an offence is defined by section 2.

s. 2 (1) A magistrates' court for a county, a London commission area or the City of London shall have jurisdiction to try all summary offences committed within the county, the London commission area or the City (as the case may be).

(2) Where a person charged with a summary offence appears or is brought before a magistrates' court in answer to a summons issued under paragraph (b) of section 1(2) above, or under a warrant issued under that paragraph, the court shall have jurisdiction to try the offence.

(3) A magistrates' court for a county, a London commission area or the City of London shall have jurisdiction as examining justices over any offence committed by a person who appears or is brought before the court, whether or not the offence was committed within the county, the London commission area or the City (as the case may be).

(4) Subject to sections 18 to 22 below and any other enactment (wherever contained) relating to the mode of trial of offences triable either way, a magistrates' court shall have jurisdiction to try summarily an offence triable either way in any case in which under subsection (3) above it would have jurisdiction as examining justices.

(5) A magistrates' court shall, in the exercise of its powers under section 24 below, have jurisdiction to try summarily an indictable offence in any case in which under subsection (3) above it would have jurisdiction as examining justices.

(6) A magistrates' court for any area by which a person is tried for an offence shall have jurisdiction to try him for any summary offence for which he could be tried by a magistrates' court for any other area.

(7) Nothing in this section shall affect any jurisdiction over offences

8 Ibid, s 1(8).

conferred on a magistrates' court by any enactment not contained in this Act.

To paraphrase the effect of these sections is to say that a magistrates' court may issue process for:

(i) any indictable offence wherever committed;
(ii) a summary offence committed within its area;
(iii) a summary offence committed outside the area where the accused is to be tried for an offence for which the court already has jurisdiction;
(iv) a summary offence committed outside the area where it is necessary or expedient to try the accused together with an accused over whom the court has jurisdiction; and
(v) in certain cases court A may issue process (but not *try* the accused) to secure the attendance at court B of an accused who resides in the area of court A.

However, it is often difficult to know just where an offence has been committed and section 3 of the Act deals with this situation by declaring that any offence committed on, or within, 500 yards of a boundary between two places, or on any stretch of water between two places shall be treated as having been committed in any of those areas. Or if an offence is begun in one area and continues until it is completed in another area, it may be treated as having been wholly committed in either of those areas. Similarly, where an offence is committed on a journey between several places it may be treated as if it had been committed in any of those areas.[9]

(d) THE STATEMENT OF THE OFFENCE

When considering how the offence should be described in the information, three provisions have to be borne in mind. In the description of the offence it is not necessary to negative any proviso or exemption which may be contained in the section creating the offence.[10] Furthermore, it is sufficient if the information describes the offence in ordinary language avoiding technical terms and not necessarily giving all the elements of the offence provided it gives reasonable information as to the nature of the charge.[11] If

9 For jurisdiction granted by other statutes, especially the Merchant Shipping Act 1894 and Territorial Waters Jurisdiction Act 1878, see the footnote to MCA 1980, s 2 in *Stone's*. Also cases such as *Treacy v DPP* [1971] AC 537, [1971] 1 All ER 110 (blackmail) the offence was committed in England where the letter containing the unwarranted demand was posted to a recipient abroad; *R v Millar, R v Robert Millar (Contractors) Ltd* [1970] 2 QB 54, [1970] 1 All ER 577 the offence of counselling and procuring takes place where the substantive offence is committed. See also *R v Baxter* [1972] 1 QB 1, [1971] 2 All ER 359 (attempting to obtain property by deception, offence takes place in England where letters making the attempt were posted to an addressee abroad).

10 Magistrates' Courts Rules 1981, r 4(3).

11 Ibid, r 100. But this is not to be read literally as there is a danger that if an element of the offence is omitted the information will be defective. Similarly where a section of the act is omitted or incorrectly cited (cf *Atterton v Browne* [1945] KB 122) and the best policy is generally to follow the words of the statute.

the offence is created by statute, the section and title of the Act creating the offence should be quoted.

Rule 12 of the Magistrates' Courts Rules 1981 provides that the court shall not proceed to the trial of an information which contains more than one offence. An information which contains more than one offence is not bad in itself, but any convictions based on such an information would be bad. The prosecutor should choose on which offence he wishes to proceed.[12] This is in effect the equivalent of the duplicity rule for trials on indictment.

DUPLICITY

The rule against duplicity is that the information must contain only one offence but although the rule appears to be quite straightforward it is hard to put into practice. An obvious example of an information alleging more than one offence would be where D was charged that he 'on the 5th November 1982 at Borchester stole one bottle of milk and destroyed a flowerpot.'

However, difficulties may be caused either because of the way the offence is alleged to have been committed or because of the drafting of the statute creating the offence.

In the former case consider the example of the shoplifter who steals goods from one counter in a department store, then moves to another counter and takes some more goods. Is this one offence of theft of several items or is it a number of separate thefts? Suppose the thief moves to another floor and takes some more goods, is this a separate theft? Clearly it would be a separate theft if the thief then went into the shop next door and stole some goods there.[13]

12 *Edwards v Jones* [1947] 1 KB 659, [1947] 1 All ER 830.

13 The question of duplicity is probably one of form, not substance, so that the information will be good provided that, on the face of it, there appears to be only one offence charged even if it appears later from the evidence that more than one offence has been committed, cf *R v Greenfield* [1973] 3 All ER 1050, [1973] 1 WLR 1151.

It is possible to commit one offence of theft by taking various items from different departments in the same store (cf *R v Wilson* (1979) 69 Cr App Rep 83, explaining *R v Ballysingh* (1953) 37 Cr App Rep 28) but it is a question of fact and degree, as it can be correct to charge in a single information one activity even though that activity may consist of more than one act (cf *Jemmison v Priddle* [1972] 1 QB 489, [1972] 1 All ER 539). The problem may well not arise so much in this situation with the information, which may appear on its face to charge one offence, but with the evidence which is elicited at the trial. As the *form* of the information is good, no question of duplicity arises but the court cannot really proceed to convict the defendant of two separate offences from the one information. Therefore the information should be amended by deleting some of the particulars and another, separate, information being laid if possible

In *Horrix v Malam* (1983) Times, 28 March the information for driving without due care and attention on several roads where the facts revealed that the two

An example of the problem caused by drafting is illustrated by the Road Traffic Act 1972, section 3.

> if a person drives a motor vehicle on a road without due care and attention, or without reasonable consideration for other persons using the road, he shall be guilty of an offence.

Here it has been decided that the disjunctive 'or' creates two separate offences and the information must define which activity is alleged.[14]

Contrast section 5(1) of the same Act.

> A person who, when driving or attempting to drive a motor vehicle on a road or public place, is unfit to drive through drink or drugs shall be guilty of an offence.

It has been held that this section creates one offence of driving when incapacitated and so not in proper control, although the information must be specific to the extent of defining whether the defendant was driving or attempting to drive.[15]

The mischief rule

Accordingly one sometimes has to look at the statute to see whether a single mischief is aimed at, although this mischief may be caused in several different ways. An example of this is where the proscribed act was emitting smoke or steam from an engine on the highway and the information reciting this was not duplicitous because there was only one mischief aimed at, the prohibition of noxious emissions.[16] Similarly a single information could be laid where several chimneys belched forth black smoke where, although unconnected, they were on the same premises.[17] In a case of fraudulently inducing persons to invest money contrary to the Prevention of Fraud (Investments) Act 1958, section 13, the essence of the offence is the inducing so that many different inducements on several different days may therefore be included on the same charge.[18] A final example in this category is the offence under Public Order Act 1936, section 5.

> Any person who in any public place . . . uses threatening abusive or insulting words or behaviour with intent to provoke a breach of the peace or whereby a breach of the peace is likely to be occasioned, shall be guilty of an offence.

where the 'or' in the 'threatening, abusive or insulting words or

incidents were separated by a ten-minute interval and two miles in distance and were witnessed by two different officers was good, as the acts complained of amounted to one activity.

For a thorough discussion of this complex subject cf *Archbold* (41st edn) paras. 1–57 ff and 18–3 ff.

14 *R v Surrey Justices, ex p Witherick* [1932] 1 KB 450, 95 JP 219.
15 *Thomson v Knights* [1947] 1 KB 336.
16 *Davis v Loach* (1886) 51 JP 118.
17 *Barnes v Norris* (1876) 41 JP 150.
18 *R v Linnell* [1969] 3 All ER 849, [1969] 1 WLR 1514.

behaviour', does not serve to create several offences; the section only creates one offence.[19]

Continuing offences

Sometimes the problem is not whether there are two or more different types of offence but whether there are several offences of the same nature committed on different days, ie is it one continuing offence lasting several days or is a separate offence committed on each occasion. An example has already been given with the offence of fraudulently inducing investments. A further example is where a defendant is charged with brothel keeping as one activity but as that activity might last over several days the information was valid.[20]

Alternative forms of mens rea

Some offences may be committed with alternative forms of mens rea. For example, criminal damage may be committed either intentionally or recklessly.[1] It is not necessary in the information to be specific as to whether the act was intentional or reckless, both may be included in the same charge. A similar principle was applied where the defendant was charged with 'wilfully or negligently' failing to comply with certain prescribed conditions.[2]

The above categories are only guidelines, they cannot in any sense be described as definitive statements of the law. The answer to any particular problem has to be sought first by searching for a decided case on the point. If one cannot be found, then resort has to be made to general principles, although these principles are often difficult to apply in view of the many conflicting and confusing decisions.[3]

Why have a duplicity rule?

The cynic might say that the duplicity rule is designed merely to keep the prosecution up to the mark. If the charge is duplicitous, the defendant may take the point at any time even after conviction and if successful, the conviction would be quashed.[4]

In favour of the rule it can be said that it is desirable that each information should contain only one offence to avoid the difficulty of trying an assortment of offences all rolled into one. Second, the defendant should know with some precision the allegation he has to

19 *Vernon v Paddon* [1972] 3 All ER 302, [1973] 1 WLR 663.

20 *Anderton v Cooper* (1980) 72 Cr App Rep 232, [1981] Crim LR 177.

1 Criminal Damage Act 1971, s 1.

2 *Newton v Smith* [1962] 2 QB 278, [1962] 2 All ER 19.

3 For examples see *Stone's* Volume III commentary on Magistrates' Courts Rules 1981, r 12.

4 *R v Molloy* [1921] 2 KB 364, but where a discretionary remedy such as certiorari is applied for, the relief sought may not always be granted: see *R v Lymm Justices, ex p Brown* [1973] 1 All ER 716, [1973] 1 WLR 1039.

meet and if he has been acquitted or convicted he should know what that verdict relates to so that if need be he can raise the plea of autrefois acquit or convict.

Several informations in one document

Although one information must relate to one offence only, there is nothing to prevent one document containing several distinct informations.[5]

Issuing process

APPLYING FOR A SUMMONS

The purpose of laying an information is to obtain the process of the court to secure the attendance of the accused. This process may consist of either a summons or a warrant.

A summons is simply a letter in a particular form from the court to the accused instructing him that an allegation (an information) has been made against him and that he should attend at court on a particular date to meet the allegation.[6]

A warrant is a document authorising the person or persons named on the warrant to arrest the accused on suspicion of the offence set out in the warrant. If the warrant is without bail, the accused will be brought to court in custody as soon as possible. If the warrant is backed for bail (which means simply that the warrant is endorsed with a direction that the person named in the warrant is to be released on bail; this endorsement may be on the front or the back of the warrant) the accused will be arrested and informed what he is being arrested for. He will then be released and informed that he is bailed to attend court on the date set out in the warrant.[7]

Although in practice when a person lays an information he makes at the same time an application for a summons or warrant to be issued, in law the laying of the information and the issuing of process are two distinct matters. The laying of an information is an act of the informant and does not require much, if any, co-operation by a magistrate. For an information to be laid it does not have to be *considered* by a justice of the peace. The considering of the information comes at the second stage when the magistrate decides whether he will issue process based on its contents.[8]

5 Magistrates' Courts Rules 1981, r 12(2).
6 The summons must be signed by the justice who received the information and must state briefly the details of the information. Magistrates' Courts Rules 1981, r 98.
7 See MCA 1980, s 117 for warrants.
8 Where the information is in writing and delivered by post or otherwise to the justices' clerk's office, the information will have been laid when it is received by a duly authorised member of the clerk's staff. Cf *R v Leeds Justices, ex p Hanson* [1981] 3 All ER 72, [1981] 3 WLR 315.

When deciding whether to issue process the magistrate is exercising a judicial discretion.[9] He must make his decision on the merits of the case and not as a result of following a general policy laid down by the bench as a whole.[10] When the magistrate is considering the information the accused has no right to be present although he may attend if the magistrate grants him permission or, in exceptional circumstances, the accused may be invited to provide more information.[11]

WHEN SHOULD A MAGISTRATE DECLINE TO ISSUE PROCESS?

When a magistrate is considering an application for a summons, he must look carefully at the information. In *R v Wilson, ex p Battersea Borough Council,*[12] Lord Goddard set out the matters to which attention should be paid:

(a) is the offence known to the law, if so are the essential ingredients present?
(b) is the information in time?
(c) does the court have jurisdiction?
(d) has the informant the authority to prosecute?
(e) the justice may and should inquire to see whether the allegation is vexatious.

Categories (a)–(d) usually give little trouble, but difficulty may be encountered in the situation where all the formalities are in order but the magistrate may nevertheless feel it is oppressive or improper to issue process. How much discretion does the magistrate have?

It is clear that the magistrate cannot interfere with the information by directing the police as to what charge to bring,[13] but it appears that a magistrates' court does have a limited power to prevent an abuse of process. Certainly the Divisional Court has the power to interfere where there has been an undue delay in obtaining process and in *Mills v Cooper*[14] the case was dismissed by the magistrates on the ground that the information was oppressive and an abuse of process. Lord Parker went on to say that 'every court has undoubtedly a right in its discretion to decline to hear proceedings on the ground that they are oppressive and an abuse of the process of the court'. But doubt was cast

9 *R v Brentford Justices, ex p Catlin* [1975] QB 455, [1975] 2 All ER 201.
10 *R v Beacontree Justices, ex p Mercer* [1970] Crim LR 103, DC.
11 *R v West London Justices, ex p Klahn* [1979] 2 All ER 221, [1979] 1 WLR 933; *R v Peterborough Justices, ex p Hicks* [1978] 1 All ER 225, [1977] 1 WLR 1371.
12 [1948] KB 43, [1947] 2 All ER 569.
13 *R v Nuneaton Justices, ex p Parker* [1954] 3 All ER 251, [1954] 1 WLR 1318.
14 [1967] 2 QB 459, [1967] 2 All ER 100. D was prosecuted for an offence of being a gipsy and encamping on a highway contrary to s 127 of the Highways Act 1959. The case was dismissed on a submission that D was not a gipsy. A second information was preferred alleging a similar offence on a later date. It was held that (i) issue estoppel did not apply (ii) there was power for the magistrates to prevent an abuse of process but there was no abuse in this case.

on this dictum by the House of Lords in *DPP v Humphrys*[15] where their Lordships felt that it might be too wide. However, in the more recent case in the Divisional Court of *R v Brentford Justices, ex p Wong,*[16] Donaldson LJ agreed with the view of Lord Salmon in Humphreys that

> it is only if the prosecution amounts to an abuse of the process of the court and is oppressive and vexatious that the judge has the power to intervene

and in the *Brentford Justices* case this was applied to proceedings in the magistrates' court. The police had laid an information and obtained a summons because the six months' time limit had nearly expired. They took this course as a 'holding operation' because they had not finally decided whether to prosecute or not. The summons was not served by them until after a considerable delay. At the hearing the magistrates decided to hear the case. On appeal the Divisional Court decided that, whilst a court could not decline to hear a case merely because as a matter of policy the case should not have been brought, it can refuse to act where the actual process of the court has been abused.[17]

If the magistrate declines to issue a warrant or summons, he need give no reasons for this refusal although it may be useful to do so where the informant can give more information.[18] Once the process has finally been refused it is doubtful whether another magistrate could reconsider the matter unless there is a change in circumstances.[19]

SHOULD A SUMMONS OR A WARRANT BE ISSUED?

The general principle is that a summons should always be issued in preference to a warrant where it would be as effectual unless the charge is of a serious nature.[20] An additional safeguard to the liberty of the

15 [1977] AC1, [1976] 2 All ER 497.

16 [1981] QB 445, [1981] 1 All ER 884.

17 This is a rapidly expanding area of law. A recent case is *R v Watford Justices, ex p Outrim* [1982] Crim LR 593, DC where, through no fault of the defendant, the summons was not served until 22 months after the information was laid. It was held that the justices had a judicial discretion to refuse to hear the case where there was substantial prejudice to the accused or there was unreasonable delay. It should be noted that in this case there was no suggestion of an abuse of process. This should be contrasted with *R v Grays Justices, ex p Graham* [1982] 3 All ER 653, [1982] Crim LR 594 where on the facts the delay was held not to merit a quashing of the committal proceedings. For a review of the recent cases see 'Abuse of Process' (1982) 146 JP 717. See also *R v Canterbury and St Augustine's Justices, ex p Turner* (1983) 147 JP 193. (Similar principles apply to the conduct of committal proceedings. Even in the absence of bad faith or inefficiency, there could be extreme cases where delay could by itself amount to an abuse of process.)

18 *R v Worthing Justices, ex p Norvell and Abbot* [1981] 1 WLR 413, [1981] Crim LR 778.

19 *R v Worthing Justices above; R v Battier* (1880) 44 JP 490. This is analogous to the rule concerning reconsidering applications for bail referred to in chapter four, where one bench should not be seen to be acting as an appeal court from a decision of their colleagues.

20 *O'Brien v Brabner* (1885) 49 JP 227. A warrant to secure the attendance of the accused at the start of proceedings is known as a 'warrant in the first instance'.

subject is that a warrant can only be issued where the information is in writing and has been substantiated on oath.[1] Nor can a warrant be issued unless the offence concerned is indictable or imprisonable, or if it is neither of these two, the person's address is not sufficiently established for a summons to be served on him.

HOW PROCESS IS GRANTED IN PRACTICE

A busy magistrates' court, especially in a large urban area, may well be responsible for the issuing of tens and even hundreds of thousands of summonses in a year. The usual informant is the police. The police will normally prepare their own informations and summonses by using multi-part carbonised stationery. The information will be typed on the top sheet and this will be transferred to several summonses below. Great bundles of these informations and summonses will be delivered to the appropriate magistrates' court where they will be examined, often in the most perfunctory way and signed either by the justices' clerk himself (exercising his power under the Justices' Clerks' Rules 1970) or after he has approved them, by a member of his staff on his behalf. Similarly, if a magistrate has considered them, they may be signed by him or by a member of staff with a facsimile signature on a rubber stamp.[2] The court will then keep a copy of the summons together with the information and the police will retain a copy of the summons and send one to the defendant.

THE SERVICE OF A SUMMONS AND THE EXECUTION OF A WARRANT

Summons

A summons has been described as a form of letter instructing the accused that proceedings have been taken against him and that he should attend court. The summons will not have achieved its purpose unless that knowledge actually reaches the defendant.

A letter can be delivered either by handing it personally to the addressee, or by leaving it at his home or by sending it through the post. Only the first mentioned ensures that the letter reaches the intended recipient (of course one cannot be sure that he will read it). The Magistrates' Courts Rules prescribe three methods of serving a summons:

> 99(1) Service of a summons issued by a justice of the peace on a person other than a corporation may be effected –
>
> (a) by delivering it to the person to whom it is directed; or
>
> (b) by leaving it for him with some person at his last known or

1 MCA 1980, s 1(3). Note the expression used is 'substantiated' on oath not 'laid' on oath. Therefore the substantiating of the information may be done at any time after the laying of the information.

2 *R v Brentford Justices, ex p Catlin* [1975] QB 455, [1975] 2 All ER 201.

usual place of abode; or

(c) by sending it by post in a letter addressed to him at his last known or usual place of abode.

(2) If the person summoned fails to appear, service of a summons in the manner authorised by sub-paragraph (b) or (c) of paragraph (1) shall not be treated as proved unless it is proved that the summons came to his knowledge; and for that purpose any letter or other communication purporting to be written by him or on his behalf in such terms as reasonably to justify the inference that the summons came to his knowledge shall be admissible as evidence of that fact;

Provided that this paragraph shall not apply to any summons in respect of a summary offence served in the manner authorised by (a) the said sub-paragraph (b); or (b) the said sub-paragraph (c) in a registered letter or by recorded delivery service.

(3)–(7) omitted.

The effect of this for criminal matters is that where a summons has been sent by post (including ordinary post) or has been left at the defendant's place of abode, then before the court can be satisfied that it has been served, there must be some evidence that the defendant is aware of the proceedings. But where the offence is a summary one, a summons sent by recorded delivery or registered post or left at the defendant's place of abode is deemed to have been served unless there is evidence to the contrary, eg the letter returned marked 'gone away'.[3]

The rest of the rule (paragraphs (3)–(7)) provides inter alia that a summons may be served on a company by delivering it to its registered office and in the case of an individual it may be delivered to an address which has been specifically given by the defendant for that purpose.

Proof of service

How service was effected may be proved simply by a certificate on the copy of the summons, in which a person declares that he has served the summons either personally or by sending the summons by recorded delivery service or whatever.[4]

Warrant

A warrant is authority for the persons named in the warrant (usually the constables for a particular police force[5]) to arrest the accused. If the warrant is backed for bail, the accused is released and informed that he is under a duty to attend court on a certain date at a specific time. The police do not need to have the warrant in their possession when arresting the accused when an offence is charged[6] but they should

3 *R v County of London Quarter Sessions Appeal Committee, ex p Rossi* [1956] 1 QB 682, [1956] 1 All ER 670.

4 Magistrates' Courts Rules 1981, r 67.

5 Ibid, r 96.

6 MCA 1980, s 117.

produce it on request as soon as practicable.[7] Once the accused has been arrested, the warrant is said to have been executed and the warrant will be endorsed to that effect by the constable and returned to the court.

The relationship between the information and summons or warrant

The purpose of laying an information is to obtain a summons or warrant but nevertheless it is the information which remains the foundation for any proceedings.[8] Summary proceedings begin when the information is laid, not when the summons is served,[9] and therefore where a summons with a particular return date on it (ie the date of the court hearing at which the accused is to attend) is not served, a fresh summons may be issued on the same information even though it may be more than six months from the date of the offence.[10] Similarly a fresh warrant may be issued where a previous one has been destroyed. The information, once laid, does not expire nor can it be withdrawn, though of course there is a discretion whether to issue process on it.[11]

The summons or warrant is the means to secure the attendance of the accused at court and any defect in the process does not render the subsequent proceedings invalid. If the accused attends court any defect in the summons or warrant which caused him to be there will be irrelevant as to whether the proceedings against him can continue (unlike a defect in the information).[12]

INFORMATIONS AND THE 'CHARGE' PROCEDURE

It has been stated above that the purpose of laying an information is to obtain a warrant or summons. However, in the situation where an accused has been arrested by the police in circumstances where they do not need a warrant, the accused is brought to court either in custody or on police bail. Accordingly, process is unnecessary and an information does not need to be laid for that purpose. But if no information were

7 Ibid, s 125.

8 *R v Godstone Justices, ex p Secretary of State for the Environment* [1974] Crim LR 110, DC (immaterial that summons did not have the date of the information on it provided that the information itself was in order).

9 *Abraham v Jutsun* [1963] 2 All ER 402, [1963] 1 WLR 658, but where proceedings are brought about by arrest and charge then proceedings begin with the charge at the police station, *R v Brentwood Justices, ex p Jones* [1979] RTR 155, [1979] Crim LR 115, DC.

10 *R v Pickford* (1861) 25 JP 549.

11 *R v Leigh Justices, ex p Kara* (1980) 72 Cr App Rep 327, [1981] Crim LR 628.

12 *R v Hughes* (1879) 4 QBD 614, *Dixon v Wells* (1890) 25 QBD 249.

laid there could be no summary proceedings before magistrates because the Magistrates' Courts Act always refers to the 'summary trial of an information'.[13] Therefore the accepted view is that the copy of the charge sheet which the police will have forwarded to the court will serve as an information in writing.[14] Of course no summons or warrant would have to be issued in these circumstances.

Amending an information

The various requirements for laying an information and issuing a summons have been described already. Occasionally, an information or summons may be defective and this section will concern itself with the question of amending these defects. Attention will be concentrated on amending an information in view of the importance that is attached to an information as the foundation of the subsequent proceedings.

The situation would seem to be covered by the Magistrates' Courts Act 1980, section 123.

> (1) No objection shall be allowed to any information or complaint, or to any summons or warrant to procure the presence of the defendant, for any defect in it in substance or in form, or for any variance between it and the evidence adduced on behalf of the prosecutor or complainant at the hearing of the information or complaint.
>
> (2) If it appears to a magistrates' court that any variance between a summons or warrant and the evidence adduced on behalf of the prosecutor or complainant is such that the defendant has been misled by the variance, the court shall, on the application of the defendant, adjourn the hearing.

Unfortunately the section is not to be read literally. So it is not the case that no objection whatsoever can be taken to a defective information no matter how fundamental that defect may be.[15] Defects in an information may fall into one of three categories: those that are so trivial as to require no amendment; those that require amendment to make the position clear; and defects so fundamental that they cannot be amended. It is important to distinguish between the first two categories because if an information needs to be amended then the court must grant the defendant an adjournment if he so requests.

DEFECTS REQUIRING NO AMENDMENT

(a) Where the defect is in a particular which is not material to the information, eg in the case of an allegation of criminal damage where the information alleges that X was the owner of the property

13 Eg MCA 1980, s 9.

14 See Paley on *Summary Convictions* (10th edn, 1953) p 40 and *Blake v Beech* (1876) 40 JP 678 cited therein.

15 *Wright v Nicholson* [1970] 1 All ER 12, [1970] 1 WLR 142.

damaged whereas the owner was in fact Y. The essence of the offence is property belonging to another; it is not material who that 'other' is.[16] Perhaps also in this category is a charge of driving with excess alcohol in the blood where the information mistakenly alleges that the specimen had been required under section 8 of the Road Traffic Act 1972 not section 9.[17]

(b) Where there is a simple spelling mistake which can mislead no-one, eg as in *Taylor v Grey*[18] where a street name was misspelt.

(c) Where although the particulars of the offence given in the information are incorrect the defence is not misled because it knows what the intended allegation is and the prosecution and defence both intend to call evidence relating to that correct allegation, eg as in *R v Sandwell Justices, ex p West Midlands Passenger Transport Executive*[19] where the information concerned a defective 'front offside' tyre which by a mistake appeared on the information as a nearside tyre. The evidence called by the prosecution concerned only the front offside tyre and the defence were in no way misled. Accordingly, there was no need formally to amend the information as the offence was correct in substance being that for a defective tyre, only the particulars were incorrect.

But with all examples in this section caution should be exercised by a magistrates' court in holding that an information does not require amendment and it is submitted that care must be taken when interpreting decisions of the Divisional Court in this respect. By the time a case reaches the appellate court it is too late to amend an information. If it does require amendment then the conviction must be quashed, accordingly there may be examples where the court has declared an error not to require amendment and thus an otherwise justified conviction may be upheld.

DEFECTS THAT CAN BE AMENDED

(a) Minor mistakes concerning the place where the offence was committed

For example where the information names the wrong parish and the defendant was not misled. This is just the sort of error that section 123 is designed for.[20] Similarly where the error is in naming the correct street.[1] The aim should be to do justice between the parties. Obviously the situation would be different where the amendment seriously misled the accused or deprived the court itself of jurisdiction.

16 *Pike v Morrison* [1981] Crim LR 492.
17 *Lee v Wiltshire Chief Constable* [1979] RTR 349, [1979] Crim LR 319, DC.
18 [1973] RTR 281, [1974] Crim LR 46, DC. Cf also *Dring v Mann* (1948) 112 JP 270, 92 Sol Jo 272, DC.
19 [1979] RTR 17, [1979] Crim LR 56.
20 *Moulder v Judd* [1974] Crim LR 111.
1 *Darnell v Holliday* [1973] RTR 276, [1973] Crim LR 366; *Cotterill v Johal* [1982] Crim LR 523.

(b) Where the defendant is incorrectly named
The criteria here is that an amendment may be allowed provided it is clear that it is still the same person that is being referred to. Therefore there would be no problem if the wrong Christian name had been used[2] or even the wrong surname provided it was clear that it was the same person.[3]

(c) The date of the offence
Amendment has been allowed where the date of the offence alleged varies from the evidence given.[4]

(d) The offence itself
Within certain limitations the information may be amended to a different offence altogether even after the six months' time limit has expired, although this would be exceptional. In *R v Newcastle upon Tyne Justices, ex p John Bryce (Contractors) Ltd*[5] the defendant was summoned for permitting the use of an overloaded lorry. A statement of facts was served under the Magistrates' Courts Act procedure (cf ch 13) (pleas of guilty by letter). The hearing took place outside the statutory time limit for the laying of a fresh information. At the hearing it was clear that the defendant was guilty of 'using' not 'permitting' and the information was amended even though 'using' is a separate offence from 'permitting'. However, the Divisional Court was at pains to point out that this was not to be taken as licence for the courts to substitute one offence for another. The particular features of this case must be borne in mind: the defence had prior notice of all the evidence, this evidence was identical for both allegations and the prosecution did not seek to depart from it in any way.

Another situation which arises is where the statute alleged to have been contravened is referred to incorrectly in the information. Here it is up to the court to decide where the interests of justice lie before deciding whether to allow an amendment. It is suggested that where it is quite apparent from the particulars of the offence in the information what offence is alleged then an amendment may be allowed. Indeed it may be appropriate in some cases where a statute has been repealed but a former offence has been re-enacted in a later statute in identical terms to allow an amendment to cite the later statutory provision.[6]

2 *R v Norkett, ex p Geach* (1915) 139 LT Jo 316.
3 *Allan v Wiseman* [1975] RTR 217, [1975] Crim LR 37, DC.
4 *Wright v Nicholson* [1970] 1 All ER 12, [1970] 1 WLR 142.
5 [1976] 2 All ER 611, [1976] Crim LR 134, DC.
6 Cf *Meek v Powell* [1952] 1 KB 164, [1952] 1 All ER 347. Cf also *Thornley v Clegg* [1982] Crim LR 523 where the information did not refer to the section or act but the wording of the information followed the wording of the statute and the information could be amended to specify the act and section.

On the other hand where the particulars of the offence are so inadequately described as to reveal no offence known to the law then it may be said that the information containing them is not really an information at all and so cannot be amended.[7]

DEFECTS THAT CANNOT BE AMENDED

(a) Substituting a different defendant
An amendment cannot be allowed to substitute a different defendant as this would in effect be starting fresh proceedings. The usual situation in which this arises is where a person has been summoned in a personal capacity whereas the real defendant should be a company. The information cannot be amended to refer to the company as this has a distinct legal personality.[8] This should be distinguished from the situation where the name is merely amended without altering the identity of the person proceeded against, eg where a company's name is incorrectly referred to as '— Ltd' instead of '—P.L.C.'

(b) Where the information does not reveal any offence known to the law (see above)

(c) Where the information is bad for duplicity
Section 123 does not apply to duplicity[9] and the prosecution must check that the information is not duplicitous before the start of the trial and if it is, they must choose on which offence to proceed.[10] Once the trial has started it will then be too late. In effect there is a special rule for duplicity in that the amendment must take place before, and not during, the course of proceedings.

GENERAL REMARKS ON THE AMENDMENT OF INFORMATIONS

If the magistrates decide that an amendment is necessary then the defence must be granted an adjournment to reconsider its position.[11]

The conviction for any offence must accord with the information. A conviction for an offence which is at variance from that in the information is bad and will be quashed. Therefore the magistrates

7 *Garman v Plaice* [1969] 1 All ER 62, [1969] 1 WLR 19.
8 *City of Oxford Tramway Co v Sankey* (1890) 54 JP 564, and see now *Marco (Croydon) Ltd v Metropolitan Police* [1983] Crim LR 395; *Tector Ltd v DHSS* (1983) Times, 29 June.
9 *Edwards v Jones* [1947] 1 KB 659, [1947] 1 All ER 830.
10 *Hargreaves v Alderson* [1964] 2 QB 159, [1962] 3 All ER 1019. Contrast the position on indictment where an amendment may be made at any time, eg *R v Dossi* (1918) 13 Cr App Rep 158.
11 If the magistrates decide of their own motion that an amendment is necessary they should inform the defendant of this so that he can make representations. *Morriss v Lawrence* [1977] RTR 205, [1977] Crim LR 170.

must exercise their power to amend the information before they are functus officio.[12]

Time and again the High Court has said that the test for the magistrates to apply when deciding whether to permit an amendment to an information is that of doing justice between the parties;[13] has anyone been misled, if so could the situation be remedied by an adjournment? Often the remedy is not to declare that the information is bad but to allow an adjournment for the defence to be supplied with further and better particulars.[14]

12 Although an appeal against conviction to the Crown Court is by way of a rehearing the information cannot be amended on appeal. Cf *Garfield v Maddocks* [1974] QB 7, [1973] 2 All ER 303; disapproving dicta in *Wright v Nicholson* [1970] 1 All ER 12, [1970] 1 WLR 142.

13 *Garfield v Maddocks* [1974] QB 7, [1973] 2 All ER 303.

14 *Hutchison (Cinemas) Ltd v Tyson* [1970] Crim LR 350, DC.

Chapter 4

The first court appearance – legal aid, bail, mode of trial

The defendant by now is either in police custody charged, or about to be charged, with an offence, or else he has been charged and bailed to court, or has been summoned. At this stage the defendant may well contact his solicitor. If the accused is at liberty he will go to his solicitor's office, otherwise his solicitor may go to see him. In either situation the solicitor will want to make sure that he will be paid for his services. An accused person may either instruct a solicitor privately, ie that work will be done for an agreed fee, or if the defendant cannot afford to pay for the services of a solicitor, recourse will have to be made to the legal aid scheme.

Legal aid

Generally speaking legal aid, which is the financial assistance offered by central government for those who require legal services but cannot afford to pay for them, falls into two categories: legal advice and assistance, and legal aid. The former category covers the matters preliminary to a court hearing, and the latter covers matters preliminary to the trial (ie preparation and travel) and proceedings at the hearing including representation by a solicitor or counsel.[1]

LEGAL ADVICE AND ASSISTANCE

At the initial interview the solicitor will want to know some details from his client: his name, address and the matter that he has been accused of. The only reliable way to discover what the charge is will be to ask the defendant to produce the copy of his charge sheet or summons provided by the police. If these are not available and the defendant is vague about the charge, the police will have to be contacted. All this costs the solicitor time and money and yet he has not even reached the stage of deciding whether the accused will need representing in court.

1 Legal Aid Act 1974, ss 2 and 30.

Having found out what the accused is charged with, the solicitor will have to take a 'proof' of the accused's version of events. Of course, if invited to relate what happened a defendant would invariably start off on a rambling narrative which would take a long time to get to the point. The solicitor should therefore guide his client to the salient parts of his story and he can do this by examining the charge sheet or summons very carefully. He should note the matters outlined in chapter 3 concerning the date of the offence, jurisdiction, the substance of the charge and the statute alleged to have been contravened. For example, in the case of a charge of theft from a shop a common defence would be a lack of dishonest intent. Therefore it is extremely relevant whether the client is admitting or denying dishonesty in the appropriation of the goods.

An example of a proof of evidence (abbreviated) might be:

Proof of evidence of John Doe, 10 Gas St., Borchester

'I am 52 years of age, married with two children. On 30 March 1983 I went into Borchester with my wife to get the family shopping for the weekend. We went to the Acme Supermarket as we do every weekend and I pushed the supermarket trolley round the aisles while my wife selected items off the shelf. My wife then recognised a friend of hers by the meat display and she went off to talk to her. I was by the display of car accessories and tools and I remember looking at a screwdriver. Suddenly my wife shouted at me to get a move on as we had to get home to prepare lunch. I became flustered and I do not remember what happened to the screwdriver. I forgot all about it until we were on our way out of the supermarket when a store detective came up to me and asked me to go to the manager's office. A policeman came and asked me some questions. I don't think I made a statement in writing. I was arrested and taken to the police station and there I was charged. I was then given a charge sheet and told I was bailed to attend court in four weeks time.

(signed) John Doe.'

It can be seen that the preparation of even such a brief statement as this entails quite some work for the solicitor and for which he would expect to be remunerated, and in reality many more probing questions would have to be asked about how the screwdriver found its way into the bag. Therefore, the client, unless he is going to pay privately, should be asked for details to complete a 'Green Form' which is the common name for legal advice and assistance.

In our case of John Doe the initial interview would be funded by the Green Form as there would have been no time to prepare an application for legal aid, nor have this application granted by the magistrates' court.

The green form scheme

This system operates quickly and efficiently (though not generously) because the solicitor and client complete the form themselves and the

LA/Rep/6A
GREEN FORM

THE LAW SOCIETY

ENGLAND and WALES

Key Card

SOLICITOR'S REPORT ON LEGAL ADVICE AND ASSISTANCE GIVEN UNDER THE LEGAL AID ACT 1974

PLEASE USE BLOCK CAPITALS

Surname	Forenames	Male/Female	AREA REF. No.
Address			

<u>CAPITAL</u>	CLIENT	£
TOTAL SAVINGS and OTHER CAPITAL	SPOUSE	£
	TOTAL	£

A

<u>INCOME</u>

State whether in receipt of Supplementary Benefit or Family Income Supplement.

<u>YES/NO</u> If the answer is YES ignore the rest of this Section.

B

<u>Total weekly Gross Income</u>

Client		£
Spouse		£
TOTAL		£

<u>Allowances and Deductions from Income</u>

Income tax	£	
National Health Contributions, etc.	£	
Spouse	£	

C D E

Dependent children and/or other dependants	Number		
Under 5		£	
5 but under 11		£	
11 „ „ 13		£	
13 „ „ 16		£	
16 „ „ 18		£	
18 and over		£	
LESS TOTAL DEDUCTIONS		→	£
TOTAL WEEKLY DISPOSABLE INCOME			£

F

NOTE TO SOLICITORS

With effect from 1st April 1977

Where advice and assistance are being given in respect of divorce or judicial separation proceedings and the work to be carried out includes the preparation of a petition, the solicitor will be entitled to ask for his claim for Costs and Disbursements to be assessed up to an amount referred to in a general authority given by the Area Committee to exceed the prescribed basic sum in such cases.

TO BE COMPLETED AND SIGNED BY CLIENT

I am over the compulsory school-leaving age.

I <u>have/have not</u> previously received help from a solicitor about this matter under the Legal Aid and Advice Schemes.

I am liable to pay a contribution not exceeding .. .. £

G

I understand that any money or property which is recovered or preserved for me may be subject to a deduction if my contribution (if any) is less than my Solicitor's charges.

<u>The information on this page is to the best of my knowledge correct and complete. I understand that dishonesty in providing such information may lead to a prosecution.</u>

Date .... Signature ....

ENGLAND and WALES

THE LAW SOCIETY

Please see over for explanatory notes.

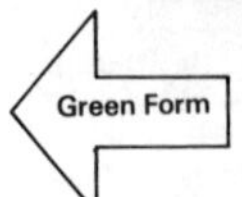

GREEN FORM KEY CARD (No. 13)

Effective from 1st April 1983

CAPITAL means the amount or value of every resource of a capital nature
In computing Disposable Capital disregard
(i) the value of the main or only dwelling house in which the client resides, and
(ii) the value of household furniture and effects, articles of personal clothing and tools or implements of the client's trade, and
(iii) the subject matter of the advice and assistance.

Maximum Disposable Capital for Financial Eligiblity
£700 client with no dependants.
£900 ,, ,, 1 dependant (whether spouse, child or other relative)
£1020 ,, ,, 2 such dependants
£1080 ,, ,, 3 such dependants
(Add £60 for each additional dependant.)

B **INCOME** means the total income from all sources which the client received or became entitled to during or in respect of the seven days up to and including the date of this application.

Note – a client in receipt of supplementary benefit or family income supplement is entitled to advice and assistance without contribution provided that his disposable capitals is within the limits set out in **A** above.

The capital and weekly income of both husband and wife must be taken into account, unless:
(a) they have a contrary interest;
(b) they live apart; or
(c) it is inequitable or impracticable to aggregate their means.
If a housewife living with her husband is seeking advice in connection with a matter in which he has a contrary interest, the money which she receives from him for normal household expenses should not be included as part of her own separate income.

In computing Disposable Income deduct:-
(i) Income Tax
(ii) Payments under the Social Security Acts 1975-80
(iii) £29.**55** in respect of either husband or wife (if living together) whether or not their means are aggregated. Where they are separated or divorced, the allowance will be the actual maintenance paid by the client in respect of the previous 7 days.

These deductions also apply to the spouse's income if there is aggregation.

(iv) £13.13 for each child under 11 years of age
£19.73 ,, ,, ,, of 11 but under 16 years of age
£23.69 for each dependant (or child) of 16 and 17 years of age
£30.83 ,, ,, ,, of 18 years of age or over

Client's Contributions

Disposable Income	*Maximum Contribution*	*Disposable Income*	*Maximum Contribution*
Not exceeding £47 a week	nil	Not exceeding £75 a week	£28
,, £55 ,,	£5	,, £79 ,,	£33
,, £59 ,,	£10	,, £83 ,,	£37
,, £63 ,,	£15	,, £87 ,,	£41
,, £67 ,,	£20	,, £91 ,,	£46
,, £71 ,,	£24	,, £95 ,,	£50
		,, £99 ,,	£55

G Where the initial green form limit is £40 client's contribution in excess of this amount can only be called for if a financial extension has been obtained from the general committee.

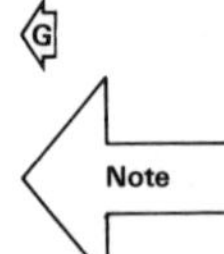

The green form must be signed by the client at the initial interview as soon as his eligibility has been determined except in the case of an authorised postal application.

PUBLISHER'S NOTE. It should be noted that some key cards contain an error which has been amended on the above form. The amount of the allowance which may be deducted in the case of a spouse is £29.55 and not £29.38 as stated on existing forms.

assistance takes the form of a fixed fee interview. The fee that is to be paid is assessed by following the guidelines on the form itself and the 'key card'. The law on the Green Form Scheme is to be found in sections 1–5 of the Legal Aid Act 1974 and the financial guidelines contained in the form itself are governed by the Legal Advice and Assistance Regulations (No. 2) 1980.

The solicitor must complete the form from information supplied by the client. The fee to be paid depends on the client's disposable income (which is calculated in accordance with Schedule 2 to the Regulations) and the scale in Schedule 3. Although the client may be eligible for assistance, the solicitor may decline to act for him without stating his reasons although he may be asked to provide information to the Law Society on request by that body.[2]

Having fixed the fee to be paid and having agreed to act, the solicitor may collect the fee from his client in full or by instalments but in either event if the costs do not reach the amount paid by the client the balance must be reimbursed.[3] In the usual case the contribution paid by the client does not cover the costs of the advice and so the deficit has to be claimed by the solicitor from the Area Committee of the Law Society who assess the bill and pay the balance.[4]

Unfortunately for the solicitor there is an overall limit to the amount of work that can be done on the Green Form.[5] Although he can apply to the local area committee for an extension of that limit, it would only be in unusual cases that the limit would be extended.[6] In the case of John Doe only preliminary work would be done on the Green Form so that an application for legal aid could be prepared and submitted without delay.

LEGAL AID

The main financial assistance provided in criminal proceedings is legal aid. This covers the preparation and conduct of the defence case in criminal proceedings. The scheme is governed by Part II of the Legal Aid Act 1974, sections 28–40.[7]

Proceedings for which legal aid may be granted[8]

Legal aid may be granted where a person is charged with an offence or

2 Legal Advice and Assistance Regulations (No. 2) 1980, regs 12 and 13.
3 Ibid, reg 22.
4 Ibid, reg 23.
5 This limit changes regularly and at the time of writing was £40 (Legal Aid Act 1974, s 3(2)).
6 Legal Advice and Assistance Regulations (No. 2) 1980, reg 15.
7 Part I of the Act deals with advice and assistance (the Green Form) and legal aid for civil cases.
8 Legal Aid Act 1974, s 28.

where he is to be dealt with by the magistrates. The expression 'dealt with' is used to cover such situations as proceedings where the defendant is brought back to the court for breach of a probation order or a community service order.[9] Legal aid may also be granted where there is a complaint for a bind over under section 115 of the Magistrates' Courts Act 1980. But it should be noted that legal aid is never available to prosecute a matter, so for example one neighbour who wished to prosecute another for common assault after a quarrel would not be able to obtain legal aid for that purpose.

Committals for sentence and trial, and appeals from the magistrates' court may be covered by legal aid which may be granted by the magistrates or the Crown Court.[10]

When will legal aid be granted?

Just because there is the power to grant legal aid for particular proceedings it does not necessarily mean that it will be granted. The power to grant legal aid is subject to the discretion of the authority granting it.[11]

The criterion for granting legal aid is that it shall be 'desirable to do so in the interests of justice'.[12] The question then prompts itself when is it in the interests of justice to grant legal aid? This is partly answered by the Act itself where certain situations are deemed to require legal aid to be granted.

The relevant situations in the magistrates' court are:

(a) where the accused is committed for trial on a charge of murder;
(b) where the accused is produced from custody on remand and may be remanded in custody again and he wishes to be legally represented, he must be granted legal aid to cover that remand appearance if he has not been represented previously in the proceedings; and
(c) where after conviction the accused is remanded in custody for inquiries to be made before sentence.

In addition to these situations where it is deemed to be in the interests of justice to grant legal aid, there are other factors which may make the grant of legal aid desirable in a particular case. Such factors are illustrated in the 'Widgery Criteria'.[13]

Legal aid shall be granted if:

(a) the charge is a grave one in the sense that the accused is in real jeopardy of losing his liberty or livelihood or suffering serious damage to his reputation; or

9 Ibid, s 30(12).
10 Ibid, s 28(5), (7).
11 Ibid, s 28(1).
12 Ibid, s 29(1).
13 See The Departmental Committee on Legal Aid in Criminal Proceedings (the Widgery Committee) 1966.

(b) the charge raises a substantial question of law; or
(c) the accused is unable to follow the proceedings and state his own case because of his inadequate knowledge of English, mental illness or other mental or physical disability; or
(d) the nature of the defence involves the tracing and interviewing of witnesses or expert cross-examination of a witness for the prosecution; or
(e) legal representation is desirable in the interests of someone other than the accused as, for example, in the case of sexual offences against young children when it is undesirable that the accused should cross-examine the witness in person.[14]

The means test

If any of the above mentioned conditions is fulfilled, it will be desirable in the interests of justice to grant legal aid. However, before legal aid will be granted it must be apparent that the applicant's means are such that he requires assistance in meeting the costs which he may incur.[15] Accordingly, there are two tests for every application for legal aid:
(a) is it necessary in the interests of justice that the accused is represented, and
(b) are his means such that he requires assistance.

Making an application[16]

An application for legal aid can be made either orally or in writing to the court, a magistrate or a justices' clerk,[17] but with the application there should be a written statement of means on a Form 4. Although there are prescribed forms in the Schedule to the Regulations, each court generally adopts its own forms, usually combining Form 1 (the application) with Form 4 (the statement of means).

The contents of the form are mainly self-explanatory but needless to say the form should be completed carefully. The grant of a legal aid order is not automatic and will only be granted after due consideration by the court. Therefore the form should be as complete and persuasive as possible. It is not enough for an applicant to repeat parrot-fashion one of the Widgery criteria and automatically expect to obtain legal aid. Just as in court an advocate would be expected to do his best to put forward his client's case, so he should do the same when assisting his client to complete his application for legal aid.

Once the application and statement of means have been completed,

14 Further guidance can be obtained from the reported cases: legal aid is appropriate for those eligible for deportation – *R v Sullivan* [1964] Crim LR 120 – and those committed for trial on serious matters – *R v Howes* [1964] 2 QB 459.
15 Legal Aid Act 1974, s 29(2).
16 Legal Aid in Criminal Proceedings (General) Regulations 1968.
17 Ibid, reg 1 and Form 1.

the form should be sent to the office of the clerk to the justices for the appropriate magistrates' court. On arrival, the application will be considered by the justices' clerk or more usually a duly authorised member of his staff. The justices' clerk has power to grant an application for legal aid but not refuse it. If he feels inclined not to grant the application he will refer it to a magistrate.

Assessment of means when considering whether to grant legal aid

Assuming the offence merits legal aid, the financial circumstances have to be considered. Unfortunately only scant assistance is afforded by the Legal Aid in Criminal Proceedings (Assessment of Resources) Regulations 1978. The salient provisions are that the following matters should be taken into account:

(a) the resources of the applicant, ie those which are reasonably available to meet the costs he is likely to incur after he has provided for all necessary commitments (disregarding any capital which could not be realised in time to obtain legal representation)[18]

(b) the resources and commitments of the applicant's spouse should be included unless it is impracticable to do so.[19]

Having considered the applicant's resources legal aid cannot be refused where:

(a) the applicant or his spouse is in receipt of a supplementary benefit or allowance; or

(b) the resources immediately[20] available to the applicant at the date of the application do not exceed £75 (or £120 if married).

If the applicant's resources are above these minima, the clerk has discretion to grant the application or refuse it until a down payment is made, which means that the legal aid order will not be issued until the required payment is made.[1] If the clerk does not feel disposed to grant the application he must then refer it to a magistrate.

Where legal aid is granted

A legal aid order will be typed and sent to the solicitor named on the order.[2] Legal aid for several defendants will normally be granted only to one solicitor unless a conflict is shown to exist between the defendants.[3]

18 Legal Aid in Criminal Proceedings (Assessment of Resources) Regulations 1978, reg 6.

19 Ibid, reg 5.

20 'Immediately' is to be interpreted literally, the court is not entitled to adjourn the proceedings so that the defendant may save up some money: *R v Selby Justices, ex p Woodcock* [1983] Crim LR 179.

1 Legal Aid in Criminal Proceedings (General) Regulations 1968, reg 1(6).

2 Ibid, reg 6(2). Note it is a legal aid *order* not a certificate which is the appropriate term for civil legal aid.

3 Ibid, reg 14 and H.O.C. 93/1976. *R v Solihull Justices* (1976) 16 March (unreported).

The scope of the order. Legal aid will cover representation by a solicitor before the magistrates' court and, where appropriate, representation by solicitor and counsel, including advice on the preparation of the case for the hearing.[4] Counsel will not be included on an order for representation before the magistrates unless the offence concerned is indictable and the case is unusually grave or difficult, making representation by solicitor and counsel desirable.[5] An order for representation for proceedings in the magistrates' court will also cover advice and assistance given by the solicitor on whether there are any reasonable grounds for appeal and if there are, assistance in preparing a notice of appeal or application for a case to be stated where the appeal is lodged within time.[6] Most importantly the order will only cover expenses incurred since the order was made as there is no power to back date the order.[7]

Remuneration (see form on p 66, below).[8] The amount allowed by the taxing authority (the Law Society) shall be 'such fees and expenses as appear . . . to be fair remuneration for work actually and reasonably done.'[9] In practice the remuneration is worked out on a time basis for different categories of work, ie preparation, travelling, hearing time and waiting time. The Law Society will fix certain agreed rates and payment will be made accordingly. The scale of fees might be

Preparation	£ a per hour
Travelling	£ b per hour
Waiting	£ c per hour
Hearing	£ d per hour

and these rates would be adjusted on a periodic basis. The rates do not mean that there will be no departure from the scales, but they are a guideline to a fair remuneration. To these amounts will be added disbursements and other necessary expenses. With the legal aid order sent from the court will come a form to claim the solicitor's costs from the Law Society. At the conclusion of the case this form (in effect a bill of costs) will be completed by the solicitor and forwarded to the

4 Legal Aid Act 1974, s 30(1).
5 As a matter of practice legal aid should be granted to counsel for committal proceedings on a charge of murder even though the case is not necessarily difficult (*R v Derby Justices, ex p Kooner* [1971] 1 QB 147, [1970] 3 All ER 399), although this should be confined to murder as the preliminary proceedings in the magistrates' court for many grave matters can be quite adequately dealt with by a solicitor alone. An exception to this of course would be where there was a good reason for conducting a full committal under MCA 1980, s 6(1). Cf *R v Guildford Justices, ex p Scott* [1975] Crim LR 286, (1975) 119 Sol Jo 237, DC.
6 Legal Aid Act 1974, s 30(5).
7 *R v Rogers* [1979] 1 All ER 693, 69 Cr App Rep 96.
8 See Legal Aid in Criminal Proceedings (Fees and Expenses) Regulations 1968 (as amended).
9 Ibid, reg 1.

LA/Rep/3B — No covering letter necessary – explanatory notes on reverse

The Law Society — Legal Aid in Criminal Proceedings (Fees and Expenses) Regulations 1968 (as amended)

A — Serial Number — **SP** — FOR OFFICIAL USE ONLY

Initials and Surname of Main Defendant

If you acted for more than one legally aided defendant, list their names overleaf and enter the total number in the right hand box

Number of Defendants if more than one

1. Name of court and date of charge — 1. — Date
2. Brief description of charge(s) — 2.
3. Type of hearing — 3. * Summary trial/Preliminary hearing (Quote section)
4. Plea – Where case tried — 4. * Guilty/Not Guilty
5. Result of trial or hearing — 5. * Guilty/Not Guilty/Committed
6. Was your client ordered to pay a contribution? If so, amount — 6. * No/Yes. Amount £
7. Was Counsel assigned? — 7. * Yes/No
8. If not, was Counsel instructed? — 8. * Yes/No

* Delete as necessary

Summary of all work done

(If there is insufficient space to enable you to provide the details required to justify your charges, continue on a separate sheet)

Personal attendances (taking statements, etc.)				Correspondence & telephone calls		Attendance at court (Apportion travelling time if more than one case)			
Client		Other persons					Time taken		
Date	Time taken	Date	Time taken	No. of letters written		Date	Travelling	Waiting	Hearing
				No. of telephone calls					

Special features (if any) ....

....

....

(Use separate letter if appropriate)

Claims for Costs

If you have advised your client in connection with this matter under a GREEN FORM which you had already submitted for assessment, please give the date of the relevent form LA/ACC/8B. If you have not yet submitted a GREEN FORM for assessment and intend to do so, please attach it together with a form LA/ACC/8B to this form. Date of LA/ACC/8B ....

	Solicitor's costs	Disbursements	Counsel's fees (Total including VAT as shown on fee note)
Basic fee		As Listed Overleaf	
Adjournment fee(s)			
Additional Defendants			
Work on appeal			
Total Fees			
Plus VAT %			
Totals	£	£	£

Do you wish to make any comment on the fee claimed by Counsel. (See explanatory Note No. 6)

Signed .... Solicitor Date .... Solicitor's reference ....

Firm name (in full) ....

Address ....

Counsel's Name & Address ....

For official use only

B — Control — Sol. A/c No. — Coun. A/c — Counsel Assigned

Authorised for Payment — Date .... Signed ....

appropriate area law society which will tax it and pay the resulting account. In order to complete the form correctly it will be apparent that the solicitor should be scrupulous to keep a record of the work he has done, especially the times he has spent on the different aspects of the case. For example, he should not only record his preparation and travelling time but also the time the court hearing began and concluded. As unsatisfactory as 'taximeter' advocacy may be, that is the system that is in use.

Legal aid and the defendant

The statement of means (Form 4) was used to determine whether the applicant should be granted legal aid or not. If legal aid is granted, the statement of means is still relevant because the grant of an order is not the end of the matter. Depending on his resources, the legally aided defendant may still be called upon to pay a contribution towards the costs of his defence at the conclusion of his case. How much that contribution will be depends on the 'maximum contribution' payable as calculated by the court.

Unfortunately again there is very little guidance on how the maximum contribution figure is to be calculated. The Legal Aid in Criminal Proceedings (Assessment of Resources) Regulations 1978 provide the following guidelines:

(a) calculate the applicant's net income for the 12 months prior to the application. If it was £815 or less (£1319 if married) and his capital at the time of the application is £75 or less (£120 if married), or he is in receipt of supplementary benefit, then no contribution is payable.[10]

(b) if the exemption from liability in (a) does not apply, then the assessor will consider the applicant's income over the next 12 months (the likely income can be based on the income over the previous 12 months) and deduct tax, national insurance etc, costs of accommodation and other matters for which he must or reasonably may provide.

    To this is added a sum for capital excluding the value of his main or only dwelling house and various other exemptions.

The resulting sum is the maximum contribution. To eke out the lack of guidance in assessing the contribution payable, the Home Office recommend that courts should have some regard to the limits and allowances applicable to the civil aid scheme.

Contribution orders[11]

Suppose that an applicant for legal aid has been assessed to have a

10 Legal Aid in Criminal Proceedings (Assessment of Resources) Regulations 1978, reg 7(2).

11 Legal Aid Act 1974, s 32.

maximum contribution of £300. At the end of the case the court might ask the defence advocate for an estimate of his costs. If he can provide such an estimate (eg £100) the court might order the defendant to pay a 'legal aid contribution order' of £100 which might be payable in instalments in the same way as a fine. This order would be completely separate from any fine or other penalty or order for costs which the court might make, and would be collected separately. The money collected would be collected by the justices' clerk and forwarded to the Law Society. If in the example above the estimated costs were £400, the defendant could not be called upon to pay more than his maximum contribution, ie £300.[12]

The possibility of a contribution order being made is a matter which the solicitor should draw to the attention of his client as it can be a shock to a client granted legal aid to be ordered to pay a substantial sum by way of a contribution order at the end of his case.

A contribution order can be made whether an accused is convicted or acquitted and as a rough guideline it is submitted that it should be made whenever an accused would not otherwise obtain his costs from central funds or the other party on the merits of his case.

REFUSAL, REVOCATION AND AMENDMENT

If an application for legal aid is refused there is no appeal as such but the applicant may renew his application at the 'court of trial or other proceedings'.[13] As 'other proceedings' refers to the hearing of appeals the regulation refers to an application at a summary trial of an information in the sense of the occasion when a case is about to be disposed of, not merely at a preliminary hearing.[14] In practice a court will often reconsider an application if fresh information is available which was not available on the original application.

A legal aid order may be amended by substituting one solicitor for another and if this is done, the original solicitor will be paid for the work done up to the time of the amendment.[15] The order may be revoked entirely either on the application of the accused or where his legal representative withdraws from the case and the court considers it undesirable in view of the accused's conduct to amend the order to substitute another solicitor.

12 The court can make an order that the defendant pay a contribution of all of the defence costs paid by the legal aid fund or a specified figure whichever is the lesser sum. The defence costs will be paid by the Law Society and the amount notified to the clerk to the justices who will then arrange for the collection of the appropriate amount from the defendant: cf reg 20 of the Legal Aid in Criminal Proceedings (General) Regulations 1968.

13 Legal Aid in Criminal Proceedings (General) Regulations 1968, reg 5.

14 *R v Macclesfield Justices, ex p Greenhalgh* (1979) 144 JP 142; *R v Cambridge Crown Court, ex p Hagi* (1979) 144 JP 145.

15 Legal Aid Act 1974, s 31.

JUVENILES

The particular problems concerning legal aid for juveniles is discussed in chapter 12.

Adjournments and bail

Unfortunately not every case can proceed on the first occasion that it is before the court. The reasons for this are many: the prosecution may not have completed their preparations, the defence may not have obtained legal aid, and so on. Even at a later stage a case may have to be adjourned to a suitable date for a trial when all the witnesses will be available, or after a conviction for the preparation of a social inquiry report and sentence. Accordingly, it is important to note the power of the court to adjourn the case and deal with the defendant in the intervening period. To understand the powers of adjournment it is necessary first of all to distinguish three categories of offences.

PURELY INDICTABLE, EITHER WAY AND PURELY SUMMARY OFFENCES

In chapter 2 offences were categorised as arrestable or non arrestable. In addition, they may be divided into purely indictable, either way or purely summary offences. Purely indictable offences can only be tried at the Crown Court, either way offences are indictable but they can be tried by the magistrates with the accused's consent, and purely summary offences can only be tried in the magistrates' court.

The two different sets of categories – arrestable/ non-arrestable, and purely indictable/either way/purely summary are not directly linked although in practice indictable matters, being serious offences, will carry a power of arrest whilst although most purely summary offences are non arrestable, some do carry the power of arrest.

Distinguishing the category of offence
The basic premise to work from is that offences are purely indictable as this was the position at common law. Before an offence can be either way or summary, there must be a statutory provision specifying this.

Either way offences. There are two statutory provisions governing this. Firstly, Schedule 1 to the Magistrates' Courts Act 1980 provides a list of either way offences, this is supplemented by Schedule 2 which deals with the special procedure for offences of criminal damage where the value is above or below £200. In addition, there are many offences where the section of the Act which specifies the penalty will stipulate a penalty if the case is tried on indictment and another penalty where the case is heard summarily, eg section 26(1) of the Vehicles (Excise) Act 1971.

if any person forges or fraudulently alters or uses, or fraudulently lends or allows to be used by any other person –

(a) any mark to be fixed or sign to be exhibited on a mechanically propelled vehicle in accordance with sections 19 or 21 of this Act; or

(b) any trade plates or replacements such as are mentioned in section 23(2) (c) of this Act; or

(c) any licence or registration document under this Act,

he shall be liable on *summary conviction* to a fine not exceeding £1,000 or on *conviction on indictment* to imprisonment for a term not exceeding two years. [Italics supplied]

This indicates that the offence is triable either way.

Summary offences. The statute which creates the offence will also prescribe the penalty and this gives the clue to the status of the offence. The penalty section will usually say 'Penalty on summary conviction £X' or words to that effect. For an example of this see Schedule 4 to the Road Traffic Act 1972. Other offences are declared to be triable only summarily by being listed in Schedule 1 to the Criminal Law Act 1977.

Committal proceedings. Although a purely indictable offence cannot be tried in the magistrates' court the case will start there because it is the magistrates' function to act as examining justices before deciding whether to commit the accused for trial at the Crown Court.

Mode of trial proceedings. Either way offences may be tried either in the magistrates' court or the accused may be committed for trial at the Crown Court as for a purely indictable offence. When an accused is charged with an either way offence, he appears before the court in mode of trial proceedings which are not concluded until the magistrates decide where the case shall be heard (and if they decide for summary trial the accused must consent to this). If the bench decide summary trial is inappropriate, or if the accused refuses to consent to summary trial, the case will then proceed in the same way as a purely indictable matter.

Summary trial. These are the proceedings where the magistrates try the offence either because there is no possibility of trial on indictment or the defendant has elected to be tried summarily.

ADJOURNMENT AND REMAND

An adjournment of a case should be a quite straightforward affair. At the hearing the case is put off to another date when all the parties should attend and carry on the proceedings, in the meantime everyone goes home. Whilst this is quite satisfactory for civil cases and minor criminal matters, what happens when the accused has committed a serious offence and is perhaps likely not to turn up at court unless he is forcibly brought to court. He may well have appeared at the first hearing from the custody of the police after his initial arrest. Is he to be released during the adjournment period? The answer is that there is a power to do something more than merely adjourn a case: the court, where appropriate, may (or must) remand the accused. A remand means that the accused is kept in custody during the period of the adjournment or is released on bail.

A release *on bail* differs from a simple adjournment in that the court may attach conditions to the bail regulating the accused's conduct, and if the accused breaches those conditions, he may be arrested and brought to the court forthwith.[16] Whether or not the bail is subject to conditions, if the accused fails to surrender at the appointed time and place he will be guilty of an offence punishable with up to three months' imprisonment and a fine of £400.[17]

Therefore a remand means an adjournment in custody or on bail with the obligations that this implies.

When can the court remand an accused?

In committal proceedings there is no choice. For every adjournment the court must remand the accused.[18] In mode of trial proceedings the court is not obliged to remand the accused except where he was initially arrested and brought to the court in custody or he was bailed to court by the police, or he was previously remanded in the proceedings.[19] In the case of purely summary matters the court has a discretion whether to remand or not at every stage.[20]

The length of an adjournment or remand

Where an accused has been remanded in custody the remand may not be for more than eight clear days if he is detained in prison: ie if he is remanded on Monday 1st the accused must not be remanded to a later date than Wednesday 10th. Where the accused has been remanded in police custody the period is three clear days.[1]

The main exceptions to this are firstly where the accused has been convicted and his case has been adjourned under section 10(3) of the Magistrates' Courts Act 1980 for inquiries to be made before determining the most suitable form of sentence, or section 30, remand for medical examination. In this case the remand may be for up to four

16 Bail Act 1976, s 7.
17 Or 12 months' imprisonment and unlimited fine if committed for sentence to the Crown Court.
18 MCA 1980, s 5(1).
19 Ibid, s 18(4).
20 Ibid, s 10(4).
1 Cf ibid, s 128. For an exception in mode of trial proceedings cf s 128(6) (c).

weeks if the accused is remanded on bail or there is simply an adjournment, or three weeks if he is remanded in custody.

Second, where the accused is already detained in custody under a custodial sentence and he is not to be released in the intervening period, section 131 of the Magistrates' Courts Act 1980 allows the court to remand him for up to 28 days. (But if the accused would have served his sentence in a shorter period, eg 15 days, the remand may only be for the period he will be in custody under his sentence.)

Remands in absence.[2] It would be ideal if all cases could be concluded forthwith, but as a case may have to be adjourned (for example, where a serious matter is to be tried at the Crown Court, the case may have to be adjourned over a period of several weeks or months) in the interim period the defendant may have to be remanded in custody. According to the usual rule that a remand in custody before conviction may not be for more than eight clear days, the defendant would have to be produced at weekly intervals even though he may not wish to apply for bail, or may not be entitled to make an application for bail on the basis of the *Nottingham City Justices* case discussed below. Therefore in prescribed circumstances, the court may determine a remand in the absence of the accused.

The conditions to be complied with are that where there is a hearing before the court and

(a) the court is adjourning committal proceedings, mode of trial proceedings or the trial of an information (ie adjourning a case before conviction); and
(b) the accused is present before the court; and
(c) he has attained the age of 17; and
(d) he is legally represented before the court (although his solicitor need not necessarily be present in the court);

the court must explain to the accused the powers of the court to hold further remand hearings in his absence. The accused must be asked if he consents to these further hearings being held in his absence. If he does not consent, he must be produced at each and every remand hearing, even if this means appearing every week for a period of several months.

If the accused does consent to the determination of applications for his remand in his absence, the court may remand him for up to three occasions in his absence. On the fourth occasion he must be produced before the court and the hearing take place in his presence, although thereafter the same sequence may be followed. But if on any determination of a remand in the absence of the accused the court is not satisfied that the above criteria are fulfilled (because for example

2 See generally MCA 1980, ss 128, 130 and 131 as amended by Criminal Justice Act 1982, s 59 and Sch 9.

the accused has withdrawn his consent to the hearings being held in his absence, or he is no longer legally represented), the accused will have to be brought before the court as soon as possible so that the application for his remand may be heard in his presence.

A sequence of remands might appear as follows:

	<8 clear days>								
Hearing:	1	2	3	4	5	6	7	8	9
	Present	Absent	Absent	Absent	Present	Absent	Absent	Absent	Present

It should be noted of course that this power does not authorise the period of the remand to extend beyond the usual period of eight clear days (or 28 days where the accused is already detained under a custodial sentence), it only provides that a remand hearing may take place in the absence of the accused.

Other provisions for remand in absence. Sometimes an accused who has been granted bail or has been remanded in custody cannot appear at the appropriate date because of accident or illness. In this case the court may further remand him in custody or on bail for a further period,[3] or even if this does not apply the court may always further remand an accused who has been released on bail.[4]

Remand courts

It is common, especially in the case of more serious offences, for the matter not to be ready to proceed on the first appearance of the accused and it would be rare indeed for committal proceedings to be heard on the first appearance of the accused. In cases where the police have arrested an accused and brought him before the court from custody a decision will have to be made by the court whether to remand the accused back into custody during the period of the adjournment or whether to release him on bail. Bearing in mind the powers of the police themselves to remand an accused on unconditional bail to attend court on the first appearance, if they have produced a prisoner from custody it is likely that they want him further remanded in custody or if bailed, for conditions to be attached to that bail. In larger courts it is usual for all cases where there is going to be an adjournment of the case of an accused who is in custody to be grouped together in one court known as a 'remand court'. But it should always be remembered that every adjournment of a case where the defendant is in custody or on bail is a remand.

THE DECISION WHETHER TO REMAND IN CUSTODY OR ON BAIL[5]

The general principle is that an accused man has a right to be released

3 MCA 1980, s 129(1).
4 Ibid, s 129(3).
5 Bail Act 1976, s 4.

on bail where he is not yet convicted of the offence charged, or even where he is convicted but his case has been adjourned for social inquiry reports or other further information to be provided for the court before sentence. However, where the accused has been convicted and committed for sentence to the Crown Court the presumption of liberty does not apply.

In summary proceedings in the magistrates' court or in committal proceedings the defendant must always be granted bail unless the court finds an exception to the right to bail. In the case of imprisonable offences these exceptions are set out in Schedule 1, Part I to the Bail Act 1976 and are summarised here:

(a) where the court has substantial grounds for believing the accused would
   (i) fail to answer to bail, or
   (ii) commit further offences on bail, or
   (iii) interfere with witnesses or otherwise obstruct the course of justice

   each of these exceptions must be substantiated by a reason given by the court such as
   (i) the nature and seriousness of the offence or default (and the probable method of dealing with the accused for it),
   (ii) the character, antecedents, associations and community ties of the defendant,
   (iii) the accused's previous record when granted bail (eg committing offences on bail or absconding),
   (iv) (except when remanding after conviction for a report) the strength of the evidence against the accused,
   (v) any other relevant reason.

The other exceptions to the right to bail are:

(b) remand in custody for the accused's own welfare,
(c) where the accused is already in custody as a result of a prison sentence,
(d) where there has been insufficient time to gather information to make the bail decision;
(e) where the accused has absconded or breached the conditions of his bail in the same proceedings already,
(f) where the case has been adjourned for reports or inquiries and it is impracticable to gain the information or prepare reports without remanding the accused in custody

These exceptions do not need a supplementary reason to be given as in exception (a).[6]

Why bail is refused

The most common exceptions for refusing bail are (a) (i) (ii) or (iii).

6 Any one of these exceptions is enough to remand the accused in custody.

Consider these examples:

(a) A dwelling house burglar with a bad previous record. There is strong evidence against him and if convicted he will inevitably receive a custodial sentence. The court may fear that if he is granted bail, he will commit as many offences as he can before he is sent to prison as he may want to obtain as much money as he can to hide away until he is released or to maintain his family in the style to which they are accustomed.

The reasons given for refusing bail might be 'fear of further offences because of his character and antecedents, the serious nature of the offence and the probable method of disposal and the strength of evidence against him.'[7]

(b) A thief stealing a bottle of whisky from an off-licence. Numerous previous convictions all over the country. No fixed abode, no connection with the place where the offence was committed. The court might remand him in custody because it feared that he might not answer to his bail in view of his character and antecedents and his lack of community ties.

(c) The defendant is part of a group of offenders. It is feared that if he is released he would 'tip off' the other accused before the police could arrest them. He might be remanded in custody because it was feared that he might obstruct the course of justice in view of the nature of the charge and the allegations made against him.

Conditional bail

In some situations the court might feel able to release the accused on bail provided there were conditions attached to the bail. Conditions commonly imposed are:

(a) residence;
(b) curfew;
(c) reporting at a police station;
(d) non-association with specified people;
(e) sureties.

Other conditions may be imposed provided they are reasonable and are enforceable.

It should be said at the outset that conditions should not be attached to bail as a matter of course. The conditions should be imposed for a reason and that reason must be stated in open court by the justices.[8] The conditions should be imposed to allow an accused to be at liberty where the only alternative would be a remand in custody.

A condition of residence might be useful when coupled with a condition of reporting at a police station where there was a fear that the accused might leave the district. A curfew might be employed to inhibit

7 *R v Phillips* (1947) 111 JP 333, 32 Cr App Rep 47.
8 Bail Act 1976, s 5(3).

the accused's nocturnal burgling activities. Non-association with the accused's spouse could be appropriate in domestic disputes. But consideration must be given whether conditions attached to bail serve any useful purpose: does a curfew really prevent a burglar going out at night? Is reporting once a week at a police station going to stop the offender committing further offences, or will it prevent him from absconding? There must surely be a suspicion that sometimes conditions are imposed (a) because the police ask for them (b) the magistrates, whilst not wishing to lock up the accused, do not want him to 'get away with it'.

Sureties

The one condition not mentioned so far is perhaps the most useful: the surety. In remand proceedings no one has to deposit a sum of money to secure the release of an accused but a third party may stand surety for the accused.[9] A surety is a person who agrees to forfeit a sum of money fixed by the court (called recognizances and pronounced 'reconnaissances') if the accused fails to surrender to custody.[10] The suretyship may be specified by the court and being limited to the next court hearing when the accused must appear or for each occasion to which the case may be from time to time adjourned.[11] The court should specify which form of suretyship is being imposed. If the surety subsequently fears that the accused may fail to answer to his bail he may notify the police in writing that he wishes to be relieved of his obligations as a surety in which case they will then arrest the accused.[12]

Forfeiting the recognizances of a surety

If the accused fails to answer his bail or the surety informs the police that the accused may abscond, the surety may be required to forfeit his recognizance. The surety should be informed by the court that it is considering forfeiting his recognizance and he should be given an opportunity to attend and explain his case. The court should inquire into the surety's culpability[13] and the onus of proving an absence of

9 *R v Harrow Justices, ex p Morris* [1973] 1 QB 672, [1972] 3 All ER 494 (unless he is likely to abscond abroad when the accused himself might be required to provide a security).

10 For the criteria governing the acceptability of proposed sureties see s 8 of the Bail Act 1976. In particular the court is to have regard to

(a) the surety's financial resources;

(b) his character and any previous convictions of his; and

(c) his proximity (whether in point of kinship, place or otherwise) to the person for whom he is to be surety.

11 MCA 1980, s 128(4) and cf *R v Wells Street Magistrates' Court, ex p Albanese* [1981] 3 WLR 694, [1981] Crim LR 771.

12 Bail Act 1976, s 7(3) (c).

13 *R v Southampton Justices, ex p Green* [1976] 1 QB 11, [1975] 2 All ER 1073.

culpability is on the surety;[14] the court will start with the assumption that the whole sum should be forfeited.[15]

It is the duty of the surety to keep in contact with the accused to see that he will attend at court and when considering the culpability of the surety the court should examine what steps he took to ensure his attendance and inform the police.[16] Even if the surety has acted diligently he is still in peril of forfeiture because by initially entering into a suretyship he was undertaking a solemn obligation from which he cannot relieve himself lightly.[17] Therefore even when the surety informs the police under section 7(3) of the Bail Act 1976 that the defendant is about to abscond he is not then automatically relieved of his obligations.[18] When deciding on the amount of recognizances to be forfeited the court should have regard to the means of the surety although of course this should have been borne in mind when fixing the original amount of the recognizances.[19]

MAKING A BAIL APPLICATION

As in all aspects of an advocate's work preparation is essential. Since the decision in *R v Nottingham City Justices, ex p Davies*[20] the accused might only have one chance to apply for bail and if remanded in custody he might remain there for several weeks or months. The *Nottingham City Justices* case decided that where an application for bail was refused the accused could not apply for bail again to the magistrates' court unless he could show there had been a change in circumstances or there was fresh information before the court which was not available at the prior hearing. If a bail application were refused by a bench of magistrates and exactly the same application were made the following week to a differently constituted bench, this second bench would in effect be asked to sit as an appeal tribunal against the decision of their colleagues. Accordingly, an advocate wishing to apply to the bench again must, as a preliminary point, satisfy the bench that there are fresh matters to consider. An alternative course of action is to apply to a judge in chambers and this is discussed below.

As there is a presumption that the accused has a right to bail the police must produce material which would lead the court to conclude

14 *R v Southampton Justices, ex p Corker* (1976) 120 Sol Jo 214.

15 *R v Knightsbridge Crown Court, ex p Newton* [1980] Crim LR 715, DC and *R v Uxbridge Justices, ex p Heward-Mills* [1983] Crim LR 165.

16 *R v Wells Street Magistrates' Court, ex p Albanese* [1981] 3 WLR 694, [1981] Crim LR 771.

17 *R v Horseferry Road Magistrates' Court, ex p Pearson* [1976] 2 All ER 264, (1976) 140 JP 382.

18 *R v Ipswich Crown Court, ex p Reddington* [1981] Crim LR 618.

19 Bail Act 1976, s 8(2) (a).

20 [1980] 2 All ER 775, [1980] 3 WLR 15.

that one of the exceptions to bail applies in the particular case. A remand application usually starts with the police either through a uniformed officer or a prosecuting solicitor outlining their objections to bail. These objections will usually be framed to accord with the exceptions to bail in the Bail Act. For example they might stress the seriousness of the offence leading to the conclusion that the defendant will abscond to avoid his punishment. The defence advocate should therefore be prepared to meet these objections. Before the hearing he should ask the police whether they are objecting to bail and if they are, what are the objections. He should ask for a copy of the accused's antecedents (never trust what the accused himself has to say about them). He should also inquire whether the police would object to bail with conditions. If the police still object to bail, he should consider their objections very carefully and decide how to counter them.

(a) The accused will fail to surrender. In this case the advocate should consider amongst other things:
(i) has the accused ever failed to surrender in the past?;
(ii) has he a permanent residence? Is there a person willing to stand as surety who will therefore keep a watch over him?;
(iii) has he a regular job?;
(iv) are his friends and relations all in the area, ie is he a 'local'?;
(v) will the penalty he is likely to receive be sufficient to frighten him away?

(b) The accused will commit offences on bail. In this situation the following matters require consideration:
(i) how bad is his record of previous convictions, has he committed offences on bail before?;
(ii) is the nature of the offence such that it is likely to be repeated because the defendant knows that he will be heavily punished and has nothing to lose, eg a burglar committing further crimes to put away money before his imprisonment?;
(iii) will a surety and a curfew curb his activities or reassure the court that he will not commit further offences?

(c) Interfering with witnesses or obstructing the course of justice. There are perhaps three situations where this objection might be raised:
(i) In the case of really serious crime where hardened criminals are involved who may interfere with witnesses.
(ii) Occasionally in assault cases where there is strong evidence that the accused will intimidate the complainant and any witnesses.
(iii) Where the police still have further inquiries to make and arrest other suspects. It is a matter of fact and degree: what inquiries are to be made and what other suspects are to be apprehended? Are the objections well founded?

If the advocate is going to produce sureties he should prepare them in advance. What financial resources do they have? have they any previous convictions? how close a contact would they have with the accused? and, most importantly, are they aware of their obligations and the peril they are in if the accused should abscond?

The bail application should be succinct and to the point
The police objections that have been made should be dealt with as well as any misgivings that the bench may have voiced. A long application that wanders from the point will do nothing except bore and annoy the bench. The magistrates will probably have heard many bail applications on past occasions and may have a full list to contend with at the present hearing, therefore they will not relish having their time wasted.

REFUSAL OF BAIL

If bail is refused by the magistrates and another application is precluded by the *Nottingham City Justices* case, the only remedy is to apply to a High Court or Circuit judge in chambers. The application to the High Court judge will not be covered by legal aid and so if the defendant is impecunious the Official Solicitor will act for him. The procedure for making such an application will be found in Rule 79 of the Rules of the Supreme Court.

More commonly, however, the accused may apply to the circuit judge.[1] The method of applying for bail is more fully described in chapter 9. With his application the accused must file a certificate of refusal of bail which the magistrates must give him when they have rejected a full application for bail.[2]

BREACH OF BAIL

Where the accused fails to surrender at the appointed time and place he will have committed a criminal offence unless he had a reasonable excuse and he made an attempt to surrender to custody as soon as reasonably practicable afterwards.[3] The magistrates can fine and imprison the defendant for his non-attendance and, even though the offence is not triable either way, they may commit him to the Crown Court for sentence.[4]

The only way in which a Bail Act offence can be committed is by failure to surrender. If the defendant breaches the conditions of his bail he does not commit an offence provided he surrenders to custody at the

1 Supreme Court Act 1981, s 81 (as amended by the Criminal Justice Act 1982, s 60).
2 Bail Act 1976, s 5(6A) et seq, and the original legal aid order will cover the application for bail at the Crown Court (Legal Aid Act 1974, s 30(1A)).
3 Bail Act 1976, s 6 for details of the offence.
4 Ibid, s 6(6).

correct time. The sanction for breach of conditions is that if he is caught in the act of breaking the conditions, he may be arrested and brought back to court where he would be in peril of being remanded in custody.[5]

Mode of trial proceedings[6]

Before the magistrates can proceed to act as examining justices or try an information summarily in the case of an either way offence, it has to be decided where the case is going to be tried, in the magistrates' or the Crown Court. This decision is taken at mode of trial proceedings.[7]

The decision is reached in a two-stage process. First the magistrates decide whether they feel able to deal with the case; if they do the defendant will be given the choice of where he wishes the case to be heard. If the magistrates do not feel able to deal with it then the defendant has no choice and committal proceedings will then take place after any necessary adjournment.

In order to help them decide which court should deal with the matter the magistrates may hear representations on the seriousness of the case both from the prosecutor and the defendant.[8] The court at this stage is only concerned with the gravity of the offence and not with the character of the defendant, and previous convictions of the accused are, therefore, irrelevant and should not be mentioned. This is because the magistrates have power to commit the accused for sentence to the Crown Court if a heavier punishment is merited in view of the accused's character and antecedents. If he has been dealt with summarily for a serious offence but after conviction it is found that he has no character and antecedents to aggravate the penalty, he cannot be committed for sentence and so the magistrates are confined to their own powers of punishment. The prosecutor should therefore give the court an outline of the prosecution case so that the gravity of the offence can be ascertained, eg in an assault case: a description of the injuries caused and whether a weapon was used. The defence may then make representations if it wishes and the magistrates make their decision.

THE DECISION TO HEAR THE CASE SUMMARILY

Section 19(3) and (4) of the Magistrates' Courts Act 1980:

5 Ibid, s 7.
6 MCA 1980, ss 17–26.
7 If the procedure is not followed the resulting proceedings are a nullity: *R v Tottenham Justices, ex p Arthur's Transport Services* [1981] Crim LR 180.
8 And any representations should be recorded: *R v Horseferry Road Magistrates' Court, ex p Constable* [1981] Crim LR 504.

(3) The matters to which the court is to have regard . . . are the nature of the case;
whether the circumstances make the offence one of serious character; whether the punishment[9] which a magistrates' court would have power to inflict for it would be adequate; and any other circumstances which appear to the court to make it more suitable for the offence to be tried in one way rather than the other.
(4) If the prosecution is being carried on by the Attorney General, the Solicitor General or the Director of Public Prosecutions and he applies for the offence to be tried on indictment, . . . the court shall proceed to inquire into the information as examining justices.

It should be re-emphasised that the magistrates are concerned with the nature of the offence and not the character of the accused or any extenuating circumstances peculiar to the defendant. Thus if the offence is serious but there is good mitigation the question of whether the court should be merciful on the defendant is a matter for the Crown Court.[10]

It is not clear whether TIC's (offences to be taken into consideration) can be mentioned at this stage. TIC's can be 'character and antecedents' justifying a committal for sentence.[11] In a case where they were introduced at the mode of trial stage this practice was passed over without comment except that they could not be used again to justify a committal for sentence as they were known to the court when mode of trial was decided.[12] It is submitted that TIC's may be relevant to mode of trial when they show that the particular offence concerned was graver than it might appear on the face of it because it was part of a wider scheme of criminal activity, eg a regular system of fraud.[13] Such offences would then be admissible in evidence on the charge before the court on the 'similar fact' principle. On the other hand TIC's that have no relevance to the particular offence which is the subject of the mode of trial proceedings but are only relevant as to the defendant's character should not be referred to until after conviction and even then they are only relevant if the accused accepts them.

After the magistrates have decided they feel able to deal with the case and that summary trial is appropriate, they will announce this and the defendant is then asked which court he wishes to try the offence. Before he is given this choice he must be warned that if he elects summary trial and is convicted he may still be committed for sentence

9 Including compensation: *R v McLean, ex p Metropolitan Police Comr* [1975] Crim LR 289, DC.

10 *R v Middlesex Justices, ex p DPP* [1950] 2 KB 589, [1950] 1 All ER 916.

11 *R v Vallett* [1951] 1 All ER 231, 34 Cr App Rep 251.

12 *R v Derby and South Derbyshire Justices, ex p McCarthy and McGovern* (1981) 2 Cr App Rep (S) 140.

13 And in *R v Harlow Justices, ex p Galway* [1975] Crim LR 288, DC it was held that it was right for the magistrates to be informed that the charge was part of a wider scheme (see P. Warboys (1982) 146 JP 69).

to the Crown Court if it is appropriate in view of his character and antecedents. This warning must be given and should be given to the defendant personally if he is present.[14]

At this stage the defendant may either elect to be tried by jury, in which case the court will proceed to inquire into the matter as examining justices, or the accused may consent to summary trial.

THE CHOICE BETWEEN SUMMARY TRIAL AND TRIAL ON INDICTMENT

Arguments in favour of summary trial

(a) Where the accused pleads guilty.

(i) *Speed.* The defendant may well be dealt with there and then after the mode of trial proceedings.

(ii) *Sentence.* The sentence imposed by the magistrates for any given offence will be likely to be less than that imposed by the Crown Court especially for the more serious offences. Although the magistrates have the power to commit for sentence there is a psychological barrier to be crossed before they will hand over jurisdiction to the Crown Court.

(iii) *Appeal.* There is an unrestricted right of appeal to the Crown Court which is speedy and convenient.

(b) Where the accused pleads not guilty.

(i) *There is no substantial evidence that magistrates are more prone to convict than a jury in ordinary cases.*[15]

(ii) *Convenience.* It may be easier to obtain an early trial date in the magistrates' court than at the Crown Court especially as there will not have to be the delay caused by committal proceedings.

(iii) *Cost.* The costs incurred will be substantially less than in the Crown Court; therefore a defendant is not in as much peril of paying a substantial sum by way of costs as he would be in the Crown Court.

(iv) *Appeal.* As above.

(v) Although the Crown Court may be a technically superior tribunal in some respects such as deciding the admissibility of evidence, trial

14 *R v Kettering Justices, ex p Patmore* [1968] 3 All ER 167, [1968] 1 WLR 1436; but cf *R v Salisbury and Amesbury Justices, ex p Greatbatch* [1954] 2 QB 142, [1954] 2 All ER 326.

15 Cf Baldwin and Hopkins (1975) 139 JP 465; Softley (1976) 140 JP 455.

in the magistrates' court will be more speedy and less of an ordeal for the accused with less of a risk of attracting publicity.

Arguments in favour of trial by jury

For an ordinary case little is to be gained where the defendant is going to plead guilty, but where the charge is contested the following matters may be considered:

(a) At the present time the prosecution is not obliged to disclose its case to the defence whereas if the accused elects trial it will have to do so at the committal proceedings.[16]

(b) The defendant has an opportunity to have the case discharged at the committal proceedings.

(c) The defendant is more likely to obtain legal aid for the Crown Court but he runs the risk of having to pay higher costs and legal aid contribution order if he is convicted of an offence which could quite easily have been dealt with in the magistrates' court.[17]

(d) In not guilty cases there is a general feeling that where police evidence is to be strongly challenged the magistrates are more likely to accept the police evidence than a jury would be.

(e) Where there are points of law to be argued concerning the admissibility of evidence, such as confessions and 'similar fact' evidence. In the magistrates' court the magistrates themselves decide whether the evidence is admissible. In the Crown Court admissibility is decided by the judge in the absence of the jury. There are no similar provisions in the magistrates' court.[18]

Where the defendant (or the prosecutor) changes his mind

The defendant may have consented to summary trial and then changes his mind. The magistrates have a discretion to allow him to withdraw his consent but they are not bound to do so: they must consider the merits of the application.[19] Sometimes the magistrates have conducted mode of trial proceedings and the defendant has elected trial by jury. The prosecution then changes its mind and decides to prefer some purely summary offences instead and withdraw the indictable offences. The prosecution can do this without the approval of the court and thus nullify the election for trial at the Crown Court.[20]

16 But it would be an abuse of process to elect trial by jury in order to secure a sight of the prosecution case and then seek to revert to summary trial: *R v Warrington Justices, ex p McDonagh* [1981] Crim LR 629.

17 *R v Hayden* [1975] 2 All ER 558, [1975] 1 WLR 852 and *R v Bushell* [1980] Crim LR 445, CA.

18 *SJF (an infant) v Chief Constable of Kent ex p Margate Juvenile Court* (1982) Times, 17 June.

19 *R v Southampton City Justices, ex p Robins* (1980) 144 JP 288, [1980] Crim LR 440.

20 *R v Canterbury and St Augustine's Justices, ex p Klisiak; R v Ramsgate Justices, ex p Warren* [1981] 2 All ER 129, [1981] 3 WLR 60.

CRIMINAL DAMAGE UNDER £200[1]

Criminal damage is an anomalous offence because although it is an indictable offence triable either way, if the value of the alleged damage is under £200 it has to be tried summarily. Therefore before any mode of trial proceedings can commence the value of the alleged damage has to be ascertained. If it is under £200 the court will proceed to summary trial, if the value is over £200 then the case will proceed as for a normal either way offence. The court does not have to be precise in its valuation provided it is clear on which side of the limit the case falls. If the value is not clear, the defendant is given a choice, he can elect summary trial and he will only be liable for the reduced penalty for small criminal damage offences with no possibility of committal for sentence under section 38 of the Magistrates' Courts Act 1980, otherwise he can elect to have the matter tried as an ordinary either way offence.

One final complication is that even if the offence is clearly under £200 and so apparently triable only summarily, it becomes an either way offence if it is part of a series of offences of a same or similar character. What amounts to 'same or similar character' is discussed in the footnote to section 22 of the Magistrates' Courts Act 1980 in *Stone's* but the general effect of the decisions appears to be that only another offence under the Criminal Damage Act will be an offence of a similar character.[2]

1 MCA 1980, s 22.
2 *Re Prescott* (1979) 70 Cr App Rep 244 criminal damage and obstructing a police officer not similar offences nor: criminal damage and burglary (*R v Considine* (1979) 70 Cr App Rep 239); criminal damage and common assault (*R v Tottenham Justices, ex p Tibble* (1981) 73 Cr App Rep 55); criminal damage and police assault or breach of the peace (*R v Hatfield Justices, ex p Castle* [1980] 3 All ER 509; sub nom *R v Hertford Justices ex p Castle* [1980] Crim LR 579).

Chapter 5

The plea

Introductory

When the defendant appears in court the next stage of the proceedings depends on the nature of the offence with which he is charged, and this was described in chapter 4. Where the offence is purely summary, the court can proceed straight to the stage of asking the defendant whether he pleads guilty or not guilty. If the offence is either way, this stage will not be reached until after the court has decided that it feels able to deal with the matter and the accused has consented to summary trial. The process of determining whether the accused is guilty or not guilty is correctly described as the trial of an information as the information is the formal accusation made against him[1] and the equivalent of the indictment for trial at the Crown Court.

Trying several informations and defendants together

It was formerly the rule that a defendant had an absolute right to demand the separate trial of each information laid against him.[2] Similarly, where there were several defendants they each had the right to separate trials unless they were jointly charged.[3] This rule could produce anomalies particularly where a court was hearing several informations against an absent defendant in a road traffic case, and the earlier authorities were overruled by the House of Lords in *Clayton v Chief Constable of Norfolk*.[4]

The position for determining whether there should be separate trials of several informations either against the same defendant or against several defendants has been assimilated to the practice for trials on indictment. The present situation is that the magistrates may determine to hear separate informations together if they think it is desirable having regard to any connection between the facts in the various informations.

1 MCA 1980, s 9(1).
2 *Brangwynne v Evans* [1962] 1 All ER 446, [1962] 1 WLR 267.
3 *Aldus v Watson* [1973] QB 902, [1973] 2 All ER 1018.
4 [1983] 1 All ER 984, [1983] 2 WLR 555.

The bench should seek the consent of the prosecution and the defence, but if this is not forthcoming they should hear submissions from both sides and then make a determination. The aim of the magistrates should be to have regard to the overall interests of justice. Unlike the previously existing law, the absence of consent by the defendant is not a bar to a joint trial although the magistrates must be concerned to see that he is treated justly and fairly.

For a detailed explanation of the rules governing joint trials on indictment reference should be made to *Archbold*,[5] but the salient points of practice concerning joinder of offences and defendants are as follows:

(a) Several offences charged against the same accused may be tried together if those charges are formulated on the same facts or form or are part of a series of offences of the same or similar character.[6] In relation to this statement it should be mentioned that two offences may form a 'series', and that to be offences of the 'same or similar character' evidence of the one offence need not be admissible on the 'similar fact' principle on the other charge.

(b) Several accused may be tried together if they are all charged with participating in the same offence.[7]

(c) Several accused who have committed distinct offences may be tried together if the charges against all the accused may be linked together in the same way as offences where only one accused is involved as described at (a), and not only where the accused all acted together in concert but also where the offences are contemporaneous or linked together in some other way.

The above rules are all subject to the right to have separate trials where the interests of justice demand it, eg where one accused might be unduly prejudiced by having his case heard at the same time as other accused, or where joint proceedings against a multiplicity of accused might be unwieldy and unnecessarily complex[8]

The plea

Having heard, if necessary, representations to have more than one

5 (41st edn) paras 1–70 to 1–84.

6 See generally *Ludlow v Metropolitan Police Comr* [1971] AC 29, [1970] 1 All ER 567.

7 It is common practice for two defendants to appear on the same information where it is alleged that they have committed a 'joint' offence. Whether an offence is a joint offence depends on the nature of the offence charged and the way the offence was committed. An example would be where two men set out to burgle a house. One stands outside as a lookout and the other enters the house. Both may be prosecuted on a single information for a joint burglary. Usually a joint charge has the word 'jointly' contained in it, but there is no magic in the formula of the words used. Whether a charge is joint or not depends entirely on the nature of the case, not on the particular words used: *R v Rowlands* [1972] 1 QB 424, [1972] 1 All ER 306.

8 Normally, however, it is in the interests of justice that co-defendants be tried together: *R v Hoggins* [1967] 3 All ER 334, [1967] 1 WLR 1223.

information tried together the clerk will then ask the accused whether he pleads guilty or not guilty.[9] This is one of the most important stages in any trial and the accused must be asked personally how he pleads and he should normally reply himself.[10] It is not necessarily an invalid plea if the defence advocate replies on the defendant's behalf but the better, and safest practice, is to let the defendant himself reply,[11] in order to avoid misunderstanding.

SPECIAL PLEAS

In reply to the question 'how do you plead?' the court would expect to receive the reply of 'guilty' or 'not guilty'. These are known as general pleas. However the defendant may raise the plea

(a) the court has no jurisdiction to try him;
(b) that he has been pardoned for the offence;
(c) that he has already been tried for this offence and been convicted or acquitted.[12]

These are known as special pleas.

None of these pleas is at all common and it is not proposed to dwell on them here. However, one situation where the plea of autrefois acquit can be a live issue is where the defendant has entered a plea of not guilty and the prosecution for some reason are not ready to proceed. The prosecution may then apply for an adjournment, which is refused, and so there is no option but to offer no evidence and the information is therefore dismissed. Can the prosecution have another go by laying a fresh information for the same offence?

AUTREFOIS ACQUIT WHERE NO EVIDENCE HAS BEEN OFFERED

In the situation where a case is listed for a contested hearing and the case is called on but the prosecution is not ready to proceed because, for example, a vital witness is not available, the prosecution has three options open to it. The proceedings may be withdrawn, or the case adjourned, or the prosecution may proceed on the evidence it has available. If it has insufficient evidence and the case proceeds, the defendant will be acquitted.

9 MCA 1980, s 9(1).
10 *R v Wakefield Justices, ex p Butterworth* [1970] 1 All ER 1181, 134 JP 347.
11 *R v Gowerton Justices, ex p Davies* [1974] Crim LR 253, DC. Cf *R v Ali Tasamulug* [1971] Crim LR 441.
12. Another example of a special plea is, in effect, that the defendant is unfit to plead. For the inapplicability of this to the magistrates' court see ch 14. The pleas based on a previous acquittal or conviction are generally known as autrefois acquit or autrefois convict, although, to be pedantic, these terms refer only to trial on indictment. Nevertheless, the same principles apply to summary trial, see *Wemyss v Hopkins* (1875) LR 10 QB 378, 39 JP 549.

The consent of the magistrates is required for proceedings to be withdrawn[13] or adjourned, but if the application to withdraw is granted, the case can be reinstated at a later date.[14] On the other hand, where no evidence has been offered and the case dismissed, the defendant cannot be prosecuted against for the same matter as he may then enter a plea of autrefois acquit. Accordingly, where the prosecution is placed in this situation it should first apply to adjourn or withdraw the proceedings and then the magistrates must exercise their judicial discretion whether to grant the application. If the application is refused and the defendant is subsequently acquitted, that will be an end of the matter.

The authority for the above proposition is to be found in the decision of *R v Pressick* a decision of the Chester Crown Court where all the authorities are reviewed and explained.[15] Although the decision is that of a circuit judge, the decision follows the reasoning in an earlier Divisional Court case[16] and *Pressick* was implicitly supported by the Divisional Court again in *British Railways Board v Warwick*.[17]

On the face of it, the plea of autrefois acquit should always apply where there has been a previous acquittal. The controversy arises from the view held by many that the defendant should have been in jeopardy at the original hearing and one of the criteria to be fulfilled for the defendant to have been in jeopardy was that the trial was 'on the merits'. In *Pressick* this phrase was explained as referring only to the doctrine of res judicata where matters could only be judicata where there had been a full hearing. However, the plea of autrefois acquit was a distinct matter and depended only on the verdict of the court. The only exception to this proposition that it was merely the verdict of the court which founded the plea of autrefois acquit was where the previous proceedings could be said to be a nullity. An example of this would be where the defendant had not been required to consent to the summary trial of an either way offence.

To summarise the position: if the defendant has been lawfully acquitted by a court of competent jurisdiction then he may plead autrefois acquit. The defendant will not have been lawfully acquitted if the earlier proceedings were a nullity. In the 'no evidence offered' cases the remedy of the prosecution is to challenge by judicial review the decision of the magistrates to refuse the prosecution application to withdraw the proceedings or to adjourn the case.[18] If the matter has

13 *R v Bedwellty Justices, ex p Munday* [1970] Crim LR 601, DC.
14 *R (McDonnell) v Tyrone Justices* [1912] 2 IR 44.
15 Cf the report in (1978) 142 JP 249.
16 *Metropolitan Police Comr v Meller* [1963] Crim LR 856, DC (a classic case of a witness failing to attend).
17 [1980] Crim LR 590, DC and now confirmed in *R v Swansea Justices, ex p Purvis* cited in (1981) 145 JP 214.
18 *R v Swansea Justices*, above, n. 17

been dismissed, the prosecution cannot lay a fresh information because this would be a back door method of circumventing the original decision of the magistrates.

The plea of guilty

If the defendant pleads not guilty, the prosecution will probably ask for the case to be adjourned so that it may produce its witnesses and there can be allocated sufficient court time for the hearing of all the evidence. The proceedings will therefore be adjourned to a date agreed by all the parties in court and the defendant would be remanded if necessary.

If the defendant pleads guilty, the case will usually proceed there and then.

PROCEDURE ON A PLEA OF GUILTY

After the accused has entered his plea of guilty, the prosecutor will then outline the prosecution case. He may produce a list of offences which the defendant may wish to have taken into consideration when sentence is passed, and also the defendant's antecedents and convictions and then he may also ask for costs and compensation.

When the prosecution has concluded its case, the defence will be called upon to present any mitigation which there may be, and to comment on any social inquiry report which the bench may have considered. In addition, if a financial penalty has been imposed the defendant will be expected to pay the fine forthwith and if not, then he may be asked for his proposals for repayment of the sums due.

Although the procedure on a plea of guilty may appear straightforward there are a few matters which need consideration.

THE PROSECUTION CASE

The prosecutor does not need to call evidence on a plea of guilty[19] unless there is a substantial disagreement with the defence over the facts of the case. Normally, the prosecuting solicitor or a police officer will provide a synopsis of the allegations and then he will produce the offences to be taken into consideration. In addition to these the prosecutor should inform the magistrates of any other outstanding cases against the defendant so that if possible and if it is desirable they can all be heard together.[20]

19 MCA 1980, s 9(3).
20 *R v Bennett* (1980) 2 Cr App Rep (S) 96, [1980] Crim LR 447, CA.

When the accused's previous convictions are being referred to, the prosecutor should be aware of the provisions of the Rehabilitation of Offenders Act 1974. This Act has the effect of 'wiping the slate clean' for spent convictions. A conviction becomes spent if the sentence is within the limits set out in the Act and the prescribed period of time has passed. Although the Act does not apply to criminal proceedings the spirit of the Act should be adhered to where possible.[1]

TAKING OFFENCES INTO CONSIDERATION (TICS)

Although the prosecution may have proceeded against the defendant on one or more charges, there may be other offences which they believe the defendant may have committed. The prosecution may be content that the defendant should acknowledge his guilt on these matters so they may 'clear up their books' without formally charging him or exposing him to a separate penalty.[2] In this event a list of these offences will be prepared and given to the accused for him to consider.

At the hearing the procedure for having offences taken into consideration should only be adopted with the consent of the accused himself. He should be explicitly informed of each offence and should be expressly asked whether he admits them.[3] The defendant should be asked personally whether he admits the offences[4] and there should be no pressure on him to accept these further offences.[5] The court should make quite sure which offences are being admitted.

In practice, both the bench and the defendant are supplied with a copy of the form by the prosecution, and the bench inquires of the defendant which offences on the form are admitted.[6]

Although the defendant may be quite willing to have an offence taken into consideration, the magistrates have the final discretion whether to consider it when sentencing, and so the question of what offences may be taken into consideration depends on what the bench in its discretion will accept, for example where the TIC offence is more serious than the substantive charge, or where (perhaps) the offence is of a different kind.[7] Normally endorsable offences should not be the subject of the TIC procedure but they may be taken into consideration where the substantive offence is endorsable.[8]

1 See the *Practice Note* [1975] 2 All ER 1072, [1975] 1 WLR 1065.
2 Except occasionally a higher liability to pay compensation on the TICs as well as the substantive offence.
3 *DPP v Anderson* [1978] AC 964, [1978] 2 All ER 512.
4 *R v Davies* (1980) 72 Cr App Rep 262, [1981] Crim LR 192; *R v Urbas* [1963] Crim LR 37, CCA.
5 *R v Nelson* [1967] 1 All ER 358n, [1967] 1 WLR 449.
6 *R v Massiah* [1961] Crim LR 605, CCA.
7 *R v Collins* [1947] KB 560, [1947] 1 All ER 147.
8 *R v Jones* [1970] 3 All ER 815, [1970] 1 WLR 1494.

If an offence is taken into consideration, the defendant cannot plead autrefois convict on that matter[9] but in practice the prosecution would never proceed on it and the courts have encouraged the use of the TIC procedure to clear up outstanding matters.[10] Offences that have been taken into consideration may be 'character and antecedents' to justify a committal to the Crown Court for sentence[11] but at the Crown Court the defendant may withdraw his acceptance of them.[12]

THE EQUIVOCAL PLEA

The defendant may utter the word 'guilty' when asked for his plea; but does he really mean it? Once a plea of guilty has been entered certain consequences follow: the defendant will be sentenced on the basis of his culpability, or he may be committed for sentence. Having been dealt with on a plea of guilty how can the defendant then appeal against conviction?

The defendant will have to lodge an appeal at the Crown Court against conviction where a preliminary point will be taken that the appeal cannot proceed as the plea was one of guilty. The Crown Court may inquire into the proceedings at the magistrates' court to determine whether there was an equivocal plea. If the Crown Court is satisfied of this, the case may be remitted to the justices who, if they are also of the opinion that the plea was equivocal, may enter a plea of not guilty and have a not guilty hearing. This procedure is discussed further below.

The court can only proceed to sentence if the defendant has been convicted either after hearing evidence or after a plea of guilty. What occasionally happens is that the defendant pleads guilty but in his mitigation he says something inconsistent with the plea. A typical example might be in an allegation of theft from a shop where the defendant says in mitigation that it was a mistake and he did not know the goods had fallen into his shopping bag. This might be difficult to believe, but nevertheless if the defendant were to persist in this tale, his plea would have to be entered as not guilty as he had not acknowledged any dishonesty which is an essential element in a charge of theft. The court has at all times to watch that the defendant is admitting all the elements of the offence and the defence advocate should always beware of putting forward a mitigation which amounts to a denial of the offence charged.

9 *R v Nicholson* [1947] 2 All ER 535, 32 Cr App Rep 98.

10 As in *R v Walter* [1956] Crim LR 840, CCA, where it was said that it was undesirable for D to be charged, on his release from prison, with an offence that could have been taken into consideration.

11 *R v Vallett* [1951] 1 All ER 231, 34 Cr App Rep 251.

12 *R v Davis* (1980) 72 Cr App Rep 262, [1981] Crim LR 192. See ch 7, under 'Committal to Crown Court for sentence'.

It is clear that a high standard is expected of the plea of guilty and the court will scrutinise anything said in mitigation which casts doubt on the correctness of the defendant's plea.[13] This scrutiny is not only confined to the mitigation as there may be material contained in the accused's statement to the police[14] or even in the social inquiry report [15] which casts doubt on the plea. Such ambiguities should be clarified before the court proceeds to sentence.[16]

THE EQUIVOCAL PLEA IN THE CROWN COURT

The question whether the original plea before the magistrates was equivocal not infrequently arises in the Crown Court either on an appeal against conviction where the defendant originally pleaded guilty, or on a committal for sentence.

The Crown Court has power to consider whether the original plea was equivocal[17] but it must conduct its investigation scrupulously and should obtain affidavits from the magistrates and their clerk covering the events in the court below.[18] If it decided that there was a prima facie case of equivocality, the matter could then be remitted to the magistrates. The Crown Court should only do this after a thorough investigation in order to

13 *R v Ingleson* [1915] 1 KB 512.

14 *R v Tottenham Justices, ex p Rubens* [1970] 1 All ER 879, [1970] 1 WLR 800.

15 *Maurice Leahy v Rawlinson* [1978] Crim LR 106.

16 Some difficulty is caused by the case of *Foster (Haulage) Ltd v Roberts* [1978] 2 All ER 751, [1978] RTR 302 where the defendant company mitigated through its solicitor on the basis that the offence was absolute and it could not deny guilt. In fact the offence did require knowledge on the part of the defendant. The view is sometimes put forward that this was not an equivocal plea because the word 'guilty' was unambiguously used by the defence and as the mitigation only subsequently revealed a mistake the magistrates had a *discretion* to allow a change of plea. It is submitted that whenever there is an ambiguity in a plea the bench are under a *duty* to resolve the ambiguity and if the defendant is in fact pleading not guilty, then a not guilty plea must be entered. It is sometimes thought that an equivocal plea cannot apply where the plea has been entered by a solicitor; this is not so. In the *Foster* case the magistrates heard evidence after the plea of guilty and themselves decided, on the evidence before them, that the company did have the requisite knowledge. The objection to an equivocal plea, that the bench does not have a factual basis for sentencing the accused because his guilt was neither admitted nor proved, did not apply in the *Foster* case.

The essence of a plea of guilty is that it must be a free and voluntary admission of guilt. The word 'guilty' usually implies acceptance of guilt but as has been seen it is not necessarily the end of the matter and the court has to scrutinise the surrounding circumstances as well. Therefore, where an apparently unequivocal plea of guilty was entered but it was later discovered it had been entered under duress, the plea was re-entered as not guilty (*R v Huntingdon Crown Court, ex p Jordan* (1981) 73 Cr App Rep 194, [1981] Crim LR 641), or where the defendant pleaded guilty by mistake, not appreciating which charge he was pleading to (*R v Phillips* [1982] Crim LR 125).

17 *R v Durham Quarter Sessions, ex p Virgo* [1952] 2 QB 1, [1952] 1 All ER 466.

18 *R v Rochdale Justices, ex p Allwork* [1981] Crim LR 719, 125 Sol Jo 587; *R v Marylebone Justices, ex p Westmister City Council* [1971] 1 All ER 1025, [1971] 1 WLR 567.

avoid the undesirable situation of the magistrates refusing to accept that the plea was equivocal and consequently declining jurisdiction. The decision of the justices will be the final decision as to whether the plea was equivocal, and after they have investigated the matter the Crown Court must accept their decision.[19]

WHY EQUIVOCALITY IS IMPORTANT

Even where the plea was not equivocal magistrates have a power to allow a change of plea up until they finally dispose of the case and are functus officio,[20] but this power is subject to the discretion of the bench which may not always be exercised in the defendant's favour. However, if the plea is equivocal the magistrates must allow the defendant to enter a plea of not guilty. The same principle applies where the defendant has been committed for sentence as the Crown Court has a discretion to allow a change of plea because the case has not finally been disposed of until the defendant is sentenced.[1]

In the case of an appeal the defendant cannot appeal against conviction where he has pleaded guilty; he can only do so where the Crown Court decides that prima facie the plea was ambiguous and remits the case to the magistrates who finally determine whether a plea of not guilty should be entered.

Social inquiry reports

The court may wish to have a social inquiry report prepared by a probation officer to help in its deliberations on sentence. This may be desirable for two reasons: either to investigate the defendant's home circumstances and any behavioural problems which he may have, or to assess the defendant's suitability for a particular sentence. The social inquiry report is not intended to do the work which a competent advocate should do and it is not a substitute for the proper presentation of the defence mitigation. Therefore in the first instance, the advocate should be sure that there is sufficient material to justify a report rather than simply to request one because he cannot be bothered to prepare his case properly.

Apart from a report prepared in order to investigate the character of the

19 *R v Plymouth Justices, ex p Whitton* (1980) 71 Cr App Rep 322.

20 *S (an infant) v Manchester City Recorder* [1971] AC 481, [1969] 3 All ER 1230.

1 *R v Mutford and Lothingland Justices, ex p Harber* [1971] 2 QB 291, [1971] 1 All ER 81. See also *R v Inner London Crown Court, ex p Sloper* (1978) 69 Cr App Rep 1. It should be noted that on a *committal for sentence* the Crown Court has jurisdiction to allow a change of plea and remit the case to the justices for trial unlike an *appeal against conviction* where it is the justices who finally decide whether a not guilty plea should be entered.

accused, a report may be necessary to see whether the accused is suitable for a certain sentence, eg community service. Where the success of a particular sentence depends on the suitability of the offender and his willingness to co-operate with the Probation Service, it is only common sense that the matter should be investigated beforehand.

It is mandatory for a social inquiry report to be prepared before a sentence of community service is imposed[2] and although the Home Secretary has power to insist[3] on a social inquiry report being available where certain sentences are imposed, at present he *recommends* that a social inquiry report be considered where the court is considering:

(a) detention in a detention centre;
(b) youth custody (formerly borstal training);
(c) imprisonment (including a suspended sentence) where the defendant has not previously *served* a sentence of imprisonment (ie a suspended sentence which was not activated does not count). This recommendation is strengthened by section 20 of the Powers of Criminal Courts Act 1973. Where the accused has not been to prison before the court 'shall obtain and consider information about the circumstances and shall take into account any information before the court which is relevant to his character and his physical and mental condition';
(d) imprisonment on a woman;
(e) committal to Crown Court for sentence;
(f) probation order.

ADJOURNMENT FOR REPORTS

In the magistrates' court it is not usual for reports to be prepared in anticipation of a plea of guilty or conviction after a trial, therefore if a report is requested an adjournment may be necessary. After conviction by plea or trial the period of an adjournment is limited to four weeks and a remand on bail is similarly limited to four weeks or three weeks in custody.[4] The phrasing of the decision to adjourn for sentence can be a trap for the bench because if the court leads the accused to understand that he will receive a certain form of sentence provided the social inquiry report is favourable, then on receipt of a favourable report it would be wrong to impose a custodial sentence.[5] The decision

2 Powers of Criminal Courts Act 1973, s 14(2) (b).
3 Ibid, s 45. Under the provisions of the Criminal Justice Act the court now has to give its reasons in open court why no social inquiry report was obtained before a custodial sentence was imposed.
4 MCA 1980, s 10(3) although this section is directory and a resulting sentence will not be quashed if, for example, by an oversight these limits are exceeded. Cf *R v Manchester City Justices, ex p Miley and Dynan* (1977) 141 JP 248.
5 *R v Gillam* [1981] Crim LR 55. See also *R v Ward* [1982] Crim LR 459 (sentence of imprisonment wrong after adjournment to assess suitability for a probation hostel where report indicated that D was suitable).

to adjourn for a social inquiry report to assess suitability for a particular sentence is in effect a provisional sentence subject to confirmation by the report. If the court does not wish to proceed on this basis it should make it clear that it has not yet made up its mind on the appropriate sentence.[6]

The social inquiry report will be prepared by a probation officer[7] and when it is presented to the court it should be considered before any mitigation[8] although in practice it is sometimes deferred until after the mitigation where the report, as is usual, is presented in writing. A copy of the report is given to the defendant or his advocate[9] and should not be read out aloud.[10] Although it is not usual for a social inquiry report to be challenged by the defence, the probation officer can be called to give evidence and may be cross-examined on the contents of the report. It is important that the rules of natural justice be observed and that any information relevant to the sentence be given in open court and with the knowledge of the accused, otherwise the sentence will be quashed.[11]

Mitigation

THE FACTUAL BASIS FOR SENTENCING

After the plea has been accepted and the prosecution case concluded, the defence may mitigate. Mitigation may be put forward on the basis either that the offence concerned was not as serious as suggested by the prosecution and that there is another version of the facts consistent with the plea of guilty but differing from the prosecution version, or the mitigation may be based on the defendant's character and social circumstances. Where the dispute concerns the nature of the offence that was committed, how is the court to resolve the conflict?

Where there has been a not guilty hearing followed by a conviction the bench will have formed their own views of the facts, but where there has

6 As in *R v Hatherall* [1977] Crim LR 755, CA, where the case was adjourned for reports to assess suitability for community service. There was nothing said by the court which would have led the defendant to expect a non-custodial sentence, and a subsequent prison sentence imposed at the adjourned hearing was upheld.

7 Powers of Criminal Courts Act 1973, Sch 3, para 8(1).

8 *R v Kirkham* [1968] Crim LR 210, CA.

9 Powers of Criminal Courts Act 1973, s 46.

10 *R v Smith* [1968] Crim LR 33, 111 Sol Jo 850, CA.

11 *R v Aberdare Justices, ex p Jones* [1973] Crim LR 45 (where the magistrates interviewed a social worker in the retiring room). See also *R v Bodmin Justices, ex p McEwen* [1947] KB 321, [1947] 1 All ER 109 (where the defendant's senior officer was interviewed without the defendant being present).

been a plea of guilty they will have heard no evidence. In the normal case no evidence is called after conviction and the sentencer bases his considerations on such facts as would appear to be consistent with the conviction.

The bench are not bound to accept the defence mitigation as the factual basis for sentencing the accused[12] and so where there is a dispute between the prosecution and defence versions this dispute has to be resolved.

(a) If there is a doubt raised about the basis on which the accused should be sentenced (for example on a charge of assault occasioning actual bodily harm where the prosecution alleges the defendant kicked the complainant and the defendant maintains he only used one punch) the bench should draw the parties' attention to this discrepancy if this has not already been referred to and invite their comment. The court may then invite the parties to call evidence which should generally be confined to the matter actually in dispute rather than a full not guilty hearing.[13]

(b) The prosecution is entitled to call evidence after conviction even to the extent of establishing aggravating circumstances. In this case however the defence should be given notice and the standard of such evidence naturally has to be high so that it must be first-hand evidence and not hearsay, and it should be sufficiently particularised so that the defence may have the opportunity to rebut it.[14]

(c) The defence may call evidence to support its mitigation[15] and it may be desirable, where there is a conflict, for the court to request the defendant to give evidence which can be tested by cross-examination.[16]

(d) Having heard any evidence that may have been called the court then has to make its decision on the factual basis on which sentence is to be passed.

The court may only sentence the accused for the offence of which he has been convicted or he has admitted (eg offences to be taken into consideration) and is not entitled to speculate that the offence concerned is part of a wider criminal activity[17] but having said that, the court is entitled to form its own view of the gravity of the offence from the evidence or admitted facts before it as it is not compelled to accept only the defence mitigation.[18] However, it is

12 *R v Campbell* [1980] Crim LR 248, CA; *R v Depledge* (1979) 1 Cr App Rep (S) 183, [1979] Crim LR 733, CA.

13 *R v Lester* (1976) 63 Cr App Rep 144 and *R v Milligan* [1982] Crim LR 317.

14 *R v Robinson* (1969) 53 Cr App Rep 314, [1969] Crim LR 207, CA.

15 *R v Cross* [1975] Crim LR 591, CA.

16 *R v Recorder of Grimsby, ex p Purser* [1951] 2 All ER 889, (1951) 35 Cr App Rep 155.

17 *R v Wishart* [1980] Crim LR 113, CA; *R v Huchison* [1972] 1 All ER 936, [1972] 1 WLR 398; *R v Morgan* [1981] Crim LR 56.

18 *R v Campbell*, n.12, above.

suggested[19] that the defence should be given the benefit of any doubt and that the court should be satisfied beyond a reasonable doubt before it accepts a version of the facts inconsistent with that put forward by the defence.[20] In any event the court should not normally conclude that the offence is more serious than is suggested by the prosecution view.[1]

Although this is the theory of how sentence should be considered, in practice apart from road traffic matters where special reasons for not endorsing a licence, or mitigating circumstances for reducing a disqualification are being considered, the calling of evidence after conviction is not very common, especially the calling of evidence by the prosecution. This is perhaps because the facts are not fundamentally in dispute on such comparatively minor matters and where they are, the court is prepared to sentence on the basis of the defendant's version of events. Also, there is a natural reluctance on the part of the defence and prosecution to have the extra trouble and delay of adjourning proceedings for evidence to be called.

SENTENCING OF CO-ACCUSED

Where there is more than one defendant involved in a case this can pose extra procedural difficulties. It is obviously desirable that all the accused should be sentenced at the same time by the same tribunal so that there can be a uniformity of treatment.[2] Occasionally where this is not done there can be an undue disparity of treatment which can be a good basis for an appeal.[3]

Co-accused may become separated for several reasons: one defendant may plead guilty and the other not guilty; co-accused may both plead guilty but one may have his case adjourned for the preparation of a social inquiry report; one accused may be an adult and another a juvenile who is subsequently remitted to the juvenile court for sentence.

Where one defendant pleads guilty and the other not guilty, the defendant who pleads guilty should normally await the outcome of the trial before being sentenced. This may not be practicable, however, where there would be a long delay before the trial takes place. Furthermore, it is

19 By D. A. Thomas.

20 *R v Taggart* (1979) Cr App Rep (S) 144. (but as regards the suggestion in *Taggart* that there should be a full not guilty hearing to determine any conflict on the facts this is doubted in *Milligan*, n. 13, above).

1 *R v Pearce* (1979) 1 Cr App Rep (S) 317, [1979] Crim LR 658, CA.

2 Cf *R v Bryant* [1964] Crim LR 553, (1964) 108 Sol Jo 338, CCA.

3 *R v Reeves* [1964] Crim LR 67, CCA (where the sentence on one appellant had to be reduced because of the ludicrously light sentence imposed on his co-accused). Cf *R v Midgley* [1975] Crim LR 469, CA for a statement of the general principles.

desirable to sentence an accused who is going to give evidence against a co-accused before he appears as a witness.[4]

If cases are split, it is desirable that the same tribunal should sentence both accused where possible,[5] and if it is not possible, the second tribunal should hear all the facts and circumstances of the case so that it may have the fullest possible picture.[6]

The fact that there is more than one accused involved may have important implications for the mitigation. The fact that there is a general principle that co-accused should not receive unduly disparate sentences, does not preclude the court from considering the relative culpability of the accused (eg was one a 'ring leader' and the other a person who was easily led?), or that one readily admitted his guilt whilst the other fought a hopeless case. In addition, one defendant might be a man of previous good character, whilst the other had a bad record.

Where one accused is going to cast blame on the other they will of course have to be separately represented because of the resulting conflict of interest.

THE MITIGATION

Mitigating can be perhaps one of the most difficult tasks for an advocate especially where the defendant seems to have little in his favour. Whilst it is not possible to have a 'pre-packaged' mitigation to be followed slavishly in every case, there are certain matters which should be borne in mind and which, when considered, may help to formulate a coherently structured mitigation. A lengthy mitigation does not necessarily entail a useful one, indeed magistrates may become alternately annoyed and bored. They hear many cases and appreciate an advocate who gets to the point. The defending solicitor should decide beforehand what he is planning to say and for what purpose. Consider these elements of a mitigation.

The facts

Where there has been a trial, the bench will have formed their own view and usually the defence can have little to say especially where the defence was that the events as described never happened at all. But where there has been a plea of guilty followed by an outline of the case by the prosecution, the defence may seek to describe the defendant's actions in a better light.[7] The solicitor should always beware in this

4 *R v Coffey* [1977] Crim LR 45, CA.
5 Ibid, and *R v Begg* [1981] Crim LR 423.
6 *R v Newham* [1970] Crim LR 705, CA.
7 See p 95, above.

situation that his client's instructions so seek to shift the blame or excuse his actions that they amount to an equivocal plea.

Mitigating circumstances

In many cases of violence the defendant may say that he was provoked. Provocation is not a defence to a criminal charge except one of murder, nevertheless it can amount to mitigation if there is sufficient evidence to show that the accused was provoked. Similarly in dishonesty cases, the defendant may have been led into temptation by the ease with which money could be taken from the victim by the victim's own recklessness, or by the financial hardship suffered by the defendant which caused him to steal.

The defendant's personal circumstances

After considering the nature of the offence and the motive for committing it the bench would consider the personal circumstances of the accused. Has he a long record of previous convictions or is he a man of previous good character? Does he have a stable background with a family to support? Is he in employment? All these matters are considerations which should be taken into account.

Not every factor described above (and other factors not mentioned here) will be relevant to every case. The defence solicitor should have some idea what form of sentence his client is likely to receive and to aim his mitigation at that sentence, or rather, if that sentence is considered by the defence to be too severe, to aim the mitigation at dissuading the bench from adopting that course of action.

In order to form a view the solicitor should consider his client's record carefully to see what sentences have been imposed in the past. Is his client committing a different kind of offence from that of which he has previously been convicted, or, most importantly, is the defendant in breach of any sentence?

The mitigation will be shaped by the sentence which may be contemplated. If imprisonment is a possibility, an adjournment for a social inquiry report may be necessary at which time the defendant's suitability for community service may be considered. Similarly, an adjournment for a report may be necessary if a probation order is contemplated. If on the other hand a fine is clearly going to be imposed, the solicitor would be well advised to address the bench on his client's financial circumstances.

Whatever else, the mitigation should have a purpose behind it: to minimise the offence, to explain the defendant's motives, to argue against a specific sentence or for a particular one, but the mitigation should not simply be a few minutes of aimless waffle, the only result of which could be to make the bench feel ill-disposed to the client.

The announcing of the sentence

Having considered the case the bench, through the chairman, will announce sentence. Sometimes, where several offences are concerned together with orders for costs, compensation and legal aid, the announcing of the sentences can be an extremely complex process and so the magistrates are quite entitled to correct any slips of the tongue without recourse to section 142 of the Magistrates' Courts Act 1980.[8]

8 *R v Newcastle upon Tyne Justices, ex p Swales* [1972] RTR 57, [1972] Crim LR 111, DC.

Chapter 6

The not guilty hearing

The accused has pleaded not guilty and, as is usual, the case is adjourned to a suitable date when there is sufficient court time for a trial to be held and all the witnesses are able to attend. The police, in the course of their investigations, will have taken statements from anyone whom they think can give material evidence in the matter. Some of these potential witnesses may turn out not to be of any help to the prosecution but they may be able to give assistance to the defence. The first question to consider therefore is the obligation on the prosecution to disclose their case to the defence.

Matters preliminary to the hearing

PRE-TRIAL DISCLOSURE[1]

Generally speaking the prosecution are under no obligation to 'show their hand' to the defence before the trial and, therefore, unlike at the Crown Court where the defence will have been served with depositions at the committal stage, the defence will have no idea upon what evidence the prosecution case depends. Nor would it be aware of any potential defence witnesses rejected by the police. This last situation is remedied by authorities which place a duty on the prosecution to inform the defence of the names of witnesses from whom they have taken statements but whom they do not intend to call as witnesses.[2] This duty does not extend, however, to supplying the defence with copies of the statements already taken (although the prosecution may oblige).[3] Occasionally, the defence may wish the prosecution to call a particular witness as it may wish to discredit him and show a conflict with the

1 See Criminal Law Act 1977, s 48 (not in force at the time of writing).

2 *R v Leyland Justices, ex p Hawthorn* [1979] QB 283, [1979] 1 All ER 209.

3 *R v Bryant and Dickson* (1946) 110 JP 267, 31 Cr App Rep 146. A practice in some areas is for there to be a 'pre-trial review' before a not guilty hearing takes place. At the pre-trial review the prosecution and defence undertake mutual disclosure of their case. Disclosure will help to narrow the points in issue and canvass any law which is to be argued. A pre-trial review also assists the listing of cases in court by ensuring that a case does not 'collapse' by the defendant suddenly pleading guilty at the date of trial, and by aiding the estimation of court time needed for the trial.

evidence of other prosecution witnesses. The prosecution has a discretion as to which witnesses it will call and this discretion should be exercised so as to further the interests of justice and to be fair to the defence, so that where no purpose would be served by calling a particular witness the prosecution may refuse to do so,[4] but if the evidence is capable of belief the witness should be called even if it conflicts with other prosecution evidence.[5]

A further duty of disclosure by the prosecution is that it must inform the defence if any of the prosecution witnesses have previous convictions,[6] but there is no obligation on the prosecution to search all their records if the evidence is not to hand.[7] In addition, the prudent defence solicitor will already have asked for a copy of his client's previous convictions and it is also wise to inquire whether any of the potential defence witnesses have previous convictions. If it has not already been done, the defendant's voluntary statement should be asked for and this will usually be supplied, and these days, especially where the prosecution is being conducted by a solicitor, the defence will usually be shown the defendant's 'verbals' or oral replies to police questioning. It is in the interests of all parties to have foreknowledge of damaging admissions either because the defendant will realise the strength of the case against him and plead guilty, or if he maintains his plea of not guilty, his solicitor will be more prepared for the cross-examination of the police officer.

Outside the court room the prosecutor may show the prosecution witnesses their statements which they made to the police so that they may refresh their memories, but not for the purpose of comparing their evidence.[8] If they are in fact shown their statements, it is desirable that the defence be informed of this before the witnesses give evidence.[9]

THE DEFENCE WITNESSES

The defence solicitor will have taken statements or 'proofs' from his witnesses in the same way as the police. When deciding to call witnesses their is a great temptation to conduct a battle of numbers with the prosecution, that is, call as many witnesses as possible. But there is a great danger in this. Consider for example a charge of breach

4 *R v Nugent* [1977] 3 All ER 662, [1977] 1 WLR 789 where the prosecution were correct in not calling a witness who would only confuse the jury by describing a third version of events as the accused described them.

5 *R v Oliva* [1965] 3 All ER 116, [1965] 1 WLR 1028.

6 *R v Chambers and Wilson* [1960] Crim LR 437.

7 Cf *R v Collister and Warhurst* (1955) 39 Cr App Rep 100 (convictions of the accused himself).

8 *R v Richardson* [1971] 2 QB 484, [1971] 2 All ER 773.

9 *R v Webb* [1975] Crim LR 159; *Worley v Bentley* [1976] 2 All ER 449, [1976] Crim LR 310.

of the peace committed at a football match. The defendant may wish to bring along several 'mates' to support his story. Apart from the fact that his 'mates' may present individually an unsavoury appearance which is not enhanced when they are seen all together, it is very wise to prepare their proofs of evidence very carefully to make quite sure that they can actually give relevant evidence. A defence case is not improved by calling witnesses who, in the witness box, cannot testify to having seen the vital incident especially if the reasons for this temporary blindness are not very convincing. There is a difference between a witness who did not see it happen and one who saw it not happen. An even worse situation is when the defence witness starts contradicting in evidence the statement he previously made to the defendant's solicitor. For this reason the reluctant witness has to be treated with care. It is possible to obtain a witness summons or warrant[10] to enforce the attendance of an unwilling witness, who can be compelled[11] to give evidence, but before taking this step consideration should be given to what the witness will or will not say in court.

The hearing itself

LISTING SEVERAL MATTERS TOGETHER

When the case is called on, the defendant will usually be asked for his name and the charge will be read again and an indication given to the bench by the clerk that the accused has already pleaded not guilty. A problem can sometimes be caused by the fact that the accused faces several charges to some of which he has pleaded guilty. The defendant can always ask for separate trials and even where the offences are still listed together, he can insist that the magistrates should not be made aware of the other charges on the grounds that they might appear to be prejudiced against him.[12] In practice the defendant is very often not at a disadvantage, especially in the situation where he has already pleaded guilty to several more serious matters, as the bench might naturally incline to the view that if a man has shown his willingness to admit his guilt, why should he persist in a not guilty plea on the remaining matter unless he is in fact innocent? In other cases the fact that other offences have been committed might be so tightly bound up with the not guilty plea that it is inevitable that evidence of the other offences will be given. In *R v Bastin*[13] (a trial at the Crown Court)

10 MCA 1980, s 97.
11 Ibid, s 97(4).
12 *R v Liverpool City Justices, ex p Topping* [1983] 1 All ER 490, [1983] 1 WLR 119. Cf *R v Sandwich Justices, ex p Berry* (1981) 74 Cr App Rep 132, [1982] Crim LR 121.
13 [1971] Crim LR 529.

evidence of guilty pleas to two offences was held to be properly admitted, though prejudicial, on the trial of the third offence as it was so directly relevant.

THE BENCH

Unless the hearing is before a stipendiary magistrate, a trial should take place before three magistrates. The minimum number is two[14] (unlike a remand or committal hearing where one is sufficient) but it is desirable that an odd number of magistrates should adjudicate (ie three) on a not guilty hearing because if two magistrates disagreed, they would have to order a rehearing.[15] Whatever number of magistrates are sitting, they must reach a decision, they cannot order a rehearing because each of them individually cannot decide whether the accused is guilty or not guilty.[16] The decision may be by a majority of the justices adjudicating.

PREVIOUS CONVICTIONS

Where a magistrate has previously sat on a remand hearing in the same proceedings and has been informed of the defendant's previous convictions, he cannot sit at the trial of the information[17] but where the magistrate may know the defendant has previous convictions, because for example he has convicted him on a previous occasion, although it is desirable that the magistrate should not adjudicate, there is no principle of law that he should not.[18] If it were otherwise, many small courts with small local populations would be in an impossible situation.[19]

THE PRESENCE OF THE ACCUSED

The general rule is that an accused is deemed to be present if he is represented by counsel or solicitor[20] (and so no warrant or summons under section 13 of the Magistrates' Courts Act 1980 would be issued[1]) except that the defendant must attend personally if he has been bailed. Accordingly, the court could quite well proceed in the absence of the accused if mode of trial and plea have been taken,[2] but it would be

14 MCA 1980, s 121.
15 *Barnsley v Marsh* [1947] KB 672, [1947] 1 All ER 874.
16 *R v Bridgend Justices, ex p Randall* [1975] Crim LR 287, (1975) 119 SJ 458.
17 MCA 1980, s 42.
18 *R v McElligott, ex p Gallagher and Seal* [1972] Crim LR 332, DC.
19 Cf the *Sandwich Justices* case where the bench conducted a series of trials against the same defendant.
20 MCA 1980, s 122.
1 *R v Thompson* [1909] 2 KB 614, 73 JP 403; *R v Montgomery, ex p Long* (1910) 74 JP 110.
2 MCA 1980, s 11.

unusual to do this in a serious case especially where the accused has instructed a solicitor and failed to arrive at court for no apparent reason. The court would normally expect the presence of the accused and in serious cases would only proceed if there were strong grounds for believing the defendant wilfully disobeyed the summons or bail to attend.[3]

EXCLUDING WITNESSES FROM COURT

In criminal trials it is usual for all witnesses to be excluded from the court room until they give their evidence. After they have given evidence they will remain in court until released by the magistrates. This prevents any collusion with witnesses who are about to give evidence. Exceptionally, the bench may grant permission for a witness who has given evidence to be released forthwith where, for instance, he has an urgent appointment to keep or he has been working on a night shift and wants to go back to bed. The bench would wish to make sure that it is unlikely that the witness will be needed again and that he will leave the building straight away without contacting other witnesses. If, through inadvertence, a witness remains in court before he gives evidence, the court cannot refuse to hear his evidence but the bench will naturally view his evidence in the light of his having had the opportunity to hear what the other witnesses have had to say.[4]

EXPERT WITNESSES

An exception to the general exclusion rule is made for expert witnesses who are called to assist the court in the interpretation of the evidence that has been given. They are usually allowed to remain in court throughout the hearing so that they can comment on what has been said.

The prosecution case

THE OPENING

After the defendant has been identified and the witnesses have been removed from the court, the prosecutor will 'open' his case. The opening is a speech in which the prosecutor outlines his case so that the magistrates have a picture of what the case is about. The prosecutor will often describe who his witnesses are and what they will say. If he expects there to be any argument on the law, he will often comment on it at this stage. The prosecutor only has one speech which must be

3 Cf articles at (1971) 135 JP 861 and (1974) 138 JP 518.
4 *Tomlinson v Tomlinson* [1980] 1 All ER 593, [1980] 1 WLR 322.

made before he calls his evidence, although he may address the magistrates again after the defence has given its evidence, but only if the bench give him leave.[5]

In his opening the prosecutor is concerned to present his case fairly; his duty is not to obtain a conviction at all costs but rather to assist the court to do justice.[6] In his opening the prosecutor is not giving evidence and so he must be careful only to mention those matters which he reasonably believes will be substantiated by the evidence he is to call. If he includes in his speech a reference to evidence of a witness which he does not subsequently wish to call, he should tender that witness so that the defence may have an opportunity of cross-examining him.[7]

CALLING THE FIRST PROSECUTION WITNESS

The trial proper only begins when the magistrates begin to hear the evidence (as opposed to the prosecution opening)[8] and the prosecution will normally call their witnesses in the chronological order of events.

In order to describe the course of a trial and the pitfalls that can be encountered, the imaginary case of shoplifting that was described in chapter 3 for the purpose of laying an information, will be presumed to have progressed to the stage of a trial. No attempt will be made to present a verbatim account of the trial, but only the more salient features of the case will be discussed.

John Doe has been alleged to have stolen a screwdriver from the Acme Supermarket. The prosecution have three witnesses: a shop assistant who saw him take the item and place it in his shopping bag, the shop manager who can testify that the store does sell the type of screwdriver in question, and PC Dixon who interviewed the accused and took his voluntary statement. The defence will call the accused and a (none too reliable) friend of his.

The first prosecution witness is the shop assistant. He is called to give evidence and steps into the witness box.

The oath

Apart from certain exceptions, eg the unsworn evidence of children of tender years received under section 38 of the Children and Young Persons Act 1933 all evidence before the magistrates is given on oath.[9] The witness (if a Christian) takes the New Testament in either the

5 For the order of speeches see Magistrates' Courts Rules 1981, r 3 and for a discussion on the role of the prosecutor read C. Humphries 'The Duties and Responsibilities of Prosecuting Counsel' [1955] Crim LR 739.

6 *Ostler v Elliot* [1980] Crim LR 584, DC.

7 *R v Sterk* [1972] Crim LR 391, CA.

8 *R v Craske, ex p Metropolitan Police Comr* [1957] 2 QB 591, [1957] 2 All ER 772; *R v Ibrahim* (1957) 42 Cr App Rep 38, [1958] Crim LR 130.

9 MCA 1980, s 98.

right or left hand and raises it and repeats the words of the oath 'I swear by Almighty God etc . . .'[10]

This oath will be administered as a matter of course unless the witness objects, in which case he must be allowed to affirm or take a religious oath binding on his conscience.[11]

THE EXAMINATION IN CHIEF

The purpose of this is to induce the witness to tell his story to the court. It can be quite difficult to keep the witness to the point especially as generally the witness cannot be 'led'. The bench are concerned to hear the witness' own version of events, not that of the prosecutor, and so the prosecutor is not allowed to ask the witness leading questions. It is almost impossible to define a leading question but it is in effect a question which suggests the answer that is desired.[12] An obvious example in the present case would be 'You saw the accused put the screwdriver in his bag didn't you?' To which the obvious answer would be 'yes'. In some contexts a question such as 'Did you see the accused put the screwdriver in the bag?' would be a leading question where there had been no prior mention of the screwdriver being taken or put in the bag. The advocate should so phrase his questions that the story comes naturally from the witness. For example, the shop assistant has been narrating how he saw the accused wandering up the aisle where the Do-it-Yourself tools were on display. The questioning might go as follows:

Prosecutor: 'And what did the accused do then?'
Assistant: 'He stopped by the tools.'
Prosecutor: 'What happened then?'
Assistant: 'He bent down and picked up the screwdriver.'
Prosecutor: 'What did he do with the screwdriver?'
Assistant: 'He looked round and put it in his shopping bag.'
Prosecutor: 'Tell the court more about this bag. What sort of bag was it . . . etc.'

Needless to say, eliciting evidence in chief can be an extremely skilful matter where the witness is taciturn or even where he is excessively garrulous.

Although leading questions should generally not be asked, it is permissible to ask them where the evidence to be elicited is not in dispute, but as soon as matters become contentious the normal rule

10 In the case of a juvenile witness or where the proceedings are in a juvenile court the words are 'I promise before Almighty God etc . . .' (Children and Young Persons Act 1963, s 28).

11 See generally the Oaths Act 1978 and *R v Chapman* [1980] Crim LR 42, CA. The Act is directive and a failure to comply with its provisions does not necessarily invalidate the oath.

12 *Cross* (5th edn) p 226.

applies. As a matter of courtesy the advocate on the other side should be consulted before the witness is led in this way.

CROSS-EXAMINATION BY THE DEFENCE

The purpose of cross-examining a witness is either to pin point a weakness in the evidence he has given, for example did he really have a good view of the accused taking the screwdriver if he was keeping observation from behind an enormous pile of tins of baked beans, or else to show that the witness is not to be believed because he is a man of bad character or is biased against the accused. The prosecution witness may have several previous convictions for dishonesty or he may have quarrelled with the accused and there may be ill-feeling between them. This form of cross-examination is said to be attacking the character of the prosecution witness and it can have serious consequences for the defendant.

PUTTING THE ACCUSED'S RECORD IN[13]

In criminal cases the prosecution is not allowed to mention the previous convictions of the accused by virtue of section 1(f) of the Criminal Evidence Act 1898. There are however three exceptions to this:

(a) where the other offences are admissible as evidence to prove the offence with which the accused is already charged (the 'similar fact' rule);
(b) where the accused gives evidence of his own good character, eg he says 'I am a pillar of respectability, I would not do such a thing as that' and he has a string of convictions for the very same offence;
(c) where he casts imputations on the character of the prosecutor (or another co-accused).

If the accused attacked the prosecution witnesses and then gave evidence, he would lose this 'shield' protecting him from having his previous convictions mentioned.

In the usual trial the cross-examination consists in merely testing the accuracy of the evidence of the witness rather than his credit, if for no other reason than that the witness and the accused are not known to each other. Nevertheless, the potential loss of the shield should always be borne in mind when pursuing a vigorous cross-examination and for this reason it is important to check whether the defendant has any previous convictions; do not rely on his word. Another principle of cross-examination is that, wherever possible, a question should only be

13 Ibid, 417. If an unrepresented accused is in danger of putting his character in, he should be warned of this by the clerk in the absence of the magistrates *R v Weston Super Mare Justices, ex p Townsend* [1968] 3 All ER 225n, [1968] Crim LR 500.

asked where the answer is known. It is wise to be careful of asking questions that will provide the prosecution witness with a reason to give really damaging evidence. If the witness says 'I noticed the accused by the display of tools and I saw him etc.', do not ask 'why did you notice my client?' because the reply might be 'because I have seen him acting very suspiciously on several occasions in the past'. A further and important function of cross-examination is to put the defence case to the witness.[14] It is only fair that if the accused or a defence witness is going to contradict the evidence of a prosecution witness, the witness should be given a chance to comment on the inconsistency when he is giving his evidence. The assistant might be cross examined:

Defence solicitor: 'My client will say that the screwdriver was found in his shopping bag because it fell from the shelf. Is that right?'

Assistant: 'That's what your client says, but I saw him take it.'

The cross-examination should not be an excuse for a display of bad temper by the advocate. He should be courteous but firm if need be, and only ask one question at a time so that the witness has time to reply in full. Under no circumstances should the witness be brow beaten, nor should the same question be repeated once an answer has been given. Remember a bench of magistrates, unlike a jury, will probably have considerable collective experience of hearing trials and will not be amused by needless repetition. Similar rules of questioning apply to cross-examination as apply to evidence in chief; the cross-examiner should not put words into the mouth of the witness, but of course cross-examination will be more direct when evidence is being challenged which has already been given in chief.

RE-EXAMINATION

After the witness has been cross-examined, he may then be re-examined by the party calling him, in this case the prosecutor. The purpose of re-examination is to clarify any points which may remain ambiguous after the cross-examination or to deal with any matters which have been freshly raised by the cross-examination and which could not reasonably have been anticipated in the examination in chief. The purpose of re-examination is not to repeat evidence already given nor to bolster up evidence that has been shaken by good cross-examination.

QUESTIONS FROM THE BENCH[15]

After any re-examination the bench will be invited to say whether they have any questions of the witness. The bench may ask questions to clear

14 *O'Connell v Adams* [1973] RTR 150, [1973] Crim LR 113, DC.

15 The most useful authority on this is *Jones v National Coal Board* [1957] 2 QB 55, [1957] 2 All ER 155.

up any ambiguities in the evidence to ensure that they have thoroughly understood what has been said. Except where the justices have to intervene, usually through their clerk, to ensure that an unrepresented accused is able to put his case properly, the justices should not interfere with the presentation of the case but should content themselves with adjudicating on the evidence before them. Excessive interference by the bench which inhibits the proper presentation of the defence case, for example, will result in a conviction being quashed.[16]

THE SECOND PROSECUTION WITNESS – THE SECTION 9 STATEMENT

In our imaginary case the second witness to be called is the manager of the shop. He is called to testify that the store sells such items and he was handed the screwdriver from the assistant and handed it to the police officer. This simple example has been chosen to illustrate the case of the use of the written statement tendered in evidence under section 9 of the Criminal Justice Act 1967. In many criminal cases formal evidence will have to be called for the sake of completeness, although the evidence will not be challenged. Obviously, it would be a waste of time and money to have the manager called to give evidence where there will be no cross-examination. To obviate this, there is a procedure (similar to the use of written statements in committal proceedings) for reducing his evidence to the form of a written statement tendered under section 9. The basic requirements of the section may be summarised as follows:

(a) the statement shall contain the maker's age if he is under 21;
(b) it shall contain a declaration that it is true to the best of his knowledge and belief and that he is liable to be prosecuted if he wilfully stated anything that was not true or believed to be true;
(c) it is signed by the maker; and
(d) it is served on the other parties at least seven days before the hearing.

The requirement of seven days' notice may be waived by agreement and at the hearing, the party who caused the statement to be prepared may always call the witness to give oral evidence instead. The court itself, or on the application of the opposing party, may call the witness if objection was not made to the admission of the statement when it was originally served.

In court the statement will usually be read out aloud either in full or in a summarised form.

PITFALLS OF THE SECTION 9 PROCEDURE

(a) For the party producing the statement

The written statement is useful and convenient but it should not be

16 *R v Welwyn Justices, ex p Jones* [1969] Crim LR 616, (1969) 113 Sol Jo 564, DC.

used for a witness who is essential to the central issue in the case as other oral evidence might be given during the course of the trial which conflicts with the written statement and might cast doubt in the mind of the bench.[17]

(b) For the party who is served with the statement

Whenever a statement is served it should be scrutinised carefully to see whether it contains prejudicial evidence which could and should be challenged. If no objection is raised to the statement, the evidence will be read out at the trial and there will be no opportunity for cross-examination and normally the bench will almost inevitably accept the evidence as it stands. An advocate in this situation has no alternative but the embarrassment of applying for an adjournment so that the witness may be called to give oral evidence.[18]

THE THIRD PROSECUTION WITNESS – THE POLICE OFFICER

Shoplifting cases provide a useful example of the idiosyncratic nature of the power of arrest. In chapter 2 it was explained that a private person only has a power of arrest for theft under section 2 of the Criminal Law Act 1967 where an offence has actually been committed. If the assistant (or a store detective) arrested a customer who was subsequently acquitted of the charge, the person making the arrest would be liable to be sued civilly for false imprisonment. Therefore the assistant would usually 'invite' (ie not arrest) the customer to return to the manager's office where he would remain (voluntarily) until a police officer arrives. The police officer will question the accused and if he has reasonable suspicion that an offence has been committed, he will make the arrest. If it later turns out that an offence has not been committed, the officer will be protected because he has the power to arrest merely on reasonable suspicion of an offence.

After he has been told by the assistant what has taken place, the officer will caution the accused,[19] ask him some questions and then arrest him and take him to the police station. At the police station he will be reminded that he is under caution, asked further questions and invited to make a voluntary statement. He will then be charged and further cautioned[20] and released on police bail to court, or if the summons procedure is used, an information will be laid by sending a prepared information and summons to the appropriate magistrates' court for issue.

The problem for the defence in cross-examining a police officer is

17 *Lister v Quaife* (1982) Times, 1 May.
18 For further examples of admitting evidence in writing without the need to call witnesses to give oral evidence see (1981) 145 JP 434.
19 The 'first' caution: see p 29, above.
20 The 'second' caution.

that the officer will almost inevitably ask permission to refresh his memory from his notebook. Any witness may refresh his memory in the witness box from notes which he made at the time of the incident or within a reasonable period thereafter. In practice, only the police use this facility, or other professional witnesses such as store detectives or officials of the Department of Health and Social Security.[1] Unfortunately, the police officer is unlikely to have made either a contemporaneous or a verbatim note of the conversation. What often happens is that the officer will make his notes afterwards from his recollection of what took place, or if there were two officers involved they will compile their notes together from their joint recollections.[2]

The objection to the officer using his notebook to refresh his memory may take two forms, whether he should be allowed to refer to his notebook at all, and then what weight is to be attached to the recollection contained in the notebook.

The use of the notebook will be permitted if the witness confirms that the events were still fresh in his memory when he compiled his record, and usually he will be allowed to refer to it when the events were recorded several hours later, or even two or three days later, but where a witness was allowed to refer to a statement made 27 days later this was definitely frowned on.[3] If the officer does use his notebook, the defence are quite at liberty to question him on how he can maintain that he has recorded verbatim a lengthy conversation held some hours beforehand as it can suggest to the bench that little weight should be attached to such evidence.

The defence may call for and inspect the officer's notebook and provided that cross-examination is confined to the parts which he has used to refresh his memory, the book should not be produced for the bench to read (ie made an exhibit).[4] It will, of course, often be very difficult for the defence advocate when faced with an officer giving evidence of very damaging 'verbals' by the accused, to avoid casting an imputation on the character of the officer so that the accused will lose his 'shield' under section 1(f) of the Criminal Evidence Act 1898, with the result that his previous convictions will be put in evidence. There is obviously a limit to the extent to which it can be alleged that the officer is 'mistaken' rather than that he is not telling the truth.[5]

1 Although a witness may use his own statement that he made to the police if it fulfils the other criteria.

2 *R v Bass* [1953] 1 QB 681, [1953] 1 All ER 1064, where the process was deemed to be a reasonable thing to do.

3 *R v Graham* [1973] Crim LR 628, CA.

4 Cf *Senat v Senat* [1965] P 172, [1965] 2 All ER 505; but also note the exception in *Bass* where the bench is entitled to see the notebooks where the two officers had denied they had made up their notes together.

5 It is one thing to dispute the accuracy or the existence of a brief conversation with the officer, and another to dispute the existence of a detailed interview lasting a long time; see *R v Britzman, R v Hall* [1983] Crim LR 106.

WHERE THE DEFENDANT'S PREVIOUS CONVICTIONS ARE INADVERTENTLY MENTIONED

If a previous conviction of the accused is deliberately elicited by the prosecution in breach of section 1(f) of the Criminal Evidence Act 1898 a resulting conviction will be quashed. However, occasionally the fact that the defendant has a previous conviction may inadvertently be let slip. In this situation it may be the best course not to make too much fuss and carry straight on as if nothing had happened.[6] The advocate should decide whether any undue prejudice has been caused to his client, eg was the conviction for a similar matter or was it something totally different such as a road traffic offence.[7]

The submission of no case to answer

After the prosecution has called all its evidence, it will formally close its case. The hearing will have reached the halfway stage sometimes colloquially known as 'half time'. At this point it is open to the defence to submit that the defendant has no case to answer. This means that the prosecution have not produced sufficient evidence to satisfy any reasonable bench of the defendant's guilt beyond a reasonable doubt. The law on this point is set out in a *Practice Note*.[8]

> Without attempting to lay down any principle of law, we think that as a matter of practice justices should be guided by the following considerations.
>
> A submission that there is no case to answer may properly be made and upheld: (a) when there has been no evidence to prove an essential element in the alleged offence; (b) when the evidence adduced by the prosecution has been so discredited as a result of cross-examination or is so manifestly unreliable that no reasonable tribunal could safely convict on it.
>
> Apart from these two situations a tribunal should not in general be called to reach a decision as to conviction or acquittal until the whole of the evidence which either side wishes to tender has been placed before it. If, however, a submission is made that there is no case to answer, the decision should depend not so much on whether the adjudicating tribunal (if compelled to do so) would at that stage convict or acquit but on whether the evidence is such that a reasonable tribunal might convict. If a reasonable tribunal might convict on the evidence so far laid before it, there is a case to answer.

6 *R v Wright* (1934) 25 Cr App Rep 35.
7 See *R v Pike (No 2)* [1962] Crim LR 40 and the cases cited in the commentary; also *R v Dickerson and Cavill* [1964] Crim LR 821, CCA.
8 [1962] 1 All ER 448 which which the bench should always have available for their guidance; *Stoneley v Coleman* [1974] Crim LR 254.

If the defendant makes a submission which is unsuccessful he is not deprived of his final speech as it is probable that these submissions are not speeches within the meaning of the rule.[9] For a similar reason it is generally accepted that the prosecutor has a right of reply on the law.

PROBLEMS WITH THE SUBMISSION OF NO CASE

The first problem is that the bench of lay magistrates is required to do a very difficult job. The magistrates have to decide not whether the prosecution has satisfied them beyond a reasonable doubt, but whether the prosecution might satisfy any reasonable bench. It might happen that the bench trying the case would be inclined to acquit the accused but nevertheless another reasonable bench might convict, therefore the submission would be rejected. If the defence called no evidence, the same bench would then have no option but to acquit as they were themselves not satisfied of the defendant's guilt beyond a reasonable doubt. However, the defence does not know on what basis the submission was rejected. Therefore it may have to run the risk of the accused giving evidence which instead of establishing his innocence, might tip the scales against him. It is submitted that the Practice Note does not take account of the differing functions of the judge and jury in the Crown Court and those of the magistrates, who decide both whether, as a matter of law, there is sufficient evidence to convict and whether, in fact, there is sufficient for a conviction.

The second problem is that the magistrates sometimes misinterpret the submission of no case to answer as the final defence speech after calling no evidence, with the result that a conviction may be prematurely announced. Although certiorari might lie to quash the conviction, in view of the provisions of section 142 of the Magistrates' Courts Act 1980 the discretionary remedy of certiorari would now probably be refused because of the magistrates' ability to order a fresh hearing before a different bench.[10]

In order to avoid any possibility of this happening, the bench should ask the defence solicitor whether he is making a final speech or is he making a submission and reserving the right to call evidence thereafter.[11]

The defence case

THE FIRST WITNESS – THE DEFENDANT

If the defence decides to call evidence, it is the general rule that the defendant will give evidence first although in exceptional cases formal evidence may be called before the accused.[12] Before calling any

9 Cf the discussion at (1980) 144 JP 228 and 286 and see A. Samuels (1975) 139 JP 493.
10 *R v Midhurst Justices, ex p Thompson* [1974] QB 137, [1973] 3 All ER 1164.
11 *R v Gravesend Justices, ex p Sheldon* [1968] 3 All ER 466n, [1968] 1 WLR 1699.
12 *R v Smith* [1968] 2 All ER 115, [1968] 1 WLR 636.

evidence the defence may make a speech but if it does it cannot address the court at the end of the defence case without the leave of the court.

The defendant will give evidence, be cross-examined and perhaps re-examined in the same way as the prosecution witnesses.

THE SECOND DEFENCE WITNESS – WHO TURNS 'HOSTILE'[13]

Whether or not the defendant gives evidence, the defence may call witnesses in the same way as the prosecution, including the use where appropriate of section 9 statements.

A problem which sometimes occurs is that a witness does not say what is expected of him or, even worse, gives evidence directly contradictory to the statement he has made earlier. In the case under discussion suppose the defendant had a witness who gives a statement to his solicitor in which he says that he saw the screwdriver slip off the shelf into the defendant's bag without the defendant touching it. What would happen if in the witness box, he were to say that he saw the accused pick up the screwdriver and place it in his bag?

The party calling a witness cannot usually cross-examine his own witness because cross-examination is designed to impeach the reliability of a witness. A party cannot put forward a witness as to the truth and then seek to show that his evidence is not to be relied on. But in the situation where the witness turns hostile – that is to say he shows a distinct hostility towards the party calling him (not merely that he is forgetful, or necessarily that he tells a story different from one told before) – the permission of the bench may be sought to have the witness treated as hostile. If this permission is granted, the hostile witness may be cross-examined by the party calling him who may produce an inconsistent statement made by the hostile witness on an earlier occasion with a view to destroying the worth of his evidence. The previous statement is usually a written proof of evidence but it could be a previous oral statement.[14]

The witness should be asked whether he has made such a statement and he should be told sufficient details to identify the occasion. If he does not admit it, proof may be given of the statement and if the statement is in writing, he may be cross-examined about its contents and the bench may examine the statement if they see fit.[15]

In the case we are considering the defence solicitor would, having received permission from the bench, ask the witness whether he had made a statement to him at his office on a specified date. If the witness

13 See *Cross* (5th edn) p 250 and 'The Hostile Witness in the Magistrates Court' (1980) 144 JP 497 and A Samuels 'The Hostile Witness in Criminal Proceedings' (1977) 141 JP 250.

14 Criminal Procedure and Evidence Act 1865, s 3.

15 Ibid, ss 4 and 5.

said no, the solicitor would have to prove that he had, but as the solicitor would have a signed copy, the making of the statement would not usually be denied. The witness would be allowed to examine the statement and if he still persisted in his contradictory evidence he could be cross-examined on his previous statement.

The previous written statement never becomes evidence in the case unless it is adopted by the witness when faced with its existence, as the only evidence the court can accept is the oral evidence given in the witness box. The purpose of cross-examining a hostile witness is to destroy the value of the oral evidence given at the trial and the effect of a totally successful cross-examination would be to expunge the hostile evidence he has just given, but unless the previous statement were adopted, it would not produce any positive evidence in favour of the accused.

If the witness is merely forgetful and so does not give evidence that is 'hostile', he cannot be impeached by the party calling him although other witnesses may be called who give a fuller version of the events to be described, or who even give evidence which is at variance with that given by the forgetful witness.[16]

Reopening the prosecution case

After the defence has called its evidence the defence solicitor will make his closing speech if he had not done so at the beginning of the case. Before this, the prosecutor might wish to call further evidence even though the prosecution case has been closed. He cannot do this without the leave of the court.

A distinction should be made between evidence in rebuttal and evidence which has been omitted owing to an oversight. Evidence in rebuttal is evidence which is given to contradict defence evidence. Where the nature of the defence evidence is something which arose unexpectedly in the course of the defence case and which no human ingenuity could foresee then clearly the prosecution must be allowed to call rebutting evidence[17], but where the evidence was obviously going to be relevant and the prosecution were in possession of it the bench would probably not exercise their discretion to allow it to be called after the defence case.[18]

Where evidence has been inadvertently omitted, the bench do have a residuary discretion to allow further evidence to be called. Even where the prosecution omits to prove a matter of substance the bench could

16 See *Cross* (5th edn) p 250.
17 *R v Whelan* (1881) 8 LR Ir 314, 14 Cox CC 595; *R v Harris* [1927] 2 KB 587, 91 JP 152.
18 *R v Levy and Tait* (1966) 50 Cr App Rep 198, [1966] Crim LR 454.

allow further evidence to be called but the magistrates should be careful not to encourage careless prosecutions.[19] This discretion should be exercised judicially and where the prosecution makes a mistake which could cause no prejudice to the defendant[20] or the omission was of evidence of a formal nature, leave should be granted.[1] Even where there has been a submission of no case to answer, the prosecution may call further evidence where it has been misled or has been guilty of a pardonable oversight.[2] Where the justices have retired to consider their verdict, although the procedural rules are not rigidly to be applied, there must be very special circumstances before the bench should hear further evidence.[3]

Sometimes neither side omits evidence but the bench itself may wish to hear a witness again to refresh its memory and this may be done.[4]

The closing speeches

At the conclusion of the defence case the defence advocate will make his closing speech before the bench retire to consider their verdict. Exceptionally, the prosecutor may ask leave to address the court a second time and if permission is granted, the defence may also address the court a second time.[5]

THE FINAL DEFENCE SPEECH

There is no point in boring the bench by reciting at great length the evidence which they have just spent perhaps several hours listening to. During the course of the trial they will probably have been taking notes and their clerk will have also done the same. The speech should be confined to what is relevant and there should be a clear perception of the legal issues involved. If it is a straight question of fact then say so, no amount of blandishment will convince a bench that a shifty-eyed witness who has been detected in telling several tall stories is a paragon of truth. The advocate may point out that a particular witness has nothing to gain by telling lies and that his story has the ring of truth about it, and he may point out inconsistencies in the prosecution case.

The golden rule should be never to irritate the bench, who are probably eager to get on and consider the evidence for themselves. One exception to the rule never to dwell on the obvious, is to remind the magistrates of the burden of proof. The fact that the burden of proof is on

19 *Middleton v Rowlett* [1954] 2 All ER 277, [1954] 1 WLR 831.
20 *Matthews v Morris* [1981] Crim LR 495.
1 As in *Royal v Prescott-Clarke* [1966] 2 All ER 366, [1966] 1 WLR 788.
2 *Saunders v Johns* [1965] Crim LR 49, DC.
3 *Webb v Leadbetter* [1966] 2 All ER 114, [1966] 1 WLR 245.
4 *Phelan v Back* [1972] 1 All ER 901, [1972] 1 WLR 273.
5 Magistrates' Courts Rules 1981, r 13.

the side of the defence is one of the most valuable assets that the defence possesses. If the defendant can raise a reasonable doubt in the minds of the bench, he will be entitled to be acquitted.

The justices' decision

THE PRESENCE OF THIRD PARTIES IN THE RETIRING ROOM

After the conclusion of the case the justices will retire to consider their verdict. Great care must be exercised to ensure that the justices are seen to be making their decision without influence from third parties. In the case of *R v Stratford upon Avon Justices,*[6] ex p Edmonds the conviction was quashed because the informant went into the retiring room for a matter of seconds to proffer a book of statutes. His action could have created the impression that he went in to make a point and thus justice was not seen to be done. It is submitted that not every entry by a third party would render a decision invalid, eg an usher delivering a cup of tea, the presence of the third party is only improper if it *creates the impression* that the course of justice is being affected. The usual cases where this problem arises is over the question of the presence of the clerk in the retiring room which is discussed in chapter 1.

JUSTICES USING LOCAL KNOWLEDGE

The justices themselves may have considerable knowledge of facts relevant to the case before them. They may use this knowledge when it is of a general nature and in effect takes the form of local judicial notice.[7] This is particularly the case with local geography as in *Borthwick v Vickers*[8] where the justices were entitled to use the knowledge which was common to all the people in the area that a particular journey must have taken place on a public road. Where the knowledge relates to a more specific matter which is particular to the case in question, the justices should rely solely on the evidence called by the parties and if they contemplate using their local knowledge they should intimate this fact to the parties and allow them to call evidence if necessary. The important point to remember is that it is the evidence called by the parties that matters, as if it is not accepted, it can be tested by cross-examination. Justice is not seen to be done if the magistrates consider their own evidence privately in the retiring room.[9]

6 [1973] RTR 356, [1973] Crim LR 241, DC.
7 For judicial notice see *Cross* (5th edn) p 153.
8 [1973] RTR 390, [1973] Crim LR 317, DC.
9 As in *R v Tiverton Justices, ex p Smith* (1981) 145 JP 177 where the justices used a tyre gauge to measure for themselves the depth of tread on the exhibit in the case. For a magistrate's specialist knowlege see *Wetherall v Harrison* [1976] 1 QB 773, [1976] 1 All ER 241 and Y. I. Cole-Wilson (1982) 146 JP 628.

For the same reason a magistrate with specialist knowledge such as a doctor should not use his specialist knowledge in order to give evidence to his colleagues but he may use it to explain and clarify the evidence given by the parties in court if his colleagues desire him to.

THE VERDICT

Magistrates make their decision on whether the evidence has satisfied them of the truth of the information laid before them. If they are not satisfied beyond a reasonable doubt that the accused committed the offence in the information, but are sure that he committed another offence, they cannot convict him of that other offence.[10] Within certain limitations the information can be amended but it is submitted this could not be done after the justices had retired and so the information would have to be dismissed. The bench might invite the prosecution then to lay a fresh information, if this is possible in view of any time limits, and then proceed on that information.[11]

The solution for the prosecution where it is not sure which of two offences the accused has committed is to lay two informations. Sometimes the prosecution lay two informations for offences which occur from the same set of circumstances such as driving without due care and attention and failing to conform to a give way sign. It would be unjust to convict the accused of both of the offences[12] and *Stones*[13] suggests that one of the matters should be marked 'not proceeded with' or withdrawn. Alternatively, it might be marked adjourned sine die if it is not an indictable offence where the accused has been remanded. The information should not be dismissed at that stage because if it were and the defendant successfully appealed against conviction he would then have been acquitted on both matters even though the justices would have acquitted on the second matter only to avoid oppression to the defendant.

When the magistrates have made their decision (which must be by a majority as the chairman has no casting vote) the decision should be announced simply as 'Guilty' or 'Not Guilty'. The justices do not need to give reasons nor should they in criminal proceedings. If the verdict is guilty the proceedings will follow a pattern similar to those for a guilty

10 With the exception of reckless and careless driving: see ch 13.

11 *Lawrence v Same* [1968] 2 QB 93, [1968] 1 All ER 1191 (substitution of a lesser offence). Note that in a charge of theft it is not necessary to prove theft of the whole amount charged, proof of theft of a part is sufficient for a conviction: *Machent v Quinn* [1970] 1 All ER 255, 134 JP 501 and *Pilgram v Rice-Smith* [1977] 2 All ER 658, [1977] 1 WLR 671.

12 Cf *Welton v Taneborne* (1908) 72 JP 419 (dangerous driving (speed) and speeding); *R v Harris* [1969] 2 All ER 599n, [1969] 1 WLR 745 (buggery and indecent assault).

13 1983 edn p 65.

plea. The prosecutor will make his application for costs and produce any antecedents. The defence will mitigate (although scope for mitigation on the facts will necessarily be limited). Then the magistrates will decide on sentence or adjourn for social inquiry reports. If the accused is acquitted, the prosecutor may still apply for his costs from central funds if the offence is indictable, and the defence may apply for their costs.

Chapter 7

Sentence

Introductory

Sentencing can pose considerable difficulties for anyone unfamiliar with criminal procedure. These difficulties may arise either from a lack of knowledge of which penalties are available for a particular offence, or from the more subtle question of which sentence is most appropriate for the particular case. The newly qualified advocate is most likely to make an embarrasing mistake through ignorance of the availability of sentences because of the limitations of the extent of the magistrates' power to punish imposed by statute. On the whole, magistrates' courts operate within a fairly rigid framework of statutory restrictions governing their sentencing powers, and because they operate within such limits and because of the lack of guidance from the superior courts, it is difficult to establish a coherent philosophy of sentencing for the justices.[1]

Appeals against sentence lie to the local Crown Court, where a decision will be announced in open court but not reported and will not be of much use to establish a precedent or guideline. However, the decision will be communicated to the magistrates who made the original order and in this way an appeal may serve to educate the magistrates in sentencing practice. What is to be applauded is the fresh emphasis that has been placed on the role of the clerk in advising the bench on sentencing principles. A good clerk should be able to assist the bench by referring them to guidance given on sentencing matters by the Court of Appeal to the Crown Court, with any necessary adaptation, and also by informing them of sentences passed for similar offences by other magistrates on that bench and thereby endeavouring to achieve a greater degree of consistency.

In a book such as this, no attempt is made to discuss the philosophical or criminological aspects of sentencing as within the limited space available emphasis will be placed more on the purely objective provisions governing the imposition of sentences and orders on an offender. The bulk of the statutory authority on sentencing matters is contained in the Powers of Criminal Courts Act 1973 and the Criminal Justice Act 1982 which should be studied thoroughly with the aim of knowing the statutory authority for all sentencing matters.

1 Cf Thomas (1981) 145 JP 467.

The powers of the court to deal with a mentally disordered defendant are discussed in chapter 14 and the court's power to bind over a defendant is also given separate treatment in chapter 11.

The sentences available for a particular offence

The sentence that a court may impose for a particular offence is governed first of all by the statute which creates the offence. (In the case of a common law offence the maximum penalty was:

(i) drawing hanging and quartering for treason;
(ii) death for felonies;
(iii) fine or imprisonment at the court's discretion (with or without whipping or the pillory) for misdemeanours.

As felonies have been abolished by the Criminal Law Act 1967 it is the misdemeanour penalty which applies).

Various statutes have prescribed maximum penalties (eg section 47 of the Offences Against the Person Act 1861 limits the maximum penalties for the common law offence of assault, the maximum depending on whether it is common assault or assault occasioning actual bodily harm[2]). In the case of either way offences the statute will give the maximum penalty for trial on indictment but in the magistrates' court there is a general limit for either way offences tried summarily.

The statute will usually provide either for a fine, or for a fine or imprisonment, or for a fine and/or imprisonment. The range of sentences open to a court is of course much wider than a choice between a fine or imprisonment but the availability of these other sentences may depend on whether imprisonment is available. If the penalty section prescribes that both a fine and imprisonment may be imposed at the same time it is possible to combine sentences of a fine and imprisonment for the same offence.

SENTENCES AND ORDERS AVAILABLE FOR A NON-IMPRISONABLE OFFENCE

Fine
Compensation
Probation
Conditional Discharge
Absolute Discharge

(Probation, Conditional Discharge and Absolute Discharge: } passed instead of sentencing the accused.)

SENTENCES AND ORDERS AVAILABLE FOR AN IMPRISONABLE OFFENCE

All the above and in addition:

2 Cf the interesting article on common assault by D. P. Gleeson (1976) 140 JP 203 and 231.

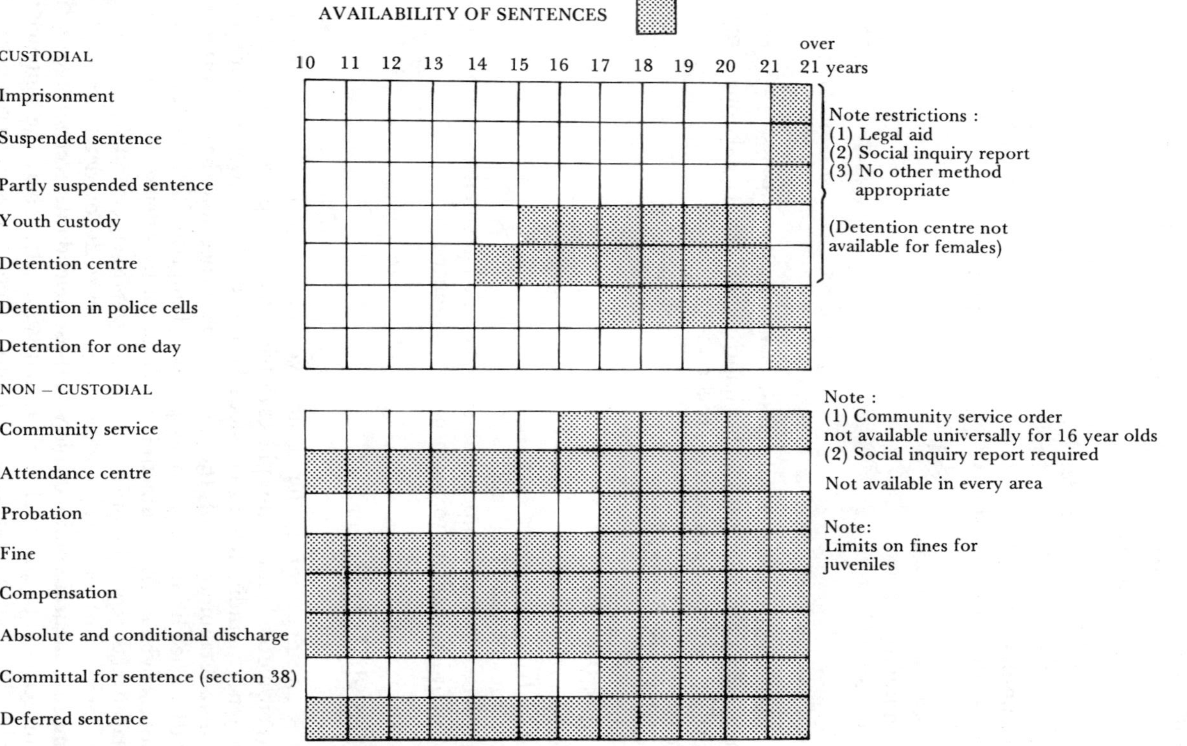

AVAILABILITY OF SENTENCES ■

	10	11	12	13	14	15	16	17	18	19	20	21 – over 21 years
CUSTODIAL												
Imprisonment												■
Suspended sentence												■
Partly suspended sentence												■
Youth custody						■	■	■	■	■	■	
Detention centre					■	■	■	■	■	■	■	
Detention in police cells								■	■	■	■	■
Detention for one day												■
NON – CUSTODIAL												
*Community service							■	■	■	■	■	■
*Attendance centre	■	■	■	■	■	■	■	■	■	■	■	
Probation								■	■	■	■	■
Fine	■	■	■	■	■	■	■	■	■	■	■	■
Compensation	■	■	■	■	■	■	■	■	■	■	■	■
Absolute and conditional discharge	■	■	■	■	■	■	■	■	■	■	■	■
Committal for sentence (section 38)								■	■	■	■	■
Deferred sentence	■	■	■	■	■	■	■	■	■	■	■	■

*Imprisonable offences only

Custodial

Imprisonment Suspended Sentence Partly suspended sentence	over 21.
Youth Custody Detention Centre	under 21.

Detention in Police Cells.
Detention in a Court House or Police Station.

Non-custodial
Community Service.
Attendance Centre.

ANCILLARY ORDERS

In addition to imposing a substantive sentence, the court may at the same time and for any offence (whether imprisonable or not) make one or more ancillary orders. Such orders are for:
Costs.
Legal Aid Contribution.
Compensation.
Restitution.
Forfeiture.
Bind Over.
Recommendation for Deportation.
It will be seen that compensation may be either a sentence in its own right or an order ancillary to a substantive sentence.

Custodial sentences

It is an important matter to deprive someone of his liberty (and an expensive one) and the law places restrictions on the power of the courts to sentence an individual to a custodial sentence. The power to imprison is generally confined to only the more serious offences and the trend of recent statutes has been to take away powers of imprisonment for less serious cases.[3] Even if imprisonment is available for the offence, restrictions are placed on the court before it can actually pass a sentence of imprisonment (in any form) or a sentence of youth custody or detention centre. Imprisonment is confined solely to those defendants over the age of 21. For defendants under 21 the alternative penalty where the sentence is more than four months is youth custody, and if the sentence is between 21 days and four months a detention centre order is made.

3 Eg vagrancy and soliciting (Criminal Justice Act 1982, ss 70 and 71).

Before passing a sentence of imprisonment on a person who has not previously *served* a sentence of imprisonment, or before making a youth custody or detention centre order, the court must have satisfied itself that the accused is legally represented or could be if he wished, and that there is no other form of sentence that is appropriate (the wording differs slightly depending on whether the court is dealing with prison, youth custody or detention centre). The court must give its reasons why no other method is appropriate and to help it in this decision, the court should have a social inquiry report unless, stating its reasons, it considers it unnecessary to do so.

Where the defendant is over 21 and has previously *served* a period of imprisonment the above restrictions do not apply.

SENTENCES OF IMPRISONMENT

There are three forms of a prison sentence.: the immediately effective prison sentence, the suspended sentence and the partly suspended sentence. The requirements for imposing each are the same, the only distinction between them being factors peculiar to the individual case before the court which enable the court to grant a partial or full suspension of the sentence.

Restrictions on imposing a sentence of imprisonment

Is imprisonment available for the offence? This may seem rather an obvious precondition, but surprisingly errors are made and defendants sent to prison for a non-imprisonable offence. This error may be caused either by using an out-of-date textbook as some offences have ceased to be imprisonable (eg soliciting and the offence of vagrancy) or by overlooking the fact that an offence is triable either way and is only punishable with imprisonment on indictment. Examples of this are offences under section 26 of the Vehicles (Excise) Act 1971 (fraudulent conduct with regard to vehicle excise licences) and offences under section 1 of the Trade Descriptions Act 1968. If summary trial has been decided on in these cases, the offence will cease to be one punishable with imprisonment.[4]

Is the defendant over 21? Imprisonment can only be imposed on a person of or over 21 years of age at the time sentence is passed, although it is possible that the accused was under 21 when he was convicted, and his age shall be deemed to be that which it appears to the court to be after considering any available evidence.[5]

Legal representation.[6] A defendant shall not be sentenced to imprisonment if he is not legally represented and has not previously been sentenced to

4 *R v Melbourne* (1980) 2 Cr App Rep (S) 116, [1980] Crim LR 510, CA.
5 Criminal Justice Act 1982, ss 1(1) and (6).
6 Powers of Criminal Courts Act 1973, s 21.

imprisonment in any part of the United Kingdom. ('Sentenced to imprisonment' does not include a non-activated suspended sentence.) However, legal representation is not obligatory where he has either applied for legal aid and it was refused on financial grounds or he was informed of his right to apply for legal aid and he failed to apply for it.

No other method appropriate. If the defendant has not previously been sentenced to imprisonment (which does not include a suspended sentence), the court cannot impose a prison sentence unless it is of the opinion that no other method of dealing with him is appropriate and to determine this the court 'shall obtain and consider information about the circumstances and shall take into account any information before the court which is relevant to his character and his physical and mental condition.'[7] Unfortunately this requirement is rather vague. It may technically be complied with by hearing the defence mitigation; but generally speaking the court should have a social inquiry report prepared for it by a probation officer.[8] The court is under an obligation to obtain a social inquiry report on an offender who has not previously been sentenced to imprisonment unless it is of the opinion that it is unnecessary to obtain a report, and if it is of that opinion it must state its reasons for not requiring the report in open court and record the reasons in the register and warrant of commitment. However a sentence passed in contravention of this requirement to obtain a social inquiry report would not necessarily be invalid.[9]

Having considered a social inquiry report and having decided that no other method is appropriate the court may pass a sentence of imprisonment, but if the defendant has not been to prison before, the court must state its reasons why it felt that no other method of dealing with the offender is appropriate.[10] The court may sometimes have to give two sets of reasons: one for not obtaining a social inquiry report and another why no other method is appropriate.

The social inquiry report

This is a report (usually, but not necessarily, in writing) prepared for

7 Ibid, s 20.

8 A social inquiry report is mandatory before making a community service order but the Home Office also recommends that a report is obtained before imprisonment for the first time on an offender (even if it is suspended), or on a woman; before a committal for sentence; where the court is considering making a probation order or where the defendant is already in touch with probation. In addition, of course, a report should normally be obtained before passing a sentence of youth custody or detention in a detention centre.

9 Criminal Justice Act 1982, s 2(8), but any other court on appeal from the original court shall obtain a social inquiry report unless it is of the opinion that in the circumstances of the case it is unnecessary to do so.

10 A failure to state the reasons why no other method is appropriate will not invalidate the sentence cf *R v Chesterfield Justices, ex p Hewitt* [1973] Crim LR 181, DC; *R v Jackson* [1966] 2 All ER 436, [1966] 1 WLR 528.

the court by a probation officer on the defendant's character and social background. As the probation officer is an officer of the court, a request for the preparation of a report must come from the court itself and not direct from the defendant. In the magistrates' court it is very unusual for a report to be prepared in anticipation of a plea of guilty or a conviction and so an adjournment after conviction is usually necessary. When the report is presented to the court a copy must be handed to the offender or his solicitor.[11]

Guidelines on the preparation of a report have been given by the Home Office in two circulars. Circular 17 of 1983 suggests the following matters should be contained in a social inquiry report.

(a) An assessment of the offender's personality, character and family and social background which is relevant to the court's assessment of his culpability and information relevant to the court's consideration of how to check his criminal career (including details of his record at educational, training or residential establishments where he has recently been, apart from penal institutions).
(b) His employment record and future prospects of employment.
(c) Information about the circumstances of the offence and his attitude to it.
(d) An opinion of the likely effect on his criminal career of probation or some specified sentence.

Of course a report is only as valuable as the information on which it is based, and so the report should specify its sources of information ie verified and unverified information, and also a distinction should clearly be drawn between fact and opinion.

The most controversial aspect of a report may be the recommendation made at the end. Home Office Circular 18 of 1983 deals with this matter. If an experienced probation officer feels able to make a recommendation for a particular form of decision, he should state it clearly in his report. The probation officer may have had more contact with the defendant and also more experience gained by dealing with a wide range of offenders at first hand. He may feel able to give a recommendation about the effects of a particular sentence on the offender and support this recommendation with a logical argument following from the contents of the report itself.

The recommendation is something to be considered carefully by the magistrates and to which they may attach great weight, but of course it is the bench which makes the final decision and it may well decline to follow the recommendation.

The length of the sentence for the offence

The maximum length of the sentence will be prescribed by statute. On summary trial the maximum sentence for offences made triable either

11 Powers of Criminal Courts Act 1973, s 46.

way by the Magistrates' Courts Act 1980, section 17 and Schedule 1 (which includes the common either way offences such as A.B.H; section 20 G.B.H. and theft etc) is six months' imprisonment.[12] For other either way offences and purely summary offences the maximum penalty will be that prescribed in the penalty section of the statute creating the offence: eg for section 146(3) of the Social Security Act 1975 the maximum penalty is three months' imprisonment.

Consecutive sentences

Where an offender is to be sentenced for two or more imprisonable offences, the sentencer contemplating a custodial sentence has a choice; he may impose the sentences to be concurrent or consecutive to each other. If he wishes the sentences to be consecutive he must state this as the presumption is that a prison sentence will start on the day it is imposed.[13] There are limits on the power of the court to make sentences consecutive. Section 133 of the Magistrates' Courts Act 1980 provides that the court cannot impose an aggregate of more than six months in total except where the offences are triable either way, in which case the aggregate may be up to 12 months. It is generally accepted that an activated suspended sentence may be imposed in addition to these maxima.[14]

Practice

The whole tenor of recent legislation and authorities has been to regard prison as very much the last resort. In a magistrates' court the typical candidate for prison will be the offender with a bad record where every other possibility has been tried, or where the offender has committed a really serious offence. Even if the offender has a bad record, his sentence should bear some relationship to the gravity of the offence, therefore no matter how bad the record a prison sentence should not be imposed merely because all other sentences have been tried as he should be sentenced for the offence and not his record.

The upper limit of the sentence is determined by the seriousness of the offence. Normally a defendant will have much mitigation which serves to reduce the penalty so that for the average defendant there will be the 'average' penalty for the offence. For the offender with no mitigation, the sentence is not aggravated, rather the sentence is not reduced from the maximum for that sort of offence. Therefore a trivial offence, even if it has been repeated on numerous occasions may not necessarily justify a custodial sentence.[15]

12 MCA 1980, s 32.

13 *R v Thornton* [1968] Crim LR 98, 122, CA; *R v Gilbert* [1975] 1 All ER 742, [1975] 1 WLR 1012 (cannot antedate a sentence).

14 The view of the editors of *Stone's* referring to *R v Lamb* [1968] 2 QB 829, [1968] 3 All ER 206.

15 *R v Clarke* (1975) 61 Cr App Rep 320, [1975] Crim LR 595, CA.

Some offences may be regarded as very grave in themselves, such as offences of serious violence,

offences involving football hooligans using violence or committing vandalism,

burglary of dwelling houses (the justices should think very carefully before even accepting jurisdiction at the mode of trial stage as 18 months' imprisonment would not be inappropriate even for a person of good character) except for 'sneak thefts'.[16]

Formerly included in this category was theft from an employer. Whilst this is still regarded as a serious offence meriting a custodial sentence, for small thefts dealt with by a magistrates' court a suspended sentence or a stiff fine is more usual now.

Where a custodial sentence has been decided upon the trend now is for shorter sentences.[17] Although most of the discussion in the authorities concerns the sentences to be imposed by the Crown Court and is about reducing sentences longer than the justices' maximum powers, nevertheless the spirit of the cases should be applied in magistrates' courts. Having reasoned that a prison sentence is unavoidable the court should ask itself what is the shortest sentence it can pass. The justification for some prison sentences is the need to protect the public. This can rarely apply in a magistrates' court because of their limited powers of sentencing. Prison in a magistrates' court is purely a punishment. For many offenders, especially first offenders and particularly an intelligent and otherwise respectable individual, the mere fact of being sent to prison is punishment enough.[18] Once the initial shock has worn off, there is little more to be gained by a long sentence. This principle might lead the court to conclude that it can pass a shorter sentence than it otherwise would. Guidance in the use of short sentences in the Crown Court is given in *R v Bibi*[19] which it is submitted might lead magistrates' courts, where prison sentences are in the range three–six months, to consider whether the court could now think in terms of weeks.

Deterrent sentences

'Deterrent' sentences do not seem to fit into the principles outlined above. A court may have trouble with an offence causing particular problems in the locality, eg attacks on bus conductors, or football hooliganism. The court may take a tough line on these offences. In principle the court cannot increase the penalty for the offence by imposing a sentence out of proportion to the gravity of the offence, but

16 *R v Stoakes* [1981] Crim LR 56, but contrast the case of the burglary consisting of a sneak theft which is quite within the justices' powers: *R v Hardman* (1983) JP Jo 59.
17 *R v Bibi* [1980] 1 WLR 1193, (1980) 71 Cr App Rep 360.
18 The 'clang of the gates principle' as in *R v Smedley* [1981] Crim LR 575.
19 [1980] 1 WLR 193, 71 Cr App Rep 360.

it is entitled, as a mark of deterrence, to decline to take account of any mitigation personal to the offender, and so offenders who would otherwise have plentiful mitigation (eg first offenders) might find themselves severely dealt with.[20]

Concurrent/consecutive

Where the sentencer is faced with the choice whether to make sentences concurrent or consecutive, he should consider the relationship between the offences. It is generally wrong to pass consecutive sentences when the offences have arisen out of the same incident,[1] although this may be less rigidly applied when the offences are of a different nature.[2] Indeed where an offence has been committed on bail the sentence for this should normally be consecutive.[3]

Even though a consecutive sentence might be justified, regard must still be had to the totality of the sentence even though this is less of a problem in the magistrates' court because of the limited power of sentencing. Where the defendant has committed multiple offences it may not be possible to reflect the gravity of each offence by making the sentences consecutive and so the better practice is to make them all concurrent.[4] It is not possible to make one sentence partly consecutive to another.[5]

Serving a sentence of imprisonment

When a defendant has been sentenced to imprisonment, the court will issue a warrant of commitment authorising the police to take him to the prison specified in the warrant and authorising the governor of the prison to detain him until he has served his sentence. The court will initially commit the offender to its local prison[6] which is a form of clearing house which holds prisoners on remand awaiting trial, and prisoners from magistrates' courts who of necessity have been sentenced to short periods of imprisonment, will serve their whole sentence in the local prison.[7]

Remission and parole Although the court may have sentenced a prisoner to a fixed term of, say, six months, he will not necessarily serve the whole of that term. Every prisoner is entitled to be released after

20 *R v Glavin, Woods and Japp* [1979] Crim LR 401, CA, but contrast with *R v Raphael* [1972] Crim LR 648, CA where the sentence seems to have been increased.
1 *R v Walsh* [1965] Crim LR 248, CCA.
2 *R v White* [1972] Crim LR 192, CA.
3 *R v Cameron* (1980) 144 JP Jo 282.
4 *R v Brown* (1969) 54 Cr App Rep 176, [1970] Crim LR 168.
5 *R v Gregory and Mills* [1969] 2 All ER 174, [1969] 1 WLR 455.
6 Ie the prison specified for that court under s 12 of the Prison Act 1952.
7 For a thumbnail sketch of the prison system *The Sentence of the Court* is a useful publication.

serving two-thirds of his sentence provided his sentence is not reduced to less than 31 days. This is known as remission. It is automatic and can only be forfeited for offences contrary to the Prison Rules.

A quite distinct power to reduce a prison sentence is that of the Home Secretary, acting through the Parole Board or a local review committee, who may release a prisoner on licence (parole) after serving one-third of his sentence or 12 months, whichever is the longer.[8] A person released on parole remains on licence until he would have been released on remission (unless he is subject to an extended sentence). The Home Secretary has power to reduce the minimum period for parole from 12 months,[9] and until this is done parole is not directly relevant to magistrates' courts but the justices do have the power to commit an offender who is in breach of parole and has committed an indictable offence punishable with imprisonment, to the Crown Court for sentence. This Court may then revoke his licence and return him to prison.[10]

Reduction for time spent in custody on remand. If the defendant has been remanded in custody before he received his sentence of imprisonment, the period previously spent in custody will serve to reduce the period of his sentence that he has to serve.[11]

THE SUSPENDED SENTENCE[12]

If the court has power to impose a sentence of imprisonment, it may order that the implementation of that sentence be suspended provided the defendant does not commit a further offence punishable with imprisonment during the period of suspension.

The suspended sentence is composed of two elements: the term of imprisonment and the period of the suspension. The maximum length of sentence which may be suspended is two years in the Crown Court or six months (or 12 months for two either way offences) in the magistrates' court, which may be suspended for a minimum of one year and a maximum of two years.

Before a court can impose a suspended sentence it must be satisfied that, unless there was the power to suspend, an immediate custodial sentence was necessary. Therefore all the restrictions on imposing a sentence of imprisonment apply with equal force to a suspended sentence.

8 When passing sentence the court should not take account of the possibility of remission and parole: *R v Black* [1971] Crim LR 109, CA.
9 Criminal Justice Act 1982, s 33.
10 Criminal Justice Act 1967, s 62.
11 Ibid, s 67.
12 Powers of Criminal Courts Act 1973, s 22.

Breach of a suspended sentence. A suspended sentence is breached if the offender commits a further offence punishable with imprisonment during the currency of the suspended sentence (note he will not be in breach if, during the term of the suspended sentence, he is sentenced for an offence committed before the sentence was imposed). If the offender breaches a suspended sentence any magistrates' court may deal with him for that breach, but if the suspended sentence was imposed by the Crown Court, the magistrates may commit him to the Crown Court to be dealt with.

A magistrates' court dealing with a breach has four options:

(a) it may order the suspended sentence to take effect with the original term unaltered (concurrent or consecutive to any term imposed for the fresh offence); or
(b) activate it as at (a) with a lesser term substituted; or
(c) further suspend the sentence for up to two years; or
(d) make no order.[13]

If the court is dealing with a breach of a suspended sentence, it is under an obligation to activate the suspended sentence with the original term unaltered unless it is of the opinion that it would be unjust to do so in view of all the circumstances, including the facts of the subsequent offence, and where it is of that opinion the court shall state its reasons.[14]

Practice

The suspended sentence is a sentence of imprisonment and so the court must fulfil all the requirements applicable to the passing of a prison sentence. The correct approach is for the court to satisfy itself that no other method of dealing with the accused other than the passing of an effective prison sentence is appropriate.[15] Having decided that imprisonment is the only appropriate disposal the court must then consider whether there are any matters which could justify suspending the sentence. The sort of case in which a suspended sentence might be justified is where the offence is serious (in the terms of the magistrates' court) but where the offender does not have a record of custodial sentences, where he has a family and a job, is otherwise respectable and has committed an offence out of character. A common example of this may be the employee who, completely out of character, steals from his

13 If the court specifically makes no order it has 'dealt with' the breach, *R v Peterborough Justices, ex p Casey* [1979] LS Gaz R 847.

14 Powers of Criminal Courts Act 1973, s 23(1) as amended by Criminal Justice Act 1982, s 31.

15 *R v O'Keefe* [1969] 2 QB 29, [1969] 1 All ER 426. It is wrong to pass an immediate and a suspended sentence of imprisonment at the same time: *R v Sapiano* (1969) 52 Cr App Rep 674, [1968] Crim LR 497 (but not necessarily wrong where they are imposed on separate occasions: *R v Gibbons* [1969] Crim LR 210, (1969) 113 Sol Jo 86).

employer on the spur of the moment. A suspended sentence may be appropriate to an offender who realises the seriousness of the situation he is in and shows genuine remorse with an appreciation of what would happen to him were he to re-offend in the future.

There are three dangers inherent in the suspended sentence. There is a danger that the court will impose a suspended sentence when it otherwise would not really have imposed an immediate custodial sentence for the offence concerned but for the power to suspend. Second, a suspended sentence should not, it is submitted, be imposed on an offender with a record which suggests that he will breach the sentence as this is only storing up problems for the future. This is coupled with the third danger that the suspended sentence is looked on as a soft option, putting off the evil day. Because the sentence is not to be immediately served the court may unwittingly tend to impose a longer sentence than it otherwise would have done, and so if the offender breaches the sentence the court may be obliged to activate an otherwise excessive sentence.

Activating a suspended sentence. If the defendant has breached a suspended sentence, the court should start by sentencing him for the fresh offence.[16] Having considered the fresh offence, the magistrates should then consider whether there are any grounds for not activating the suspended sentence. The general principle is that a suspended sentence should be activated unless the subsequent offence was both different in nature *and* trivial but in view of the amendments made by the Criminal Justice Act 1982 the principle may not be so rigid and the triviality of the subsequent offence may be sufficient not to activate the suspended sentence. The court is now required to consider all the circumstances, including the facts of the subsequent offence.

If the court decides to activate the sentence, normally the whole of the suspended sentence will be activated and in general this should be consecutive to any imprisonment for the fresh offence.[17] The court should not take account of any period spent in custody before the original suspended sentence was imposed[18] but there may be factors which influence the court to reduce the period of imprisonment subsequently imposed. For example, the fresh offences may have been committed towards the end of the term of suspension and it is usual to give credit for this.[19] An important principle is that the totality of the

16 *R v Ithell* [1969] 2 All ER 449, [1969] 1 WLR 272. If a probation order or discharge is imposed for the subsequent offence the accused will not be in breach of the suspended sentence because he will not have been 'convicted': see Powers of Criminal Courts Act 1973, s 13.

17 *R v Brown* [1969] Crim LR 20, CA.

18 *R v Deering* [1976] Crim LR 638.

19 *R v Beacock* (1979) 1 Cr App Rep (S) 198, [1979] Crim LR 797 but contrast *R v Gunn* [1971] Crim LR 551, CA where the defendant had abused his chance and thus the whole sentence was activated.

sentences imposed on a given day should be in proportion to the offences concerned. Thus if a suspended sentence is activated in full consecutive to the sentence for the fresh offence and the resulting combined sentence would be excessive, the sentences might be reduced,[20] and for this reason the court should have adequate information concerning the circumstances of the original offences.[1]

Where a breach of a suspended sentence has been dealt with. If the sentence is activated either fully or in part, there can be no question of any further breach of the original sentence. But if the court has chosen option (d) above and has not activated the sentence, it has also 'dealt' with the breach. Therefore the defendant will only be in breach of the suspended sentence again if he commits another offence punishable with imprisonment during the currency of the suspended sentence.

This means that if court A has imposed a suspended sentence and the accused is convicted of a further offence by court B which specifically orders no action to be taken on the breach of the suspended sentence, court A cannot then summon the accused back before it to be dealt with for the breach under section 25 of the Powers of Criminal Courts Act 1973. Court B must quite specifically announce that it is taking no action rather than by saying nothing at all, in which case court A might have power to take action. If no action is taken on the breach of the suspended sentence and the defendant is placed on community service for the fresh offence, a breach of the community service order will not render the defendant in breach of his suspended sentence again because he has not committed a further offence.[2]

If the court has dealt with the breach by extending the period of suspension and the defendant subsequently appears before the court for an offence committed during the original term of the sentence, he will still be in breach of the suspended sentence.[3]

Suspended sentence supervision order.[4] There is a power to place an offender under the supervision of a probation officer during the term of a suspended sentence but as it is only applicable in the case of a sentence of more than six months for a single offence (which is beyond the powers of the magistrates) it is not available for a magistrates' court.

20 *R v Smith* [1972] Crim LR 124, CA.
1 *R v Munday* [1972] Crim LR 195.
2 *R v Folan* [1980] 1 All ER 217, [1980] 1 WLR 1 perhaps aliter for breach of probation. Cf commentary to *R v Temperley* in [1980] Crim LR 511.
3 *R v McDonald* [1971] Crim LR 550.
4 Powers of Criminal Courts Act 1973, s 26.

PARTLY SUSPENDED SENTENCES

The court has a power under section 47 of the Criminal Law Act 1977 (as amended by section 30 of the Criminal Justice Act 1982) to impose a prison sentence where the defendant will serve a part and the rest will be held in suspense provided he does not commit a further imprisonable offence during the period of suspense.

Criteria for imposing a partly suspended sentence

A partly suspended sentence is a sentence of imprisonment and so all the restrictions on passing a sentence of imprisonment apply. Therefore the court has to consider:

is imprisonment available for the offence?
is the defendant over 21?
legal representation?
social inquiry report?
no other method appropriate?

} for a defendant who has not previously served a sentence of imprisonment

The partly suspended sentence may be a sentence of not less than three months and not more than two years (in the Crown Court) of which the defendant may be required to serve a minimum of 28 days or of which a minimum of one-quarter of the whole term may be suspended. If the defendant commits an imprisonable offence during the whole period of the original sentence he is liable to be sentenced for the fresh offence he has committed and to have the unserved part of the partly suspended sentence activated. Therefore if a defendant receives a four months' sentence,

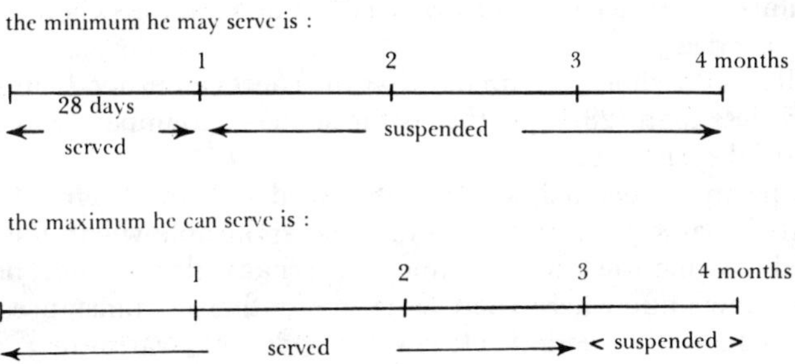

(a month means a calendar month (Interpretation Act 1978, Schedule 1) which, with the exception of February, is more than 28 days).

It should be noted that there is a sharp distinction between the period of suspension for a fully suspended sentence and a partly suspended sentence. The maximum period of suspension for a fully suspended sentence is two years, the period of suspension for a partly suspended sentence is only the residue of the original sentence which is to be held in suspense.

In the example above the defendant is under the threat of the suspended part of the sentence for four months from the date when the sentence was passed but the court which deals with the subsequent offence is not obliged to restore the part of the original sentence held in suspense either in full or in part where it is of the opinion that in view of all the circumstances, including the facts of the subsequent offence, it would be unjust to restore the part of the sentence held in suspense and so it may restore a lesser part, or, stating its reasons, make no order of restoration.[5] Once a partly suspended sentence has been restored, it may not be restored again for a further breach.

Practice

The partly suspended sentence is not common in the magistrates' court. When section 47 of the Criminal Law Act 1977 was first enacted the minimum sentence was six months, that is the maximum sentence which could be imposed by a magistrates' court for a single offence, and the minimum period which could be suspended was one-quarter. Now that the minima are three months and 28 days respectively the sentence is now theoretically more suited to the magistrates' court.

Guidelines for the use of the partly suspended sentence were given in *R v Clarke*[6]

(a) is a custodial sentence really necessary? If not pass a non-custodial sentence;
(b) if a custodial sentence is necessary will an alternative to custody suffice, such as community service, or can the whole term be suspended?
(c) what is the shortest sentence that the court can properly impose? If it is less than (28 days) that is the sentence to impose without any partial suspension.

If a partly suspended sentence is considered, the Court of Appeal suggested that such a sentence might be applicable where the offence merited six months' imprisonment (perhaps this should be three months now) but where there were mitigating circumstances which could reduce the period of custody without warranting a total suspension. Examples might include some serious 'one-off' acts of violence; some frauds on government departments; some cases of handling or thefts in breach of trust and some thefts from employers.

The partly suspended sentence seems to be appropriate to the offender who has no previous convictions (or at least someone who last

5 Criminal Law Act 1977, s 47(4).
6 [1982] 3 All ER 232, [1982] Crim LR 464.

served a sentence of imprisonment a long time previously) who has committed a serious offence meriting an immediate custodial sentence. The offence should be serious enough to necessitate the imposition of an immediate custodial sentence to show public disapproval, but include sufficient mitigation to reduce the period of custody. The offender being a person of previous good character (or virtually so) will nevertheless suffer the shock of being incarcerated even for the short period not suspended, and will be deterred from reoffending by the threat still hanging over him.[7]

Nevertheless, it is submitted that the partly suspended sentence will never be a common form of sentence in the magistrates' court. Magistrates do not deal with serious offences of a nature which will always demand a custodial element in spite of any mitigation except in the case of deterrent sentences where mitigation is not relevant. The defendant who usually receives a custodial sentence in the magistrates' court is one with a long previous record who has come to the end of the line and is not a candidate for the partly suspended sentence. It is rare for a first offender to have committed an offence so serious that there is no option but to commit him to custody forthwith and if he had, the magistrates would probably have declined jurisdiction at the mode of trial stage. If a first offender has committed a really serious offence, eg theft from an employer, the tendency is for a wholly suspended sentence to be passed if the mitigation is strong enough. If magistrates' courts were to become enthusiastic users of the partly suspended sentence it is submitted that there would be a danger of more custodial sentences, albeit partly suspended, being passed. Further, the threat hanging over the defendant subject to a partly suspended sentence is having the part held in suspense restored if he commits a further imprisonable offence during the currency of the sentence. This may be satisfactory for the longer sentences passed in the Crown Court but it is hardly sufficient for a six-month sentence in the magistrates' court where two months is effective and four months is suspended because the deterrence will last only for the four or so months remaining after the defendant is released. It is submitted that many magistrates' courts would prefer a wholly suspended sentence for a period of up to two years.

YOUTH CUSTODY

Imprisonment is not available for any defendant under the age of 21.

7 An example is *R v Salter* [1982] Crim LR 698 where the defendant was a consultant psychiatrist who dishonestly obtained drugs for his own use. The sentence of three years' imprisonment was reduced on appeal to 12 months' imprisonment with 9 months suspended; there was the need for the deterrent element of 12 months' imprisonment to show others they could not criminally meddle with drugs, but on the 'clang of the gates' principle the defendant should serve only three months.

The custodial options open to the court for a defendant under this age are: for sentences of 21 days – four months inclusive, Detention Centre; more than four months, Youth Custody. Also available is custody for life under section 8 of the Criminal Justice Act 1982 (equivalent to life imprisonment) and detention under section 9 for contempt or failure to pay a fine.

Restrictions on imposing a sentence of youth custody[8]

(a) The offender must be between the ages of 15 and 21 and may be male or female.
(b) He must have been convicted of an offence punishable in the case of an adult with imprisonment.
(c) No other method is appropriate because it appears to the court that he is unable or unwilling to respond to non-custodial penalties or because a custodial sentence is necessary for the protection of the public, or because the offence was so serious that a non-custodial sentence cannot be justified and these reasons have been stated in open court.
(d) The court feels that a sentence of more than four months is appropriate (unless the defendant is ineligible for detention centre or the defendant is female and over 17, when a term of less than four months may be imposed).
(e) The court has consulted a social inquiry report, unless it has stated its reasons why a social inquiry report was felt to be unnecessary.
(f) The accused is legally represented or has had the opportunity to be represented.

The maximum sentences of youth custody are the same as the maxima which apply to imprisonment in the case of an adult, ie generally no more than six months where summary offences are concerned and up to 12 months where two either way offences carrying six months each are made consecutive.[9]

The minimum term is a term of more than four months[10] except where the court feels that a term of less than this would be appropriate and the offender is a female over 17, or is male and ineligible for detention centre in which case the minimum term is 21 days.[11]

Youth custody is designed to replace the former indeterminate sentence of Borstal Training; it is like imprisonment in the duration of its sentences and carries remission.[12]

Young offenders will now be completely separated from older offenders as imprisonment for those in the 17–20 age group has been abolished. The idea of 'training' embodied in the old borstal sentence

8 Criminal Justice Act 1982, ss 1 and 6.
9 Ibid, s 7.
10 Which may be composed of an aggregate of sentences, ibid, s 7(4) and (9).
11 Criminal Justice Act 1982, s 7(6) and cf s 15(11).
12 Ibid, s 10.

has been dropped but in practice it is difficult to envisage any difference in regime especially as the 'youth custody centres' will be the former borstals under a new name. Nevertheless for the practitioner it does mean a tidying up of the custodial provisions for defendants in the 17–20 age group as the choice is reduced from prison, borstal and detention centre to youth custody and detention centre, dependent on whether the custodial sentence is to be over four months or four months or less. Also the trap created by the restriction on passing a prison sentence of between six months and three years contained in section 3 of the Criminal Justice Act 1961 has been abolished.

When the offender is released he will be under the supervision of a probation officer for three months after his release but no later than his twenty-second birthday,[13] and if the offender fails to comply with the requirements of his supervision he may be convicted of an offence and fined up to £200 or receive an appropriate custodial sentence (including youth custody) of up to 30 days.[14]

DETENTION CENTRE[15]

This is available for male defendants between the ages of 14 and 20 inclusive and the minimum sentence which can be passed is 21 days and the maximum is four months (or the maximum term which an adult could receive for the offence whichever is the less).

The requirements for making a detention centre order are:

(a) The offender is male, over 14 and under 21.

(b) The offence is punishable in the case of an adult with imprisonment sufficient to cover the period of detention.

(c) The only appropriate sentence is a custodial one not exceeding four months because the court is of the opinion that no other method of dealing with him is appropriate because it appears to the court that he is unable or unwilling to respond to non-custodial penalties or because a custodial sentence is necessary for the protection of the public, or because the offence was so serious that a non-custodial sentence cannot be justified, and the court has stated its reasons.[16]

(d) The court has considered a social inquiry report or given its reasons why a report is unnecessary.[17]

(e) The accused is legally represented or has had the opportunity to be represented.

(f) A detention centre order is not precluded because of the

13 For longer sentences imposed by the Crown Court the defendant may be released on licence in which case in certain circumstances the supervision may last up to 12 months from release.

14 Criminal Justice Act 1982 s. 15.

15 Ibid, ss 4 and 5.

16 Ibid, s 1.

17 Ibid, s 2.

defendant's mental or physical condition or he is serving or has served a sentence of

(i) imprisonment,
(ii) detention under section 53 Children and Young Persons Act 1933,
(iii) borstal training,
(iv) youth custody,
(v) custody for life

unless there are special circumstances which warrant the making of such an order.

Concurrent and consecutive sentences

Terms of detention in a detention centre can be made concurrent or consecutive to each other (and to an existing term) provided in aggregate they do not total more than four months.[18] If the total term does exceed four months the sentence will automatically be treated as one sentence of youth custody if the offender is over 15 years of age (otherwise the excess will be remitted).

Supervision after release

An offender released from a detention centre is subject to supervision by a probation officer in the same way as an offender released from a sentence of youth custody with the same penalties for failing to comply with a requirement of the supervision.[19]

The detention centre

Detention centres, unlike youth custody, have only been affected to a limited extent by the Criminal Justice Act 1982. The major changes have been that the maximum term has been reduced from six months to four months[20] and the minimum term reduced to 21 days instead of three months. It remains to be seen what the new 'average' sentence will be, if any. Generally the detention centre deals with offenders who have not received a custodial sentence before. Instead of cells, the inmates sleep in dormitories and are subject to a certain amount of discipline. The punitive element for most offenders is the fact that they are being taken away from home but once at the detention centre the regime is in many ways similar to that at an army cadet camp. One aspect of the work of a detention centre that is very important is the need to safeguard the education of the offenders. Some may still be at school and obviously their studies should be interrupted as little as possible but even with those who are no longer at school remedial

18 Ibid, s 5.
19 Ibid, s 15.
20 Six months was not a common term anyway, the usual penalty was three months.

education may still be necessary, and ironically the teaching available at the detention centre, with a low pupil-teacher ratio may be more effective than they have hitherto received.

One reason for the reduction in the minimum period of detention is the introduction, or reintroduction, of the idea of the 'short, sharp, shock' regime in certain detention centres and the retreat of the philosophy of 'training', although the tougher regime is not available throughout the country at present.

At all detention centres there is a probation officer who takes an interest in the offender and who will prepare him for release and liaise with the appropriate probation area to arrange for supervision after release.

OTHER FORMS OF CUSTODIAL SENTENCE

Mention should be made of two other forms of custody: detention in police cells and detention for one day in a court house or police station.

Detention in police cells[1]

Where the court would have power to imprison (or impose a sentence of youth custody on a person over 17), it may instead order him to be detained for up to four days in police cells or some other suitable place provided the cells have been approved for that purpose by the Secretary of State. It should be noted that this is not a sentence of imprisonment.

Detention for one day in a court house or police station[2]

Where the court would have power to commit the offender to prison (or if aged 17–20 inclusive to commit to detention for default or contempt under section 9 of the Criminal Justice Act 1982 but not simply as a sentence for an *offence*) it may order him instead to be detained within the precincts of the court house or at any police station until a specified time not being later than 8 o'clock in the evening. The court must not however make such an order if it would prevent the offender from having a reasonable opportunity of returning to his abode on the day of the order.

Non-custodial sentences

COMMUNITY SERVICE

A community service order is an order requiring an offender to perform unpaid work for the number of hours specified in the order.

1 MCA 1980, s 134.
2 MCA, s 135.

Community service is only available for an offence punishable with imprisonment in the case of an adult and where a community service scheme is in force for the relevant area. If the offender is over 17 community service is available throughout the country.

The requirements for making a community service order[3]

(a) The offence is punishable with imprisonment in the case of an adult.
(b) The offender is 16 years or older.
(c) A community service scheme is available for the area where the offender will reside.
(d) The court has considered a social inquiry report regarding the suitability of the offender to perform community service (this is obligatory).
(e) The offender consents.

When sentencing an offender to community service the court must consider a report by a probation officer about the offender's circumstances and it must be satisfied that he is a suitable person to undertake such an order. It should be noted that a report is obligatory and in this case it is a more strict requirement than that for imposing a sentence of imprisonment, but the requirements about legal aid and representation do not apply in the case of a community service order (although for reasons that will become apparent a defendant would usually be represented).

If the court decides that community service is appropriate, it will make an order for the number of hours it feels to be suitable being between 40 and 240 hours in the case of an offender over 17. If there is more than one offence concerned, the orders can be made concurrent or consecutive but the aggregate must not exceed 240 hours.[4] An order can even be made consecutive to an existing order but it is undesirable for there to be a total of more than 240 hours in existence at any one time.[5] The meaning of the order must be explained to the offender and he must be asked whether he consents to the making of the order. If he does, a copy of the order will be given forthwith[6] to the court liaison probation officer who will in turn give a copy to the offender and a copy to the appropriate probation officer and clerk to the justices for the petty sessional division specified in the order, being the place where the offender resides.

After an order has been made the offender will have an appointment with a probation officer responsible for community service in that particular area. The officer will assess the offender's suitability for the

3 Powers of Criminal Courts Act 1973, s 14.
4 Ibid, s 14(3).
5 *R v Evans* [1977] 1 All ER 228, [1977] 1 WLR 27.
6 For this procedure see *R v Dugdale* [1981] Crim LR 105 (Crown Court).

various schemes which are in operation. Such schemes might include helping in a youth club or renovating or repairing old people's homes or landscaping derelict areas. It is the probation service that decides what work is to be done: the court has no power to direct the work which will be done. Nevertheless, the probation service will be at pains to ensure that offenders are only given suitable work as they wish to ensure the credibility of community service as a sentence. If the court loses faith in community service, orders will simply stop being made. In fact the only problem with community service in some areas appears to have been caused by its popularity occasionally causing a scheme to be overburdened.

If the offender fails to turn up for his work sessions without good cause the probation officer will start proceedings for breach.

Breach of community service

Whatever numbers of hours are imposed under a community service order, they must be completed within 12 months of the making of the order. A community service order is breached by the offender failing to report to the relevant probation officer and notify him of any change of address or failing to perform the number of hours specified in the order.[7]

If the offender is in breach, the probation officer will lay an information before the magistrates' court named in the order and the offender will be summoned to explain himself. The court may then fine him up to £200, or revoke the community service order and re-sentence him for the original offence, or where the community service order was made by the Crown Court, commit him to be dealt with there.[8] An offender in breach of a community service order is in a perilous position as a community service is high up on the tarriff and in default of any other sentence a custodial sentence is a distinct possibility,[9] although credit should be given where the defendant has completed a substantial number of hours.[10]

Amendment and revocation[11]

As opposed to proceedings for breach, the offender or the probation officer may apply to the court to extend the period of 12 months for completing the order having regard to the circumstances which have arisen since the order was made, or the court may hear an application for revocation of the order, or for the offender to be re-sentenced for the

7 Powers of Criminal Courts Act 1973, s 15.
8 Ibid, s 16.
9 *R v Howard and Wade* [1977] Crim LR 683, DC, and see now *R v Lawrence* [1982] Crim LR 377.
10 *R v Anderson* [1982] Crim LR 835 and *R v Paisley* (1979) Crim App Rep (S) 196.
11 Powers of Criminal Courts Act 1973, s 17.

original offence. An application might be made under this provision when, for example, an offender has subsequently become physically unable to complete the order. Another common situation is where the offender has subsequently been sentenced to imprisonment by another court and thus cannot complete the order. The court which imposes the custodial sentence may, even if it is not the court acting for the petty sessional division specified in the order, on the application of the relevant probation officer, or the offender, revoke the order if it was made by a magistrates' court, or commit him to the Crown Court if the order was originally made there.

Community service and the tariff

In many respects community service is looked on as an alternative to a custodial sentence as it is, in effect, quite high up on the tariff of sentences. But it is not analogous to the suspended sentence in the sense that the court must have contemplated a custodial sentence and then pulled back from the brink, as it were. It now seems clear from the case of *Lawrence*[12] that the court does not have to be contemplating a custodial sentence before it may make a community service order but it is also apparent that the magistrates may make orders which are too long. The maximum number of hours is 240 and a community service order may be appropriate in the Crown Court for offenders who would otherwise receive a custodial sentence in the range of 18 months to two years. Magistrates have passed sentences for up to 240 hours for offences where the maximum sentence of imprisonment would have been 12 months. Whilst it is dangerous to draw a strict mathematical correlation between the number of hours' community service ordered and the equivalent months of imprisonment, *Lawrence* does suggest a trend in the magistrates' court to err on the high side.

ATTENDANCE CENTRE[13]

Section 16 of the Criminal Justice Act 1982 provides for the continued existence of attendance centres. These are establishments (often school buildings) open on Saturdays where offenders are required to attend for a maximum of three hours per session. An attendance centre order is available for an offender under the age of 21 who has been convicted of an imprisonable offence or for non-payment of a fine or breach of a probation order and whose home is accessible to a suitable attendance centre. The court may order him to attend for any period between 12 and 36 hours. No order may be made, however, where a defendant has previously been sentenced to:

12 [1982] Crim LR 377.

13 For a description of the Nottingham Attendance Centre see N. Stone (1982) 146 JP 484.

imprisonment;
detention under section 53 of the Children and Young Persons Act 1933;
borstal training;
youth custody or detention for life;
detention in a detention centre;
unless there are special circumstances which warrant the making of an attendance centre order.

The procedure on making a typical attendance centre order might be that the court would announce the sentence, eg 18 hours' attendance, and the defendant would be told the first occasion on which he is to attend. The defendant must attend on that date at the centre and remain there for a period of three hours. During that time he will be under the supervision of police officers (or off-duty prison officers) who will expect a certain degree of tidiness and clean presentation. There will be some drill and physical training and also some work in class such as life saving courses and car maintenance. The idea is to use the time as constructively as possible and also to instil a certain amount of discipline. After the session is over the defendant will be required to return at fortnightly intervals until he has completed the order.

If the offender breaches the order by failing to attend or by failing to comply with the rules of the attendance centre, section 19 of the Criminal Justice Act 1982 provides that he may be brought back before the magistrates' court for the area in which the attendance centre is situated or which made the order, and if the order was made by a magistrates' court it may revoke the order and sentence him afresh, or if the order was made by the Crown Court it may commit him for sentence. In addition there is a power to vary or discharge an order on the application of either the offender or the attendance centre. Variation consists of varying the date or hour of the offender's first attendance, and varying the location of the attendance centre having regard to any change of his residence.

PROBATION[14]

Where a defendant of or over 17 years of age has been convicted of any offence (except an offence where the penalty is fixed by law ie murder or treason) the court may, having regard to the circumstances including the nature of the offence and the character of the offender, if it is expedient to do so, *instead of sentencing him* (so that it may not, for example, be combined with a fine for the same offence), make a probation order placing him under the supervision of a probation officer for a period of not less than six months or more than three years. The defendant must consent to the making of the order.

14 Powers of Criminal Courts Act 1973, s 2.

The probation order may in addition contain certain requirements which the court, having regard to the circumstances of the case, considers necessary for securing the good conduct of the offender or for preventing a repetition by him of the same offence or the commission of other offences. The Powers of Criminal Courts Act 1973 does not provide for any particular requirements to be automatically included in the order although courts commonly attach 'standard' conditions even going so far as to pre-print them on the order. Such common conditions are notifying the probation officer of any change of address and reporting to him when required, and of being of good behaviour and living an 'honest and industrious life' even though the last condition was criticised for its vagueness as long ago as 1952.[15]

The Powers of Criminal Courts Act 1973 does make provision for certain specific conditions to be included if these are felt to be necessary.

Section 3 provides for a probation order with a condition of medical treatment for a mental condition and this is discussed in chapter 14.

A commonly occurring condition in a probation order is a condition of residence at a probation hostel. In a probation hostel the residents have their own accommodation and the hostel is under the supervision of a warden. The idea behind this is to allow the probationers their liberty but at the same time ensuring a certain amount of supervision within the rules of the hostel, for example it might be used for those who are not wholly institutionalised but may not be trusted entirely to be left to their own devices. If the court does require the offender to live in a hostel, it must specify the period of that requirement in the order.

Before the amendments introduced by the Criminal Justice Act 1982, the court had power to include a condition in a probation order that the probationer attend at a day training centre to receive training in various skills that might prove useful to him. Unfortunately there were only two of these centres set up under the 1973 Act and which were funded by the Home Office. Consequently many probation committees set up their own schemes which were outside the ambit of the Powers of Criminal Courts Act 1973. Case law held that attendance at these local centres was invalid[16] but now the new sections 4A and 4B of the Powers of Criminal Courts Act 1973 provide that a probation order may contain conditions that an offender attend at one of these centres for a total of up to 60 days and comply with the instructions of the supervisor or comply with other conditions requiring participation or non-participation in activities. Before making such a condition the court must consult a probation oficer and be satisfied that arrangements do exist for the activities specified in the order and that the

15 By Lord Goddard (1952) 116 JP 145 and see the article (1978) 142 JP 529.
16 *Cullen v Rogers* [1982] 2 All ER 570, [1982] 1 WLR 729.

conditions would not interfere with the probationer's attendance at school or work.

Breach of probation

A probation order is, in a sense, a strengthened form of conditional discharge. The order may be breached either by failing to comply with the terms of the order, in which case the offender may be brought back to the original magistrates' court or the supervising court and fined, or be made subject to an attendance centre order or be sentenced again for the original offence,[17] or the order may be breached by the commission of a further offence during the currency of the order[18]

In the case of orders made by the Crown Court the offender must be dealt with for the breach by that court but in the case of probation orders made by a magistrates' court the breach may be dealt with either by the original court which made the order, or by the court named in the order as the supervising court being the court for the area where the defendant resides, or by any magistrates' court if the original or supervising court consents.

When dealing with a breach the court should put the breach to him in the clearest possible terms pointing out when he was convicted, what happened to him and how the breach took place – the date of conviction and the adjudication of the court. The defendant should then be asked whether he admits the facts and the breach.[19] When considering whether the defendant is in breach by the commission of an offence it is the date of the offence which is important as the conviction itself may not take place until after the probation order has expired.[20] When re-sentencing after a breach it is possible to impose a further probation order even though it extends beyond the maximum of three years from the making of the original order,[1] but whatever order is made the court should inquire about the circumstances of the original offence.

FINES

The fine is by far the most popular sentence imposed by the magistrates' court (indeed for road traffic offences a fine is almost invariably the penalty) and is available for every offence dealt with by the justices.[2] The level of the fine is determined by three factors which have a close interrelationship: the maximum penalty allowed by statute; the gravity of the offence; and the ability of the offender to pay.

17 Powers of Criminal Courts Act 1973, s 6.
18 Ibid, s 8. Note the distinction from a community service order, which is not breached by the commission of a further offence.
19 *R v Devine* [1956] 1 All ER 548n, [1956] 1 WLR 236.
20 *R v Lee* [1976] Crim LR 521.
1 *R v Havant Justices, ex p Jacobs* [1957] 1 All ER 475, [1957] 1 WLR 365.
2 Note MCA 1980, s 34.

Maximum fines

Every fine in a magistrates' court has a maximum penalty imposed by statute. Generally the maximum fine for an either way offence is £1,000 although some such offences, for example offences of criminal damage where the damage is less than £200 and some offences under the Misuse of Drugs Act 1971 carry a lesser penalty.[3]

Purely summary offences have a maximum penalty prescribed by the statute which creates the offence and these maxima varied from, for example £10 for having a dog without a licence[4] to £1,000 for an offence of breach of the peace.[5] Since the Criminal Law Act 1977 there has been a gradual tidying up of the levels of maximum fines which could have been imposed for purely summary offences. Section 31 of that Act provided that where the maximum penalty was less than £20 and was provided for in an Act passed before 1949 and had not been increased since 1949, it was increased to £25 and where it was more than £20 it was increased to £50. This process has been carried further now by Part III of the Criminal Justice Act 1982. Maximum fines for *summary* offences are now determined by reference to a point on a scale. This standard scale is as follows:[6]

Level on the scale	Amount of fine
1	£25
2	£50
3	£200
4	£500
5	£1,000

In future, statutes will prescribe the maximum penalty by reference to a point on the scale rather than to a set figure.[7] In this way the bewildering variety of maximum fines will be reduced to five and these maxima can be increased in line with inflation by the expedient of altering the amounts on the scale.[8]

Existing penalty provisions are amended and simplified by abolishing those provisions which provide for enhanced penalties on a second or subsequent offence so that an offence will only carry one maximum penalty.[9] There is also a general increase in the level of fines for summary offences. For offences in statutes passed before 29 July 1977 (when the Criminal Law Act 1977 came into force) which have not had their maximum penalty increased under section 31 of the

3 There are some offences such as oil pollution and fisheries offences which carry maximum penalties in excess of the usual amount.
4 Dog Licences Act 1959, s 12.
5 Public Order Act 1936, s 5.
6 Criminal Justice Act 1982, s 37.
7 Ibid, s 46.
8 MCA 1980, s 143 (Criminal Justice Act 1982, s 48).
9 Criminal Justice Act 1982, ss 35 and 36.

Criminal Law Act 1977, the fine is increased to the next level up on the scale, so for example the fine for not having a dog licence is increased to £25. The only exception to this is that a fine of £400 is increased not to £500 but to £1,000.[10]

There are exceptional increases not provided for by the general scheme outlined above, which are contained in Schedule 3 to the Criminal Justice Act 1982. For some offences listed in Schedule 2, the penalties are to remain the same. However, after this initial adjustment, it is to be hoped that all maximum penalties will thereafter be determined by a general adjustment to the standard scale with the minimum of alteration to the position of a particular offence on the scale.

Part II of the Criminal Justice Act also provides for amendments to the penalty provisions of the more esoteric offences such as shipping and oil pollution infringements.

Gravity of the offence and the means of the offender

The upper limit to a fine in a particular case is established by the maximum for the offence provided by statute and by the gravity of the particular example of the offence. A fine shall only be used where the offence is not grave enough to merit a custodial sentence as it should not be seen as a way for the rich man to buy his way out of custody.[11] If the particular offence is suitable for a financial penalty, the court should tentatively fix in its mind the amount of the fine in relation to the gravity of the offence, then the court should consider the means of the offender.

> In fixing the amount of a fine, a magistrates' court shall take into consideration among other things the means of the person on whom the fine is imposed so far as they appear or are known to the court.[12]

The means of the offender may be apparent from a social inquiry report or the court may ask him for financial details. The defendant is not obliged to answer what may be embarrassing questions, although it may be advantageous to do so in certain cases.

If the defendant is a man of small means, this may serve to reduce the level of the fine as the fine must be within his capacity to pay although the court can take account of his potential earning capacity.[13] Problems may be caused when the defendant is of really limited means. The court may be in an impossible situation, but if an offender is unable to pay a fine that is no reason to impose imprisonment; imprisonment would have to be justified on its own merits.[14] If the

10 Ibid, ss 38 and 40.

11 *R v Markwick* (1953) 37 Cr App Rep 125, CCA; *R v Thompson* [1974] Crim LR 720 CA. Equally, a fine should not be increased above the level merited by the offence because the defendant is wealthy *R v Fairbairn* [1981] Crim LR 190.

12 MCA 1980, s 35.

13 *R v Lewis* [1965] Crim LR 121.

14 *R v Gillies* [1965] Crim LR 664, (1965) 109 Sol Jo 737, CCA.

offence is not serious, the usual alternative would be a conditional discharge but where this is not practicable (because for example the defendant has previously breached a discharge) a much reduced fine coupled with a long period to pay would be the only possibility.[15] If a court is ordering a fine much below the average it should make its reasons for adopting that particular course quite plain otherwise a lack of means might appear to be a licence to commit crime.[16]

Continuing offences

Some offences have a penalty prescribed as being a fine of £X, and £Y for each day the offence continues. The maximum penalty for a first conviction will be £X, the daily penalty only applies on the second or subsequent conviction.

COMPENSATION

Section 35 of the Powers of Criminal Courts Act 1973 provides:

> (1) . . . a court by or before which a person is convicted of an offence, instead of or in addition to dealing with him in any other way, may, on application or otherwise, make an order . . . requiring him to pay compensation for any personal injury, loss or damage resulting from that offence or any other offence which is taken into consideration by the court in determining sentence.
>
> (1A) Compensation . . . shall be of such amount as the court considers appropriate, having regard to any evidence and to any representations that are made by or on behalf of the accused or prosecutor.
>
> (4) In determining whether to make a compensation order against any person, and in determining the amount to be paid by any person under such an order, the court shall have regard to his means so far as they appear or are known to the court.
>
> (4A) Where the court considers:
>
> (a) that it would be appropriate both to impose a fine and to make a compensation order but
>
> (b) that the offender has insufficient means to pay both an appropriate fine and appropriate compensation
>
> the court shall give preference to compensation (though it may impose a fine as well).

The basic idea behind the power to award compensation is simple enough. An offender may have assaulted the victim and in the course of the assault he may have damaged the victim's clothing or spectacles. If the offender is punished by a fine for example, that will not recompense the victim for a new jacket he has had to buy. The victim has a right to sue the offender for damages in the civil courts but this can be expensive and troublesome. In order to avoid this, the criminal courts are given the power to order the offender to pay compensation.

15 *R v Ball* [1982] Crim LR 131.

16 *R v Botfield* (1982) 146 JP Jo 388.

For what damage can compensation be ordered?

The consequences of a given act can be never ending. Suppose a victim was assaulted at a bus stop, apart from having his clothing damaged he may also have missed his bus and failed to keep an appointment thereby losing an opportunity to obtain a job. Should the defendant pay compensation for the loss of this opportunity? Even in civil law there is an attempt made to limit liability for all the consequences of a wrongful act and in criminal cases this limit tends to be more closely drawn. Compensation is designed for 'simple, straightforward cases where the amount of compensation can be readily ascertained',[17] the court should not concern itself with complicated questions of law.[18]

Some guidance is given by section 35 itself: where the offence is theft and the stolen article has been recovered but is damaged, any damage is treated as having been caused by the thief even though it may have been occasioned by a third person. Second, dependants of a victim cannot claim compensation for loss occasioned by his death nor can any claim be made in respect of injury, loss or damage due to an accident arising out of the presence of a motor vehicle on a road except arising from an offence under the Theft Act 1968. This means that where a motor vehicle is taken without the owner's consent and collides with another motor vehicle, compensation may be claimed for the vehicle taken without consent but not for the damage to the other vehicle which was not involved in the offence under section 12 of the Theft Act 1968.[19]

Normally claims for compensation relate to the replacing of things which have been stolen or have been damaged or destroyed, but the magistrates can order compensation to victims of assault for the pain and suffering they have been caused, for example, £X for a black eye and £Y for a damaged tooth. This may be appropriate where the extent of the injury would not justify a claim being made under the criminal injuries compensation scheme. In the case of *Bond v Chief Constable of Kent*[20] compensation was awarded for the fright and distress caused to the complainant by the criminal damage caused to the house by the defendant. The Magistrates' Association publishes guidelines from time to time on the amount of compensation that may be awarded. Where a substantial amount of compensation is contemplated for personal injury such matters are best left to the county court.[1]

When should compensation be awarded?

The court may order compensation for any loss arising from the offence or any offences taken into consideration whether an application is

17 *R v Donovan* [1981] Crim LR 723.
18 *R v Kneeshaw* [1975] QB 57, [1974] 1 All ER 896.
19 *Quigley v Stokes* [1977] 2 All ER 317, [1977] 1 WLR 434. **20** (1983) 147 JP Jo 49.
1 *R v Cooper* [1982] Crim LR 308 and for the Magistrates' Association guidelines see (1980) 144 JP 698.

made or not. In practice the prosecution will submit a claim form which it has prepared, asking for a specific amount. If the amount was not in dispute, the court would proceed to make the order. However, the defence might raise an objection and dispute either the amount of compensation or whether it should be awarded at all. This could put the court in difficulty. Formerly the claim for compensation had to be agreed or proved by the applicant which might effectively deny an effective remedy to a claimant to a modest amount of compensation.[2] The court is now (since the enactment of section 67 of the Criminal Justice Act 1982 which inserted subsection (1A) into section 35 of the Powers of Criminal Courts Act 1973) not so strictly bound; it may listen to representations and evidence, if any, and make the order it feels to be appropriate. This is not to say that the court should ride rough shod over any objections or should entertain an application where there are complex points of law involved;[3] but it should enable the court to reach a fair result in the majority of applications before it.

How much compensation?

The magistrates can only award up to £1,000 compensation for each offence.[4] If there are offences to be taken into consideration compensation may be awarded for them, but the global sum of compensation cannot exceed the limit for the substantive offences. Thus if there are two substantive offences and five TICs and £2,000 compensation is awarded on the substantive offences no compensation can be awarded on the TICs but if say £500 compensation is awarded on one offence and £700 on another there will be £800 left from the overall limit which can be awarded to the TICs.

However the largest difficulty which usually faces a magistrates' court is not that of quantifying the amount of compensation but overcoming the fact that the defendant may have little ability to pay. The court has two ways of tackling this.

There is the power given by the rather curiously worded provisions of section 35 of the Powers of Criminal Courts Act 1973 reproduced above to treat compensation as a sentence in its own right or as an order ancillary to (another) sentence. Formerly the courts could not make a compensation order on its own and this could cause difficulty. If the only appropriate penalty was a fine (as it very often was) the court was in the dilemma of either imposing a realistic fine and no compensation, or a derisory fine with a full compensation order, as the court had to have regard to the defendant's ability to pay.

There are strong moral reasons for the court wishing to give

2 *R v Vivian* [1979] 1 All ER 48, [1979] 1 WLR 291; *R v Carnwell* (1978) 68 Cr App Rep 58, [1979] Crim LR 59.

3 *R v Kneeshaw* [1975] QB 57, [1974] 1 All ER 896.

4 MCA 1980, s 40.

preference to a compensation order rather than a fine and this has now been recognised. In those quite common situations where a fine and a compensation order would be appropriate the court must now give preference to compensation even to the extent of reducing or dispensing with a fine.

Even where the court does not impose a fine the compensation order must still be within the ability of the defendant to pay. The court must try to steer a middle course between obtaining compensation and ordering a realistic amount which is not going to be counter-productive by driving the defendant to despair and possible further criminal activity. Orders which require payments to be made over a long period are wrong.[5] The remedy in this situation is to reduce the amount of the compensation ordered. Thus, for example, an order for £7,500 of compensation to be paid at £20 per week was reduced to an amount which could be paid off at £20 per week in approximately two years.[6]

Where there are several claimants and the means of the offender are not sufficient to satisfy all their claims, the court could either reduce all their claims on a pro rata basis or, in exceptional cases, if this would work without injustice, the court may make such adjustment to the claims as is felt to be reasonable.[7]

The problem of lack of means is often felt acutely when an order for compensation is coupled with an immediate custodial sentence. Whilst these are not mutually incompatible, nevertheless there is a great danger that an order will be made that cannot be complied with, thus a sentence of nine months' imprisonment (in the Crown Court) for defrauding the Department of Health and Social Security coupled with a compensation order on a man who had no savings was held to be wrong in principle.[8] The basic question which the court must ask itself is whether the order is going to be paid within a reasonable period or is it unrealistic and will only serve to bring the defendant back before the enforcement court and result in his committal to custody for default.[9]

The making of an order

Where one offender has committed several offences it is possible to make one order to cover the offences provided the victim in each case is the same.[10] Where two offenders have committed the same offence it is the usual practice to make a separate order against each offender for half the amount unless there was a difference in responsibility or the

5 *R v Bradburn* (1973) 57 Cr App Rep 948, [1973] Crim LR 705.
6 *R v Making* [1982] Crim LR 613.
7 *R v Amey* (1983) Times, 6 January where an order was made in favour of individuals who were claiming compensation whilst a bank was left to seek its remedy in the civil courts.
8 *R v McCullough* [1982] Crim LR 461.
9 *R v Oddy* [1974] 2 All ER 666, [1974] 1 WLR 1212.
10 *R v Warton* [1976] Crim LR 520.

ability to pay was markedly different.[11] It is possible to make joint and several orders but this is usually inappropriate and could cause considerable problems in enforcement.[12]

Appeal and review of compensation orders

If the defendant appeals against conviction or sentence the order for compensation is suspended and compensation for an offence taken into consideration will be quashed if all his convictions are overturned on appeal. A defendant may appeal against compensation awarded on a TIC as if it were a sentence on a substantive offence.[13]

At any time before the compensation order has been complied with, or fully complied with, the defendant may apply to have the order reviewed on the basis that subsequent civil proceedings have determined the value to be less than originally thought, or that the property has been recovered.[14]

ABSOLUTE AND CONDITIONAL DISCHARGE

Section 7 Powers of Criminal Courts Act 1973 provides:

> (1) Where a court by or before which a person is convicted of an offence . . . is of the opinion, having regard to the circumstances including the nature of the offence and the character of the offender, that it is inexpedient to inflict punishment and that a probation order is not appropriate, the court may make an order discharging him absolutely, or, if the court thinks fit, discharging him subject to the condition that he commits no offence during such period, not exceeding three years from the date of the order, as may be specified therein.

An absolute discharge releases the offender from all further obligations although he may be ordered to pay costs and compensation[15] but an absolute discharge can only follow a finding of guilt and must be distinguished from the dismissal of an information. A conditional discharge is similar except that if the offender commits an offence during the specified period, he is liable to be sentenced again for the offence for which he was conditionally discharged and this possibility must be explained to him at the time the order of conditional discharge is made. If the offender is sentenced again for the original offence after the breach of a conditional discharge the conditional discharge will cease to be of effect.[16]

Any magistrates' court may deal with a breach of a conditional discharge imposed by another magistrates' court with that court's

11 *R v Amey* (1983) Times, 6 January.
12 *R v Grundy and Moorhouse* [1974] 1 All ER 292, [1974] 1 WLR 139.
13 Powers of Criminal Courts Act 1973, s 36.
14 Ibid, s 37.
15 Ibid, s 12 and disqualification and endorsement of a driving licence may be ordered, s 102 of the Road Traffic Act 1972.
16 Powers of Criminal Courts Act 1973, s 7(4).

permission, but if the order was made by the Crown Court, the magistrates may only, if they feel it appropriate, commit him on bail or in custody to the Crown Court.[17]

COMMITTAL TO CROWN COURT FOR SENTENCE

Committals under section 38 of the Magistrates' Courts Act 1980

The magistrates may have considered all their sentencing options and decided that they did not have enough powers to sentence the accused – for example they would like to send him to prison for longer than their powers would allow.[18] In this case they do have a power in certain circumstances to commit him to the Crown Court to be sentenced by the judge who has the same powers of punishment as if the defendant had just been convicted on indictment.[19] This power to commit for sentence is provided by section 38 of the Magistrates' Courts Act 1980:

> Where on the summary trial of an offence triable either way[20] . . . a person who is not less than 17 years old is convicted of the offence, then, if on obtaining information about his character and antecedents the court is of the opinion that they are such that greater punishment should be inflicted for the offence than the court has power to inflict, the court may, . . . commit him in custody or on bail to the Crown Court for sentence . . . .

It will be noted that this power is only available for either way offences and therefore for purely summary offences there is no provision for any court to impose a penalty greater than that prescribed as the maximum for the offence on summary conviction, although as will be seen below, there is a power to commit summary offences to the Crown Court for the purpose of dealing with them at the same time as an either way offence.

The problem with section 38 is caused by the words 'then, if on obtaining information about his character and antecedents . . .'. This presupposes, rightly, that at the mode of trial proceedings which determine whether the offence will be heard in the magistrates' court or the Crown Court, the court is only concerned about the seriousness of the offence and not with whether the defendant has a bad criminal record. It would be wholly wrong for the prosecution to adduce

17 Ibid, s 8.

18 Or, for example, to commit him with a view to a restriction order being made under s 41 of the Mental Health Act 1983. The bench may wish a sentence to be passed on one particular offence which is in excess of their powers even though the defendant has been convicted of two offences and the aggregate maximum would be within their powers: *R v Rugby Justices, ex p Prince* [1974] 2 All ER 116, [1974] 1 WLR 736 (D convicted of two either way offences, maximum sentence 12 months, committed for sentence because the bench wished him to be made the subject of a suspended sentence supervision order).

19 Powers of Criminal Courts Act 1973, s 42.

20 Note offences of criminal damage where the value is under £200 which are purely summary.

evidence of the defendant's previous convictions at this stage. The scheme of the section is apparently simple: the magistrates decide that they can deal with the *offence*, if the defendant is convicted they can sentence him themselves but if they discover that he has such a bad criminal record, they may commit him for sentence so that the judge may inflict greater punishment.

Generally speaking, once the magistrates have assumed jurisdiction to deal with a particular case, for example assault, they cannot then commit the accused for sentence simply because the offence turns out to be more serious than they originally thought.[1] (However, if the court assumes jurisdiction and the defendant pleads not guilty the court may revert from summary trial to acting as examining justices at any time before the end of the prosecution case. This will result in a committal for *trial* rather than a committal for *sentence*.[2]) The problem is most apparent in cases of assault where the bench is only informed after the plea of guilty of the true nature of the injuries inflicted. Therefore the prosecution are under a duty, especially in assault cases, to give the bench full details of the allegations[3] (unless the charge speaks for itself as when the prosecutor may simply assert that the charge is one of theft from a shop with no aggravating features).

In considering character and antecedents a record of previous offences would obviously constitute 'character and antecedents' but the definition is not confined to this. The word 'antecedents' is as wide as can be conceived, and includes offences to be taken into consideration[4] when sentencing for the substantive offence. Therefore a defendant with no previous convictions could be committed for sentence on the basis that he had asked for other offences to be taken into consideration and this principle has been extended to cover the situation where there was in fact a long series of transactions involved behind the apparently single substantive offence.[5] But a limit is placed on this in that if nothing new appears from the facts stated by the prosecution to aggravate the defendant's character more than the charges themselves revealed, he cannot be committed for sentence.[6]

1 *R v Hartlepool Justices, ex p King* [1973] Crim LR 637, DC.
2 MCA 1980, s 25.
3 *R v Harlow Justices, ex p Galway* [1975] Crim LR 288, DC.
4 *R v Vallett* [1951] 1 All ER 231, (1951) 34 Crim App Rep 251, provided of course they have not already been mentioned at the mode of trial proceedings: *R v South Derbyshire Justices, ex p McCarthy* (1980) 2 Cr App Rep (S) 140.
5 *R v King's Lynn Justices, ex p Carter* [1969] 1 QB 488, [1968] 3 All ER 858.
6 *R v Tower Bridge Magistrate, ex p Osman* [1971] 2 All ER 1018, [1971] 1 WLR 1109 where it was apparent from the charges that the accused had been pilfering over several months. It is rather curious that in the case of *R v Lymm Justices, ex p Brown* [1973] 1 All ER 716, [1973] 1 WLR 1039 where the magistrates discovered after a plea of guilty that the accused was an airport policeman stealing whilst on duty, there was a power to commit for sentence on the basis of his character. His status as a policeman surely aggravated only the *offence*; his character and antecedents were exemplary.

Committals for sentence under other provisions
There are other powers to commit to the Crown Court for sentence but these relate generally to situations where the defendant is in breach of a Crown Court sentence such as probation (section 8(6) of the Powers of Criminal Courts Act 1973) or a suspended sentence (section 24(2)) or to commit a person in breach of parole (section 62(6) of the Criminal Justice Act 1967). There is also a power to commit for sentence an offence under the Bail Act 1976 (section 6(6)).

The 'tidying-up' committal – section 56 of the Criminal Justice Act 1967. If a defendant has been committed for sentence on one either way offence he may also face several summary matters. It would be wrong to deal with him separately for these offences in the magistrates' court and commit him for sentence on the either way offence and so there is provision under section 56 of the Criminal Justice Act 1967 to commit these along with the either way offence for sentence. At the Crown Court the judge may only pass a sentence which could have been passed by the magistrates on any offence which has been committed under section 56.

Committals for sentence generally
If the magistrates decide to commit for sentence there is no appeal against that decision, the only way to challenge the decision would be by judicial review.[7] Once the decision has been made the magistrates cannot make any ancillary orders such as compensation or restitution,[8] although they may impose an interim disqualification under section 103(1) of the Road Traffic Act 1974.

When the defendant is at the Crown Court the Crown Court may entertain an application for change of plea as the defendant has not yet been sentenced and the case would be remitted to the magistrates to proceed on the basis of a not guilty hearing.[9]

Although the defendant technically has a right to apply for bail, in view of the the circumstances of the committal it must be rare for bail to be granted.[10]

DEFERMENT OF SENTENCE

The magistrates do have a power to defer passing sentence for a period of up to six months.[11] Once sentence has been deferred it may not be

7 *R v London Sessions, ex p Rogers* [1951] 2 KB 74, [1951] 1 All ER 343.
8 *R v Brogan* [1975] 1 All ER 879, [1975] 1 WLR 393 (compensation); *R v Blackpool Justices, ex p Charlson and Gregory* [1972] 3 All ER 854, [1972] 1 WLR 1456 (restitution).
9 *R v Inner London Crown Court, ex p Sloper* (1978) 69 Crim App Rep 1 reported sub nom *R v Camberwell Green Justices, ex p Sloper* [1979] Crim LR 264.
10 *R v Coe* [1969] 1 All ER 65, [1968] 1 WLR 1950.
11 Powers of Criminal Courts Act 1973, s 1.

deferred again (although it will be possible to adjourn under section 10 of the Magistrates' Courts Act 1980) but on the other hand the court may bring forward the date for sentencing. A deferment is like an adjournment but there are two differences: there is a power to 'adjourn' for more than four weeks after the conviction and there is no power to remand.[12]

The question then prompts itself: 'Why defer sentence?' The answer must not be that the court cannot think what to do with the accused and so it is putting off the evil day of sentencing. The power of deferment should be used:

> 'for the purpose of enabling the court to have regard, in determining his sentence, to his conduct after conviction (including, where appropriate, the making by him of reparation for his offence) or to any change in his circumstances.

and

> 'only if the offender consents and the court is satisfied, having regard to the nature of the offence and the character and circumstances of the offender, that it would be in the interests of justice to exercise the power.[13]

Therefore the power should not be used where the offences are so serious as for example a clever and deliberate fraud[14] or where the defendant should really be dealt with at the Crown Court because he is in breach of a Crown Court order. But a deferred sentence may be appropriate where there have been recent developments in the offender's history or there are future changes which materially affect his situation and which suggest that the court would be in a better position to deal with him then. The deferred sentence is not another form of suspended sentence hanging over the head of the defendant. Because of the aims of deferment the court, when sentencing the accused to a deferred sentence, should spell out its object in deferring sentence (eg to see how the defendant settles down in his new job and copes with his family responsibilities). After the deferment it is desirable that the same bench of magistrates should pass sentence or if this is not possible, the new bench should be made aware of the reasons for the deferment.[15]

If the defendant has substantially complied with the court's expectations for the period of the deferment, he should not receive a custodial sentence[16] but obviously he can have no complaint about receiving a custodial sentence if he has committed offences during the period of the deferment.[17] The magistrates may decide at the end of the

12 Cf M. Wasik (1981) 145 JP 754.
13 Powers of Criminal Courts Act 1973, s 1(1).
14 *R v Crosby* (1974) 60 Cr App Rep 234, [1975] Crim LR 246.
15 *R v Gurney* [1974] Crim LR 472.
16 *R v Fletcher* [1982] Crim LR 462 sentenced to borstal training after period of deferment. Sentence quashed because the defendant had committed only one peccadillo and had complied with the aims of the original sentencer.
17 *R v Hope* [1980] Crim LR 314, CA (further offences during period of deferment).

period of deferment, if it is appropriate, to commit him for sentence to the Crown Court under section 38 of the Magistrates' Courts Act 1980.[18]

COMBINATIONS OF SENTENCES

A problem which can present itself in court is the compatability of the varying forms of sentence which are available to the court. This may present itself in one of two ways: can the court order two forms of sentence for the same offence; and can the court pass different sentences for different offences at the same time.

The only guidance given by the statute which creates the offence or provides for its punishment is whether the offence is punishable by a fine *or* imprisonment and, in the case of most either way offences, a fine *and/or* imprisonment.

In the case of an offence carrying a fine or imprisonment only one disposal would be appropriate, but where a fine and imprisonment is available difficulties may present themselves.

Combining sentences for the same offence

Absolute or conditional discharge. This sentence cannot be combined with another penalty such as fine or imprisonment because the court must already have decided that it is expedient not to inflict punishment.[19]

Probation order. This cannot be combined with another sentence for the same offence because it is made instead of sentencing him for that offence.[20]

Community service. This was intended by parliament to stand as a sentence by itself and thus cannot be combined with another sentence for the same offence.[1]

Attendance centre. Attendance can probably not be combined with a fine.[2]

Fine and suspended sentence. There is nothing wrong with this in principle,[3] and it would ensure that the defendant did not think he was being let off but the court must be sure of his ability to pay the fine otherwise he would go to prison for default.[4]

18 Powers of Criminal Courts Act 1973, s 1(8) as amended by Criminal Justice Act 1982, s 63.
19 Powers of Criminal Courts Act 1973, s 7(1) (and therefore should not be combined with a restitution order).
20 Ibid, s 2(1): Cf *R v Hunt* [1978] Crim LR 697, CA.
1 *R v Carnwell* (1978) 68 Cr App Rep 58, [1979] Crim LR 59.
2 See discussion at (1979) 143 JP 698, aliter (1979) JP 427.
3 *R v King* [1970] Crim LR 478; *R v Scarlett* [1978] Crim LR 241, CA.
4 For these difficulties see *R v Sisodia* [1980] Crim LR 114, CA and *R v Whenman* [1977] Crim LR 430, CA.

Combining sentences for several offences
Where there are several offences involved, the court must pass sentence separately for each offence. However even in this situation there are combinations of sentences which are undesirable.

Probation order. Probation orders cannot be made at the same time as a suspended sentence[5] and it is inappropriate where the defendant receives a custodial sentence,[6] but there is no reason why a defendant cannot be fined for another offence[7] and there is probably nothing wrong in ordering community service and probation.

Community service. This should not be combined with a custodial sentence for the obvious reasons that the defendant would not be at liberty to complete his tasks and that community service is an alternative to a custodial sentence. Nor should community service be combined with a suspended sentence[8]

Imprisonment. Apart from the above examples it is inappropriate to combine an immediate and suspended sentence together[9] although the court now does have the power to pass a partly suspended sentence where appropriate.[10]

REMITTING TO ANOTHER COURT FOR SENTENCE

Apart from the duty on the court to remit a juvenile to the juvenile court for sentence in prescribed circumstances,[11] the court may remit the defendant to another magistrates' court where the offence is punishable with imprisonment or for which the defendant may be disqualified from driving.[12] The other court must already have convicted him of another offence but not yet have sentenced him or committed him for sentence to the Crown Court, so that any remittal has to be carefully timed to slot into this intervening period. During this period the accused may be remanded in custody or on bail.

ANCILLARY ORDERS

So far, this chapter has been concerned with substantive sentences, but the court also has the power to make certain ancillary orders in addition to passing those sentences.

5 Powers of Criminal Courts Act 1973, s 22(3). If it is done, the suspended sentence is valid but the probation order is void: *R v Wright* [1975] Crim LR 728.
6 *R v Bainbridge* [1979] LS Gaz R 209.
7 *R v Evans* [1958] 3 All ER 673, [1959] 1 WLR 26.
8 *R v Starie* (1979) 69 Cr App Rep 239, [1979] Crim LR 731.
9 *R v Sapiano* (1969) 52 Cr App Rep 674, [1968] Crim LR 497.
10 Criminal Law Act 1977, s 47.
11 See ch 12.
12 MCA 1980, s 39.

Costs
There is the power to order the costs of the litigation to be paid by one party to another, or from government funds. This is discussed in chapter 8.

Legal aid contribution order
If the defendant is legally aided the court may order him to pay a contribution towards the costs of his legal aid. This is discussed in chapter 4.

Compensation
Since the Criminal Justice Act was brought into force this can be a sentence in its own right or an order made in addition to another sentence and is discussed earlier in the chapter.

Restitution[13]
Where goods have been stolen (and stolen for this purpose includes property obtained by deception or blackmail) the magistrates, if the accused has been convicted of any offence with reference to the theft (whether or not the stealing is the gist of his offence) or has such an offence taken into consideration may:
(a) order anyone having possession or control of the goods to restore them to any person entitled to recover them from him; or
(b) on the application of a person entitled to recover from the person convicted any other goods directly or indirectly representing the first mentioned goods order those goods to be delivered to the applicant; or
(c) order that a sum not exceeding the value of the first mentioned goods shall be paid out of any money of the person convicted which was taken out of his possession on his apprehension, to any person who, if those goods were in the possession of the person convicted, would be entitled to recover them from him.

or the court may make a suitable combination of orders under (b) and (c).

The court can only make a restitution order where the facts appear to be sufficiently clear from the evidence given, or from admissible evidence in the form of documents, or the admissions of the defendant. As with compensation orders a restitution order should only be made in straightforward cases. Where the goods have been passed on to an innocent party there may be complications about whether ownership has passed under the civil law and problems can particularly occur where restitution is ordered under paragraph (a). In this case the defendant may be ordered to pay money to the innocent third party

13 See generally Theft Act 1968, s 28.

from money found in his possession on his apprehension (the victim of the crime will of course have had his goods returned to him). Where there are competing claims between the victim and the innocent third party and there are questions of law involved about ownership the justices should hesitate before making an order.[14]

A restitution order is really a means of restoring the situation to what it was before the offence was committed where the only loser, if any, should be the accused if he has had to pay out from money in his possession.

Where sentence has been deferred the court may still make a restitution order at the time of conviction and it need not wait until it finally passes sentence.

Forfeiture

Where the defendant has been convicted of an offence punishable on indictment with imprisonment for two years or more, if the court is satisfied that any property[15] in his possession or under his control at the time of his apprehension was used to commit or facilitate the commission of any offence or was intended for that use (or for concealing the crime or avoiding apprehension or disposing of the property) the court may make a forfeiture order. The effect of the order is to deprive the defendant of any rights in the property and place it in the possession of the police.

The purpose of this order is to be an additional punishment;[16] it is not intended to be a form of distress warrant to realise assets to satisfy a claim for costs or compensation.[17]

Other statutes provide for the forfeiture of articles used in the course of crime, the most common powers being those for the forfeiture of firearms, offensive weapons and articles used for poaching; also a very common power is that to seize drugs under the Misuse of Drugs Act 1971 (section 27).

Recommendation for deportation[18]

The magistrates' court does have a power to make a recommendation for deportation under section 6 of the Immigration Act 1971 in respect of persons over the age of 17 convicted of an offence punishable with imprisonment but it should be remembered that this is only a power to make a *recommendation* to the Home Secretary and the final decision

14 *Stamp v United Dominion Trust (Commercial) Ltd* [1967] 1 QB 418, [1967] 1 All ER 251; *R v Ferguson* [1970] Crim LR 538.
15 Excluding real property *R v Khan; R v Crawley* [1982] Crim LR 752.
16 *R v Buddo* [1982] Crim LR 837. It should be treated as part of the whole sentence.
17 *R v Kingston-upon-Hull Justices, ex p Hartung* [1981] Crim LR 42; *R v Thibeault* (1983) 147 JP Jo 60.
18 Immigration Act 1971, ss 3(6) and 6.

rests with him. When the court makes a recommendation for deportation it may direct that the defendant be released (with or without conditions of reporting to the police and a condition of residence) or detained in custody until his case is considered by the Secretary of State. If a court is considering such a recommendation reference should be made to the extensive law on the subject contained in the footnotes to *Stone's* on the Immigration Act.

Bind over

Following a conviction for a criminal offence the court cannot simply order a bind over on its own as the court is under a duty to sentence for the offence as well. However, when the court passes sentence it may order a bind over in addition to the penalty and this power of bind over is discussed in chapter 11.

Chapter 8

Costs

Introductory

The subject of costs is a matter which tends to be overlooked by the student of criminal law and procedure. There may be several reasons for this. It may be that the advocate is more concerned with tackling the question of substantive law involved in the case, or it may be that he is anxious about whether his client is convicted or acquitted of the charge against him. The question of costs is raised when the verdict is given and it may be overlooked in the aftermath of the case. However, for the client it can be of extreme importance whether he is awarded his costs or not. For example, consider a defendant of impeccable character who has been charged with theft of some items from a shop. He pleads not guilty and on the merits of the case he is acquitted. The defendant will naturally feel relieved and may be most anxious to leave the court. But will he be so satisfied when later he receives a bill from his solicitor for a considerable sum being the solicitor's costs for defending him? In these circumstances it can be a pyrrhic victory for a defendant to have to pay a bill for being acquitted which is larger than the fine he could have expected to be imposed had he been convicted. Accordingly it is of the utmost importance for any advocate, whether for the prosecution or the defence, to be thoroughly versed in the law of costs. It is not an edifying sight to see an advocate shuffling to his feet and inquiring nervously if he is entitled to costs, and if he is, that he would like to apply for them from somebody or other.

The bulk of the law of costs is to be found in one Act, the Costs in Criminal Cases Act 1973, and this Act should be studied and learned thoroughly. In this chapter a summary will be given of the law relating to costs in the magistrates' court, both from the point of view of the prosecution and the defence. However, mention must be made first of the sources from which costs can be paid.

CENTRAL FUNDS

It is obvious that most litigation costs money: there are lawyers to be paid, travelling costs to the court and payment to any witnesses for any loss of wages, etc, that they have incurred in giving up their time to

AVAILABILITY OF COSTS

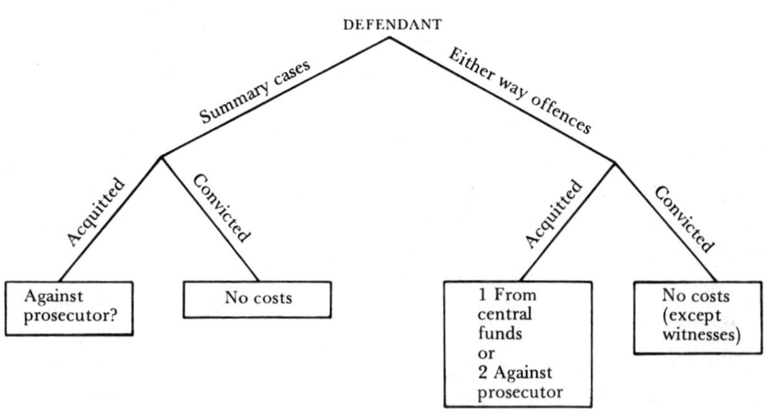

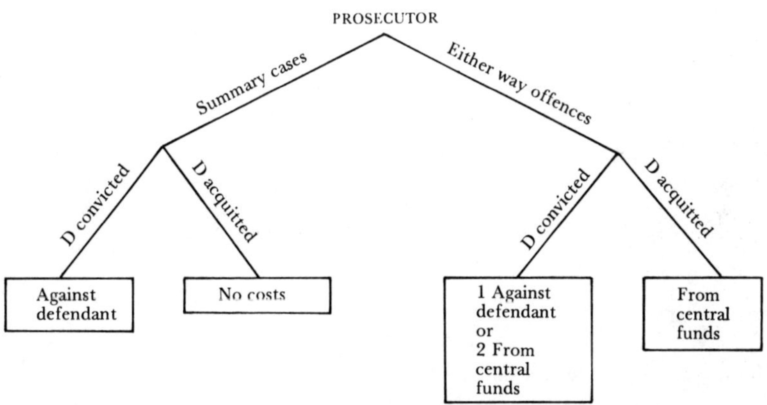

come to the trial. The obvious source for reimbursement of these costs incurred by a party to proceedings is the opposing party, that is that the loser pays the winner's costs. This rule applies generally in civil proceedings and can apply in criminal matters as well. However, there is money available from government funds, administered by the Home Office and paid out by magistrates' courts, to finance criminal litigation, this is known as central funds. The existence of these funds is perhaps linked to the involvement which the Crown has in prosecuting the more serious, indictable, criminal offences. It is extremely important for an advocate to know whether these central funds are available in his particular case for two reasons: as will be described below, a successful party will be more likely to have his costs awarded from central funds than against the other party, and second, in many cases he will have them paid more quickly, especially where the other party does not have a lump sum available.

Central funds are available in any case involving an indictable offence.[1] An indictable offence is an offence which is triable only at the Crown Court or which is triable either in the magistrates' court or the Crown Court (an 'either way' offence). Therefore it is important for the advocate to know the status of the offence he is concerned with. The exact definition of an indictable offence is given in section 64 of the Criminal Law Act 1977 and one anomaly arising from that definition is that an offence of criminal damage where the value involved is under £200 and which is triable only summarily is, for the purposes of costs, treated as being an indictable offence.[2]

It is proposed now to discuss the award of costs in a trial before the magistrates.

Costs in a summary trial before magistrates

THE PROSECUTION[3]

Where central funds are available

The situation will be considered first of all where the prosecution has been successful and the defendant has been convicted. In these circumstances the prosecutor may seek his costs either against the defendant or from central funds. It is the general rule that the

1 Costs in Criminal Cases Act 1973, s 1(1) and (2).

2 Criminal Law Act 1977, s 64(2).

3 Although it will naturally be assumed that the prosecution is being conducted by the police, the same principles will apply to a private prosecution where there is a serious charge: *R v Esher and Walton Justices ex p Victor Value & Co Ltd* [1967] Crim LR 475, (1967) 111 Sol Jo 473, DC (private prosecution for theft).

prosecution looks first towards the defendant to reimburse its costs. This may be thought to be a fair rule because it is the defendant who has brought about the expense of a prosecution.

However, there are a number of factors which may dictate that the defendant should not pay either all, or part of the prosecution costs. The court must have some regard to the defendant's means.[4] If the defendant is being ordered to pay the prosecution costs then he should be told what those costs are, not that he will pay, for example, one-half of the costs (whatever they may be).[5] But on the other hand, if the defendant has the ability to pay and has wasted the court's time by pursuing a hopeless case, he could not complain if he were asked to pay all of the prosecution's costs, even if they were considerable.[6] The costs awarded, though, must be costs that have genuinely been incurred and the court must not seek to impose a penalty disguised in the form of costs.[7] Furthermore it would be wrong to order the defendant to pay the costs where he has received a considerable prison sentence unless he has private capital available.[8]

If it is inappropriate to order the costs against the defendant, then recourse must be made to central funds if the prosecution is to have its costs. Several general points should be made about the awarding of costs from central funds or against the defendant. Very often the sum claimed by the prosecution for its costs is something of a conventional figure because the prosecutor is often a prosecuting solicitor working for the local authority and doing it for a living. The prosecutor is entitled to 'such sums as appear to the court reasonably sufficient to compensate the prosecutor . . . for the expenses properly incurred by him in carrying on the prosecution . . .'.[9] In practice the prosecutor and the justices' clerk may agree a scale rate which will normally be accepted by the magistrates as being fair recompense for the prosecution costs.

When costs are awarded from central funds, the magistrates make the decision whether to award costs to the prosecution from central funds or not. Once the decision to award costs has been made, it is for the clerk to ascertain the amount of costs that will be paid from central

4 *R v Wright* [1977] Crim LR 236, CA, ie a defendant should not be ordered to pay a sum by way of costs which is beyond his ability to pay. The fact that the defendant has been convicted does not mean that he must automatically pay the costs of the prosecution even where he has pleaded not guilty and has been convicted after a trial. For a discussion of this see D. A. Thomas (1982) 146 JP 4 and *R v Singh* [1982] Crim LR 315.

5 *R v McKenzie* [1970] Crim LR 594, CA.

6 *R v Yoxall* (1972) 57 Cr App Rep 263, [1973] Crim LR 63, CA.

7 *R v Highgate Justices, ex p Petrou* [1954] 1 All ER 406, [1954] 1 WLR 485; cf *R v Tottenham Justices, ex p Joshi* [1982] 2 All ER 507, [1982] Crim LR 307.

8 *R v Gaston* [1971] 1 All ER 128n, [1971] 1 WLR 85.

9 Costs in Criminal Cases Act 1973, s 1(3).

funds.[10] The question of quantum is purely one for the clerk as the magistrates cannot order only a part of the costs to be met from central funds. In the usual case where the prosecution is claiming a conventional sum, the figure will be agreed there and then by the clerk. In the remaining cases the amount of costs will be ascertained by the clerk afterwards.

Two final points may be made. First, if the defendant is ordered to pay a fixed sum for prosecution costs which is less than the whole of the prosecution costs, the court may also order the prosecution costs from central funds and the prosecution will be reimbursed initially from central funds and any monies recovered from the defendant under his order for costs will be paid back into central funds. In fact in all cases where central funds are available it is the practice to make the prosecution costs payable initially from central funds so that the prosecution receives its costs straight away. Any costs paid by the defendant are then paid straight into central funds as and when they are collected.[11]

The discussion so far has been concerned with the award of costs to the prosecution where it has been successful. If the prosecution is unsuccessful and the defendant is acquitted, the prosecution cannot claim its costs against the defendant. However it may still claim its costs from central funds and this claim would usually be accepted where the court felt that the prosecution had been properly brought. If the court felt that the prosecution had not acted reasonably in bringing the case then not only would the prosecution not have its costs awarded from central funds but it would probably have to pay the defence costs as well.

Where central funds are not available

In a case involving a purely summary offence, that is an offence that cannot be tried on indictment,[12] central funds are not available. Accordingly if the prosecution is successful, it can only obtain its costs from the defendant. The criteria for deciding whether the defendant shall pay the prosecution costs and if so, how much he should pay, are the same as those cases where central funds are available and the defence is ordered to pay the costs. It will be seen therefore that the prosecution is in a less advantageous position in dealing with a purely summary case because if the defendant is unable to pay its costs, there are no central funds to fall back on. There is also another disadvantage

10 *R v Chertsey Justices, ex p Edwards & Co (The Provision Market) Ltd* [1974] 1 All ER 156, [1973] 1 WLR 1545.

11 Costs in Criminal Cases Act 1973, s 16.

12 With the exception of criminal damage offences under £200 which, although triable only summarily are treated as being indictable offences Criminal Law Act 1977, s 64(2).

for the prosecution because if the case is dismissed, the prosecution cannot have its costs paid by the defendant, nor can it have its costs paid by central funds. Thus if the prosecution is unsuccessful, the prosecution itself has to bear the costs it has incurred. Furthermore it can be argued for reasons that will become apparent later, that the prosecution is more likely in purely summary cases to have to pay the costs of an acquitted defendant who has no recourse to central funds for his costs.

Costs where the prosecution is withdrawn

When the prosecution withdraws a case it may not have its costs paid by the defendant as he can only be ordered to pay costs if he is convicted, which he is not if the case against him is withdrawn. Neither can the prosecution have its costs from central funds because the court can only make such an order when *dealing* with a case summarily, and the court is not *dealing* with a case when it is withdrawn.[13] Therefore when a case is withdrawn the prosecution will have to pay its own costs.

THE DEFENCE

Where central funds are available

The first and obvious point to remember when considering the question of defence costs is that no application can be made by the defence for its costs either from central funds or from the prosecution, when the defendant is convicted. The only exception to this is that costs can be awarded from central funds to compensate a defence witness for his attendance at court.[14] Therefore as a general rule the defence can only make an application for costs when the defendant has been acquitted. In a case where central funds are available and the defendant has been convicted the prosecution would normally seek their costs against the defendant and from central funds if the defendant were not able to meet an order for costs. In the case of a successful defendant on the other hand he would normally make his application from central funds. An application for costs would only be brought against the prosecutor directly where it was alleged that the prosecution had acted improperly in some way. The reason for this is that the prosecution, whether it be the police or a local authority, is under a duty to prosecute breaches of the law and in bringing the prosecution to act fairly and impartially. The State recognises the importance of these prosecutors being able to operate without fear of being penalised in costs if they make a genuine mistake in bringing a

13 *R v Phipps, ex p Alton* [1964] 2 QB 420, [1964] 1 All ER 972, DC.
14 Costs in Criminal Cases Act 1973, s 1(4).

case which they were unable to prove *beyond a reasonable doubt* and central funds have been provided to cover the cost of litigation in these circumstances. Therefore if the court makes a deliberate decision to award the defence costs against the prosecution rather than from central funds, it is impliedly criticising the prosecution and indicating that the prosecution should never have been brought.

These principles underlie the 1982 Practice Note on the award of costs in the magistrates' court which is as follows:[15]

> It should be accepted as normal practice that such an award be made (for the payment of the costs of an acquitted defendant out of central funds) unless there are positive reasons for making a different order. Examples of such reasons are:
>
> (a) where the prosecution has acted spitefully or has instituted or continued proceedings without reasonable cause, the defendant's costs should be paid by the prosecutor . . .;
>
> (b) where the defendant's own conduct has brought suspicion on himself and has misled the prosecution into thinking that the case against him is stronger than it is, the defendant can be left to pay his own costs;
>
> (c) where there is ample evidence to support a conviction but the defendant is acquitted on a technicality which has no merit, here again the defendant can be left to pay his own costs.
>
> (d) where the defendant is acquitted on one charge but convicted on another, the court should make whatever order seems just having regard to the relative importance of the two charges and the conduct of the parties generally.

Where costs from central funds are awarded to the defendant then as with the prosecution costs the defendant must be awarded the whole of his costs which have been reasonably and properly incurred.[16] The decision as to what has been reasonably incurred being that of the clerk.

Where central funds are not available

In proceedings for a purely summary offence where no central funds are available, defence costs, if the defendant is acquitted, can only come from the prosecutor. However, there are two views concerning the circumstances in which costs should be awarded against the prosecution in purely summary cases. The two opposing principles can each be found in the Practice Note[17] referred to above:

(a) an acquitted defendant should normally receive his costs (from central funds) unless there are positive reasons for making a different order, and

(b) that costs should not be awarded against the prosecution unless it has in some way acted improperly.

15 [1982] 3 All ER 1152, [1982] 1 WLR 1447.
16 *R v Bow St. Magistrate, ex p Palmer* [1969] Crim LR 658, (1969) 113 Sol Jo 735, DC.
17 [1982] 3 All ER 1152, [1982] 1 WLR 1447.

Unfortunately it is difficult to state authoritatively the correct position owing to a lack of authority on the subject and the varying practice in different courts. The longer held view, and the position favoured by the prosecution, is that an acquitted defendant in a summary case should not be awarded his costs against the prosecution unless the prosecution should not have been brought or it has acted improperly. The basis for this argument is that the prosecution, that is the police, are only doing their duty in the interests of the public. In addition the prosecution and the defence are not in the same position regarding their chances of success. Unlike civil proceedings the prosecution has to satisfy the court of the defendant's guilt beyond reasonable doubt not on the civil standard of the balance of probabilities. Therefore the scales are weighted against the prosecution. Finally some support for this view can be adduced from the case of *R v Lytham Justices, ex p Carter.*[18] This case emphasised that every application for costs must be looked at on its merits and it was wrong to have a blanket policy of not awarding costs against the police. This would have been enough to dispose of the case but the judgment, as briefly reported, went on to say that the justices should first decide whether the prosecution had been properly brought and then decide the question of costs.

The contrary view is that it is wrong for a defendant to have to pay to prove his innocence when he is presumed to be innocent unless proved guilty. Although in a case where central funds are available it is clearly a criticism of the police to award costs against the prosecution, that argument cannot be sustained where the defendant has no other remedy than an order for costs against the prosecution. Given that the loss cannot fall on central funds, on whom should it fall, the prosecution or the defence? By analogy with civil litigation it should fall on the prosecution, especially as generally it is the police who are themselves financed out of public funds and do not dip into their own pockets.

It is submitted that the preferable view is that a successful defendant in a purely summary case should be awarded his costs against the prosecution unless he has debarred himself from such relief by his conduct in the manner outlined in the Practice Note on costs from central funds. The decision to award costs can be crucial in many minor summary matters where a defendant might have to pay his own solicitor several times the amount of any fine he would incur if convicted. Is it fair that he should be forced to appear unrepresented when the prosecution is now almost certainly (outside London) conducted by a solicitor?

Defence costs when the prosecution is withdrawn

When a prosecution is withdrawn, the defence may have its costs awarded from central funds or against the prosecution in indictable cases, and against the prosecutor alone in purely summary cases.[19]

18 [1975] Crim LR 225, (1975) 119 Sol Jo 341.
19 Costs in Criminal Cases Act 1973, s 12.

Committal proceedings

Rather similar principles apply to the awarding of costs in committal proceedings as apply to summary trial. Central funds will always be available of course by the very nature of the proceedings.

The prosecution may be awarded its costs from central funds whether the committal proceedings are successful or not[20] but unlike a summary trial it cannot be awarded its costs against the defendant.

The defendant if he is discharged, may be awarded his costs from central funds[21] or, if the justices are satisfied that the charge was not made in good faith, they may order the defence costs to be paid by the prosecutor.[1]

Committal for sentence

When a defendant has been committed for sentence at the Crown Court the view favoured by the Home Office is that the prosecution may make an application for its costs before the magistrates' court and need not delay the application until the Crown Court.[2]

Costs and the legally-aided defendant

COSTS AGAINST A LEGALLY-AIDED DEFENDANT

Where the costs are awarded against a legally-aided defendant, he will have to pay them out of his own pocket in the same way as any other defendant as legal aid is an arrangement between him and the legal aid fund to finance his own defence.[3]

COSTS IN FAVOUR OF A LEGALLY-AIDED DEFENDANT

If the defendant is successful, he should apply for his costs in the usual way. If he is awarded his costs these will be paid to the legal aid fund.[4] The advantage to the defendant is that if the legal aid fund is reimbursed in this way there will be no reason for him to be called upon to pay a contribution towards his legal aid bill.

20 Ibid, s 1.
21 Ibid, s 1(2).
1 Ibid, s 2(4).
2 Home Office Circular Mag 71, 26 November 1974.
3 Although if the prosecution costs are awarded against him he will have to pay whatever sum the court has ordered, his legal aid contribution is a separate matter referring only to the defence costs and is ordered separately.
4 *R v Arron* [1973] 2 All ER 1221, [1973] 1 WLR 1238.

Consider these examples which assume that the defendant is legally aided with a maximum contribution of £50. The costs of preparing the defence are assumed to be £100.

(a) The defendant is acquitted. He applies for costs of £100 from central funds. If these are ordered they will be paid to the legal aid fund.[5]

(b) The defendant is acquitted but the court does not consider that he deserves his costs. In this case it might be appropriate to order the defendant to pay a contribution of up to £50 towards his own costs which are being paid by the legal aid fund.

(c) The defendant is convicted. He may be ordered to pay the costs of the prosecution personally and the court may order him to pay up to £50 of his costs. Unlike the non-legally aided defendant there are no circumstances when he can be ordered to pay the whole costs of the defence.

However it is suggested by the editors of *Stone's Justices' Manual*[6] that it would simplify the payment of costs to a legally-aided defendant if, when costs are awarded, the legal aid order was revoked and so the costs would be paid directly to the defence, instead of to the legal aid fund which then has to reimburse the defence solicitor.

Appeals against the ordering of costs

Ordinarily there is no appeal to the Crown Court against the award of costs but there is an exception in favour of the prosecutor who may appeal where committing justices have awarded costs exceeding £25 to the defendant.[7] The committing justices may only order costs against the prosecution in these circumstances where they feel that the charge was not made in good faith. There is no right of appeal where an information is withdrawn and the defence costs are awarded against the prosecutor by virtue of section 12(3) of the Costs in Criminal Cases Act 1973.[8] However, if an award of costs is made which is clearly fundamentally wrong and an abuse of the court's jurisdiction, the situation can be remedied by an application to the High Court for a writ of judicial review.[9]

The assessing and payment of costs

Most of this chapter has been concerned with the question of when and

5 *R v Arron* [1973] 2 All ER 1221, [1973] 1 WLR 1238.
6 (115th edn, 1983) p 639.
7 Costs in Criminal Cases Act 1973, s 2(5).
8 *R v Crown Court at Lewes, ex p Rogers* [1974] 1 All ER 589, [1974] 1 WLR 196.
9 See, eg *R v Tottenham Justices, ex p Joshi* [1982] 2 All ER 507, [1982] 1 WLR 631 (in excess of £700 costs awarded in a plea of guilty by letter case).

to whom an order for costs can be made. This section is concerned with the question of how much costs will be awarded under an order.

It has been explained that there is a distinction between costs ordered to be paid from central funds and costs paid between the parties.

COSTS BETWEEN THE PARTIES

Costs between the parties are fixed at the court by the magistrates, as a specific sum; they cannot be assessed afterwards by the justices' clerk.[10] The magistrates must decide what they consider to be 'just and reasonable' which can be a somewhat rough and ready figure. When the order has been made the parties must comply with it. If the prosecutor fails to comply with an order for payment of defence costs then the order can be enforced as a civil debt.[11] If the defendant fails to comply with an order against him, the order may be enforced as a sum adjudged to be paid on a conviction.

THE ASSESSMENT OF COSTS AWARDED FROM CENTRAL FUNDS

The amount of these costs is 'ascertained' by the justices' clerk who is by statute the appropriate officer of the court.[12] When the costs have been ascertained the appropriate certificates (known as 'Forms') are completed to authorise the payment from central funds;[13] in committal proceedings: Form A for witness expenses, Form B for the prosecutor's (or defendant's) expenses; in summary trials of indictable offences: Form C for witness expenses, Form D for the prosecutor's (or defendant's) expenses.

When the case has been heard summarily or the defendant has been discharged in committal proceedings, the justices' clerk will pay out the money forthwith but when the defendant is committed for trial the witness expenses will be paid forthwith (Form A) but the prosecution's costs (excluding witness expenses) will be certified on Form B and will be considered by the Crown Court at the trial.

HOW THE COSTS PAYABLE OUT OF CENTRAL FUNDS ARE ASCERTAINED

It is important to note first of all that the word used in the Costs in Criminal Cases Act 1973 is 'ascertained'; it does not use the word 'taxed'. It may well be that the process of ascertaining costs in summary cases is a less exact one than that of taxation in the superior courts. This could be the case as most justices' clerks will not have the experience of taxation enjoyed by taxation officers.

10 *Bunston v Rawlings* [1982] 2 All ER 697, [1982] Crim LR 306.
11 Administration of Justice Act 1970, s 41.
12 Costs in Criminal Cases Act 1973, s 1(6).
13 Costs in Criminal Cases Regulations 1908.

Guidelines for the use of a justices' clerk are set out in *Stone's* (1983) at page 78. For a defence advocate it is suggested by *Stone's* that it is essential to supply the clerk with a properly itemised bill as he would do when supplying his bill to the Law Society. It is the usual practice for a clerk when determining whether the costs claimed are reasonable to have regard to the rates payable on legal aid. Therefore he needs to know how much time has been spent on preparation, waiting and hearing, how much travelling has been necessary and how much has been spent on telephone calls and correspondence.

WITNESS EXPENSES

Apart from the costs incurred by the solicitor, his witnesses may have incurred expenses, for example in bus fares and having to buy meals, and loss of wages for time off work. The witness will look initially to the solicitor for the party calling him to reimburse him. If the party obtains his costs from central funds or the opposing side he may claim his witnesses' expenses as part of his general costs in the usual way. However where the costs have been awarded from central funds there is a limit to what may be awarded. The various allowances that may be claimed are set out in circulars issued from time to time by the Lord Chancellor's Department under the provisions of the Costs in Criminal Cases (Allowances) Regulations 1977. These allowances provide for limits on the amounts to be claimed for subsistence and travelling, loss of earnings and, where appropriate, professional fees claimed by expert witnesses such as doctors. On the other hand, where the costs have been awarded between the parties, there is no limit on the amount that may be claimed, although the justices will be concerned to award what is just and reasonable. If no costs are awarded then each side must pay its own witnesses (or in the case of a legally aided defendant, claim them as part of his legal aid bill).

Conclusions

The advocate should start his preparation for the matter of costs before the case begins. He should discover whether the offence is an indictable offence. If it is then central funds will be available. For the prosecutor this fact is important because he may have his costs ordered whether the defendant is convicted or acquitted.

Whilst the prosecutor may be seeking a more or less conventional sum for his costs, the defence advocate will have to be more precise. This is particularly so in a purely summary case where almost invariably the magistrates will determine the amount of costs on the spot rather than adjourn the matter. Therefore it is useful for the defence to calculate their costs when the court has retired to consider its verdict. In this way if the defence is awarded its costs, a specific sum can be claimed and justified. Furthermore if a defendant is legally-aided he may be required to pay a legal aid contribution order in which case the court would wish to know the defence costs in order to ascertain what, if any, contribution he should make to the legal aid fund.

Chapter 9

Appeals and other forms of redress

Introductory

When the court has announced its decision, not all parties may be satisfied with the result. There are two stages at which either the prosecution or defence may feel aggrieved: the verdict (of guilty or not guilty), and the sentence which may follow. In addition, the court may itself not be satisfied with the outcome of the proceedings; it may have announced the wrong sentence by a slip of the tongue, or it may have passed a sentence which is either not allowed by law or which the court feels, on reflection, to have been inappropriate. This chapter is intended to deal with the means of redressing grievances which arise from the judgments of magistrates' courts.

The power of a magistrates' court to alter its own decisions

An appeal is strictly speaking an application to a superior court to rectify the decisions of an inferior court, and in due course the various means of appeal to the Crown Court and High Court will be described. However, an appeal to another court has its disadvantages, the main one being that it can take some time before the case can be listed for a hearing. Therefore the first recourse should always be to the magistrates' court itself to see whether the court can, or will, alter its own decision where there has been a mistake. The magistrates' power to alter their own decisions can be divided into three main sources: the mandatory requirement to set aside proceedings where the defendant was unaware of them, the inherent power to rectify mistakes until the court has completed its duty by finally disposing of a case (when the court is said to be functus officio) and the statutory power to rectify mistakes, which is available after conviction.

WHERE THE ACCUSED WAS UNAWARE OF THE PROCEEDINGS

It has already been described how in certain circumstances the magistrates may proceed to hear an information in the absence of the accused.[1] Although the requirement of the law regarding service of the

1 P 49, above.

summons may have been complied with and the conviction is otherwise valid, it can still happen that the accused is unaware of the hearing. For example, it is sufficient service of a summons for a summary offence that it is sent to the accused's address by recorded delivery service and is not returned marked 'gone away' etc, but service by this method is no guarantee that the accused has actually received the summons. In these circumstances he may avail himself of the provisions of section 14 of the Magistrates' Courts Act 1980, subsection (1) of which provides:

> . . . if
> (a) the accused, at any time during or after the trial, makes a statutory declaration that he did not know of the summons or the proceedings until a date specified in the declaration, being a date after the court has begun to try the information; and
> (b) within 21 days of that date the declaration is served on the clerk to the justices, . . .
>
> without prejudice to the validity of the information, the summons and all subsequent proceedings shall be void.

The statutory declaration[2] is not made on oath and can be simply a proforma completed by the accused which is sent by registered letter or recorded delivery to the justices' clerk. Although it is not made on oath, any deliberate falsification is caught by section 5 of the Perjury Act 1911 and carries a penalty of up to two years' imprisonment on indictment. The declaration can be made at any time during or after the trial (but not before), but must be served on the justices' clerk within 21 days of the accused becoming aware of the proceedings. So, a declaration can be made as much as a year or more after the trial if it is only then that the accused became aware of the proceedings, but once he has become aware of them he must serve the declaration within 21 days of his discovery. However, the accused may apply for permission to a court or a single magistrate to serve this declaration outside the 21-day period if he can show it was not reasonable for him to serve it within the specified period.

THE EFFECT OF A STATUTORY DECLARATION

Once a statutory declaration has been served, the original proceedings fall to the ground with the exception of the information. Accordingly a fresh summons may be issued and proceedings started over again even though by then it is outside the time limit for laying an information for a purely summary offence.

Although section 14 is not confined to proceedings for purely summary offences, in practice its use is confined to fairly trivial summary cases. More serious cases are usually instituted by the charge and bail procedure, and where a summons has proved ineffective a warrant would have been issued.

2 See Appendix A to this chapter.

After the statutory declaration has been received, the court must abandon proceedings already instituted and then issue a fresh summons according to the usual principles. Where the accused was unaware of the proceedings this is the course that he should adopt and not seek a writ of judicial review to quash the proceedings.[3]

The magistrates' power to rectify mistakes

The magistrates have an inherent power to rectify mistakes right up to the moment that the case is finally disposed of. This is because until that point they are still seized of the case and have not finally discharged their duty when they are said to be functus officio. At one time the law was very strict and when magistrates made an error which was recognised by all concerned, the only remedy was by way of a review in the High Court. To circumvent this unfortunate situation, the doctrine of functus officio (that is, the magistrates had not finally exhausted their powers and could correct their mistakes) was developed and extended to the position stated above.[4] However, there was one situation not covered, that was where the magistrates had announced sentence and thus it could fairly be said that they had disposed of the case. Although they could change a decision announced in court where there had been a slip of the tongue, they could not change the actual intended result. To remedy this deficiency and to put the matter beyond doubt, the magistrates' powers were put into statutory form in the precursor of section 142 of the Magistrates' Courts Act 1980, which provides as follows:

> (1) Subject to subsection (4) below, a magistrates' court may vary or rescind a sentence or other order imposed or made by it when dealing with an offender; and it is hereby declared that this power extends to replacing a sentence or order which for any reason appears to be invalid by another which the court has power to impose or make.
>
> (2) Where a person is found guilty by a magistrates' court in a case in which he has pleaded not guilty or the court has proceeded in his absence under section 11(1) above, and it subsequently appears to the court that it would be in the interests of justice that the case should be heard again by different justices, the court may, subject to subsection (4) below, so direct.
>
> (3) Where a court gives a direction under subsection (2) above –
>
> (a) the finding of guilty and any sentence or other order imposed or made in consequence thereof shall be of no effect; and
>
> (b) section 10(4) above shall apply as if the trial of the person in question had been adjourned.
>
> (4) The powers conferred by subsections (1) and (2) above shall be exercisable only within the period of 28 days beginning with the day on

3 *R v Brighton Justices, ex p Robinson* [1973] 1 WLR 69, [1973] Crim LR 53, DC.
4 *S (An Infant) v Recorder of Manchester* [1971] AC 481, [1969] 3 All ER 1230.

which the sentence or order was imposed or made or . . . the person was found guilty, as the case may be, and only –

(a) by a court constituted in the same manner as the court by which the sentence or order was imposed or made, or as the case may be, by which the person in question was found guilty, or

(b) where that court comprised 3 or more justices of the peace, by a court which consists of or comprises a majority of those justices.

(5) Where a sentence or order is varied under subsection (1) above, the sentence or other order, as so varied, shall take effect from the beginning of the day on which it was originally imposed or made, unless the court otherwise directs.

A general observation may be made about section 142 – it can only be used where the accused has been convicted, never when he has been acquitted.[5]

The section can be divided into two main parts: section 142(2) deals with the position where the accused has not admitted his guilt but has been found guilty after a trial and section 142(1) provides for the case where the defendant is guilty but the bench wish to reconsider sentence.

Section 142(2). It is important to note that the magistrates can only change their minds about the defendant's guilt where he has been convicted after evidence has been called either with the accused being present or in his absence. If the accused has pleaded guilty, then unless the plea was equivocal and in effect amounted to a plea of 'not guilty', the court cannot reopen the case and the defendant will remain convicted with the exception that the magistrates may allow him to change his plea up until they have sentenced him and are functus officio.

Section 142(1). This is the power to alter a sentence or order, eg for compensation. It is most commonly used where the court has passed a sentence which it could not lawfully pass such as imposing a fine above the statutory maximum.

Section 142 in practice

Section 142(2). When the court wishes to have a rehearing of the trial it is as if an ordinary trial were being adjourned, and accordingly notice must be served on both parties of the hearing date for the fresh trial. It should of course be remembered that this procedure is to be used where the accused has been convicted. If an irregularity has occurred in the course of the trial the magistrates may direct a fresh trial of their own motion at any time before conviction without recourse to section 142.

Section 142(1). Where the magistrates have passed sentence they may wish to change their minds about the sentence they have imposed. This may be because they have had second thoughts about the degree of culpability

5 *R v Gravesend Justices, ex p Dexter* [1977] Crim LR 298, DC.

of the accused or the suitability of his sentence, or more commonly because they have passed a sentence not authorised by law, for example a prison sentence in excess of their statutory powers.

Section 142 was enacted to deal with the situation where the magistrates made an obvious error which was quite plain and indisputable; it was not intended to allow a defendant to seek to persuade magistrates to change an otherwise lawful sentence. Therefore, it is submitted that a decision to change a lawful sentence should only come from a change of heart by the magistrates themselves. But where they have passed a sentence which can be shown to be unlawful then it is right for either party to point this out to the court. Notice of this fact should be sent to the court forthwith and if the court decides to exercise its own powers of review under section 142, it is submitted that notice of this, and a hearing date, should be given to both the defence and the prosecution. The defendant should be informed because he is the person most directly concerned by the decision, and his consent may be required if an alternative form of disposal is contemplated. Furthermore, it is suggested that he should be allowed to address the court again as the court may have proceeded on mistaken assumptions at the earlier hearing. The prosecutor should be informed if only for the practical reason of ensuring that the criminal records are amended as a result of an alteration made to the sentence.

The same bench must exercise the power to rescind or vary. The powers under this section can only be exercised by the bench constituted in the same way as that which adjudicated at the original hearing, or a majority of those adjudicating. The decision cannot be altered by another bench of magistrates even though they are from the same petty sessional division.

TIME LIMITS

The decision to order a retrial under section 142(2) or the varying of the sentence must take place within 28 days of the conviction or sentence as the case may be. Time starts to run from the date of the conviction or order.

For example:

If D is convicted on 1 June and sentenced on 8 June the bench may order a retrial at any time up to and including 28 June, and they may vary the sentence up to and including 5 July.

It should be noted that this power must actually be exercised inside this period; it is not sufficient for the clerk to the justices to notify the parties within time that the justices will hold a hearing to exercise the powers on a date outside the 28-day period.[6]

6 *Bradburn v Richards* [1976] RTR 275, [1976] Crim LR 62.

Appeals to the crown court

Where the accused is aggrieved by a decision of the magistrates' court, he has an unfettered right to challenge that decision at the Crown Court subject to the time limits restricting the right to appeal. Only the defendant may appeal, and he may appeal against conviction where he has pleaded not guilty, and against sentence whether he has pleaded guilty, or been found guilty. It is important to remember the right of appeal is unrestricted, and the appeal may be based on an allegation that the magistrates erred in law or acted contrary to the weight of the evidence, or simply imposed a sentence that was too heavy.

The principal statutory provisions regulating the right to appeal are contained in sections 108–110 (the right to appeal) and section 113 (bail on appeal) of the Magistrates' Courts Act 1980 and rule 74 of the Magistrates' Courts Rules 1981 and rule 7 of the Crown Court Rules 1982.

THE RIGHT TO APPEAL[7]

Section 108 of the Magistrates' Courts Act 1980 (as amended by section 66 of the Criminal Justice Act 1982)

> (1) A person convicted by a magistrates' court may appeal to the Crown Court –
> (a) if he pleaded guilty, against his sentence;
> (b) if he did not, against the conviction or sentence.
>
> (1A) Section 13 of the Powers of Criminal Courts Act 1973 (under which a conviction of an offence for which a probation order or an order for conditional or absolute discharge is made is deemed not to be a conviction except for certain purposes) shall not prevent an appeal under this section, whether against conviction or otherwise.
>
> (2) A person sentenced by a magistrates' court for an offence in respect of which a probation order or an order for conditional discharge has been previously made may appeal to the Crown Court against sentence.
>
> (3) In this section 'sentence' includes any order made on conviction by a magistrates' court, not being –
> (a) repealed;
> (b) an order for the payment of costs;
> (c) an order under section 2 of the Protection of Animals Act 1911 (which enables a court to order the destruction of an animal); or
> (d) an order made in pursuance of any enactment under which the court has no discretion as to the making of the order or its terms.

It can be seen that there is no appeal against the conviction where the defendant has pleaded guilty. However, the defendant can raise the matter of the equivocality of his plea in the magistrates' court at the

7 Apart from certain exceptions for convictions under particular statutes, the prosecution does not have a right of appeal to the Crown Court. For these exceptions see the footnote to the MCA 1980, s 108 in *Stone's*, Volume I.

Crown Court.[8] In this case the Crown Court should make a proper investigation of the proceedings before the magistrates before remitting the case to them.[9] For this purpose the Crown Court should obtain affidavits from the magistrates' court.[10] If the Crown Court is satisfied that the plea was equivocal it may then remit the case for a rehearing before the justices,[11] who may in their discretion allow the defendant to withdraw his consent to summary trial.[12]

THE NOTICE OF APPEAL[13]

If the accused has a right of appeal which he wishes to use, he should first draft his notice of appeal as this notice must be in writing. The notice of appeal should state whether the appeal is against conviction or sentence or both but it need not, in the normal run of crime or road traffic offences, state the grounds of appeal although it is common to specify general grounds such as that the conviction was against the weight of evidence or that the sentence was too severe.[14] A common form of appeal notice is contained in Appendix B to this chapter.

When the notice of appeal has been drafted it must be served on the clerk to the appropriate magistrates' court usually by leaving it at, or sending it to, the court office.[15] Only one copy need be served and this must be done within 21 days of the termination of the proceedings in the magistrates' court, ie where a conviction is announced and the case adjourned for a week for sentence, time to appeal against conviction will only run from the date when the accused is sentenced.[16]

EXTENSION OF TIME TO APPEAL[17]

If the notice has not been served in time, an application can be made to the Crown Court for leave to appeal out of time. The notice of appeal may be sent to the Crown Court in support of the application for leave to appeal out of time, and when leave is granted, then submitted to the magistrates' court, or it may be lodged directly with

8 *R v Durham Quarter Sessions, ex p Virgo* [1952] 2 QB 1, [1952] 1 All ER 466, Supreme Court Act 1981, s 48.
9 *R v Marylebone Justices, ex p Westminster City Council* [1971] 1 All ER 1025, [1971] 1 WLR 567.
10 *R v Rochdale Justices, ex p Allwork* [1981] 3 All ER 434, [1981] Crim LR 719. Cf (1980) 144 JP Jo 537.
11 *R v Tottenham Justices, ex p Rubens* [1970] 1 All ER 879, [1970] 1 WLR 800.
12 *R v Southampton Justices, ex p Briggs* [1972] 1 All ER 573, [1972] 1 WLR 277.
13 See Crown Court Rules 1982, r 7.
14 The grounds must be specified in the case of appeals under more specialised enactments such as betting and gaming, and liquor licensing. A full list is contained in Sch 3, Part III to the Crown Court Rules.
15 Crown Court Rules 1982, r 28.
16 Ibid, r 7(3).
17 Ibid, r 7(5).

the magistrates' court. The application for leave to appeal may be made in writing but the application should set out clearly why the appeal notice was not served in time, eg through a genuine mistake or that the solicitor had only just received instructions from a client who was unrepresented before the magistrates. If leave is granted, the Crown Court will inform the magistrates' court but the appellant should inform the respondent to the appeal that he has leave to appeal out of time.

PROCEDURE ONCE NOTICE OF APPEAL IS SERVED

When the notice has been served within the time allowed or, with leave, outside that period, the appeal is regarded as being under way. Therefore those provisions which are dependent on there being an appeal in existence come into play at that stage. Such provisions include the right to apply for bail pending appeal and the right to apply for legal aid.

When the notice of appeal is received by the clerk to the justices he must send to the Crown Court the notice of appeal and a statement of the decision appealed against together with a copy of any decision made as regards bail and, where the appeal is against conviction, any written admissions made by the defendant under section 10 of the Criminal Justice Act 1967 and any notes of evidence taken in the proceedings.[18] He must also inform the Crown Court of the names and addresses of the parties to the appeal. Where legal aid has been granted the clerk should supply a copy of the notes of evidence to the solicitor acting for the legally-aided party on request. A copy of any legal aid order and statement of means are sent to the Crown Court as well.[19]

The Crown Court, on receipt of the notice, will inform the magistrates' court and the two parties to the appeal of the date set aside for the hearing.[20] A defence solicitor may obtain an idea of the waiting period for an appeal to be heard by contacting the Crown Court. Where the defendant is in custody, he may expect an earlier hearing than, for example, a defendant appealing against the level of a fine as enforcement of the payment of the fine will be suspended pending the hearing of the appeal.

LEGAL AID

Legal aid is available for an appeal and may be granted by either the magistrates' court or the Crown Court.[1] When a notice of appeal has

18 Magistrates' Courts Rules 1981, r 74 and *Practice Note* [1956] 1 QB 451, [1956] 1 All ER 448.

19 Legal Aid in Criminal Proceedings (General) Regulations 1968, rr 16 and 17.

20 Crown Court Rules 1982, r 8.

1 Legal Aid Act 1974, s 28(5).

been served the appellant may submit an application for legal aid either to the magistrates' or the Crown Court together with a statement of means. The criteria for granting legal aid are the same as for proceedings in the magistrates' court but also taking into account the desirability of the defendant's being represented in the Crown Court and the increased cost of being legally represented there.[2]

BAIL PENDING APPEAL

Once a valid notice has been served the accused, if he has received a custodial sentence, may apply for bail during the period until his appeal is heard at the Crown Court. The application may be made either to the Crown Court, the magistrates' court or the High Court.[3] The usual practice is to make the application to the Crown Court or the magistrates' court. An application may be made by contacting the court and making the request for the hearing and at the same time giving the prosecutor notice of the appellant's intentions.

APPLICATION TO THE CROWN COURT FOR BAIL

Where the application is to the Crown Court for bail the procedure is governed by rules 19 and 20 of the Crown Court Rules 1982.

An accused or his solicitor should contact the Crown Court and arrange a hearing which should be at least 24 hours ahead. When the hearing is arranged the accused should inform the prosecutor of his intentions to apply for bail by sending him a notice (see Appendix C to this chapter) as the prosecutor may wish to be present or send in written reasons for his objection to bail. A copy of the notice to apply for bail should also be sent to the Crown Court. Although as a general rule the accused is not entitled to be present at his bail application without the leave of the court, in practice legal aid will probably have been granted and he will be represented by a solicitor. In certain circumstances the Official Solicitor may be assigned to represent an accused instead. An application for bail will be heard in chambers and at the application the appellant's solicitor must inform the judge of any previous applications to the High Court or Crown Court.

A similar procedure will apply where it is the prosecutor who wishes to make an application to the Crown Court to vary or impose conditions of bail under section 3(8) of the Bail Act 1976, with the necessary modifications.[4]

THE DECISION TO GRANT BAIL PENDING APPEAL

Although the general provisions of the Bail Act 1976 apply, section 4 (the general presumption of a right to bail) does not. If an accused has received a

2 See ch 4 generally for legal aid.
3 Supreme Court Act 1981, s 81; MCA 1980, s 113; Criminal Justice Act 1967, s 22.
4 See also Crown Court Rules 1982, r 19.

custodial sentence, it would be unusual to grant him bail pending the appeal being heard. The general position is that the court will not grant bail unless there are exceptional circumstances which would force the court to conclude that justice could only be done by granting the appellant bail.[5] There are, it is submitted, two basic principles:
(a) the court dealing with the bail application should not fetter the court which eventually has to hear the appeal. It is hard on an appellant to be released on bail pending an appeal and then to be returned to custody. The appeal court would be quite prepared to do this where appropriate, nevertheless it should not generally be placed in this invidious position;[6]
(b) where the sentence is clearly appropriate to the offence then personal matters which are the basis for an appeal for clemency should not influence the court considering the bail application.[7]

Accordingly, the court considering the bail application is mainly concerned with whether the sentence imposed was unreasonable, it is not concerned with whether it would have imposed the same sentence.

An example of where bail was granted exceptionally was *R v Neville*[8] where the defendant had no previous convictions and there would be a delay before the appeal was heard so that he might serve his sentence before the appeal was heard, and also the sentence was more severe than usual. But the normal remedy where the accused appeals against a custodial sentence, especially a short one, is an expedited appeal hearing.

THE HEARING IN THE CROWN COURT

An appeal against conviction takes the form of a complete rehearing and the order of speeches and the calling of evidence takes the same form as in a summary trial. The prosecutor (not the appellant) begins first and the appellant makes the final closing speech. Similarly in an appeal against sentence, the prosecution outlines the case, then mitigation is heard and sentence pronounced. The hearing takes place before a judge and one or two justices who take a full part in the decision and may out vote the judge.

There are certain features of this rehearing that should be borne in mind:

(a) The prosecution cannot amend the information at the appellate stage[9] although the court can exercise the power which the

5 *R v Watton* (1978) 68 Cr App Rep 293, [1979] Crim LR 246, CA.
6 *R v Lancastle* [1978] Crim LR 367, CA.
7 *R v Priddle* [1981] Crim LR 114, CA.
8 [1971] Crim LR 589, CA.
9 *Meek v Powell* [1952] 1 KB 164, [1952] 1 All ER 347; *Garfield v Maddocks* [1974] QB 7, [1973] 2 All ER 303.

magistrates have to reduce a charge of reckless driving to careless driving.[10] Apart from this exception, the Crown Court cannot substitute a conviction for another offence.[11]

(b) The same rules regarding the right of the accused to make representations on separate trials of separate informations apply to the hearing of an appeal.[12]

(c) Because the appeal is a complete rehearing, the Crown Court should take no account of the decison in the magistrates' court.[13] Unfortunately for the appellant, this does mean that the Crown Court is at liberty to increase the sentence if it wishes, though only up to the limit of the magistrates' powers.

COSTS

On hearing the appeal the Crown Court may make such orders regarding the costs of the parties as it considers just.[14]

Where the appeal is concerning an indictable offence the prosecution may always have its costs from central funds. The defence may only have its costs from central funds if the appeal is against conviction (but not where the appeal is only against sentence) and the appeal is successful.[15] The Crown Court may also make an order regarding costs in the court below. As regards costs between the parties, the Crown Court may order costs to be paid by one party to another as it thinks just[16] although it would be exceptional to order the prosecution to pay the defence costs.

For an accused contemplating an appeal the question of costs must loom large and in many cases, especially where he is not legally aided, an appeal becomes very much a question of judicial double or quits.

ABANDONING AN APPEAL[17]

An appeal may be abandoned by giving notice in writing not later than the third day before the hearing of the appeal. If the appeal is to be abandoned any closer to the hearing, then the leave of the Crown Court must be sought. The notice must be served on the Crown Court, the other party to the appeal and the clerk of the appropriate magistrates' court.

If the appeal is abandoned without leave being required the question of

10 *Killington v Butcher* [1979] Crim LR 458, (1979) 123 Sol Jo 320, DC.

11 *Lawrence v Same* [1968] 2 QB 93, [1968] 1 All ER 1191.

12 *Sedwell v James* [1980] Crim LR 110, Reading Crown Court and see now *Clayton v Chief Constable of Norfolk* [1983] 1 All ER 984, [1983] 2 WLR 555.

13 *R v Justices for the Court of Quarter Sessions for the County of Leicester, ex p Gilks* [1966] Crim LR 613, DC.

14 Crown Court Rules 1982, r 12.

15 Costs in Criminal Cases Act 1973, s 3.

16 Crown Court Rules 1982, rr 12 and 13.

17 Ibid, rr 11, 12(2), (5) and (6) and MCA 1980, s 109.

costs thrown away by the respondent to the appeal will be decided by the magistrates' court, if indeed the respondent (usually the police) raises the matter at all. If the respondent does seek his costs, the magistrates may order the appellant to pay the just and reasonable expenses incurred by him in resisting the appeal. Where the leave of the Crown Court has been required, the Crown Court will determine what costs should be paid.

PREPARING A CASE FOR APPEAL IN THE CROWN COURT

Although solicitors do have a right of audience in the Crown Court on an appeal from a case in which their firm appeared in the magistrates' court,[18] most solicitors prefer to brief counsel either because of unfamiliarity with that tribunal or because periodic appearances in the Crown Court would interrupt their regular business in the magistrates' court.

An appeal in these circumstances will be a complete rehearing and so similar preparations must be made to those for the original hearing. If the appeal is against conviction, for example, the same witnesses may be called again but unlike at the original hearing the defence will have knowledge of the prosecution case.

The backsheet of the brief will describe the nature of the proceedings, ie appeal to the Borchester Crown Court against the conviction by the Borchester Magistrates of the appellant of an offence of theft, and will be marked legal aid or have a fee stated on it. The brief should refer to the enclosures in it such as:

original charge sheet,
certificate of conviction,
record of previous convictions,
notice of appeal,
proofs of defence evidence,
notes of prosecution evidence given at the trial.

As well as giving a general description of the case, the instructing solicitor may well be able to give counsel helpful information about the original hearing: were there any legal problems, or were there any matters of interest which arose in cross-examination?

When the case has been listed for hearing, the solicitor will be 'warned' that the case is due for hearing and he should ensure that his witnesses will be available when the case is set down for hearing.

Appeals to the High Court

CASE STATED AND PREROGATIVE ORDERS

Strictly speaking the title to this section of the chapter is incorrect as an application for a prerogative order is not an appeal. Nevertheless, it is

18 Practice Direction (Crown Court) [1972] 1 All ER 144 and 608 and see Supreme Court Act 1981, s 83.

convenient to deal with them together if for no other reason than that in practice it is often difficult to decide which is the more appropriate remedy to use. Both an application for a prerogative order and an appeal by way of case stated are made to the Queen's Bench Division of the High Court.

Appeals by way of case stated

Section 111(1) of the Magistrates' Courts Act 1980 provides:

> Any person who was a party to any proceedings before a magistrates' court or is aggrieved by the conviction, order, determination or other proceeding of the court may question the proceeding on the ground that it is wrong in law or in excess of jurisdiction by applying to the justices composing the court to state a case for the opinion of the High Court on the question of law or jurisdiction involved . . . .

The section seems quite clear: it gives either party to the proceeding (both prosecutor and defendant) the right to appeal to the High Court where his grievance against the decision of the magistrates is that they have erred in their application of the law or have exceeded their jurisdiction. An appeal cannot lie under these provisions where the party is aggrieved because the magistrates have made an adverse finding of fact. For example a defendant may have been charged with the theft of a bottle of milk. In his evidence he may have said that he took the bottle in the belief that the owner would have consented if he had known of the circumstances of the taking. If the magistrates convicted him because they did not believe him and found that he knew the owner would not have consented, the defendant could not challenge the conviction by way of case stated, he would have to appeal to the Crown Court. However, if the magistrates convicted him because, although they believed his evidence and found as a fact that he was not dishonest, they concluded that the offence of theft did not require an element of dishonesty, they would clearly have erred in law. If it was legally doubtful whether dishonesty was an essential element of the offence, the most appropriate remedy would be an appeal by way of case stated so that the authoritative opinion of the High Court could be obtained on the point of law in issue.

In order to give its opinion on the law, the High Court must be provided with a set of facts to formulate its opinion of the law. As will be seen, the proceedings in the Divisional Court are concerned exclusively with matters of law, the facts are provided by affidavits or the case stated. No witnesses are called or cross-examined. Accordingly a case stated is only appropriate where the facts are not in dispute and the only issue is one of law.

The prerogative order

The High Court has a general supervisory jurisdiction over inferior tribunals to ensure that justice is done. This is referred to as judicial review. The purpose of the prerogative order is to ensure that the magistrates' court has followed the rules of procedure and natural justice. It is not so much concerned with the result arrived at by the magistrates, rather with the way in which the decision was reached.

The judicial review of the magistrates' decision can take one of three forms: correcting the error that has been made (certiorari), compelling the magistrates to do their duty (mandamus) and forbidding the magistrates from exceeding their jurisdiction (prohibition).

The first principle governing the use of this power is that its exercise is purely a matter of discretion and it will be refused where there has been undue delay,[19] or where an appeal or action under section 142 of the Magistrates' Courts Act 1980 would be more appropriate.[20] Second, the proceedings in the lower court should be allowed to run their course as the procedure for judicial review depends on evidence in the form of agreed facts in the affidavits. Therefore it would be wrong, for example, to adjourn a trial for judicial review of a decision to treat certain evidence as inadmissible.[1] Third, the High Court will not consider a hypothetical point, eg where subsequent events have overtaken the original decision.[2]

Here are some examples where judicial review might be appropriate:

(a) Breach of natural justice. Where the defendant is denied a closing speech[3] or the clerk tries to influence the decision of the magistrates.[4]

(b) Error of law. Judicial review might be appropriate where the magistrates have erred in applying a point of law which is agreed by the prosecution and the defence, so that an appeal by way of case stated to ascertain the High Court's opinion of the law would be inappropriate. In the example of the theft of a bottle of milk that was mentioned earlier, there would be in reality no question that dishonesty was an essential element of theft. If the magistrates perversely insisted that it was not, then the most appropriate remedy would be judicial review.

(c) Excess of jurisdiction. The magistrates' court may have done something in excess of its powers, for example imposing a fine above the statutory maximum. A review by the justices themselves under

19 *R v Leeds Justices, ex p Hanson* [1981] QB 892, at 907, [1981] 3 All ER 72 at 82 b.
20 *R v Brighton Justices, ex p Robinson* [1973] 1 WLR 69, [1973] Crim LR 53.
1 *R v Rochford Justices, ex p Buck* (1978) 68 Cr App Rep 114, [1978] Crim LR 492, DC.
2 *R v Rees, ex p Bull* [1963] Crim LR 638, (1963) 107 Sol Jo 556, DC (challenge to issue of search warrant rendered pointless by the intervening execution of the warrant).
3 *R v Horseferry Road Stipendiary Magistrate, ex p Adams* [1977] 1 WLR 1197, [1977] Crim LR 482, DC.
4 *R v Stafford Borough Justices, ex p Ross* [1962] 1 All ER 540, [1962] 1 WLR 456.

section 142 would be more appropriate, but if this is not available the High Court can intervene and substitute a more appropriate sentence.[5]

PROCEDURE ON AN APPLICATION TO THE HIGH COURT

Prerogative order

Only a skeletal outline of the procedure will be given here where a prerogative order is sought. The general procedure is contained in Order 53 of the Rules of the Supreme Court (contained in volume III of *Stone's*).

The first step is to apply for leave to apply for judicial review by filing a completed form 86A in the Crown Office at the Royal Courts in the Strand together with an affidavit setting out the facts. The application will be considered by a single judge with or without a hearing, and in criminal matters the applicant may renew his application for leave to a full court of the Queen's Bench Division if leave is refused by the single judge.

Once leave has been granted, the proceedings commence by way of a notice of motion (similar to a summons) which must be served on all the parties directly affected together with a copy of the form 86A setting out the relief claimed and, if requested, a copy of the affidavit in support. The other parties may then in their turn file affidavits for the hearing.

Case stated

This is of more direct concern to the magistrates because application is made to the justices themselves to state a case. The procedure is set out in the Magistrates' Courts Act 1980, sections 111–114 and the Magistrates' Courts Rules 1981, rules 76–81 and the Rules of the Supreme Court, Order 56.

The applicant should make his request in writing to the clerk of the appropriate magistrates' court and should identify the point of law on which he wants the opinion of the High Court. The application must be made within 21 days of the decision appealed against and the date of the decision in criminal proceedings is taken to be the date of sentence.[6] This time limit is mandatory in that a notice must be served within that period.[7] However, if a notice is served in time but is found to be defective, it may in certain circumstances be corrected outside that period. The usual defect in an application is a failure to identify the point of law involved. If it is not possible to identify the point of law in issue from the notice and it is not corrected within 21 days, then the appellant's application must fail *in limine*, but if it is clear what question

5 Supreme Court Act 1981, s 43.
6 Magistrates' Courts Rules 1981, r 76.
7 *Michael v Gowland* [1977] 2 All ER 328, [1977] 1 WLR 296.

the appellant is trying to ask although it is not phrased felicitously and it can be said that there is substantial compliance with the rules, the notice may be amended even outside the 21-day period.[8]

When the application is received, the justices may either state a case or refuse to do so on the ground that the application is frivolous. If they refuse to state a case their decision may be challenged by judicial review,[9] otherwise the clerk must send a draft case to the parties within 21 days of the receipt of the application. They in turn make representations in writing to the clerk within a further 21 days and then the final case is prepared and signed.[10] In fact although it is the justices who state a case, the actual case will be drafted by the clerk.

At any time before the case is finally submitted to the High Court, the magistrates can require an appellant to enter into recognizances to prosecute the appeal because if he abandons the appeal, he may prejudice the respondent with regard to any costs thrown away.[11] Once the appellant has received the case stated, the procedure he should adopt will be found in Order 56 of the Rules of the Supreme Court.

THE CONTENT OF THE CASE

The case stated procedure is essentially one for obtaining the decision of the High Court on a point of law. It is not an appeal on the facts. The High Court needs to be presented with a set of facts found by the magistrates upon which the High Court can base its conclusions on the law. Therefore there should be no reciting of the evidence in the case, only the conclusions which the magistrates arrived at after hearing the evidence.[12]

The precedent for drafting a case stated set out in *Stone's*, Volume III has received judicial approval in the *Croydon Justices'*[13] case and in the appendix to this chapter will be found the case stated in *Bennett v Richardson*, the drafting of which was commended by the Lord Chief Justice.[14]

8 *R v Croydon Justices, ex p Lefore Holdings Ltd* [1981] 1 All ER 520, [1980] 1 WLR 1465.
9 MCA 1980, s 111(6).
10 In certain circumstances these time limits may be extended, Magistrates' Courts Rules 1981, r 79.
11 MCA 1980, s 114.
12 There is an exception of course when the point of law involved is that there was in law insufficient evidence to support the finding of fact made by the magistrates. Here the evidence relied on to make the finding must be stated. However, it must be remembered that the findings of fact can only be challenged on the basis that in *law* there was insufficient evidence, ie that no reasonable court could have made that finding of fact based on that evidence.
13 *R v Croydon Justices, ex p Lefore Holdings Ltd* [1981] 1 All ER 520, [1980] 1 WLR 1465.
14 [1980] RTR 358. I am obliged to Mr David Speed, the clerk in the case, and to the justices concerned, for supplying me with a copy of the case stated, which is reproduced in Appendix D to this chapter.

The relationship between the various forms of redress

Where circumstances permit, a defendant should use the provisions of the Magistrates' Courts Act 1980, section 14 to make the proceedings void, as once the defendant has made his declaration, it is mandatory for the proceedings to start over again. If proceedings have been concluded and an error occurs which is quite apparent and beyond dispute, the magistrates should consider using their powers under section 142 to rectify the situation, but where the magistrates' court cannot be said to have erred fundamentally but the defendant's view of what should have been decided differs from that of the magistrates, he should appeal to the Crown Court for a rehearing. However, if there is a pure point of law in issue where an appeal to the Crown Court would still not satisfy the parties, then an appeal by way of case stated is the appropriate remedy but where an appellant makes an application for a case stated he loses his right to appeal to the Crown Court. There may be an appeal by way of case stated from the Crown Court in a similar manner to an appeal by way of case stated from a decision of the magistrates' court.[15]

Finally, where the procedure adopted by the magistrates is challenged as being fundamentally defective and they cannot or will not remedy the defect, a review of the proceedings by the High Court may be appropriate in order to have the offending proceedings quashed.

Case stated and judicial review

The relationship between these two forms of redress is very difficult to describe. A clue is given by the nature of the hearing in the High Court. The evidence is given in the form of affidavits and so there is no scope for a conflict of evidence. Where a person is aggrieved with the finding of fact he must appeal to the Crown Court. The only occasion when a finding of fact could be disputed in the High Court is when it is argued as a matter of law that there was insufficient evidence for a reasonable tribunal to make the finding of fact which is in dispute. Even if the facts are not in dispute, case stated will be the more appropriate remedy where the facts are complicated as the justices themselves will prepare a list of the facts which they found in the case itself, whereas for judicial review the parties themselves are responsible for preparing their own affidavits without any contribution from the magistrates' court.[16]

15 Supreme Court Act 1981, s 28. Formerly where a conviction was not involved it was in the discretion of the Crown Court whether to state a case. The appellant should beware that as soon as he applies for a case to be stated by the magistrates he loses all rights to appeal to the Crown Court: *R v Winchester Crown Court, ex p Lewington* [1982] Crim LR 664.

16 *R v Ipswich Crown Court, ex p Baldwin (Note)* [1981] 1 All ER 596, (1981) 72 Cr App Rep 131.

Although both case stated and judicial review are concerned with matters of law rather than fact, a case stated deals with 'textbook' law ie pure matters of legal principle. Judicial review on the other hand deals with how the court conducted itself: have the magistrates acted in accordance with natural justice by, for example, allowing a prosecutor the chance to prove his case instead of simply dismissing a case without hearing him?[17] However, the boundaries can be, and often are, blurred. Mandamus might be ordered where the bench have not issued a summons because they feel they do not have jurisdiction but it might also be appropriate to have a case stated at the conclusion of the case where the issue is one of jurisdiction, such as where an offence of blackmail is committed where the letter containing the demand is posted in England to someone living abroad.[18]

There are cases where the High Court has commented that the appellant has used the wrong procedure but nevertheless the court has gone on to hear the appeal and made the best it could of the situation, and so the alternative procedures do not seem to be mutually exclusive.[19]

The effect of a case stated

On hearing a case stated the High Court may:

> reverse, affirm, or amend the determination in respect of which the case has been stated, or remit the matter to the justices, with the opinion of the court thereon, or make such other order in relation to the matter, and may make such orders as to costs as to the court may seem fit . . . .[20]

The effect of judicial review

Orders of mandamus and prohibition are fairly clear in their application. The former directs the justices to do something, eg issue a summons, and the latter directs them to refrain from acting any further. The effect of certiorari is normally to quash a decision, this follows from the nature of the proceedings. Certiorari is usually

17 *R v Birmingham Justices, ex p Lamb* [1983] 3 All ER 23, [1983] 1 WLR 339.

18 On this point cf cases such as *Treacy v DPP* [1971] AC 537, [1971] 1 All ER 110; and *R v Baxter* [1972] QB 1, [1971] 2 All ER 359.

19 *R v Ipswich Crown Court*, n 16, above; and *Rigby v Woodward* [1957] 1 All ER 391, [1957] 1 WLR 250 where the accused appealed by way of case stated because he was not allowed to cross-examine a co-accused who had given evidence against him. Although the Divisional Court entertained the appeal, it was said obiter that the appeal should really have been an application for judicial review (presumably because the principle of law involved was beyond dispute; it was the justices' application of that principle that was challenged).

20 Summary Jurisdiction Act 1857, s 6. It is generally held, on the authority of *Rigby v Woodward*, above, that there is no power to order a retrial but it can be argued from that case that there is nothing in principle to prevent the Divisional Court ordering a retrial, it was only the impracticability of obtaining the witnesses which did prevent it in the case before the court.

appropriate when the appellant is aggrieved with the way a case has been conducted, and with its outcome. If the case has been so badly handled that certiorari is necessary the result is in effect a nullity, and is quashed. But this is not necessarily always the result. By statute the court, when dealing with an application where the magistrates have imposed an improper sentence, eg a sentence in excess of the maximum, instead of quashing the sentence entirely may substitute an appropriate penalty. Where the decision has been quashed by certiorari the High Court may remit the matter with a direction to the magistrates to reconsider it and reach a decision in accordance with the findings of the High Court.[1]

The prosecution

Unusually, the prosecution has a right of appeal by way of case stated and a right to apply for judicial review, even where the defendant has been acquitted.[2]

1 Supreme Court Act 1981, s 31(5).

2 Where the accused had appealed to the Crown Court against conviction and his appeal was successful because he caused perjured evidence to be given, certiorari was issued to quash the decision of the Crown Court leaving the defendant still convicted by the magistrates. But generally judicial review will not lie to quash an acquittal as this would be deemed to subject the defendant to double jeopardy. Cf *R v Crown Court at Wolverhampton, ex p Crofts* [1982] 3 All ER 702, [1983] 1 WLR 204, and see *R v Dorking Justices, ex p Harrington* [1983] 3 All ER 29.

Appendix A

Statutory declaration

I, of in the (County) of
do solemnly and sincerely declare that: [Insert the details of the declaration: the nature of the proceedings, and when the declarant first became aware of them]

And I make this solemn declaration, conscientiously believing the same to be true, and by virtue of the provisions of the Statutory Declarations Act 1835.

Declared at , in the County of , this day of , 19 , before me, one of Her Majesty's Justices of the Peace in and for the said (County) of

Justice of the Peace

Appendix B

IN THE COUNTY OF
To the Clerk of the Magistrates' Court sitting at in the said County
TAKE NOTICE THAT I,
of
intend to appeal to the next practicable Crown Court in and for the said County against (The sentence imposed on) a certain conviction of me by the Magistrates' Court aforesaid, on the day of 19 , for that I, on the day of 19 , at
in the said County did

and that the general grounds of my appeal are:

and that (I am not guilty of the said offence)
(My sentence was too severe)
I HEREBY APPLY for (bail the names and addresses of my sureties are shown overleaf) (the suspension of the driving disqualification imposed on the day of 19) pending the determination of the appeal.
Dated the day of 19
Appellant's signature

Notice of Appeal/
Application for bail/
Suspension of driving
disqualification
pending the Appeal.

Appendix C

Form of notice of application relating to bail in the crown court

Take notice that an application relating to bail will be made to the Crown Court
at
on at a.m./p.m.
on behalf of the defendant/appellant/prosecutor/ respondent.

Name of defendant/appellant: Crown Court No.
(Block letters)

Solicitor for the *Applicant:*
Address:

If defendant/appellant is in custody:
state place of detention and
give Prison No. if applicable

State particulars of proceedings
during which defendant/appellant
was committed to custody or
bailed [un]conditionally:

Enter details of any relevant previous
applications for bail or variation of conditions of bail:

Nature and grounds of application:
(State fully facts relied on and list previous convictions (if any). Give details of any proposed sureties and answer any objections raised previously):

Notes
The appropriate officer of the Crown Court should be consulted about the time and place of the hearing before this notice is sent to the other party to the application.
A copy of this notice should be sent to the Crown Court.

Appendix D

IN THE HIGH COURT OF JUSTICE QUEEN'S BENCH DIVISION

BETWEEN	CLIVE BENNETT	APPELLANT
	AND	
	ROY RICHARDSON	RESPONDENT

Case stated by Justices for the County of Nottingham in respect of their adjudication as a Magistrates' Court sitting at the Shire Hall, Nottingham.

CASE

1. On the 19th day of August, 1977 an information was preferred by the appellant against the respondent that he, on the 23rd day of May, 1977 at Loughborough Road, Ruddington did unlawfully,

(a) Use a motor vehicle, the braking system not maintained in good and efficient order, and properly adjusted.
Section 40(5) Road Traffic Acts 1972 and 1974 and Motor Vehicles (Construction and Use) Regulations 1973 Regulation 94(1).

(b) Use a motor vehicle, the steering gear fitted thereto not being maintained in good and efficient working order.
Section 40(5) Road Traffic Acts 1972 and 1974 and Motor Vehicles (Construction and Use) Regulations 1973 Regulation 95(1).

(c) Use a motor vehicle, the rear suspension of which was in such condition that danger was likely to be caused.
Section 40(5) Road Traffic Acts 1972 and 1974 and Motor Vehicles (Construction and Use) Regulations 1973 Regulation 90(1).

(d) Use a motor vehicle with defective windscreen washers.
Section 40(5) Road Traffic Acts 1972 and 1974 and Motor Vehicles (Construction and Use) Regulations 1973 Regulation 26(1).

(e) Use a motor vehicle, there not being in force in relation to the user of the vehicle by the respondent, such policy of insurance as the law requires.
Section 143 Road Traffic Acts 1972 and 1974.

2. We heard the said information on the 25th day of November, 1977 and found the following facts:

(a) Bedford 10 cwt Ice Cream Van registration number 776 VHT, was stopped by a police officer on the A60 road at Ruddington on 23rd May, 1977.

(b) The driver of the vehicle was one John Diuk.

(c) The respondent, Roy Richardson, was a passenger in the back of the vehicle.

(d) The respondent's part in the business venture was to help serve and to keep the van clean.

(e) The van in question was on hire from one Sansom.

(f) John Diuk and Roy Richardson were partners, and both were equally liable under the hire terms.

(g) The vehicle was being used on partnership business.

(h) The defendant was a registered blind person.

3. It was contended by the appellant that the respondent was guilty of using the said vehicle within the meaning of the Road Traffic Acts, 1972 and 1974, Section 40(5) and Section 143.

4. It was contended by the respondent that a partner in a partnership could only be convicted of using a vehicle owned by the partnership within the meaning of the Road Traffic Acts 1972 and 1974, where that partner was driving the vehicle.

It was further contended that as a blind person, the respondent could in no way control the movements of the vehicle, and could not therefore be said to be using the vehicle.

5. We were referred to the following cases:

Crawford v Haughton [1972] RTR 125.

Garrett v Hooper [1973] RTR 1.

Cobb v Williams [1973] RTR 113.

6. We were of the opinion that the general principle laid down by Lord Parker CJ in *Carmichael & Sons (Worcester) Ltd v Cottle* [1971] RTR 11, and adopted by Lord Widgery CJ in *Crawford v Haughton* applied, namely,

> 'It has long been held that, when the offence is not merely an offence of user, but can be an offence of causing or permitting the user, a restricted meaning should be given to 'use' . . .'

We were confirmed in this view by a further dictum of Lord Parker CJ in *Windle v Dunning & Son Ltd* [1968] 2 All ER 46 cited with approval by Lord Widgery CJ in *Garrett v Hooper*.

> '. . . in my judgement 'using' when used in connection with causing and permitting has a restricted meaning. It certainly covers the driver; it may also cover the driver's employer if he, the driver, is about his master's business, but beyond that I find it very difficult to conceive that any other person could be said to be using the vehicle as opposed to causing it to be used'.

In the case before us the defendant could have been summoned for 'causing' or 'permitting' the user of the vehicle with each of the alleged defects. As the defendant was simply summoned for 'using' the vehicle, we felt constrained to follow the general principle outlined above.

The case of *Garrett v Hooper* in our opinion adds further weight to the contention that the word 'use' has a restricted meaning, and does not extend to a co-partner, where his partner is driving the vehicle.

> 'a co-partner does not use a vehicle merely because it is driven by his partner on partnership business'.
> Lord Widgery CJ.

It was argued before us by the appellant that the respondent could be convicted of 'using' the vehicle on the authority of *Cobb v Williams*. We were of the opinion that this case was a narrow exception to the general rule as explained in *Crawford v Haughton*, and applied only in the situation where . . .

> '. . . the owner was in the car, and he was in the car because he wanted to make a journey, and the car was being used in order that he might make that journey'. Lord Widgery CJ *Cobb v Williams*, page 115D.

In the light of the decisions in *Crawford v Haughton* and *Garrett v Hooper* we were of the opinion that a partner, being a passenger in a van hired for partnership business and being driven by a co-partner on partnership business, could not be convicted of 'using' a vehicle with certain defects within the meaning of the Road Trafic Acts 1972 and 1974, Section 40(5) and Section 143.

We were further of the opinion that the respondent's blindness and, therefore, his inability to control the movement of the van was irrelevant. We based this opinion on the fact that a company, an inanimate object, can be convicted of using a vehicle with certain defects.

7. The question for the opinion of the High Court is whether having regard to the decision in *Cobb v Williams* a partner, being a passenger, in a motor vehicle hired by the partnership and being driven on a road on partnership business by a co-partner, was using the vehicle within the meaning of Section 143 and Section 40(5) Road Trafic Acts 1972 and 1974, and regulations relating to the braking system, steering gear, parts and accessories and windscreen washers.

Dated the day of 19

Justice of the Peace for the County aforesaid, on behalf of the Justices adjudicating.

Signed on behalf of the above mentioned Justices at their direction.

Justices' Clerk for the Petty Sessional Division of

Chapter 10

Committal proceedings[1]

Introductory

THE NATURE OF COMMITTAL PROCEEDINGS

Earlier chapters have described how offences may be divided into three categories: purely indictable, either way and purely summary offences. All the categories of offences are heard first in the magistrates' court but not all offences proceed to a trial before the justices. When a defendant is apprehended for an offence and is not released on bail by the police, he must be brought before the magistrates to determine whether he should be given his liberty in the intervening period before the case is prepared for trial. This is so, no matter how serious the charge, eg murder.

However, in the case of a purely indictable offence there is no question of a trial of the defendant's guilt by the magistrates, nor can there be a summary trial of an either way offence where the magistrates have declined to accept jurisdiction or a law officer of the Crown has requested trial on indictment. In these examples it might be thought that the magistrates simply pass the case papers over to the local Crown Court and remand the defendant there to face his trial. In fact this 'handing over' process is formalised into committal proceedings, the formal process of transferring proceedings against an accused from the magistrates' court to the Crown Court.

WHY HAVE COMMITTAL PROCEEDINGS?

Originally, the justices of the peace were more involved in the investigation of offences and the apprehension of criminals than they are now when their function is to decide judicially on the evidence presented to them by the prosecution. The committal proceedings were part of this process of collecting evidence. Today, committal proceedings serve as a form of 'filter' to prevent hopeless cases reaching the Crown Court, so saving the time and expense involved in a trial on indictment and also to avoid unnecessary suffering to the accused. In addition, the committal proceedings enable the defence to have

1 See MCA 1980, ss 4–8; Magistrates' Courts Rules 1981, rr 5–11.

advance notice of the case it will have to meet as the prosecution must either produce its witnesses to give oral evidence or serve the evidence on the defence in the form of statements. The hearing at which the decision is made to transfer proceedings to the Crown Court is known as 'the committal' or 'committal proceedings' with a view to 'committal for trial'. 'Trial' in this context covers all the proceedings at the Crown Court whether there is to be a plea of not guilty and a trial by judge and jury, or a plea of guilty at the Crown Court and sentencing by the judge alone.

When should the magistrates commit for trial?

The purpose of committal proceedings is to inquire into the evidence of the prosecution, and the magistrates when dealing with committal proceedings are referred to as examining justices. They examine the prosecution case to decide whether there is sufficient evidence to put the defendant on trial by jury.[2] The sole test for the justices to apply is whether the prosecution has adduced sufficient evidence to satisfy them that there is a triable issue to be put before a jury

The form of committal proceedings

Committal proceedings are similar in form to a summary trial though with modifications as there are two types of procedure, the 'long committal' and the 'short committal'.

In a long committal the prosecutor may make an opening speech and call his witnesses who may be cross-examined by the defence. Then the defence may call evidence, be cross-examined, and make a closing speech. However, it must always be remembered that the purpose of committal proceedings is not to try the accused's guilt or innocence but to test the weight of the evidence against him. Accordingly, in practice, the defence tends to adopt a more passive role than in a summary trial.

Committal proceedings are required for all offences, either purely indictable or either way, which are to be heard at the Crown Court. This is so even where the accused is going to plead guilty or where he admits there is a prima facie case against him. Obviously in these circumstances it would be a waste of time to have a full committal hearing where the outcome of those proceedings would be a foregone conclusion. Consequently there is the shorter form of committal available at the option of the defence.

2 MCA 1980, s 6(1); *R v Carden* (1879) 5 QBD 1; *R v Epping and Harlow Justices, ex p Massaro* [1973] 1 QB 433, [1973] 1 All ER 1011.

The two forms of committal are known as the 'long' committal or the 'short' committal or by their section numbers in the Magistrates' Courts Act 1980: section 6(1) and 6(2) respectively. Occasionally, the long committal is also known as an 'old style' committal as the short committal was only introduced in 1967.

General provisions concerning committal proceedings

WHEN DO COMMITTAL PROCEEDINGS START?

In the case of a purely indictable offence the only jurisdiction which the magistrates have apart from the power to issue a warrant or summons, is that of examining justices, so that committal proceedings start in effect with the first appearance of the accused before the court. In the case of an either way offence, committal proceedings will not start until either the magistrates have declined to accept jurisdiction or the accused has elected to be tried on indictment.[3]

THE HEARING

The committal proceedings may take place before only one magistrate, but any hearing must take place in open court unless for any part, or the whole of the proceedings, the ends of justice would not be served by having a sitting in open court. Any evidence given before the examining justices shall be in the presence of the accused unless his disorderly conduct has made it impracticable for him to remain in court, or he is ill and is represented by an advocate and has consented to the evidence being given in his absence.[4]

PUBLICITY

There are very important restrictions imposed on the press reporting (or broadcasting) of any committal proceedings which will apply automatically unless an application is made to lift those restrictions.[5] The restrictions are that only the following matters may be contained in any report of committal proceedings:

(a) the identity of the court and the names of the examining justices;
(b) the names, addresses and occupations of the parties and witnesses and the ages of the accused and witnesses;[6]
(c) the offence or offences, or a summary of them, with which the accused is or are charged;
(d) the names of counsel and solicitors engaged in the proceedings;

3 *R v Manchester Stipendary Magistrate, exp Hill* [1983] AC 328, [1982] 2 All ER 963.
4 MCA 1980, s 4.
5 Ibid, s 5.
6 Note the provisions for anonymity of complainants and defendants in rape cases contained in the Sexual Offences (Amendment) Act 1976.

(e) any decision of the court to commit the accused or any of the accused for trial, and any decision of the court on the disposal of the case of any accused not committed;
(f) where the court commits the accused or any of the accused for trial, the charge or charges, or a summary of them, on which he is committed and the court to which he is committed;
(g) where the committal proceedings are adjourned, the date and place to which they are adjourned;
(h) any arrangements as to bail on committal or adjournment;
(i) whether legal aid was granted to the accused or any of the accused.

Any possible doubt as to when the committal proceedings commenced is covered by a provision that these restrictions apply even to any proceedings before the magistrates begin to act as examining justices (except where examining justices have first proceeded to summary trial and then switched to committal proceedings). These restrictions are mandatory and any infringement of them carries a criminal sanction, but there are two exceptions. First if the accused is discharged, or if there are more than one accused, all the accused are discharged; or if the accused is or are committed for trial, the accused is acquitted or if there are several accused, they are all acquitted, the press may report the full details of the committal proceedings. Second, the accused may himself choose to have reporting restrictions lifted.

THE LIFTING OF REPORTING RESTRICTIONS

In what circumstances would an accused wish to have reporting restrictions lifted? Normally an accused would not wish to have restrictions lifted because the reporting of his case might predjudice his trial. Yet there might be occasions when he wanted as much publicity as he can obtain for several reasons:

(a) he might hope to trace a potential witness who has been alerted to the existence of the case by what he has read in the newspapers;
(b) in a politically sensitive case the accused might wish to have maximum publicity for his cause;
(c) in a few cases the accused might wish to arouse as much public sympathy as he could before his trial.

Any one or more of such motives as these might prompt one accused to want reporting restrictions lifted, but what if he is only one of a number of accused jointly charged? If reporting restrictions are lifted against one, they are lifted against all the accused. In these circumstances all the accused are entitled to make representations to the court which will only lift the restrictions if it considers it to be in the interests of justice to do so.[7] Details of these applications may not be reported. If

7 MCA 1980, s 8 (2A). An accused must present a 'powerful' case for the lifting of restrictions especially where there are other co-accused who object. See *R v Leeds Justices, ex p Sykes* [1983] 1 All ER 460, [1983] Crim LR 180.

reporting restrictions are lifted, they apply to all the charges against the accused unless they are expressed to be in restricted terms.

THE JOINDER OF DEFENDANTS AND OFFENCES IN COMMITTAL PROCEEDINGS

It has been mentioned earlier that in the summary trial of an information the defendant may make representations to have a separate trial of each information against him. If this is accepted there will be a separate trial of each offence and if he is summonsed or charged with several other defendants each defendant can make representations for a separate trial for himself.[8]

The joinder of offences and defendants in committal proceedings is governed by the same rules, which are of course the rules applicable to trial on indictment.[9] For a detailed explanation of these rules reference should be made to *Archbold*,[10] and chapter 5.

The long committal (Magistrates' Courts Act 1980, section 6(1))[11]

This is the full committal hearing where the justices examine the evidence presented to them in order to decide whether there is sufficient evidence to commit the accused for trial. The sole issue is whether there is sufficient evidence which is capable of belief and upon which a reasonable jury, properly directed, could convict the accused. It is not for the committing magistrates to decide whether they would convict the accused, it is a lower test than that required for determining guilt or innocence.

After any application has been made by the defence concerning the lifting of reporting restrictions, the prosecutor may open his case and then proceed to call his evidence, which may be oral evidence or in certain circumstances, evidence in the form of statements.

If oral evidence is to be given by a witness, he will be sworn and will give his evidence in the same way as at a summary trial. However, his evidence will be recorded in the form of a written statement called a deposition. The witness will usually give his evidence in the form of an answer to a question put by the advocate. The usual practice is for the question and answer to be synthesised into one statement. For example:

8 See p 85, above and *Clayton v Chief Constable of Norfolk* [1983] 1 All ER 984, [1983] 2 WLR 555.

9 *R v Camberwell Green Stipendiary Magistrate, ex p Christie* [1978] QB 602, [1978] 2 All ER 377.

10 (41st edn) paras 1–70 to 1–84.

11 See Magistrates' Courts Rules 1981, r 7.

Question: 'Where were you on Saturday night?'
Answer: 'At home.'

might be recorded as:

'I was at home on Saturday night.'

The evidence must be recorded in writing. This may be done by the clerk taking down the evidence in manuscript, but it is preferable on the grounds of legibility for the evidence to be typewritten. In some courts a skilled typist will take down the evidence directly on her typewriter, or she may type the deposition outside court from a shorthand note she has taken, or from notes taken on a dictaphone. It would appear that all these methods are within the rules, provided the next stage of the proceedings is followed.

The witness may be then cross-examined by the defence. Any evidence given as a result of cross-examination must also be recorded. When the witness has given his evidence, his deposition must be read over to him in the presence of the accused (unless his presence has been dispensed with) and he should sign his deposition.[12]

The evidence of several witnesses may be taken in this way but it may not always be necessary to call a witness to give oral evidence.

EVIDENCE IN THE FORM OF WRITTEN STATEMENTS

There is no point in calling a witness to give evidence, often of a formal nature, that is not in dispute. Therefore to save expense, his evidence is prepared beforehand in the form of a deposition. These depositions are admissible in committal proceedings by virtue of section 102 of the Magistrates' Courts Act 1980. In two further examples the evidence may be inadmissible under section 102 but the evidence may be still admitted by virtue of specific statutory provisions: the evidence of children in sexual cases, and the evidence of a dangerously ill witness.

Witness statements under section 102

Depositions in committal proceedings are admissible by virtue of section 102 in the same way that similar statements are admissible in summary trials by section 9 of the Criminal Justice Act 1967. At the committal proceedings the statement will be read aloud in its entirety, or if the court directs, a summary may be given of those parts which are not read aloud.[13]

Evidence in sexual cases, section 103

Alternatively, in sexual cases the evidence of children may be received as evidence in a written statement tendered under section 103 of the

12 Although the requirement to sign the deposition is directory rather than mandatory: *R v Holloway* (1901) 65 JP 712.

13 MCA 1980, s 102(5).

Magistrates' Courts Act 1980. This section provides a similar system for the reception of evidence as that for statements received under section 102 in that the written statement becomes evidence unless the defence objects, in which case oral evidence must be given so that the witness may be cross-examined. The question presents itself, why are there two sections which appear to do the same thing? The answer may be that when the forerunner of section 103 was enacted there was no equivalent of section 102 so that section 103 was enacted to spare young children the ordeal of giving oral evidence about sexual matters in circumstances where it was not necessary. Where a child is to give evidence in a sexual case then, if applicable, section 103 must be used instead of section 102 owing to the wording of section 103.[14] Furthermore, the section is salutory in that it declares that a child shall not be called as a witness for the prosecution at the prosecution's instigation unless it can be justified for the purposes of identification of the accused, or where it has not been possible to prepare a statement, or where the defence has requested the presence of the witness by objecting to the statement. In other words the presumption is that a child witness will not be called to give evidence unless it is established that there is a good reason for doing so.

There is no requirement of seven days' notice of intention to use statements under sections 102 or 103 but in the case of statements tendered under section 103, if the defendant is unrepresented, the court must explain the effect of the provisions of the section in ordinary language to the defendant and if the defendant does not object to the use of the section he may still ask questions about the circumstances in which the statement was made.[15]

The deposition of a person dangerously ill (section 105)[16]

Where a witness is certified by a doctor to be dangerously ill *and* unlikely to recover and it is not practical to take the evidence in any other way, eg under section 102 because the other party will object to the contents of the deposition, a magistrate may attend on the witness and take his evidence on oath.

Section 105 provides that both parties must be given notice of the intention to take the deposition and be allowed to cross-examine the witness. The section therefore allows the reception of evidence in committal proceedings in the form of a written statement even though that evidence may be disputed by one party.

When the prosecution has tendered all the evidence it proposes to

14 The words of the caution in a s 102 statement which warn the witness making the statement that if he wilfully misstates any evidence he may be prosecuted are also clearly inappropriate to a child under the age of criminal responsibility.

15 Magistrates' Courts Rules 1981, r 7(4).

16 Ibid, r 33.

offer either by witnesses giving oral evidence or evidence in the form of written statements, the prosecution case will be concluded.

The nature and conduct of the prosecution case

The purpose of committal proceedings is to test whether a prima facie case has been made out against the accused. Accordingly, the prosecution need not adduce at the committal proceedings all the evidence which it has available; it need only produce enough evidence to establish a prima facie case. For example, the prosecution might have three witnesses, A, B and C. If it can establish a prima facie case by calling only A and B it need not, and is under no duty to, call witness C. The defence cannot compel the prosecution to call witness C.[17]

The magistrates are also only concerned with evidence *capable of belief*, that is evidence which a reasonable jury might believe. Some evidence adduced by the prosecution might be ruled inadmissible by the magistrates in a summary trial, or by the judge in a trial on indictment, because for example its probative value is outweighed by its prejudicial effect. Nevertheless it is *capable* of being evidence until in the exercise of judicial discretion it is ruled inadmissible. In committal proceedings the discretion to rule evidence admissible or otherwise is not exercised by the committing justices, the ruling on admissibility is made by the judge at the trial in the Crown Court.[18] Of course if the material tendered is, in law, incapable of being evidence, the magistrates should reject it, eg hearsay statements.

The depositions should record the evidence given by the witness and if prejudicial or inadmissible evidence has been given that should be recorded but the magistrates may mark against it 'treated as inadmissible'.[19]

After each witness has given his evidence orally, the defence may cross-examine him. Any cross-examination should have a purpose behind it as a blundering and aimless cross-examination is more likely than anything to ensure that the accused is committed for trial.

If the witness, left to his own devices, has not given evidence which incriminates the defendant, then the only result likely to accrue from any defence cross-examination may be that the memory of the witness

17 *R v Epping and Harlow Justices, ex p Massaro* [1973] 1 QB 433, [1973] 1 All ER 1011; *R v Grays Justices, ex p Tetley* (1979) 70 Cr App Rep 11.

18 *R v G. Weaver, R v J. Weaver* [1968] 1 QB 353, [1967] 1 All ER 277; *R v Horsham Justices, ex p Bukhari* (1982) 74 Cr App Rep 291, [1982] Crim LR 178 (the prosecution does not need the consent of the magistrates for a dock identification).

19 Magistrates' Courts Rules 1981, r 70(5).

is stirred to recall damaging testimony. If the prosecution witness has given incriminating evidence, the cross-examination should be directed at either destroying the evidence or explaining the evidence in a way favourable to the accused. But it should be remembered that it will take a great deal to destroy a witness' evidence, especially as the examining justices are only concerned with whether the evidence is *capable* of belief, not with whether they themselves believe it. Furthermore, committal proceedings are a test of the prosecution evidence, not that of the defence and that an overlong cross-examination of the prosecution witnesses may not advance the defendant's case and may reveal the defence to be used so as to enable the prosecution to be more able to meet it at the trial.

One final comment on the nature of the proceedings is to say that they are, so far as is possible, a clinical sifting of whatever evidence is presented to see whether there is a prima facie case. In view of this the High Court has gone so far as to hold that it is not improper for an examining magistrate to be given the prosecution papers in advance in order that he may be prepared for the hearing.[20]

The defence case

SUBMISSIONS OF NO CASE

After the prosecution evidence has all been received, the defence may submit that there is insufficient evidence to commit the accused for trial, and if the submission is accepted, the accused will be discharged (as opposed to being acquitted after a summary trial or a trial on indictment). The submission would be made on the same lines as those already described when discussing a submission of no case in the summary trial of an information (p 113, above).[1]

If the accused is not discharged at this stage, the charge is formulated in writing if this has not already been done, and in the case of an unrepresented defendant it should be explained to him in ordinary language. The defendant is then asked if he has anything to say in answer to the charge, and if unrepresented, is cautioned that he is not obliged to say anything. If the accused does say something, this is recorded in writing and is admissible in evidence at his trial when taken in accordance with the rules.[2]

By this stage of the proceedings the prosecution have established a

20 *R v Colchester Stipendiary Magistrate, ex p Beck* [1979] QB 674, [1979] 2 All ER 1035.

1 Including the possibility of granting the prosecution an adjournment to clear up an ambiguity in their evidence revealed by a defence submission: *R v West London Metropolitan Stipendiary Magistrate, ex p Kaminski* [1983] Crim LR 40.

2 Criminal Justice Act 1925, s 12(4).

prima facie case and the charge has been formulated. However, the accused is not yet committed for trial; he will be allowed to call witnesses and give evidence himself. But before he does so he is given an alibi warning.

THE ALIBI WARNING

The alibi warning is given to inform the accused that he may not give evidence of an alibi at his trial unless he gives notice to the prosecutor of that alibi within seven days from the end of the committal proceedings, unless the nature of the charge makes it unnecessary to give the warning.

The Criminal Justice Act 1967, section 11(8) provides:

> In this section:
> 'evidence in support of an alibi' means evidence tending to show that by reason of the presence of the defendant at a particular place or in a particular area at a particular time he was not, or was unlikely to have been, at the place where the offence was alleged to have been committed at the time of its alleged commission.

The term 'alibi', of course, should not be confused with the popular but erroneous use of the word to refer to any defence offered to an accusation.[3]

The second matter that must be referred to is that the alibi warning need not be given if it is unnecessary having regard to the charge. It should be noticed that, strictly speaking, it is the nature of the charge that is important, not the nature of the defence, ie the warning should still be given even where the defence intimates that there will be a plea of guilty.[4] An example of an offence which would not, by its nature, require an alibi warning would be living off immoral earnings; also perhaps blackmail, as the commission of these offences is not usually bound together with being in a particular place at a particular time.

The alibi warning is required even if only the defendant is giving evidence at the trial.[5] If the alibi warning is not given or the provisions are not complied with, the evidence of alibi is inadmissible at the trial unless the judge exercises his discretion to admit it, although he will usually exercise his discretion in favour of the defence after granting an

3 For a discussion of some of the problems of defining an alibi defence see T. M. S. Tosswill 'The definition of an alibi defence' [1978] Crim LR 277 and see also *R v C. Young, R v M. Young* [1979] Crim LR 651 where on a charge of taking and driving away no alibi warning was required when the defence raised was that the defendant was sitting in the passenger seat. *R v Gibbs* [1974] Crim LR 474 where a negative averment that the defendant was not at a particular place did not fall within the requirements of an alibi notice. The warning, if given, may be administered by the clerk instead of a magistrate: see *R v Horseferry Road Justices, ex p Farooki* (1982) Times, 29 October.

4 But see the view at (1975) 139 JP 475.

5 *R v Jackson and Robertson* [1973] Crim LR 356.

adjournment if necessary.[6] Therefore, if details of the alibi are not available at the committal, notice should be given as soon as possible afterwards to the prosecution. The purpose of the defence being required to give notice of an alibi is to prevent the prosecution being taken by surprise and to enable it to check the authenticity of the alibi without the waste of time and money involved in adjourning a trial on indictment.

CALLING DEFENCE EVIDENCE

After the alibi warning has been given (or not as the case may be), the defendant has a right to give evidence himself and call witnesses,[7] and if he is represented he may make a speech before or after the evidence or with the leave of the court he may do both.

Although committal proceedings are a test of the prosecution evidence, the magistrates have to look at the totality of the evidence and although the prosecution do not have to satisfy a heavy burden of proof, the prosecution evidence may be fatally weakened when looked at in the light of compelling defence evidence, especially when the bulk of the prosecution case is accepted and the defence rely on a defence which it has to raise, eg self-defence. An example of a defendant who was discharged after giving evidence was *Re Roberts*[8] where the defendant was charged with having unlawful sexual intercourse. He raised the statutory defence to such an allegation and the magistrates found that no reasonable jury could convict the accused and he was discharged. A subsequent application for a voluntary bill of indictment was refused. Another such example might be where the accused adduces evidence of a coach load of credible witnesses to establish that he was with them, miles away from the scene of the crime at the time it was committed.

THE DECISION TO COMMIT FOR TRIAL

After the defence evidence, if any, has been given the magistrates must determine whether there is sufficient evidence for the accused to stand his trial; could a reasonable jury, properly directed, convict on the evidence before it. The same test is applied as is used for a submission of no case to answer in a summary trial.[9] If there is sufficient evidence the magistrates are under a duty to commit for trial, as there would

6 *R v Sullivan* [1971] 1 QB 253, [1970] 2 All ER 681.

7 Even if he has already made an unsuccessful submission that there is insufficient evidence to commit him: *R v Horseferry Road Stipendiary Magistrate, ex p Adams* [1977] 1 WLR 1197, [1976] Crim LR 482, DC.

8 [1967] 1 WLR 474 [1967] Crim LR 304.

9 *R v Tobin* [1980] Crim LR 731 and for a recent discussion of the requirements for a successful submission in the Crown Court see *R v Galbraith* [1981] 2 All ER 1060, [1981] 1 WLR 1039.

appear to be no residual power to refuse to commit because, for example, of a feeling that the prosecution was oppressive and contrary to natural justice[10] (although it does happen). However, the magistrates are not obliged to commit the accused on the original charge read to him. In the light of the evidence they have heard, they might determine that an amended charge might be more appropriate.

PROCEDURE AFTER IT HAS BEEN DECIDED TO COMMIT THE DEFENDANT FOR TRIAL

When the magistrates have announced the decision to commit the accused for trial they should specify the court of trial. This will be the court specified by the Presiding Judge of the Crown Court circuit for that magistrates' court having regard to the category of offence and the tier of Crown Court required.[11] The date of the trial will be a matter to be fixed by the Crown Court itself which will be notified to the parties later. Then the prosecutor may apply for his costs to be certified on form B so that he may claim them later at the Crown Court although his witnesses may be reimbursed at the committal hearing on form A.

The defence should then assist the court by informing it of the nature of the witness orders required for the prosecution witnesses. At the committal proceedings, witnesses for the prosecution will have given evidence either orally or by written statement. The question to be settled is which prosecution witnesses will be required to give oral evidence at the trial at the Crown Court and which witnesses need not attend the Crown Court, either because their evidence will be dispensed with entirely, or because their evidence will be presented in the form of written statements. Prosecution witnesses whose attendance is required are made the subject of absolute witness orders, those whose attendance is not required are made the subject of conditional witness orders. The absolute order informs the witness that he must attend at the trial, the conditional order informs him that he need only attend if he is informed later that he must attend. The magistrates' court informs the witness of the order to which he is subject but he is not informed of the trial date until he receives further instructions from the Crown Court. If at the committal proceedings the position is not clear, conditional witness orders should be asked for and then the Crown Court contacted to inform the witnesses to attend if necessary.

The second defence application is usually to extend the accused's

10 *Atkinson v US Government* [1971] AC 197, [1969] 3 All ER 1317.

11 See the Practice Directions of the Lord Chief Justice in Volume 3 of *Stone's*. The magistrates will forward a certificate to the Crown Court certifying that the accused has been properly committed, although if it is inadvertently omitted the resulting trial will still be valid: see *R v Carey* [1983] Crim LR 111.

legal aid to cover his trial at the Crown Court. If the defendant is already covered by legal aid and his financial circumstances have not changed the court will usually automatically extend legal aid; if his circumstances have changed the court will have to consider whether to extend legal aid in view of the accused's financial circumstances. If the accused is applying for legal aid for the first time, he may apply for legal aid there and then, or he may apply afterwards to the Crown Court.

The final application usually covers the remand of the accused in the intervening period before his trial. If the accused has previously been on bail there is usually no problem. If he has previously been remanded in custody, the decision in *R v Nottingham City Justices, ex p Davies*[12] will apply as the mere fact that the accused is now being remanded for an indefinite period for trial is not in itself a change of circumstances entitling the accused to apply for bail.[13] No date for trial is fixed by the committing justices and the remand period is indefinite and only terminated when the Crown Court has listed the case for trial. Nor does the accused appear weekly, once remanded in custody he remains there until his trial. If the accused is remanded in custody he may apply to a High Court judge or a circuit judge in chambers. Usually an application is made to a circuit judge. In the usual straightforward case where the prosecution is conducted by the police this can be done expeditiously by the defence contacting the court to fix an appointment then completing the notice of application for bail and serving it on the prosecutor who can require 24 hours' notice of the application for bail.[14]

THE 'READ THROUGH' COMMITTAL

It is possible to have full committal proceedings where the examining justices consider the prosecution evidence but where no witnesses are called to give oral evidence. This may be done where all the evidence is in the form of written statements (usually under section 102). The statements are read through by the prosecution, and after the evidence is read the defence may submit that there is insufficient evidence to commit the accused for trial. The magistrates must consider the evidence and if they consider that it is insufficient, they must discharge the accused.[15]

If the submission is unsuccessful, the defence may call evidence in the usual way and make a further submission.

12 [1981] QB 38, [1980] 2 All ER 775.
13 *R v Slough Justices, ex p Duncan and Embling* (1982) 147 JP1.
14 See ch 9.
15 *R v Pontypool Justices, ex p McCann* [1969] Crim LR 148, (1969) 113 Sol Jo 52.

Committal without consideration of the evidence – the 'short' committal (section 6(2))

If there had to be a full committal hearing for every indictable offence which was to be heard at the Crown Court, the magistrates' courts would be over burdened by the extra demands made on them. Furthermore, it would be a waste of time and money to have such a hearing where all parties agreed that there was a case to answer. To meet this situation the Magistrates' Courts Act 1980, section 6(2) provides that the magistrates may commit the accused for trial without considering the evidence where certain criteria are fulfilled. The criteria are:

(a) every accused has a solicitor or barrister acting for him whether present in court or not;[16]

(b) the accused agrees to this form of committal;

(c) all the evidence is in the form of statements prepared under section 102.[17]

Normally at remand proceedings prior to the committal proceedings the prosecution and the defence will have agreed on what form the committal proceedings will take, always remembering that the defence has an absolute right to insist on a full committal. If a short committal has been arranged, the case will only require a few minutes of court time whereas a full committal may require a special court lasting several hours or even days.

PROCEDURE

The procedure for a short committal is as follows:[18]

Before the hearing the prosecution must supply the accused with copies of the written statements prepared in accordance with section 102.[19] At the hearing the prosecutor will make an application that the proceedings be in the short form as the initiative must come from him. He will then hand the original statements to the magistrates. The defence advocate must then consent to the short form committal by indicating that he does not wish to object to the statements being tendered in evidence, or wish to call evidence himself or submit that

16 Criminal Justice Act 1982, 61.

17 Evidence in the form of s 103 statements (evidence of children in sexual cases) cannot be used in short committals. This may be circumvented, where appropriate, by the police officer taking the statement making a s 102 statement with the child's statement being referred to and produced as an exhibit. Similar difficulties arise with a statement under s 105.

18 See Magistrates' Courts Rules 1981, r 6.

19 It is sufficient compliance if the statements are handed to the defence solicitor: *R v Bott; R v Baker* [1968] 1 All ER 1119, [1968] 1 WLR 583, and the defendant need not even see them: *R v Wells* [1969] Crim LR 47, (1968) 112 Sol Jo 839, CA.

there is insufficient evidence to justify a committal for trial. The alibi warning will be given, if appropriate, and the accused committed for trial. The defence may then make applications for the appropriate witness orders, legal aid and bail during the remand period.

What is important about the short form of committal is that the magistrates do not consider the evidence. They do not consider the statements for the purpose of deciding whether the accused should be committed for trial.[20] Accordingly, if the defence objects to the content of a particular statement it cannot ask the magistrates to excise the offending part, it can either delay any objection until the trial at the Crown Court, or it can insist on a full committal.

Which form of committal is more appropriate?

This is an almost impossible question to answer because each case will of course depend very much on its own facts. However, certain guidelines are offered which may prove useful in reaching the decision on which mode of committal proceedings is more suitable.

It is fair to say that the normal form of committal is the short committal. This is so for one or more reasons:

(a) the majority of cases end in a plea of guilty and the accused accepts the evidence against him;
(b) the accused, whilst denying his guilt accepts that there is a prima facie case against him, eg he may have made a confession to the police which he will seek to retract in due course at his trial;
(c) the short form of committal has been in existence for some years now and especially with younger advocates there may be a tendency to avoid the unfamiliar form of the long committal;
(d) the prosecution costs will be less and so will the risk of having a substantial order for costs made against him.

The question therefore usually resolves itself into one of when should an accused opt for a long committal.

A long committal is obligatory:

(a) where the accused has instructed no solicitor;
(b) where identity is in issue;[1]

and may be useful:

(a) where the defence has an overwhelmingly strong case;
(b) where, although the defence is not overwhelming, the charge may be extremely trivial and the prosecution case not too strong so that either the prosecution may be embarrassed and the magistrates

20 *R v Brooker* [1976] Crim LR 573, (1976) 120 Sol Jo 250, CA where a committal in this form was not invalid even though it appeared later that there was no reference at all to the defendant in the statements.

1 See *Archbold* (41st edn) para 14–1.

faced with this situation would naturally not be inclined to overlook any weakness in the prosecution case albeit unconsciously; (However the defence should not adopt a long committal even in these circumstances, where there is clear unimpeachable evidence against the accused even if the charge is trivial.)

(c) where although the accused might be committed for trial, the prosecution after seeing the performance of their witnesses at the hearing might proceed no further with the case or reduce the charges to those to which the accused might be willing to plead guilty;

(d) if the full hearing enables the defence to test certain prosecution witnesses in the absence of the jury so that if a line of questioning should misfire, the defence is not embarrassed at the trial;

(e) where the prosecution evidence can be so discredited by cross-examination that the evidence would be treated as worthless, eg where the prosecution evidence is that of criminals or dubious characters who could be shown to be manifestly unreliable;

(f) where it is apparent from the statements themselves that there is not a prima facie case, a 'read through' committal might be appropriate;

(g) where the prosecution witnesses may turn hostile, eg assault cases between relatives and spouses;

(h) in some circumstances (admittedly not common) where the defence may gain information from the evidence of prosecution witnesses which may unearth potential sources of evidence favourable to the accused, eg a witness may let slip the name of another person who has not been previously mentioned and who may be of use to the defence case.

But as a general rule mere 'fishing' expeditions are to be discouraged and may lose any value by the fact that the prosecution are not obliged to call all their witnesses.

Changing from committal proceedings to summary trial

Where the court is acting as examining justices and during the course of the inquiry it appears appropriate that summary trial would be more suitable, it may revert to summary trial if the accused agrees and is warned about the power to commit for sentence (p 81). Any oral evidence already given in the proceedings may be used in the summary trial.[2]

2 But not written statements tendered under s 102 (s 102(9)), s 103 (s 103(3)) nor probably evidence tendered under s 105.

Proceedings after the committal

After the committal proceedings have been concluded, if the accused has been committed the statements which are now the depositions for the trial are transmitted from the magistrates' court to the appropriate Crown Court. The formal charge at the Crown Court, the indictment, is a separate document drafted in most cases by an officer of the Crown Court from the charges on which the accused was committed. In more complex cases counsel may draft the indictment which may include counts for offences for which the accused was not committed provided the evidence to substantiate those counts appears on the depositions.

Redress against the decision to commit or not to commit

STARTING COMMITTAL PROCEEDINGS AFRESH

If the prosecution is dissatisfied with the decision of the examining justices to discharge the accused, it can in theory start proceedings once more. A decision in committal proceedings is not the final disposal of the case and therefore the accused cannot plead autrefois acquit as a plea in bar to further proceedings for the same offence. But although the prosecution may start proceedings again, if the proceedings became vexatious and in effect an abuse of the process of the court, the High Court can intervene to prevent any further prosecution.[3]

JUDICIAL REVIEW

There is no appeal as such against the decision of examining justices,[4] but in certain limited circumstances judicial review may be applicable. Judicial review will only lie to force magistrates to exercise their jurisdiction, for example, mandamus would lie if the magistrates refused to exercise their jurisdiction as examining justices. Generally though, judicial review will not lie to control the exercise of their jurisdiction by the examining justices, ie their conduct of the proceedings.[5] The basis for this is that committal proceedings are not a

3 *R v Manchester City Stipendiary Magistrate, ex p Snelson* [1978] 2 All ER 63, [1977] 1 WLR 911; *R v Horsham Justices, ex p Reeves* [1981] Crim LR 566. In the *Horsham Justices'* case, Ackner LJ went so far as to say that the examining justices themselves have power to intervene when matters became vexatious or oppressive, but the other judge concerned reserved his opinion on this point.

4 *Card v Salmon* [1953] 1 QB 392, [1953] 1 All ER 324; *Atkinson v US Government* [1971] AC 197, [1969] 3 All ER 1317.

5 *R v Wells St Stipendiary Magistrate, ex p Seillon* [1978] 3 All ER 257, [1978] 1 WLR 1002 where the magistrate had refused to allow certain cross-examination and the High Court refused to intervene to control the exercise of the magistrates discretion. See also *R v Wells St. Stipendiary Magistrate, ex p Deakin* [1980] AC 477, [1979] 2 All ER 497.

complete procedure in themselves but part of the whole trial process which is not complete until the trial is concluded.

VOLUNTARY BILLS OF INDICTMENT AND FRESH COUNTS

The practical effects of the unavailability of an appeal against the discharge of an accused in committal proceedings are mitigated by the procedure under section 2(2) (b) of the Administration of Justice (Miscellaneous Provisions) Act 1933.[6] By this procedure the prosecution may apply to a High Court judge for a 'voluntary bill of indictment' without the necessity for committal proceedings. An important use of this procedure is to 'tidy up' proceedings where an accused has been committed on some charges and it is desirable to ensure that other matters are before the Crown Court at the same time. It can also be used even where the accused has previously been discharged by the magistrates although it will not lightly be granted in these circumstances.[7]

An alternative possibility for the prosecution is in the situation where the accused has been committed on some charges and discharged on others. If the depositions transmitted to the Crown Court contain evidence on which fresh counts in the indictment may be founded, the prosecution may add these to the indictment, with the same proviso that caution should be exercised in allowing these fresh counts to stand.[8]

6 *Archbold* (41st edn) para 1–96.
7 Ibid, para 4–95.
8 Ibid, paras 4–94 and 1–97.

Appendix A

Suggested procedure for long committal proceedings (where the accused is represented).

(a) Magistrates' clerk identifies the accused, and explains the restrictions on the reporting of the case and his right to have those restrictions lifted.

(b) The prosecutor opens his case and calls his evidence.

(c) A witness giving oral evidence is sworn and proceeds to give his evidence which is recorded in the form of a deposition.
The defence cross-examines the witness and the evidence is recorded.
After the witness has finished giving his evidence the deposition is read aloud to him by the clerk in the presence of the accused and then the witness initials any amendments and alterations and signs the deposition at the foot of each page.

(d) In the case of a witness giving evidence by means of a written statement, the prosecutor reads the statement or summarises those parts that are not read in full and hands the original to the magistrates.

(e) At the conclusion of the prosecution case, the defence may submit that there is insufficient evidence to commit for trial.

(f) If the case proceeds further, the charge is put into writing if this has not already been done, and read to the accused who may make a statement in reply.

(g) The court then gives the alibi warning if appropriate.

(h) The defence advocate may address the court.

(i) The defence may call the defendant and/or other witnesses for the defence.

(j) The defence advocate may address the court after the defence case, but if he has already addressed the court at (h) above, he may only address the court a second time with leave. If leave is granted, the prosecutor must be allowed to address the court a second time and if he does so this will be before the second defence address.

(k) If the magistrates commit the accused, he is then committed at this stage.

(l) The prosecutor applies for his witness expenses to be certified and paid on form A, and his costs to be certified on form B.

(m) The defence advocate applies for the appropriate witness orders, legal aid to be extended to cover the Crown Court proceedings, and for bail if appropriate.

Appendix B

Suggested procedure for a short form committal.

(a) The accused is identified by the magistrates' clerk and the charges read to him. The clerk ascertains that the accused is legally represented.

(b) The prosecutor applies for a section 6(2) committal and states that all the evidence is in the form of written statements prepared in accordance with section 102.

(c) The defence advocate indicates that the defence has been served with the statements, does not wish to call any evidence or make any submissions.

(d) The magistrates announce that the accused is committed to stand his trial at the appropriate Crown Court and give the alibi warning if appropriate, together with a written copy of the warning.

(e) The defence advocate applies for the appropriate witness orders and for legal aid to be extended to cover the Crown Court proceedings and bail if appropriate.

Chapter 11

Binding over

Introductory

A bind over is an order by the court that a person must enter into a recognizance for a specified period to do, or abstain from doing, a certain activity.[1] Entering into a recognizance means that the subject of the bind over promises to forfeit a certain sum of money if he breaches the terms of the bind over. It should be noted that the person does not pay over the money immediately, he only pays the money if he forfeits his recognizance. Initially, he is making a promise to the Crown that if he breaches the terms of the order he will forfeit money to the Crown. Furthermore, a bind over can only be made if the person being bound agrees to the order being made. However, if the court wishes to make the order and the subject of the order refuses to enter into a recognizance, the court may imprison him until he does agree to be bound. If he has agreed to be bound, then no question of imprisonment arises for a breach of the terms of the recognizance, only for failure to pay the sum of money forfeited.

An example of a bind over might be where a person is bound over to be of good behaviour in the sum of £100 for a period of one year.

The origins of the power

The power to bind over a person emerged in the twelfth and thirteenth centuries when, in the absence of a police force, worthy men were appointed by the Crown to keep the peace (and the sheriff in check). Throughout this period there were various statutes appointing these justices of the peace, the most famous one being 34 Edw III, c 1 (Justices of the Peace Act 1361). Subsequent Acts increased the number of justices appointed for each county.

1 The power to bind over to keep the peace or be of good behaviour should be distinguished from the bind over to come up for judgment, a power exercisable only by the Crown Court.

The Act of 1361 provides:

> First, that in every County of England shall be assigned for the keeping of the peace, one lord, and with him three or four of the most worthy in the County, with some learned in the law, and they shall have power to restrain the offenders, rioters, and all other barators and to pursue, arrest, take, and chastise them according to their trespass or offence; and to cause them to be imprisoned and duly punished according to the law and customs of the realm, and according to that which to them shall seem best to do by their discretions and good advisement; . . . and to take and arrest all those that they may find by indictment, or by suspicion, and to put them in prison; and to take all of them that be (not)[2] of good fame, where they shall be found, sufficient surety and mainprise of their good behaviour towards the King and his people, and the other duly to punish; to the intent that the people be not by such rioters and rebels troubled nor endamaged, nor the peace blemished, nor merchants nor other passing by the highways of the realm disturbed, nor put in the peril which may happen of such offenders . . .

The magistracy as a whole derives its authority to bind over a person from these statutes, and an individual justice is empowered to do so from his name being on the commission for his county or London Commission Area. Strictly speaking, there is not a common law power to bind over; the magistrates are exercising a statutory power to enforce a common law obligation to keep the peace.[3]

The distinction between binding over to keep the peace and to be of good behaviour[4]

Originally, the power to bind over was intended to be used against 'rioters' and 'rebels' to prevent internal disorder caused by soldiers returning from the French wars of that period. In later times the procedure was extended to include misbehaviour in lesser forms where a bind over was necessary to prevent an offence although a breach of the peace as such was not feared.[5] The terms 'bind over to keep the peace' and 'bind over to be of good behaviour' are, in essence, to be

2 The 'not' does not appear in the original Norman French text but is conventionally inserted in the English version. In the author's view this is unnecessary as it is submitted that the intention was to bind over only those wrongdoers of basically good character, the really serious criminals would receive much harsher treatment. See *Lansbury v Riley* [1914] 3 KB 229, 77 JP 440.

3 See especially *Lansbury v Riley* [1914] 3 KB 229, 77 JP 440; and *Everett v Ribbands* [1952] 2QB 198, [1952] 1 All ER 823 where Denning LJ, citing old textbooks on the subject, expressed the view that the authority to bind over to keep the peace came from the Justices of the Peace Act 1361 and that for binding over to be of good behaviour came from the Commission of the Peace.

4 Glanville Williams 'Preventive Justice and the Rule of Law' (1953) 16 MLR 417.

5 'for causes of scandal, contra bonos mores, as well as contra pacem' per Humphrey J (following Blackstone) *R v Sandbach, ex p Williams* [1935] 2 KB 192, 99 JP 251.

found in the 1361 Act used as synonymous terms but in later periods distinctions seemed to have developed between the two. In chapter 2 mention was made of the power of arrest for a breach of the peace or an apprehended breach of the peace and it may be that there is no power of arrest for an allegation of bad behaviour simpliciter without an apprehended breach of the peace.

THE EVIDENCE REQUIRED FOR A BIND OVER

Bind over to keep the peace

A breach of the peace has been defined as occurring:

> . . . whenever harm is actually done or is likely to be done to a person or in his presence to his property or a person is in fear of being so harmed through an assault, an affray, a riot, an unlawful assembly or other disturbance. . . .[6]

And if the court fears that there may be a breach of the peace, it may bind over the accused to keep the peace.

Bind over to be of good behaviour

It appears that there is a power to bind over a defendant to be of good behaviour where he has committed an act which would not have occasioned a breach of the peace. The problem is to decide which anti-social activities are within the ambit of the bind over. In the old cases there are all sorts of activities which could be restrained, such as 'night walking', activities which were in breach of the laws or byelaws of the period, as for example, the curfew. Most of these examples are now obsolete but even as late as 1962 there could be a bind over for sending insulting letters to bishops.[7]

But although the bind over is a 'wide discretionary power', it is 'to be exercised with great caution and not capriciously, and as it is capable

6 *R v Howell* [1981] 3 All ER 383, [1981] 3 WLR 501. See also *R v Dunn* (1840) 12 Ad & El 599, 4 JP 728.

7 See for example *Bamping v Barnes* [1958] Crim LR 186, (continued breach of a byelaw); *Sawyer v Bell* [1962] Crim LR 390, (1962) 106 Sol Jo 177, DC (sending insulting letters to Bishops); *Wilson v Skeock* (1949) 113 JP 294, 65 TLR 418 (where the defendant used insulting words which probably would not have been sufficient to convict him of a criminal offence).

For a list of situations where the bind over might be used contained in old text books see *R v London County Quarter Sessions, ex p Metropolitan Police Comr* [1948] 1 KB 670, [1948] 1 All ER 72, and for a comprehensive review of the use of the bind over in public order situations see D. G. T. Williams *Keeping the Peace* (Hutchinson, 1967).

The view has been expressed, however, that in spite of the decision in *Wilson v Skeock* it remains doubtful whether a bind over would be appropriate in a case where a breach of the peace was not feared nor was a bind over necessary to prevent an offence against either statute or a byelaw. The activities catalogued in the *London Quarter Sessions* case, above. would all at one time have been breaches of the law or local regulations, eg night walking would have been in breach of the curfew.

of being abused, to be jealously watched over' (by the High Court).[8] Further limitations are placed on the justices by the fact that any apprehended fear of a breach must be a real one and that not all bad behaviour is within the jurisdiction of the bind over. Even in Hawkins it is said:

> it seems to be the better opinion, that no one ought to be bound to the good behaviour for any rash, quarrelsome or immannerly words, unless they either directly tend to a breach of the peace, or to scandalize the government, by abusing those who are intrusted by it with the administration of justice or to deter an officer from doing his duty; and therefore, it seems, that he who barely calls another a rogue, or rascal, or teller of lies, drunkard, etc., ought not, for such cause, to be bound to be of good behaviour.[9]

Since the time of Hawkins when the accepted theory was that any public criticism of the government was seditious libel, the categories of activity for which a bind over could be imposed in the absence of a breach of the peace seem to have narrowed. The only common occurrences today would be to restrain activities such as that of a peeping Tom (and even here a breach of the peace might well be imagined) and to restrain the repetition of a particular offence. No one in modern times would be bound over for scandalising the government, indeed some publications and broadcasters would go out of business if it were so, although bishops still seem to have retained this protection of the law.

Although the situations may be limited when a bind over can be imposed in the absence of an apprehended breach of the peace, a bind over to be of good behaviour will include a restraint on breaching the peace and so, for good measure, courts often bind over a defendant not only to keep the peace but also to be of good behaviour.

Situations where the bind over is commonly used

It is not proposed here to give an exhaustive list of the situations where a bind over may be appropriate, but merely to mention some of the commonly occurring situations in the magistrates' courts where bind overs are imposed.

(a) Where a charge under the Public Order Act has been dismissed but the magistrates apprehend from what they have heard, that the defendant may cause trouble in the future.

(b) Where a charge of assault is heard and it is clear that the incident may be repeated. This is particularly the case where the assault was occasioned between parties who knew each other, for example neighbours or spouses. It is quite common in these situations for

8 Per Fitzgerald J in *R (Feeham) v Queen's County Justices* (1882) LR 10 Ir 294 at 303.

9 Hawkins *Pleas of the Crown* (8th edn) Bk 1, Ch 28, section 3.

the police, although they have brought the defendant before the court on a criminal charge, to be content to withdraw the charge on the defendant being bound over. If the complainant is in court, he may also be bound over, or if absent the police may lay a complaint under section 115 of the Magistrates' Courts Act 1980 for him to show cause why he should not be bound over.

(c) The police may initiate the procedure under section 115 instead of preferring criminal charges in such cases as allegations of indecent exposure or being a peeping Tom, or in neighbour disputes where they have decided not to prosecute.

(d) Some offences, eg under local byelaws, may carry a small maximum penalty. The penalty imposed by the statute may not be a sufficient deterrent for the determined offender. Where the defendant has had several convictions for the same offence and has evinced an intention to repeat the offence, it is within the justices' power to bind him over with a recognizance set at a figure significantly greater than the maximum for the particular offence concerned.[10]

The legal status of the bind over

A bind over is not a conviction as the 1361 Act does not create an offence.[11] The proceedings are civil in nature and where there is a complaint the person laying the complaint is a complainant not a prosecutor.

In reality this may be of scant comfort to the person bound over.

> Whatever be the technical position, in the minds of innumerable people who read the report in a local newspaper there is the belief that the person who has been ordered to enter into recognizances, with or without sureties, to be of good behaviour or to keep the peace, has been convicted; and even where there is more legal knowledge there is a general feeling that behind this order is a piece of discreditable conduct.[12]

However, it follows that a bind over is not a sentence and in criminal cases where the defendant has been charged with an offence the magistrates may not bind him over *instead* of sentencing him, they must sentence the defendant even if it is only an absolute discharge although they may bind him over *in addition*.

10 *R v Sandbach, ex p Williams* [1935] 2 KB 192, 99 JP 251; *Bamping v Barnes* [1958] Crim LR 186.

11 Per Lord Goddard in *R v London County Quarter Sessions, ex p Metropolitan Police Comr* [1948] 1 KB 670, [1948] 1 All ER 72.

12 Viscount Kilmuir, cited in D. G. T. Williams *Keeping the Peace* (Hutchinson, 1967) ch 4 'Preventive Justice'.

Procedure

PROCEDURE AT COMMON LAW AND UNDER SECTION 115 MAGISTRATES' COURTS ACT 1980

To have an understanding of the procedural aspects of binding over it is necessary to consider again the historical development of the binding over jurisdiction.

It has been suggested that the authority to bind over comes from the statutes of the middle ages, of which the Act of 1361 is an example, and from the extensions of that jurisdiction in the succeeding centuries made by case law. But it is one thing to create a jurisdiction and another to administer it. The administration of modern statutes is governed by subordinate legislation in the form of statutory instruments, but there is no equivalent for regulating the procedure under the 1361 Act. The courts themselves have been left to create their own procedure. As a result the procedure for bind overs under the 1361 Act is governed by common law.

COMMON LAW

The procedure at common law was summary in the extreme and, to modern eyes, in breach of natural justice. The defendant could be arrested under the common law powers of arrest[13] or an information might be laid before a magistrate and a warrant issued. Once before the magistrate, the complainant gave evidence on oath and called his witnesses, if any. If the magistrate was satisfied of the matters complained of, then the defendant was bound over; he had no right to cross-examine the complainant or his witnesses, or give evidence himself.[14]

This was felt to be unjust and in 1879 the precursor of section 115 of the Magistrates' Courts Act 1980 was enacted.[15]

SECTION 115 OF THE MAGISTRATES' COURTS ACT 1980

Section 115 provides:

> The power of a magistrates' court on the complaint of any person to adjudge any other person to enter into a recognizance, with or without sureties, to keep the peace or to be of good behaviour towards the complainant shall be exercised by order on complaint.

This means that a summons must then be issued to the defendant and a hearing of the application take place where both sides may give evidence and the issue will be decided on its merits.

13 See ch 2.
14 Cf *Lort v Hutton* (1876) 4 5LJMC 95, 40 JP 677.
15 Summary Jurisdiction Act 1879, 25.

Although section 115 provides for the situation where the application is for the defendant to be bound over in his conduct towards the complainant, it is clear that the necessity for a proper complaint and hearing equally applies to the situation where it is intended that the defendant be bound over in respect of his behaviour towards people generally.[16] For example, if the police arrest a drunkard, they are not seeking that the defendant be bound over to be of good behaviour towards the police as complainants, but towards all the subjects of the Queen. Even if the defendant is brought before the court not by summons but by virtue of the power of arrest at common law where the defendant is committing the breach of the peace, it is submitted that a complaint must be laid although it need not be a formal, written, complaint.

THE COMMON LAW PROCEDURE TODAY: PERSONS ALREADY BEFORE THE COURT

The situation has been described where the defendant has had to be brought to the court to answer for conduct which is alleged to require a bind over. However, it may happen that the defendant is already before the court on another matter. He does not need to be brought to court because he is already there. It appears that in this situation the old common law procedure still applies. Provided the magistrates have heard sufficient to merit a bind over[17] they may bind over the defendant without warning him of their intentions or a complaint having been laid.[18] The justification for this procedure is to be found in the judgment of Lord Widgery in *R v Woking Justices, ex p Gossage*:[19]

> [T]he defendant comes before the court knowing that allegations are to be made against him, knowing that he can be represented if appropriate, and knowing that he can call evidence if he wishes. It seems to me that a rule which requires a witness to be warned of the possibility of a binding-over should not necessarily apply to a defendant in that different position.
>
> That is not to say that it would not be wise, and indeed courteous in these cases for justices to give such a warning; there certainly would be absolutely no harm [in giving a warning].

BINDING OVER A WITNESS OR COMPLAINANT

The magistrates have the power to bind over anyone who is before them. Those persons may be present either because they have been summoned there to answer a complaint under the provisions of section 115 of the Magistrates' Courts Act 1980, or because they have been

16 *Everett v Ribbands* [1952] 2 QB 198, [1952] 1 All ER 823.
17 Cf *R v South West London Magistrates' Court, ex p Brown* [1974] Crim LR 313 and the authorities mentioned in the commentary.
18 *Ex p Davis* (1871) 24 LT 547, 35 JP 551.
19 [1973] 1 QB 448, [1973] 2 All ER 621 at 623.

arrested under common law powers, or because they are in court answering a charge for a criminal offence. In this latter case the complainant may also be present and witnesses may be there to give evidence. For example, the defendant may have been charged with assaulting the complainant. The complainant gives evidence and witnesses are called by the prosecution and defence. At the conclusion of the case the magistrates may have heard evidence from which they conclude that it is necessary to bind over not only the defendant but also the complainant, and also perhaps one or more of the witnesses.

In the extract of Lord Widgery's judgment in the *Woking Justices'* case referred to above, mention was made of the rule which requires a witness to be warned if the magistrates are contemplating binding him over. The complainant and witnesses are in a different position from the defendant in these circumstances; they are not before the court to answer a criminal charge, and they cannot be legally aided or separately represented to answer the proposed exercise of the magistrates' common law power to bind them over. Accordingly, if after the trial has concluded, the bench are contemplating binding over persons other than the defendant, the magistrates must give the complainant[20] and the witnesses[1] an opportunity to be heard in opposition to the proposed bind over. The requirement to give the warning is mandatory and failure to comply with this will render the bind over liable to be quashed by the Divisional Court.[2] However, a warning need not be given where there has been a disturbance in the face of the court and the persons involved need not be given an opportunity to address the court.[3]

It is doubtful whether the bench could adjourn the case at the request of the complainant or a witness. There has been no complaint laid and so there are no 'proceedings' to be adjourned under the Magistrates' Courts Act 1980, nor would there be any point in adjourning for legal aid which is only available for proceedings under section 115 of the Magistrates' Courts Act 1980. If the proceedings were adjourned there would be no power to compel the complainant or witness to attend court on the subsequent occasion. Finally, it appears that magistrates may bind over a person during an adjournment in any event, provided there is sufficient material before them to justify such a course of action.

20 *R v Wilkins* [1907] 2 KB 380; *R v Hendon Justices, ex p Gorchein* [1974] 1 All ER 168, [1973] 1 WLR 1502. It is only in exceptional circumstances that a complainant should be bound over where the facts emerge on a plea of guilty by the defendant: *R v Preston Crown Court, ex p Pamplin* [1981] Crim LR 338.

1 *Sheldon v Bromfield Justices* [1964] 2 QB 573, [1964] 2 All ER 131.

2 Eg as in *R v Keighley Justices, ex p Stoyles* [1976] Crim LR 573, DC.

3 *R v North London Justices, ex p Haywood and Brown* [1973] 3 All ER 50, [1973] 1 WLR 1965.

Procedure in court

A COMPLAINT UNDER SECTION 115 OF THE MAGISTRATES' COURTS ACT 1980

Where a complaint has been laid under this section proceedings follow the normal pattern for the hearing of a complaint and are very similar to the summary trial of an information except that these are civil proceedings and the rules of criminal evidence do not apply. As in other civil proceedings in the magistrates' court therefore, if the defendant 'admits' the complaint that does not give the magistrates jurisdiction in the way that a plea of guilty would; it only relieves them of the duty to allow the defendant to show cause why he should not be bound over. They must still have material before them to satisfy them that there is a genuine fear of a breach of the peace or good behaviour in the future. But where the defendant is not objecting to the bind over, an outline of the facts in the case by the complainant will be sufficient. There is no need for a formal trial of the complaint.

COMMON LAW PROCEEDINGS

Where no formal complaint has been laid and the defendant appears before the court on a criminal matter, if he pleads guilty he will be allowed to put his case in mitigation. If the magistrates are minded to bind him over they should warn him of their intentions and allow him to address the court. The prosecutor present in court may also be bound over, even where the defendant has pleaded guilty. In this event, the bench will not have heard evidence, only an outline of the prosecution's case. But this should only be done in exceptional circumstances.[4]

Sureties of the peace and for good behaviour

In addition to the power to order a person to be bound over in his own recognisance to keep the peace and be of good behaviour, the magistrates may order him to find other people to stand as sureties for his own behaviour. The principles to be applied are similar to those for imposing a bind over on the defendant himself, but such an order as this places on the defendant an extra burden of finding other persons who will stand by him. Injustice may be done to a person if he is required to find sureties and he is friendless and does not know anyone who can stand surety for him. In these circumstances he will be committed to prison in default of finding the sureties.

4 *R v Preston Crown Court, ex p Pamplin* [1981] Crim LR 338, DC.

The possible drastic effects of imposing an order requiring a person to find sureties was recognised by Denning LJ in *Everett v Ribbands*[5] where he expressed the view that sureties should only be required where there has been a threat by words or conduct to breach the law of the land or to do something which is likely to result in a breach, and also a reasonable fear that this threat will be carried into effect. The bind over must be based on something actually done by the defendant such as threats of violence, interference with the course of justice or other conduct which causes an apprehension of a breach of the law. In other words the test may be more strict in the sense that mere apprehension of future conduct is insufficient, there must already have been some untoward conduct. In practice, however, a bind over even without sureties is never made without evidence of some form of reprehensible conduct.

Where sureties have been required, the surety has to acknowledge that he is a surety and accordingly has certain obligations and that if the principal breaches the terms of his recognizance the surety will be liable to forfeit some or all of his recognizance. The obligations of the surety can be undertaken either at the court hearing or later outside court before prescribed persons.[6]

VARYING, DISCHARGING OR DISPENSING WITH SURETIES

Varying or dispensing with a requirement for a surety

Where the defendant has been ordered to find sureties and has been committed in default of finding them, he may if he produces fresh evidence, apply to the court to vary the terms of the suretyship required, or to dispense with the requirements for sureties altogether.[7]

Where a surety wishes to be relieved of his obligation

A surety may apply to the court by way of complaint to be relieved of his obligation where the principal has breached, or is about to breach, the terms of the recognizance imposed on him.[8]

THE FORM OF THE BINDING OVER AND ITS DURATION

There is not a prescribed form of words for the binding over order, although naturally most courts adopt some form of set wording which they use. It is better that archaic and incomprehensible phraseology is not employed, and that the order is expressed in a way that the defendant easily understands. The essential meaning that must be

5 [1952] 2 QB 198, [1952] 1 All ER 823.

6 MCA 1980, s 119 and Magistrates' Courts Rules 1981, rr 86–88. (For the principles governing the forfeiture of recognizances see ch 4).

7 MCA 1980, s 118.

8 Ibid, s 116, and see ch 4 for the criteria to be considered when deciding to forfeit recognizances.

conveyed is that the person being bound over is under an obligation to pay all, or part of, a specified sum of money to the court if he breaches the terms of the bind over.

The terms of the order will be to keep the peace and be of good behaviour or either of the two, as the case may be. Conditions cannot be imposed on a bind over, eg a condition not to associate with X or not to visit a specified public house. However, the requirement of good behaviour may be emphasised to be towards a named person, eg 'to be of good behaviour especially towards Y'.[9]

The length of the bind over may be whatever the court prescribes, from one day onwards. But the court must act judicially and only impose the bind over only for as long as it is necessary. Although periods of up to five years have been upheld on appeal, the usual period is a year or less.

The enforcement of the bind over

There are two distinct stages in enforcing a bind over, first when the bind over is ordered, the accused may consent or refuse to be bound over (or, to be more correct, 'acknowledge' that he is bound over). Second, when the accused has been bound over and has breached the terms of that bind over the court may take sanctions against him.

WHERE THE ACCUSED REFUSES TO BE BOUND OVER

The court cannot impose a bind over unilaterally, it may only make the order with the accused's consent.[10] In reality, the choice is only illusory because if the accused refuses to be bound over, the magistrates may imprison him for up to six months or until he does agree to be bound over, whichever is the sooner.[11]

WHERE THE ACCUSED FAILS TO COMPLY WITH THE TERMS OF THE BIND OVER

Where a person has been bound over but subsequently breaches that order, then he will be liable to forfeit some or all of his recognizance.[12]

9 *R v Ayu* [1958] 3 All ER 636, [1958] 1 WLR 1264; *Lister v Healey Morgan* [1978] Crim LR 292, Birmingham Crown Court; *Goodlad v Chief Constable of South Yorkshire* [1979] Crim LR 51 (Sheffield Crown Court).

10 *Veater v G* [1981] 2 All ER 304, [1981] 1 WLR 567.

11 MCA 1980, 115(3). Although this provision, strictly speaking, only applies to a bind over made in a s 115 proceeding, in practice a limit of six months is applicable to a bind over made peremptorily in court: see Glanville Williams 'Preventive Justice and the Rule of Law' (1953) 16 MLR 417.

12 But a surety will only be liable to forfeit his recognizances if the accused has acted in a way which the recognizances were conditioned to prevent, eg a surety for the peace will not necessarily be forfeited if the principal commits an act which is unlawful but not a breach of the peace; see *Bamping v Barnes* [1958] Crim LR 186, 225 LT 241; obiter.

He should thereupon pay over the sum of money forfeited. If he refuses to pay his recognizances, the court may enforce the payment of the sum owing as if it were a fine.[13]

Accordingly, imprisonment is available only in two situations: where the person refuses to be bound over in the first place, or where having been bound over, he forfeits his recognizances and fails to pay them. Mere breach of a bind over does not carry imprisonment, only failure to pay the recognizances forfeited as a result of the breach.[14]

Legal aid

Legal aid is available to defend (but not to pursue) a complaint made under the Magistrates' Courts Act 1980, section 115. Whether in practice it would be considered to fall within the criteria for granting legal aid is another matter. Legal aid is not available where a bind over is to be imposed under the common law procedure.[15]

Appeal

A person bound over may appeal to the Crown Court against the order in the same way as any other appeal to the Crown Court.[16]

Summary

The justices' power to bind over derives from the Justice of the Peace Act 1361 or its precursors as extended by case law.

There is no difference in procedure between binding over to keep the peace and to be of good behaviour, and good behaviour includes keeping the peace. However, keeping the peace does not include all activities which would be covered by a binding over to be of good behaviour.

There are two bind over procedures: the Magistrates' Courts Act

13 See generally MCA 1980, s 120. It is not clear whether any court may forfeit the recognizances, or only the court which imposed the recognizances. It is submitted that it is only the court which made the order which may forfeit the recognizances, even where the breach occurred outside that court's petty sessional division; Cf MCA 1980, s 120(1), 'the court' (meaning the court which imposed the recognizances) and s 119(2); also (1978) 142 JP 668, (1979) 143 JP 42; and for a contrary view (1979) 143 JP 133.

14 See [1959] Crim LR at 57 and 305 and A. J. Chislett 'Recognizances and Conditions' [1958] Crim LR 734.

15 Legal Aid Act 1974, s 30(1).

16 Magistrates' Courts (Appeals From Binding Over Orders) Act 1956.

1980, section 115 where there is a complaint, summons and an adversarial hearing; and that at common law, where the parties are already before the court. Here there is no complaint or summons, but as a matter of good practice the defendant, and as a matter of law, the complainant and witnesses, are warned of the justices' intention to bind over and are invited to state their case why they should not be bound over.

A bind over can only be made with the consent of the person concerned. If he refuses to consent, he may be imprisoned for up to six months or until he does consent, whichever is the sooner.

When a person is in breach of a bind over, the only sanction against him is to estreat his recognizances. Only if he fails to pay those recognizances may imprisonment be imposed, if on conducting enforcement proceedings in the same way as for a fine, no other method of enforcement is appropriate.

Chapter 12

Juvenile offenders[1]

To even the most cynical observer it would appear incongruous that a child of ten years of age should be tried before a magistrates' court or before a judge and jury on anything but the gravest of charges, such as murder. English criminal procedure recognises that different treatment should normally be given to children below the age of 17 and so cases involving juveniles are generally heard in a specialised form of magistrates' court known as the juvenile court.

The juvenile court[2]

THE MAGISTRATES

This court is essentially a magistrates' court which is staffed by magistrates in the same way as the adult court, except that the lay magistrates are selected from among the whole bench because it is felt that they are 'specially qualified' to deal with juvenile offenders.[3] These justices must be under 65 years of age and are appointed to the 'juvenile panel'. The panel elects a chairman and a number of deputy chairmen as each juvenile court should (except in unforeseen circumstances) consist of three juvenile magistrates, at least one of whom should be male and one female and the court should be presided over by the chairman of the panel or a deputy chairman.

THE COURTROOM

It is a general principle, applicable to all criminal proceedings, that juveniles should be kept separate from adult offenders both in police stations and in court buildings. The exceptions to this rule are when the adult is the juvenile's relative or where the juvenile is jointly charged with the adult.[4] For juvenile courts there is in addition a particular provision that a juvenile court shall not sit in a room which

1 See in particular the Children and Young Persons Acts 1933, 1963 and 1969.
2 See the Children and Young Persons Act 1933, s 45.
3 Juvenile Courts (Constitution) Rules 1954, r 1 and for Inner London see Children and Young Persons Act 1933 Sch II.
4 Children and Young Persons Act 1933, s 31.

is used for normal criminal proceedings within one hour before or after those proceedings.[5]

Apart from these restrictions designed to protect juveniles by separating them from the normal criminal business of the courts, a restriction is also placed on the publicity that can be given to proceedings before the juvenile court. Only certain persons are allowed to be present during the hearing. These are:

(a) members and officers of the court;
(b) parties to the case before the court, their solicitors and counsel, and witnesses and other persons directly concerned with that case;
(c) bona fide representatives of newspapers or news agencies;
(d) such other persons as the court may specially authorise to be present.[6]

Therefore it should be noted that solicitors who are waiting for their case to be called on would generally be excluded, but the court would have power to admit persons who are in training either for social work or articled clerks if it were felt to be appropriate.

Although the press are permitted to be present, their reporting of the case is limited by section 49 of the Children and Young Persons Act 1933. The press may not report details of the name, address or school of a juvenile who is a defendant or witness in any proceedings before the juvenile court or any other details including the printing of a photograph which would identify him.[7]

Jurisdiction of the juvenile court

CHILDREN AND YOUNG PERSONS

So far offenders under the age of 17 have simply been referred to as 'juveniles' but to be precise this category should be divided into two further categories.

An offender over the age of 17 is an adult, and a child under the age of 10 years is conclusively presumed not to be guilty of an offence.[8] The offenders in the group 10 to 16 years of age inclusive are juveniles who are 'children' if they are 10–13 inclusive and 'young persons' if they are 14–16 inclusive.[9]

MODE OF TRIAL OF OFFENCES

All criminal proceedings start in the magistrates' court even where the offence is purely indictable such as a charge of murder. In the case of a juvenile, however, the matter is complicated because there is an initial choice

5 Ibid, s 47(2).
6 Ibid, s 47 as amended by the Children and Young Persons Act 1963, s 17(2).
7 Although the Secretary of State may make an exception in appropriate individual cases. See also s 10 of the Children and Young Persons Act 1969 where the juvenile attains 17.
8 Children and Young Persons Act 1933, s 50.
9 Ibid, s 107.

of whether the proceedings should be in the juvenile or the adult magistrates' court.

The basic principle is that a charge against a juvenile must be heard by a juvenile court.[10] The exceptions to this are:[11]

(a) where the juvenile is jointly charged with an adult; or
(b) where the juvenile is charged with an offence arising out of circumstances which are the same as, or connected with those giving rise to an offence with which a person who has attained the age of 17 is charged at the same time; or
(c) where an adult is charged with aiding, abetting, causing, procuring, allowing, or permitting the offence by the juvenile; or
(d) where the juvenile is charged with aiding, abetting, causing, procuring, allowing or permitting the offence by the adult; or
(e) where proceedings against the juvenile are started in the adult court and it only becomes apparent later that the defendant is a juvenile; or
(f) where the court is conducting remand proceedings.

Where exception (a) (joint charge with adult) applies the case shall be heard in the adult magistrates' court, but where any of the other exceptions (b)–(e) apply the decision is discretionary. Exception (f) enables an adult court, where necessary, to hear a remand of a juvenile.[12]

Remitting a case from the adult court to the juvenile court

If the case against the juvenile has found its way to the adult court because exception (a) has applied, ie the juvenile was jointly charged with an adult, the adult magistrates' court can send the case of the juvenile to the juvenile court in certain circumstances. This obviates to some extent the difficulty that there is no discretion where a joint charge is concerned as the juvenile's case must be heard initially in the adult court.

If the adult court, having heard representations on mode of trial for the adult, deals with the case summarily and the adult pleads guilty, or if it is decided by the court or on the accused's own election, to send the case for trial at the Crown Court and it is not felt to be in the interests of justice[13] for the juvenile to be committed for trial as well, the adult magistrates' court may remit the juvenile to the juvenile court for a trial to take place as to his innocence or guilt, where he pleads not guilty.[14] If the juvenile in these circumstances pleads guilty, the adult

10 Ibid, s 46 (and any other matters specifically assigned to a juvenile court such as care proceedings under section 1 of the Children and Young Persons Act 1969).

11 Children and Young Persons Act 1933, s 46 and Children and Young Persons Act 1963, s 18.

12 Children and Young Persons Act 1933, s 46(2).

13 The justices have a judicial discretion: *R v Newham Justices, ex p Knight* [1976] Crim LR 323.

14 MCA 1980, s 29.

court may exercise its limited powers of sentence, or if it feels that these are inappropriate, it may remit the juvenile to the juvenile court for sentence where all the powers of disposal open to a juvenile court may be exercised.[15]

The powers of an adult magistrates' court to sentence a juvenile are limited to:[16]

(a) an absolute or conditional discharge; or
(b) a fine (subject to the overall limits for juveniles); or
(c) an order requiring his parent or guardian to enter into a recognizance to take proper care of him and exercise proper control over him;

(as well as any of the normal ancillary orders such as costs, forfeiture, etc).

Committing a juvenile for trial

So far the discussion has been limited to the circumstances determining whether the juvenile should appear in the adult or juvenile magistrates' court, but there are situations where although proceedings may begin summarily, the juvenile may be committed for trial at the Crown Court.

Where a juvenile is charged with an indictable offence (which includes an either way offence) he must be tried summarily, which of course means tried in the juvenile court unless one of the exceptions applies making it either necessary (where there is a joint charge with an adult) or discretionary for the case to be heard in the adult magistrates' court. The only occasions when a juvenile must be committed for trial from the adult or juvenile court to the Crown Court are:[17]

(a) where he is charged with homicide; or
(b) where he is a young person (ie 14–16 years) and the court considers it ought to be possible to sentence him, if found guilty of the offence, under the provisions of section 53 of the Children and Young Persons Act 1933; or
(c) where he is jointly charged with an adult and the court considers it necessary in the interests of justice to commit them both for trial.

Section 53 of the Children and Young Persons Act 1933 gives the Crown Court power to detain a juvenile during Her Majesty's Pleasure either for life if he is convicted of murder, or where he has been convicted of a grave offence, that is an offence carrying a maximum sentence of 14 years' imprisonment or more, to detention for a period not exceeding the normal maximum for that offence.

15 Children and Young Persons Act 1933, s 56.
16 Children and Young Persons Act 1969, s 7(8).
17 MCA 1980, s 24. When making this decision it is unnecessary for the magistrates to consider the evidence in the case; it is sufficient if they consider the nature of the charge and hear representations from the parties: *R v South Hackney Juvenile Court, ex p RB (a minor) and CB (a minor)* (1983) Times, 23 March. In the case of homicide there is, of course, no choice, the juvenile must be committed for trial.

JUVENILES ATTAINING THE AGE OF 17 DURING THE PROCEEDINGS

The problems in this area might conveniently be divided into five.

(a) Where the defendant is a juvenile when he commits the offence but will be an adult before his first appearance in court. In this situation the police must be careful to ensure that any bail or summons is made returnable to the adult court and then the proceedings will continue in the usual way for an adult.

(b) Where the defendant is a juvenile on his first appearance in court but during the course of proceedings he becomes 17 and is charged with an either way offence. Does he then have a right to elect trial at the Crown Court? In this situation the defendant's right to elect trial will depend not on the date when proceedings were begun nor on the date of his first appearance in court, but on his age when the Court has to determine the issue of mode of trial.[18] This interpretation will cover such situations where the defendant does not appear on the return date of the summons but sends in a letter intimating a plea of not guilty so that the case is adjourned in his absence to a trial date. If when he appears at court on the day set down for trial, he has attained the age of 17 the court would have to conduct mode of trial proceedings. The crucial tests seem to be whether the summary trial has actually begun and whether a plea of guilty has been entered or evidence been called; if neither of these has occurred and the defendant has reached the age of 17 he is entitled to have mode of trial proceedings.[19]

(c) Where a juvenile is properly before the juvenile court but attains the age of 17 before the conclusion of the proceedings. In this event the juvenile court can carry on with the proceedings and although he may now be liable to penalties appropriate to a defendant over 17, the juvenile court may also make an order which it could have made if he were still a juvenile.[20]

(d) If the court has acted on the basis that it was believed that the defendant was a juvenile and it is discovered subsequently that he is over 17, the juvenile court may proceed with the hearing and determination of the charge.[1]

(e) Where a juvenile has been conditionally discharged by a juvenile court and subsequently commits a further offence when an adult

18 *Re Daley* [1982] 2 All ER 974.

19 Ibid at p 979. By analogy it is submitted that where the offence is purely indictable in the case of an adult, if proceedings have not reached the stage of a plea of guilty or evidence being called, the defendant, if he has attained 17, must be committed for trial at the Crown Court.

20 Children and Young Persons Act 1963, s 29.

1 Children and Young Persons Act 1933, s 48 but this does not enable the juvenile court to deal with a matter preferred after it is known that the defendant is 17: *R v Chelsea Justices, ex p DPP*]1963] 3 All ER 657, [1963] 1 WLR 1138.

during the currency of the discharge he may be dealt with by the juvenile court for the breach.[2]

Preliminary proceedings against a juvenile

It should always be borne in mind that the essential framework of the law of criminal procedure as it applies to juveniles is the same as for adult offenders. The procedure is modified to a greater or lesser extent at different stages of the proceedings, but it is still true to say that the best way of approaching the subject is to consider the procedure involving juveniles as the same as that applicable to adults with modifications rather than as a wholly separate code.

INVESTIGATION OF OFFENCES AND APPREHENSION OF OFFENDERS

In chapter 2 the police powers of investigation of offences are outlined and these procedures, including arrest, are just as applicable to juveniles. However, in the case of a child or young person it will usually be inappropriate to issue a warrant of arrest as a summons would be equally effective and the summons procedure is generally more common than the arrest and charge method. When a juvenile is arrested the police must take such steps as are practicable to inform at least one person whose attendance might be required at court along with the juvenile, ie his parent or guardian[3] and it is undesirable for a juvenile to be arrested or interviewed at his school.[4]

Where a juvenile is being interviewed the Home Office Administrative Directions, paragraph 4, provide that as far as practicable the juvenile should only be interviewed in the presence of a parent or guardian or a person not being a police officer and of the same sex as the juvenile. Failure to comply with these requirements may result in any confessions made by the juvenile being rendered inadmissible.[5]

2 Children and Young Persons Act 1933, s 48(2).

3 Ibid, s 34(2).

4 Para 4 of the Home Office Administrative Directions on Interrogation and taking of statements (see ch 2).

Where a juvenile has been arrested without warrant and cannot be brought before a court without delay there is a duty on the police to inquire into his case and release him unless the police consider it to be in his own interests to be detained, or unless he has committed homicide or another grave offence, or that his release would defeat the ends of justice or that he would fail to appear to answer the charge. Where the juvenile is not released, he must be placed into the care of the local authority (if the accused is not too unruly or it is not impracticable to do so) and brought before the court within 72 hours (Children and Young Persons Act 1969, s 29).

5 In *R v Roberts* [1970] Crim LR 464, (1970) 114 Sol Jo 413, a boy was questioned in the absence of his parent and although this was in breach of the Administrative Directions, the evidence was held to be admissible because it was voluntary.

Cautions

Instead of instituting criminal proceedings against a juvenile the police may be content that the juvenile should come to a police station and be formally 'cautioned' by a senior police officer. However, this procedure will only be adopted if the juvenile admits his guilt. If a caution is administered, no criminal proceedings will be instituted but the police will keep a record of the caution.[6]

If the police decide to institute proceedings against a juvenile they will normally lay an information against him with the view to obtaining a summons rather than arresting him and bringing him to court in custody or on bail, although, of course, in serious cases this procedure would have to be employed.[7]

An information against a juvenile is laid in the same way as in the case of an adult with the exception that a parent or guardian of his may be 'required' to attend at the court hearing[8] and this requirement may be incorporated on the summons so that not only the juvenile but the specified adult may be summoned to court.[9] When the police have decided to lay an information, it is their duty to notify the local authority for the area where the defendant lives and if the defendant has attained 13 the probation service must be notified as well.[10] This provision enables social inquiry reports to be more easily obtained for the juvenile court.

Once the summons has been issued the procedure follows that for adult offenders with the exception that the return date will be that for the juvenile court. In keeping with the general philosophy of separating juvenile offenders from other criminal proceedings, a particular magistrates' court will either try to ensure that there is a court room physically separate from the rest of the court rooms, or if this is not possible, it will attempt to list all juvenile court matters on a day when no other criminal cases are listed so that, for example, all domestic and juvenile cases are heard on the same day, when no petty sessional business is to be heard.

Contrast this with *R v Glyde* [1979] Crim LR 385 where a statement was excluded in circumstances where there was a breach of the Directions probably because the court was not satisfied of its voluntary nature.

6 For arguments whether cautions should be cited in court see (1974) 138 JP 661 and for cautioning generally see Ian Tweedie [1982] Crim LR 168 and Home Office Circular 49/1978.

7 The police need not consult anyone before they start criminal proceedings although they may have a juvenile bureau which would consult with other parties before bringing criminal proceedings in preference, for example, to a caution or a local authority bringing care proceedings.

8 Children and Young Persons Act 1933, s 34.

9 Magistrates' Courts (Children and Young Persons) Rules 1970, r 26.

10 Children and Young Persons Act 1969, s 34.

Procedure in the juvenile court

MATTERS PRELIMINARY TO THE HEARING

Legal aid

A juvenile is just as eligible to apply for legal aid as an adult but there is one major difference. A juvenile is unlikely to have any means of his own if he is under the school leaving age of 16 and even if he is over 16, he is unlikely to have a large income. Therefore the normal legal aid scheme is modified in the case of juveniles.

The scheme is modified to the extent of making different requirements for the submitting of a statement of means and the making of a legal aid contribution order.

Applicants under 16 years. The court may require a statement of means to be submitted both by the applicant (the juvenile) and the 'appropriate contributor'. An appropriate contributor means his father, or putative father, and his mother. The power to order a statement of means from the defendant and an appropriate contributor is discretionary and usually the court will require a statement only from the appropriate contributor and not from the juvenile and the application is determined on the means of the appropriate contributor.[11] If legal aid is granted and a contribution order is made at the end of the case, the appropriate contributor will have to pay the sum ordered.[12]

Applicants aged 16 years. In this situation the applicant will make his own application and there is no appropriate contributor. However, the statement of means would usually show either no income because the applicant was still at school, or a very low income. The court cannot 'require' a person to provide a statement of means for an applicant of this age but the court may take into account the means of a person who is liable to maintain the infant under section 17 of the Supplementary Benefits Act 1976 or would be so liable if the child were under 16, when deciding the application for legal aid or whether to make a contribution order. This would, it is submitted, take into account the situation of an infant applicant of 16 years of age who has little income of his own but is being supported by wealthy parents who themselves, because of the applicant's age, are not appropriate contributors.

In practice where a juvenile is concerned, if he is under 16 years, the means of his parents are included on a form 5 and if he is 16 years of age the juvenile himself completes the application unless the court asks for the further details under regulation 5 of the Legal Aid (Assessment of Resources) Regulations 1978.

11 See Legal Aid (Assessment of Resources) Regulations 1978, reg 6(4).
12 Legal Aid Act 1974, s 32(2).

Remanding a juvenile

In chapter 4 the decision whether to remand an adult accused in custody or on bail was based on whether one of the exceptions to the right to bail in the Bail Act 1976 applied. If an exception did apply, the accused was remanded in police or prison custody for the requisite period. A juvenile may be remanded in the same way, the decision whether the remand should be in custody or on bail being governed by the Bail Act. However, there is an important difference if the remand is to be in custody, because a juvenile defendant will not be remanded in police or prison custody but instead he will be remanded into the care of the local authority.[13] There are two exceptions to the rule that a juvenile custodial remand is into the care of the local authority:

(a) where he is committed for sentence under the provisions of section 37 of the Magistrates' Courts Act 1980 (committal with a view to a youth custody sentence being imposed in excess of the magistrates' powers) this will be to a prison establishment ie remand centre or youth custody centre;
(b) where the juvenile is male, has attained the age of 15 and is 'certified as unruly'.

Certificates of unruliness[14]

The court can certify under section 23 of the Children and Young Persons Act 1969 that the defendant is too unruly to be remanded into the care of the local authority and then he will be remanded to a remand centre or if one is not available, a prison establishment. A defendant may be certified unruly if he is male, aged over 15, and

(a) he is charged with an offence which carries 14 years imprisonment or more for an adult over 21 convicted on indictment, or
(b) he is charged with an offence of violence or has a previous finding of guilt for violence

and (in the case of (a) or (b)) either,

(i) it is the first remand and there is insufficient time to obtain a written report from the local authority on the availability of suitable accommodation, or
(ii) there is a report which declares that there is no suitable accommodation where he could be accommodated without substantial risk to himself or others, or
(c) he has persistently absconded from a community home or whilst he has been accommodated in a home he has seriously disrupted the running of the home and on the basis of a written report from the local authority the court is satisfied that no suitable

13 Children and Young Persons Act 1969, s 23.
14 Certificates of Unruly Character (Conditions) Order 1977.

accommodation is available without a risk of his absconding or seriously disrupting the running of the home.

The hearing in the juvenile court

The usual procedure in magistrates' courts for the hearing of an information is modified in the case of juveniles by the Magistrates' Courts (Children and Young Persons) Rules 1970 and the normal Magistrates' Courts Rules 1981 are subject to these provisions.[15]

The general principle applicable to all juveniles who appear before any court is that the court should have regard to the welfare of the child or young person,[16] and the general philosophy of the juvenile court rules is to modify the procedure to ensure that the defendant understands the proceedings.

As has already been explained, the proceedings are conducted in private (although the press may be present) and there may be more informality than in the petty sessional court, including calling the defendant by his Christian name. The defendant may well not be legally represented and if this is the case, the court may allow his parent or guardian to assist him in his defence, including cross-examining witnesses. If his parent or guardian is not available, a relative or any other responsible person may fulfil this function.[17] Whereas in the adult court the charge would be read to the accused, in the juvenile court the charge should be explained to him in simple language so that he can understand it, a complicated exposition of the legal technicalities should be avoided at all costs.[18]

The next rule then prescribes that the accused shall be asked whether he admits the charge and courts often use this terminology of 'admitting' or 'denying' offences instead of the more usual 'guilty' or 'not guilty'. The rules themselves are not clear on this as they use the term 'plea of guilty'[19] and although the words 'conviction' and 'sentence' are not to be used in the juvenile court or magistrates' court,[20] no limitation is put on the words 'guilty' or 'not guilty' and it may be the case that juveniles, familiar with crime stories on television, understand guilty and not guilty more easily and expect them to be used in court.

In the case of a trial, proceedings would follow the usual sequence

15 See Magistrates' Courts (Children and Young Persons) Rules 1970, r 3(2).
16 Children and Young Persons Act 1933, s 44 but note this does not mean that his welfare is the only or paramount consideration.
17 Magistrates' Courts (Children and Young Persons) Rules 1970, r 5.
18 Ibid, r 6.
19 Ibid, r 10.
20 Children and Young Persons Act 1933, s 59.

although there is express provision that where an unassisted juvenile makes assertions when cross-examining witnesses, those assertions may be translated by the court into relevant questions to be put to the witness. Furthermore, if the prosecution make out a prima facie case, the defendant must be informed that he may call evidence. Although these principles are spelled out in the case of juveniles, even in the adult court when dealing with unrepresented defendants, the court will quite commonly have to help the accused phrase his questions to be put by way of cross-examination and also at the conclusion of the prosecution case the defendant will be advised as to the courses of action open to him, namely whether to call evidence or not.

EVIDENCE OF MISCHIEVOUS DISCRETION

An important difference between the trial of an adult or a young person (ie a person aged 14–16 years inclusive) and the trial of a child is that there is a necessity for the prosecution to establish that the child not only had the mens rea to commit the particular offence with which he is charged but also that he knew that what he was doing was wrong. 'Wrong' in this context means knowledge of legal wrong or (probably) knowledge of moral wrong.[1] The burden of proof lies on the prosecution and there is a presumption (which lessens as the child approaches 14 years) that he is incapable of knowing right from wrong and the prosecution must disprove this presumption with the same standard of proof as they would in any other criminal proceedings. To summarise then:

(a) there is a requirement that the defendant must have known that he was doing wrong before he can be found guilty of an offence;
(b) there is a presumption that he did not know right from wrong which may be rebutted by the prosecution.

The practical effects of this are difficult to describe because the courts themselves find difficulty in applying the presumption and differ in the way in which evidence to displace the presumption of *doli incapax* should be presented. Let us consider three types of offence: an offence requiring no mens rea such as riding a motor cycle on common land; an offence requiring mens rea concerning the commission of the offence but not concerning the broader moral aspects of the act; and an offence of dishonesty.

Where the offence requires no mens rea in the normal sense, ordinarily the prosecution would merely have to prove that the accused did the act complained of and his knowledge of its lawfulness or

1 Cf the argument by G. Williams [1954] Crim LR 493 and *J. B. H. and J. H. (Minors) v O'Connell* [1981] Crim LR 632. In *R v Gorrie* (1918) 83 JP 136 the test was held to be even stricter, namely knowledge that the action was 'gravely or seriously wrong': cf the article cited for a comment on this.

otherwise would be irrelevant, but in the example of riding a motor cycle on common land, if the defendant were a child the prosecution would have to prove also that he knew that what he was doing was wrong, a matter which would be unnecessary in the case of an older defendant.[2]

In the second example, eg criminal damage, the juvenile under 14 may intend to damage or destroy the property but unless the prosecution proved that he also knew it was wrong to damage or destroy the property in question, he would be acquitted.

In the case of dishonesty offences the prosecution have to prove dishonesty (ie a knowledge that the action is wrong) in any event, but the problem may still arise because dishonesty as a concept is not altogether dependent on the defendant's view of the morality of his own actions.

Usually if the prosecution proved that the defendant acted dishonestly, it would logically follow that it had proved that he knew what he was doing was wrong. But what about the situation where the defendant knows that other people would disapprove of his actions but he himself believes he is acting quite justifiably. In *R v Ghosh*[3] dishonesty is defined as knowledge by the defendant that what he was doing was dishonest by the ordinary standards of reasonable and honest people, ie although the defendant may believe he is acting honestly, he is dishonest if he knows that ordinary people would consider his actions to be dishonest. This definition would include the actions of a 'Robin Hood' character who himself thought that it was morally sound to steal from the rich and give to the poor, but who *knew* that this conduct was regarded as dishonest by the standards of ordinary people. However, what if the 'Robin Hood' were under 14? The prosecution would have to show that the accused knew either that he was committing a legal wrong or that he was committing a moral wrong. Does the prosecution have to show that the accused thought he was acting *immorally*? If so, this is a distinction from the definition of dishonesty employed for adult offenders.

It can be appreciated that the prosecution may be in great difficulty in proving that a child had mischievous discretion. The commission of the crime itself is no evidence of the guilty mind which is essential before a child can be convicted of an offence although evidence of the way in which the offence was committed, eg concealment, may provide the necessary evidence.[4] Nevertheless, acts committed by the defendant which in the case of an adult would amount to a prima facie case and

2 *R v Kershaw* (1902) 18 TLR 357.

3 [1982] QB 1053, [1982] 2 All ER 689. See Glanville Williams *Textbook of Criminal Law* (1st edn) pp 660 et seq, and Smith and Hogan *Criminal Law* (4th edn) pp 517 et seq.

4 See 11 Halsbury's Laws of England (4th edn) para 33.

call for some explanation by the defence would not be sufficient to prevent a case being thrown out at the end of the prosecution case where there was a presumption that the accused did not know right from wrong. Accordingly, as the prosecution will have to adduce evidence to rebut the presumption of *doli incapax* as part of the prosecution case, there will be great pressure on the police to obtain some sort of admission of liability.[5]

In default of evidence that the offence was committed in such a way that negatives the presumption, or of a confession, the prosecution may adduce evidence of the defendant's background and education so that the court can decide having regard to his upbringing and schooling whether the defendant knows right from wrong.[6] Previous findings of guilt might be highly relevant to this issue because a defendant charged with an offence of theft could hardly deny that he knew it was wrong to steal if he had a previous court appearance for theft.[7] However, whilst it might be satisfactory for a judge to decide the question of mischievous discretion in the absence of the jury, it would cause severe problems in the juvenile court if the issue were decided by the same bench who were trying the general issue of guilt, although the procedure is quite lawful.

The doctrine has been heavily criticised and the continued existence of the principle is objected to on the grounds that:

(a) the courts are in great difficulty in applying it;
(b) the principle can put the prosecution into an impossible situation;
(c) conversely the defence might be gravely prejudiced by the admission of previous findings of guilt;
(d) the doctrine is inappropriate today because
    (i) the notion of mens rea generally is more highly developed,
    (ii) the philosophy of the juvenile court is to have regard to the welfare of the juvenile. The doctrine of *doli incapax*, by possibly rendering it more difficult to find the case proved in correspondence to the lack of moral education which the child has received (because the worse the home circumstances of the child, the less likely is he to know right from wrong), will keep the child away from the guidance he needs rather than from punishment.

PROCEDURE AFTER A FINDING OF GUILT[8]

It was mentioned earlier in this chapter that the words 'conviction' and 'sentence' are not to be used in proceedings involving juveniles in the magistrates' courts. Instead of convicting the defendant, the magistrates

5 *W (An infant) v Simpson* [1967] Crim LR 360, (1967) 111 Sol Jo 273.
6 *B v R* (1959) 123 JP 61, 44 Cr App Rep 1, and *F v Padwick* [1959] Crim LR 439, DC.
7 *R v B, R v A* [1979] 3 All ER 460, [1979] 1 WLR 1185. This case should be read in detail as it contains a clear account of the position and a review of some of the authorities.
8 Magistrates' Courts (Children and Young Person) Rules 1970, r 10.

would make a finding of guilt and then proceed to 'make an order' in respect of him rather than passing sentence.

If the defendant is found guilty or has pleaded guilty he and his parent will be given an opportunity to make a statement to the court and then the court

> shall take into consideration such information as to the general conduct, home surroundings, school record and medical history of the child or young person, as may be necessary to enable it to deal with the case in his best interests and, in particular, shall take into consideration such information as aforesaid which is provided in pursuance of section 9 of the Act of 1969.

SOCIAL INQUIRY AND SCHOOL REPORTS

By virtue of section 5(8) of the Children and Young Persons Act 1969 if the police (or indeed any other informant) lay an information against a young person (and by the direction of the Secretary of State, a child as well[9]), the local authority must be informed. The authority will then be under a duty to prepare a social inquiry report for the court under section 9 of the 1969 Act. Although the section prescribes that the local authority should prepare the report it will usually only prepare the report in the case of a child or young person below a certain age which is dependent on local arrangements, the probation service being responsible for providing reports for the older juveniles unless the local authority already has prior involvement with the family or the defendant.

There is an important difference between the provision of social inquiry reports in the juvenile court and in the adult court. In the case of adults it is rare for reports to be prepared in anticipation of a plea of guilty or of a conviction whereas in the juvenile court reports will be prepared in advance for most cases.

In rule 10(b) of the Magistrates' Courts (Children and Young Persons) Rules 1970 provision is made for the court to receive a report from the juvenile's school, and the justices can attach considerable importance to what is contained in this report. The report will contain details of the defendant's attendance at school, his educational attainment and progress and his relationships with the school staff and his contemporaries.

REMAND FOR FURTHER INQUIRIES

Although a social inquiry report and a school report should be available at the first hearing of nearly every case involving a juvenile, the information contained in them may be insufficient. The information contained in the social inquiry report may be limited because of the time

9 Children and Young Persons Act 1969, s 34 and SI1970/1882.

available between the issue of the summons and the court hearing date. The information will probably be substantially based on interviews with the juvenile and his parents and sometimes it may be felt that a more thorough examination of the juvenile's problems may be called for. In this case the initial social inquiry report at the hearing may recommend that the juvenile should be remanded into the care of the local authority for observation and assessment.[10] The effect of this is that the juvenile will be kept in a specialised local authority home and at the end of the period of remand reports would be presented to the court from the local authority covering such aspects of the juvenile's welfare as education and psychological and behavioural problems.

THE PRESENTATION OF REPORTS IN COURT

At the court hearing the various reports will be presented to the court. The reports need not be read out aloud[11] and are usually not. At this stage of the proceedings the juvenile or his parent may be required to withdraw from court if it is felt to be necessary in the interests of the child or young person.

If the report is not read out aloud or the juvenile or parent is required to withdraw from the court, the defendant or his parent will not know the allegations that have been made against them, unlike in the adult court where a copy of a probation report must be given to the defendant or his solicitor or in the case of a juvenile, his parent.[12]

Considerable importance, naturally, is attached to the views expressed in a report prepared for the juvenile court, and the effect of a recommendation in a report can be very important as the juvenile court could make a care order on the juvenile which could have the result of taking him away from his parents until the age of 18. To mitigate the injustice of any lack of disclosure if the report is not handed to the defendant, his parent or solicitor,

> the child or young person shall be told the substance of any part of the information given to the court bearing on his character or conduct which the court considers to be material to the manner in which the case should be dealt with unless it appears to be impracticable so to do having regard to his age and understanding.[13]

A similar provision is made where anything is contained in the report which has a bearing on the parent. If as a result of what is said the parent or juvenile wishes to call more evidence, the court, if it considers it to be relevant, may grant an adjournment to allow more

10 See Children and Young Persons Act 1969, s 23 and MCA 1980, s 10(3).
11 Magistrates' Courts (Children and Young Person) Rules 1970, r 10(1)(d).
12 Powers of Criminal Courts Act 1973, s 46.
13 Magistrates' Courts (Children and Young Person) Rules 1970, r 10(2)(a).

evidence to be presented and shall if necessary require the maker of any report to attend at the hearing.[14]

Although there is this provision in rule 10 for the court to give a précis of matters contained in the report which have influenced them, there must nevertheless be a feeling of injustice if the defendant and parent cannot see the reports themselves, and as a consequence some courts will allow a defence solicitor to have a copy of the report, or a parent if the juvenile is unrepresented, although even these courts will be coy of revealing the school report arguing the reluctance of school authorities to speak frankly if they know that their pupils will be made aware of the contents of the report.[15]

Before an order is made the court will (unless it is felt to be undesirable) inform the defendant and his parent of the manner in which it proposes to deal with the case and ask if there are any further representations. When an order is made the court will (again unless it is felt to be undesirable) explain the general nature and effect of the order.[16]

Orders which can be made by a juvenile court in criminal proceedings

DEFERRED SENTENCE

This option is open to a juvenile court.[17]

IMPRISONMENT

This is not available for any offender until the age of 21 years and therefore its variants, suspended and partly suspended sentences, are also not available.[18]

YOUTH CUSTODY

As described in chapter 7, youth custody is available for defendants of not less than 15 years of age. The juvenile court may pass a sentence of youth custody with the maximum term limited to that for imprisonment, ie six months for a single indictable offence and twelve months when there are two indictable offences. Of particular importance to the

14 Ibid, r 10.
15 There may also be matters of a delicate nature in the report which it is better that the child is not made aware of eg his illegitimacy.
16 Magistrates' Courts (Children and Young Persons) Rules 1970, r 11.
17 But for the problems connected with this course of action, see (1980) 144 JP 330 and 635.
18 Criminal Justice Act 1982, s 1.

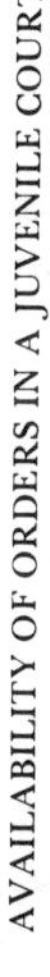
AVAILABILITY OF ORDERS IN A JUVENILE COURT

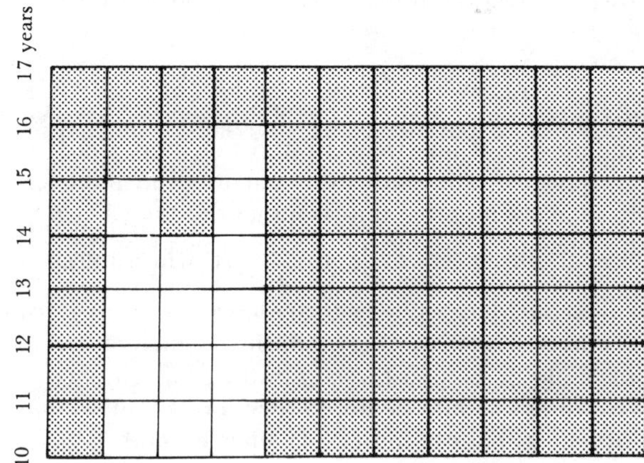
10
11
12
13
14
15
16
17 years
Deferred sentence
Youth custody
Detention centre order
Community service
Attendance centre
Care order
Supervision order
Fine
Compensation
Absolute and conditional discharge
Parental recognizances

juvenile court will be the restrictions imposed on sentencing any defendant under the age of 21 to youth custody.

COMMITTALS FOR SENTENCE – SECTION 37 OF THE MAGISTRATES' COURTS ACT 1980

Section 37 (as amended and substituted by paragraph 49 of Schedule 14 to the Criminal Justice Act 1982) provides that a court can commit a defendant of not less than 15 and not more than 16 years[19] who has been convicted of an indictable offence punishable on indictment with more than six months' imprisonment to the Crown Court for sentence with a view to youth custody. The Crown Court has an overall limit of 12 months' youth custody for a person under 17[20] and so where the juvenile court has a power to sentence for up to 12 months by making consecutive sentences of six months on each of two indictable offences there would be no point in committing for sentence.

Two things should be noted therefore about section 37:

(a) it only applies to indictable offences; and

(b) only to defendants not less than 15 years old and not more than 16 years.[1]

If an accused is committed to the Crown Court for sentence, the usual provisions about the remand to the care of the local authority and unruliness certificates do not apply. Where the accused is remanded in custody he will be detained in a remand centre or prison.[2]

DETENTION CENTRE

The juvenile court may pass a sentence of detention in a detention centre on an offender over the age of 14 years in the same way as the adult court, but two comments need to be made. As a matter of prison administration juveniles (ie offenders under the age of 17) are kept separate from seniors (ie those between 17 and 21 years) and so for administrative reasons the court may be directed by the Home Office to send its juveniles to one detention centre and its seniors to another. Furthermore, the principle behind section 5 of the Criminal Justice Act 1982, which governs the use of consecutive or aggregate detention centre orders, is that no offender under the age of 15 years should be subject to more than four months' detention in a detention centre at any one time. Section 5(1) provides that a detention centre order may be made consecutive to another detention centre order. Also, of course, an order may be made which will run concurrent to an existing order

19 This means *under 17* years of age.
20 Criminal Justice Act 1982, s 7(8).
1 See note 19, above.
2 MCA 1980, s 37(2).

which the defendant may already have been serving for some months. If, because of these circumstances, the offender under 15 years of age would suffer a total order exceeding four months the excess will automatically be remitted.[3] A sentence of more than four months would be equivalent to youth custody and this is not available for defendants below the age of 15.

In the case of an offender over 15 the same restrictions apply – consecutive detention centre orders may not be passed if the total will be more than four months, and if the court does inadvertently make such an order it will be treated as a sentence of youth custody,[4] since the restrictions on imposing youth custody and detention are the same, with the exception of the term of four months being the borderline between detention in a detention centre and in a youth custody centre.

In the situation where the defendant is in a detention centre already and the aggregate sentence will exceed four months the court is enjoined by section 5(5) to reflect whether it really intends him to be subject to an order exceeding four months in total as the court may not be so aware of the totality of the sentence to which the defendant is subject when it has not passed the whole of the sentence itself. If the court is still decided that he should have a custodial sentence exceeding four months in total, a youth custody order for the term which the sentencing court wishes to impose should be passed under section 5(5) which will convert the existing detention centre order into one continuous youth custody order.

There are no detention centres for girls, so in the case of female offenders over 17 a sentence of youth custody of between 21 days and four months may be imposed instead (of course females are also eligible for the normal terms of youth custody exceeding four months). There is no similar provision for females under the age of 17 and so the minimum custodial sentence for them will be a youth custody order in excess of four months.

COMMUNITY SERVICE

By virtue of section 68 of and Schedules 12 and 13 to the Criminal Justice Act 1982, sections 14 and 17 (inter alia) of the Powers of Criminal Courts Act 1973 are amended to provide for the availability of community service as an option for offenders aged 16 years. Two matters should be noted with respect to the availability of community service for juveniles. Although community service is now available throughout the country, schemes for offenders aged 16 will not be universally available immediately and so community service will only

3 Criminal Justice Act 1982, s 5(3).
4 Ibid, s 5(4).

be available where the court has been notified by the Secretary of State that a scheme has been provided in that area; furthermore, where it is available, the maximum number of hours which may be ordered for a juvenile offender will be 120. Otherwise the restrictions on imposing community service are the same as those for an adult.

ATTENDANCE CENTRE

Attendance centre orders are available for juvenile defendants in the same way as for adults, ie where the offence would carry imprisonment in the case of an adult over 21 years of age. As in the case of detention centres, the attendance centre will usually segregate junior offenders (ie those under 17) from the offenders attending the senior attendance centre by requiring them to attend the centre at different times.

The major differences between attendance centre orders for juveniles and those over 17 years are:

(a) no attendance centre order shall exceed 24 hours for an offender under 17 (as opposed to 36 hours for an offender above that age);[5]

(b) where the offender is under 14 years the aggregate number of hours ordered may be less than the usual minimum of 12 if the court is of the opinion that 12 hours would be excessive, having regard to his age or any other circumstances;[6]

(c) the maximum number of hours for which attendance may be required on any one occasion on one day is three, but where the offender is a juvenile, the attendance centre may require a shorter period of, for example, two hours for each session.[7]

When the juvenile court is imposing detention centre orders consecutive to each other or concurrent to existing orders, making the defendant liable to more than four months' detention in all, section 5 of the Criminal Justice Act 1982 provides that where the defendant was under 15 the excess period would be remitted, or if he were over 15 the whole term to be served would be treated as a term of youth custody. In the case of an attendance centre order there appears to be no authority to make it consecutive to another attendance centre order, but it is clear nevertheless that an order can be made whilst there is already a similar order in existence. If this is proposed, the court may make the new order without regard to the number of hours specified in the previous order, or to the fact that the other order is still in effect.[8]

CARE ORDERS

The care order is an order which is unique to juveniles. The effect of a care order is to give the same parental powers and duties to the local authority as

5 Ibid, s 17(5).
6 Ibid, s 17(4).
7 Ibid, s 17(11).
8 Ibid, s 17(6).

those enjoyed by the parents until the juvenile becomes 18 (or 19 if he was 16 or over when the order was made)[9] and the local authority has the duty to retain the juvenile in its care notwithstanding any claims by the parents whilst the care order is in force.[10] When the child is in its care, it is the duty of the local authority to give first consideration to the need to safeguard and promote the welfare of the child throughout his childhood except where it is necessary to exercise the power in a way inconsistent with this in the interests of protecting the public.[11]

When the child is in the care of the local authority he may be boarded out with foster parents or in a voluntary home or other appropriate arrangements may be made. The authority may even allow the child to be under the charge of a parent, guardian, relative or friend.[12]

The power to make a care order

In criminal proceedings[13] a care order may be made where:

(a) a child or young person is found guilty of an offence punishable in the case of an adult with imprisonment;[14] and

(b) a care order is appropriate because of the seriousness of the offence;[15] and

(c) the child or young person is in need of care or control which he is unlikely to receive unless the court makes a care order;[16] and

(d) the child or young person is legally represented, but an order may be made where he is not legally represented if he was refused legal aid on the ground that his means were such that he did not require assistance or having been informed of his right to apply for legal aid he refused or failed to apply.[17]

The making of a care order

Before the enactment of the Criminal Justice Act 1982 the magistrates simply made a care order, and the treatment of the person who was the subject of that order was at the discretion of the local authority. Although the local authority had, and still has, the power to restrict the liberty of the offender to the extent that it feels appropriate[18] there was some disquiet among magistrates that they were making care orders

9 Children and Young Persons Act 1969, s 20(3).
10 Child Care Act 1980, s 10.
11 Ibid, ss 18–19.
12 Ibid, s 21.
13 A care order may also be made in care proceedings brought under s 1 of the Children and Young Persons Act 1969 which are civil in nature.
14 Children and Young Persons Act 1969, s 7(7).
15 Children and Young Persons Act 1969, s 7A (s 23 of the Criminal Justice Act 1982).
16 Ibid.
17 Children and Young Persons Act 1969, s 7A (s 24 of the Criminal Justice Act 1982).
18 Child Care Act 1980, s 10(2) but note s 21A (as included by s 25 of the Criminal Justice Act 1982) (authorisation of use of secure accommodation).

and the local authority was letting some of the offenders return straight home. Accordingly, in some circumstances the court which makes the care order has the power to restrict the discretion of the local authority. This is provided for by section 20A of the Children and Young Persons Act 1969.[19]

Where a person is already the subject of a care order and is subsequently found guilty of an offence punishable with imprisonment, the court which finds him guilty may add a condition in the existing care order that the power of the local authority under section 21(2) of the Child Care Act 1980 to allow the juvenile to be in the charge and control of a parent, guardian, relative or friend, shall not be exercisable, or shall be exercisable only in respect of a particular parent or friend, etc, for a period of up to six months. This power is only exercisable where:

(a) the juvenile has been found guilty of an offence punishable with imprisonment in the case of a person over 21;[20] and
(b) the offender is already subject to a care order; and
(c) the court is of the opinion that it is appropriate to exercise this power because of the seriousness of the offence and that no other method of dealing with the person to whom the care order relates is appropriate; and
(d) for the purpose of deciding whether any other method is appropriate the court shall obtain and consider information about the circumstances; and
(e) the defendant is legally represented and if he is not then he must either have been refused legal aid on the ground that it did not appear his means were such that he required assistance or having been informed of his right to apply for legal aid he had the opportunity to do so but refused or failed to apply.

If the court does add such a condition to a care order, at any time during the currency of the restriction the juvenile, his parent or guardian or the local authority, may apply to the juvenile court to revoke or vary the condition[1] but only the local authority may appeal to the Crown Court against the initial decision to impose the restriction.[2]

Discharging a care order[3]

A care order may be varied in its terms but in particular the local

19 Inserted by the Criminal Justice Act 1980, s 22.
20 The Act is not specific whether the offence for which the defendant has just been found guilty must have been committed during the currency of the existing care order, but it is submitted that the provision is designed to be used on those offenders in care who abscond and commit further offences, and that it would be inequitable to use a conviction for a pre-existing offence as a basis for imposing this restriction on liberty.
1 Child Care Act 1980, s 20A(6).
2 Ibid, s 20A(7).
3 Children and Young Persons Act 1969, s 21.

authority or the juvenile or his parent may apply to the juvenile court for the care order to be discharged. If the application is successful, the order will be discharged either completely, or a supervision order will be substituted. If the application is unsuccessful, the person to whom the care order relates may appeal to the Crown Court or any of the persons who are entitled to apply for discharge may renew their application after a period of three months (or less with the consent of the juvenile court).

PROBATION ORDERS

These are not available for juveniles as their use is confined to offenders over the age of 17,[4] but a similar form of disposal is provided by the supervision order.

SUPERVISION ORDERS

A supervision order may be made where a juvenile has been found guilty of any offence (not necessarily only an offence punishable with imprisonment).[5] The juvenile will be under the supervision of a local authority (ie a social worker) or a probation officer, as the court directs,[6] and usually the younger juveniles will be supervised by the local authority and the older ones by the probation service if a probation officer has already had or is currently involved with the family.[7] The duty of the supervisor is to advise, assist and befriend the supervised person[8] and the supervision order when made will last up to three years or such shorter period as is specified by the court. All the supervision orders start on the day they are made so there is no such thing as a consecutive supervision order.[9]

Conditions in a supervision order

A supervision order may contain such prescribed provisions as the court considers appropriate for facilitating the performance by the supervisor of his duty under section 14 of the 1969 Act to advise, assist and befriend the supervised person. The prescribed conditions to be included in an order made under section 7(7) of the 1969 Act, if the court thinks they are appropriate, are requirements:

(a) to inform the supervisor of any change of address; and
(b) to keep in touch with the supervisor and comply with his instructions and receive visits from him at home if the supervisor desires this.[10]

4 Powers of Criminal Courts Act 1973, s 2.
5 Children and Young Persons Act 1969, s 7(7).
6 Ibid, s 11.
7 For the selection of supervisors see Children and Young Persons Act 1969, s 13.
8 Ibid, s 14.
9 See ibid, s 17.
10 Magistrates' Courts (Children and Young Person) Rules 1970, r 28(2).

In addition to these general provisions the supervision order may contain additional requirements.

(a) Residence. A general condition of residence with a specified individual may be imposed provided the said individual agrees to that provision being made.[11] This condition will be subject to any conflicting requirements of residence contained in the following conditions.

(b) Intermediate treatment. The supervision order may contain conditions that the supervised person should participate in activities organised by the supervisor and further conditions may require that the supervised person must attend on the required occasions and also, if necessary, live at a specified place. These conditions might be appropriate, for example, where the juvenile is away at an adventure camp. If the juvenile is also subject to the general condition of residence under section 12(1), that will temporarily be overridden by the condition of residence under this provision in section 12(2). The conditions imposed under this subsection can only last for a maximum of 90 days or such shorter period as the court specifies, and such conditions are known generally as a supervision order with a condition of intermediate treatment as the order is 'intermediate' to a full care order. A court can only make such a condition of intermediate treatment if it is satisfied that the local authority have made available a suitable scheme and it is the duty of each local authority to prepare a scheme.[12]

The scheme of intermediate treatment under section 12(2) described above can apply to supervision orders made after a finding of guilt and also to supervision orders made in civil care proceedings, but where the court is concerned with criminal proceedings it has more comprehensive powers of imposing conditions, including a condition of intermediate treatment under section 12(3C) of the Children and Young Persons Act 1969.

Conditions under section 12(3C). The previous paragraphs discussed the power of a court to impose a condition of intermediate treatment in a supervision order under section 12(2) of the 1969 Act. This power is available in all supervision orders whether made in criminal proceedings or not. If this condition is imposed under section 12(2) the directions given must be part of a scheme set up by the relevant local authority. However, where a supervision order is made in criminal proceedings, conditions may be imposed under section 12(3C) as an

11 Children and Young Persons Act 1969, s 12(1).
12 Ibid, s 19 (s 21 of the Criminal Justice Act 1982).

alternative but not in addition to intermediate treatment under section 12(2). The conditions available include a power for the court to require the supervised person to do particular things of a nature which a supervisor could direct under section 12(2) (intermediate treatment). It would, however, appear that the requirements would have to be spelled out in detail rather than merely requiring the offender to do as the supervisor directs, and these requirements are not limited to activities which are part of a local authority scheme. If conditions are imposed which fall outside the local authority scheme they may not require:

(a) the absence of the supervised person from home for more than two consecutive nights and more than two nights in any one week; or
(b) participation in activities in school hours if the supervised person is of school age (but if this is part of an arrangement made by the local education authority the restriction would not apply).

Further conditions which may be imposed under section 12(3C) are:

Night restriction order. This is a condition that the supervised person should remain at a specified place or places (which means the place or places where he lives) between the hours of 6 pm and 6 am as the court shall require, provided that the period of restriction on any one night does not exceed ten hours. The night restriction condition can only last for a maximum of 30 nights and these nights must be within the first three months of the order. The purpose of this 'curfew' is to keep the erring juvenile at home with his parents and thus it is hoped depriving him of the opportunity to commit offences with other friends of his, therefore although there may be a night restriction order in force, the juvenile may nevertheless leave the house provided he is accompanied by his parent or guardian, his supervisor or some other person specified in the supervision order.

Prohibition on participating in certain activities. The subsection further provides that the supervision order may contain a condition prohibiting the supervised person from participating in specified activities either

(a) on a specified day or days during the currency of the order, or
(b) during the whole of the order or a specified part of it.

An obvious use for this would be a condition prohibiting the juvenile's attendance at certain football matches. Unlike intermediate treatment or a night restriction order there is no overall limit of 90 or 30 days.

Requirements for the inclusion of conditions under section 12(3C). Before any condition under this subsection can be included in a supervision order (and the conditions may be combined together) the court must

(a) consult the supervisor about the offender's circumstances and whether it is feasible to secure compliance with the conditions and if it is feasible then,
(b) consider the conditions necessary for securing the good conduct of the supervised person or for preventing a repetition of the offence,

and then the supervised person, or, if a child (ie under 14), his parent or guardian, must consent to the inclusion of the conditions.

The relationship between conditions under section 12(2) and 12(3C)
On the face of it there appears to be a duplication between the provisions of section 12(2) and 12(3C). An intermediate treatment condition under section 12(2) means that the court, having made the order, is leaving it entirely to the discretion of the supervisor what activities, if any, the offender should participate in. Section 12(3C) gives the court power to spell out in the order what activities the offender *must* participate in, and the supervisor and supervised juvenile must comply with the order. In addition, the supervised activities under section 12(3C) may be combined with a night restriction order and a condition to refrain from certain activities. Therefore, the conditions under section 12(3C) are seen as bolstering the court's confidence in the supervision order as a credible alternative to a care order or custodial sentence. Indeed, such conditions or supervised activities would certainly be more rigorous than a short detention centre order.

The cynic may suggest that as the condition of supervised activities might be left to the supervisor's discretion under section 12(2), the court will only make an order under section 12(3C) if it lacks confidence in the supervisor, ie the social services department of the local authority. In fact the social services will probably welcome the conditions being spelled out so that the offender knows where he stands, and that the conditions are part of a scheme designed specifically for juveniles which provides a rigorous supervision order, possibly combined with the other conditions under section 12(3C).

Conditions of medical treatment (section 12(4)). If the court is satisfied after hearing the evidence of a medical practitioner approved under section 12 of the Mental Health Act 1983 that the supervised person is suffering from a mental condition which is susceptible to treatment but which does not require the making of a hospital order the court may attach one of the following conditions to a supervision order:
(a) treatment by a specified practitioner;
(b) treatment as a non-resident patient at a place specified in the order; or
(c) treatment as a resident patient at a hospital (but not a special hospital) or a mental nursing home;

and before such a requirement can be included the court must be satisfied that arrangements can be made for the treatment and that the supervised person, if over 14 years of age, consents to the condition.

Breach of a supervision order

A supervision order is similar in some respects to a probation order but there is at least one important distinction. If a person who has been placed on probation commits an offence during the currency of that probation order, he is automatically in breach of the probation order. This is not the case with a supervision order, a fresh offence does not automatically breach the supervision order rendering the offender liable to be sentenced again for the original offence, as the supervisor must bring proceedings for breach of the conditions of the order or on some other ground on which the court would consider it appropriate to revoke or vary the order. If the supervised person has breached a condition he may, instead of the order being revoked, be fined up to £50 or be sent to an attendance centre.

FINE

A juvenile may be fined for an offence in the same way as an adult except that there is an overall limit to the fine for each particular offence of £200 for a young person and £50 for a child.[13]

Enforcement of fines against juveniles

Although a juvenile may have been fined by a court, he may not have very much money. If the court feels that a fine, or an order for costs or compensation would nevertheless be the best way of dealing with the case the court has the duty to order the parent or guardian to pay the sums due unless either:

(a) the parent or guardian cannot be found; or
(b) it would be unreasonable to make such an order having regard to the circumstances of the case;

and such an order can be made in the parent's absence if he has been required to attend and has failed to do so.[14]

If the fine, etc has been ordered to be paid by the parent any enforcement action will be taken against him as if it were his fine and his responsibility[15] but if the juvenile was originally ordered to pay, if

13 MCA 1980, s 36.

14 See the Children and Young Persons Act 1933, s 55 (s 26 of the Criminal Justice Act 1982).

15 When a child is in care, the local authority does not become the parent or guardian for the purpose of being ordered to pay his fine under s 55 of the Children and Young Persons Act 1933: *Re Leeds City Council* [1982] Crim LR 364; although de facto control may be given to the natural parent if the child is at home on leave. If the magistrates find as a fact that the natural parent is in de facto control the *Leeds City Council* case may suggest that the provisions of s 55 may apply to the parent.

he has defaulted in payment he will be summoned to the arrears court.[16] If, after a means inquiry, the court is satisfied the defaulter has had the means to pay and has neglected or refused to pay the court may either:

(a) order the parent to enter into a recognizance if he consents, to ensure that the juvenile will pay, or
(b) if it is considered reasonable in all the circumstances, direct that the unpaid sums be paid by the parent or guardian as if it were his fine.[17] If such an order is made the adult may appeal to the Crown Court.[18]

If the court decides not to make the parent responsible for payment it can order that the juvenile defaulter attend at an attendance centre if one is available.[19] The court will fix the number of hours to be served, as with an ordinary attendance centre order, but the number of hours to be served will be reduced thereafter in proportion to any payments made of the sums due.

CONDITIONAL AND ABSOLUTE DISCHARGE

These may be made in the same way as in the adult court.

BIND OVER

Although it is technically possible to bind over a juvenile there is no power to send him to prison if he refuses to acknowledge that he is bound over. Therefore in practice no attempt should be made to bind over a juvenile, unless he is willing to be bound over.[20]

COMPENSATION

This is available as in the case of adults.

ORDER REQUIRING A PARENT TO ENTER INTO A RECOGNIZANCE[1]

Where a juvenile has been found guilty of an offence the court may, instead of making an order in respect of him, order his parent or guardian with their consent, to enter into a recognizance to take proper care of him and exercise proper control over him.

16 Which may be the adult court, though in practice juvenile defaulters would be summoned to a juvenile court.
17 The local authority is not the child's parent or guardian for these purposes if the child is in its care: *R v Barnet Juvenile Court, ex p Barnet London Borough Council* [1982] Crim LR 592, DC.
18 Children and Young Persons Act 1933, s 55.
19 Criminal Justice Act 1982, s 17.
20 *Veater v G* [1981] 2 All ER 304, [1981] Crim LR 563; *C v Oxford* (1983) Times, 18 July.
1 Children and Young Persons Act 1969, s 7(7).

COSTS

A juvenile can be ordered to pay costs (and of course in his turn he can claim them from central funds or against the prosecutor where appropriate) but if the juvenile is ordered to pay the costs himself (as opposed to making his parent or guardian responsible) the amount of costs that can be awarded cannot exceed the amount of any fine that was imposed.[2]

FORFEITURE

Available as in the case of an adult.

2 Costs in Criminal Cases Act 1973, s 2(2)(b).

Chapter 13

Road traffic

The bulk of the work of a magistrates' court is concerned with road traffic cases, ie prosecutions arising out of the use of a motor vehicle on a road. Prosecutions under the various statutes governing the use of motor vehicles are of course brought under the same procedure as for any other criminal case, usually by way of an information and summons, or where appropriate, arrest and charge. However, road traffic cases do exhibit one or two unusual features and as such prosecutions are so common and can constitute a considerable part of a criminal practice, it is worthwhile to study their procedure in more detail.

Legislation

Road traffic law is a creature of statute and so it is important to acquire a knowledge of the relevant statutes and regulations and to be able to find one's way round the various sections. Once the relevant section has been found, it should then be studied intensively as road traffic law is one of the most technical branches of the criminal law.

The main source of this law is the Road Traffic Act 1972 (which has been amended by the Road Traffic Act 1974 and the Transport Acts 1981 and 1982). This Act contains most of the commonly occurring offences and their penalties, and any references to sections of an Act in this chapter are, unless further qualified, references to this statute.

The scheme for setting up local parking regulations and the payment of fixed penalty notices is to be found in the Road Traffic Regulation Act 1967 which also includes speeding offences and motorway offences. Commercial affairs such as the regulation of drivers' hours and the compiling of records for heavy goods vehicles are to be found in the Transport Act 1968, and motor taxation offences, eg failure to pay for the road fund licence, are found in the Vehicles (Excise) Act 1971. Mention should also be made of theft of a motor vehicle and taking a motor vehicle without the owner's consent, and going equipped for such purposes, as these offences under the Theft Act 1968 are liable to an obligatory endorsement and discretionary disqualification.[1]

1 Road Traffic Act 1972, (Sch 4, Part III).

Road traffic law will be found in Volume 2 of *Stone's* and in the various text books on the subject,[2] but most of all the practitioner should make himself familiar with the contents of Schedule 4 to the Road Traffic Act 1972.

Procedure at commencement of proceedings

POWERS OF ARREST

As traffic offences are criminal matters proceedings start with the laying of an information. Most of the offences are minor, summary matters and do not carry a power of arrest, therefore the summons is the only method of securing the attendance of the accused at court unless exceptional circumstances apply. Some arrestable road traffic offences are:

(a) Causing death by reckless driving (section 1). This carries a maximum of five years' imprisonment and is thus an arrestable offence by virtue of section 2 of the Criminal Law Act 1967.
(b) Reckless and careless or inconsiderate driving carry a power of arrest if section 164 applies, ie the offence is committed in the view of the constable and the driver fails to give his name and address or produce his driving licence.[3]
(c) Driving whilst disqualified carries a power of arrest by virtue of section 100.
(d) The various alcohol offences under sections 5–9.
(e) Offences under the Theft Act 1968, eg section 12 (taking a conveyance without the owner's consent).

NOTICES OF INTENDED PROSECUTION

An unusual feature of some prosecutions is that for the road traffic offences specified in Schedule 4 a 'notice of intended prosecution' must be given to the accused within a certain period after the alleged offence was committed. The offences for which such a notice is required can be summarised as follows:

(a) reckless driving (section 2).
(b) careless or inconsiderate driving (section 3).
(c) failing to comply with traffic directions (section 22).
(d) leaving a vehicle in a dangerous position (section 24).
(e) speeding offences under the Road Traffic Regulation Act 1967.

If a notice was required, the accused must have been warned at the time the offence was committed either orally or in writing. Otherwise a

2 For example *Wilkinson* (11th edn).
3 Similar provisions apply to offences under the Road Traffic Act 1972, ss 17 and 18 (reckless and careless cycling).

summons must have been served on him within 14 days from the offence, or if this is not practicable, a written notice must be sent.[4]

The requirement of a notice of intended prosecution will be waived, however, if the vehicle concerned was involved in an accident or the police, having exercised all due diligence, could not discover on whom to serve the notice or the accused himself contributed to the failure.[5]

Where it is alleged by the defence that the notice is defective either in its form or its service, the burden of proving (on the balance of probabilities) that the notice was not served properly will be on the defence, as it is presumed by section 179(3) that all the requirements have been complied with. The purpose of the notice is to bring to the attention of the accused the fact that he might be prosecuted while the events are still fresh in his mind. Therefore although the notice might have a defect in it, provided the accused was not in fact misled or in doubt, he can take no objection to it.[6] Where the defence does wish to raise an objection to the notice it is often convenient to raise this as a preliminary point although it can be left to the point when the appropriate prosecution witness is called.[7]

THE LAYING OF THE INFORMATION – TIME LIMITS

The normal time limit for the laying of an information is six months from the commission of the offence[8] but for offences referred to in Schedule 4 the limit is extended by section 180 to a period of six months from the time when evidence sufficient in the opinion of the prosecutor to warrant proceedings came to his knowledge, and a certificate by the prosecutor concerning the appropriate date is conclusive of that fact.

Procedure at the hearing

MODE OF TRIAL

The vast majority of road traffic offences are summary. The offences under the Theft Act 1968 which carry endorsement under Schedule 4 to the Road Traffic Act 1972 are of course either way offences. The principle exceptions to the purely summary nature of traffic offences are:

(a) causing death by reckless driving (section 1) – purely indictable;

4 For service of these notices see Road Traffic Act 1972, s 179(2).
5 Ibid, s 179(4).
6 *Goody v Fletcher* [1962] Crim LR 324, (1962) 106 Sol Jo 222, DC.
7 *R v Edmonton Justices, ex p Brooks* [1960] 2 All ER 475, [1960] 1 WLR 697.
8 MCA 1980, s 127.

(b) driving whilst disqualified (section 99) – either way;
(c) forgery of licence etc (section 169) – either way; and
(d) offences of fraudulent use, alteration, etc of an excise licence (Vehicles (Excise) Act 1971, s 26) – either way.

It should also be remembered of course that the following offences are purely summary:

(a) offences of driving with excess alcohol (ss 5–9); and
(b) taking a pedal cycle without the owner's consent (Theft Act 1968, s 12(5)).

EVIDENCE

Because of their technical nature, road traffic cases often require the proof of matters which are either rarely disputed – such as the defendant's record at the Driver and Vehicle Licensing Centre at Swansea, or matters which are difficult, if not impossible, for the prosecution to prove. Accordingly, some of the normal rules of evidence are amended by specific statutory provisions.

(a) *The identity of the driver*

A constable has a power to stop a motor vehicle (section 159) and he may request the driver to produce his driving licence so as to ascertain his identity, name and address and date of birth (section 161). If the driver cannot produce his licence forthwith (eg he has left it at home), the constable would issue him with a form H.O.R.T.1 to produce it at a named police station within five days.

Other people may be required to give evidence which would help to identify the driver: section 167 requires the owner of the vehicle to give information to the police so that they can decide whether the vehicle was being driven without insurance, and for prescribed offences section 168 requires the keeper of the vehicle to give information required by the police, or any person to give information that is in his power to give, to help identify the driver.

(b) *Evidence in writing*

The normal rules of evidence are modified by such sections as section 182 which provides for the proof of records at the Driving and Vehicle Licensing Centre and section 181 which provides for the proof of certain matters by certificate.

(c) *Burden of proof on the defendant*

Mention has already been made of the burden of proving that a notice of intended prosecution was served. In addition it should be remembered that occasionally the defence may have to prove matters which are peculiarly within the defendant's own knowledge, such as whether he was insured.[9]

9 *Leathley v Drummond* [1972] RTR 293, [1972] Crim LR 227, DC.

Finally there are certain presumptions to be acknowledged, eg that the owner of the car is the person using it.[10]

ALTERNATIVE VERDICTS

In a previous chapter reference was made to the undesirability of convicting a defendant of two matters arising out of exactly the same facts and this is equally true, if not more so, in road traffic cases. A common example is where the accused is summoned for driving without due care and attention and failing to conform to a 'Give Way' sign. If the lack of due care is nothing more than the failure to comply with the sign then a conviction should only be entered in respect of the offence of driving without due care and attention. Indeed section 13 specifically provides that a person charged with an offence under section 5 (driving whilst unfit through drink or drugs), section 6 (driving with excess alcohol) or section 9 (failure to provide a specimen to ascertain whether an offence under section 6 has been committed) shall not be prosecuted for an offence under section 12 of the Licensing Act 1872 (drunk in charge of a carriage).

Substituting a different offence

Magistrates may, of course, only convict or acquit on the information before them. If they feel that the defendant is not guilty of the offence charged but guilty of an alternative matter, they cannot convict the defendant of that other matter. They may only intimate to the prosecution that the prosecution might lay a fresh information if the time limits allow. An exception to this general rule is contained in Part IV of Schedule 4. Where the accused is charged with an offence of reckless driving[11] and the bench feel that he is not guilty of that offence they may direct a charge under section 3 (careless or inconsiderate driving) [12] and may proceed on the new charge although the defence must be allowed to re-examine the witnesses if desired, or be granted an adjournment if necessary. This substitution of a fresh charge under this provision will not be caught by the usual time limits in section 127 of the Magistrates' Courts Act 1980.[13]

TICS

The matter of offences to be taken into consideration does not usually occur so often in purely road traffic cases as the police tend to charge all misdemeanours as substantive offences.

10 *Watson v Patterson* (1949) (unreported), cited in (1957) 121 JP Jo 300, 337.
11 Or an offence of reckless cycling (Road Traffic Act 1972, s 17).
12 Or s 18 (reckless or inconsiderate cycling where the prosecution is under s 17).
13 *R v Coventry Justices, ex p Sayers* [1979] RTR 22, [1978] Crim LR 364.

Procedure after conviction

If the defendant has been found guilty after a trial, the prosecution will make their usual applications for costs and witness expenses. If the defendant has himself pleaded guilty, the prosecution will outline the facts to the magistrates. In a normal criminal case the prosecution would also produce a record of the defendant's previous convictions but in simple road traffic matters the police may not record such convictions on their local records. Accordingly, proof of any previous convictions for motoring matters is often confined to endorsements on the defendant's licence and in default of that, to a print-out from the Driving and Vehicle Licensing Centre at Swansea.[14]

Endorsements

From a reading of Schedule 4 it will be apparent that the more serious road traffic offences, together with certain thefts involving cars, going equipped for such thefts and taking motor vehicles without the owner's consent, carry an endorsement. An endorsement is similar to an entry on a criminal record card. The endorsement is placed on the appropriate part of the licence in the following manner:

ENDORSMENTS

Court code	Date of conviction DD	M	YY	Offence code	Date of offence DD	M	YY	Fine ££££	pp	Disqual. period		Penalty points
2558	01	12	82	CD10	03	10	82	60	00			3
2558	01	12	82	CU10	05	10	82				JOOO	3

The court code is a number which represents a particular magistrates' court and a practitioner would become familiar with the codes for his local courts.

The offence code refers to a Home Office code for each particular endorseable offence, in this example CD 10 refers to careless driving and CU 10 to defective brakes. The number 3 refers to the number of penalty points awarded by the bench for the particular offence. It will of course be noted that some offences carry a discretionary number of points within a prescribed range. The number of points to be awarded is at the discretion of the magistrates after hearing the case and any mitigation. The second offence in the example above also shows that the defendant was given an absolute discharge, as the various penalties which the court may impose can also be recorded on the licence by the use of the codes. All these codes will be found in Volume 3 of *Stone's* at the beginning of the Statutory Instruments for road traffic law.

14 Road Traffic Act 1972, s 184.

The various endorsements will remain on the licence for four years with the exception of drink driving offences when the period is 11 years.[15]

SPECIAL REASONS[16]

Endorsement is mandatory where the defendant has been convicted of an offence carrying obligatory endorsement as prescribed in Schedule 4. The only exception to this is where the court finds that there are *special reasons* for not endorsing the licence. The usual definition of a special reason is that quoted by Wilkinson from *R v Crossan* [1939] 1 NI 106.[17]

> A 'special reason' within the exception is one which is special to the facts of the particular case, that is special to the facts which constitute the offence. It is, in other words, a mitigating or extenuating circumstance, not amounting in law to a defence to the charge, yet directly connected with the commission of the offence and one which the court ought properly to take into consideration when imposing punishment. A circumstance peculiar to the offender as distinguished from the offence is not a 'special reason' within the exception.

Obviously it is not always easy to apply this principle in practice. An example may be taken of driving with excess alcohol (section 6). It might be a special reason for not endorsing (and not disqualifying) that, unknown to the defendant, his drinks were laced with alcohol as this is a circumstance relating directly to the commission of the offence.[18] It would not be a special reason for not endorsing (and not disqualifying) that the defendant would lose his job if his licence were endorsed or he were disqualified, as this is not a matter concerning the commission of the offence but only something which arises as a result of the conviction.[19]

Whenever the possibility of special reasons occurs, the advocate should consult the discussions and examples of what can amount to special reasons in the text books.

THE IMPORTANCE OF SPECIAL REASONS

If the bench find there are special reasons for not endorsing the licence, then no penalty points will be awarded and this becomes vitally important when the question of disqualification for 'totting' arises. Furthermore, if special reasons for not endorsing the licence are found, the defendant will not become liable to disqualification where this is mandatory. If the court does find special reasons it should state them in open court.[20]

15 Ibid, s 101(7).
16 See *Wilkinson* (11th edn) pp 662 et seq.
17 Approved in *Whittal v Kirby* [1947] KB 194, [1946] 2 All ER 552.
18 *Pugsley v Hunter* [1973] 2 All ER 10, [1973] 1 WLR 578.
19 *Gordon v Smith* [1971] Crim LR 173, [1971] RTR 52, DC.
20 Road Traffic Act 1972, s 105.

PRODUCTION OF THE DRIVING LICENCE

Where the defendant has been convicted of an endorseable offence, in the absence of special reasons, the court will order the production of the defendant's driving licence. In fact, where he is prosecuted for an endorseable offence, the defendant is obliged to deliver or send by post his licence to reach the court the day before the hearing or to bring it with him to court.[1]

Before the court orders the endorsement it will require him to produce the licence and it may consider the details of any previous endorsements before deciding what sentence to pass.[2] If the defendant fails to produce his licence, the licence will be suspended until it is produced unless he satisfies the court that he has applied for a new licence and has not yet received it. This provision, of course, if applied rigorously, would be extremely hard on all the thousands of people whose licences are perpetually stuck at Swansea awaiting a change of address or other such amendment. If their licence were suspended and they continued to drive, they would commit the offence of driving without a licence (not the offence of driving whilst disqualified).

Disqualification

MANDATORY DISQUALIFICATION (SECTION 93(1))

On conviction for some offences it is mandatory for the defendant to be disqualified for a minimum period. These offences are:

Section 1 Causing death by reckless driving (purely indictable).
Section 2 Reckless driving (but only if committed within three years of a previous conviction under sections 1 or 2).
Section 5(1) Driving or attempting to drive whilst under the influence of drink or drugs.
Section 6(1) Driving or attempting to drive with alcohol concentration above the prescribed limit.
Section 9(1) Failing to provide a specimen of breath or blood or of urine for analysis, (where the offender was driving or attempting to drive on a public road or in a public place).

The defendant must be disqualified unless there are special reasons for not disqualifying him.

DISCRETIONARY DISQUALIFICATION (SECTION 93(2))

For those offences which carry an endorsement the magistrates may also, in their discretion, disqualify the offender. Discretionary

1 Ibid, s 101(4).
2 Ibid, s 101 (4A).

disqualification is not common as most drivers are disqualified either because it is mandatory or because the defendant is liable to be disqualified under the totting provisions. Nevertheless it may be used for the serious offence where the defendant is not a 'totter'.

DISQUALIFICATION UNDER THE TOTTING PROVISIONS (SECTION 19 OF THE TRANSPORT ACT 1981)

This is a form of disqualification which is frequently encountered and is often the cause for an advocate to be involved in a road traffic case. An advocate with a criminal practice should, therefore, make himself thoroughly conversant with the provisions of section 19 of the Transport Act 1981 (replacing section 93(3) of the Road Traffic Act 1972).

Earlier, when discussing endorsements, reference was made to endorseable offences carrying a certain number of points. For example, the offence of speeding carries three points. An endorsement for speeding would look something like this:

ENDORSEMENTS

Court code	Date of conviction DD	M	YY	Offence code	Date of offence DD	M	YY	Fine ££££	pp	Disqual. period	Penalty points
2558	01	12	82	SP30	03	10	82	50	00		3

What happens if the defendant is convicted of several endorseable offences? For the offences *committed* on the *same occasion* the number of points to be endorsed would be the number of points which would have been ordered for the offence carrying the highest number of penalty points, eg

ENDORSEMENTS

Court code	Date of conviction DD	M	YY	Offence code	Date of offence DD	M	YY	Fine ££££	pp	Disqual. period	Penalty points
2558	01	12	82	SP30	03	10	82	50	00		3
2558	01	12	82	PL10	03	10	82	25	00		
2558	01	12	82	PL20	03	10	82	15	00		
2558	01	12	82	SP30	02	10	82	30	00		3

The number of points which is arrived at by this method is treated as belonging to each of the offences committed on that occasion and is recorded as such on the licence. The question which then must be considered is that of what amounts to the 'same occasion'. It is suggested that it refers to offences which are connected closely either in time or space, but that for example an offence committed at the beginning of a long journey would not be on the same occasion as an offence committed at the end of the same journey.[3]

The points revealed on a defendant's licence are then added up (hence the term 'totting') and if they make 12 in all, the defendant is liable to be disqualified. The penalty points to be taken into account are those which have been awarded for offences committed within three years of each other.

ENDORSEMENTS

Court code	Date of conviction DD	M	YY	Offence code	Date of offence DD	M	YY	Fine ££££	pp	Disqual. period	Penalty points
2558	05	2	80	SP30	03	1	80	20	00		
2675	03	5	81	CD10	07	2	81	40	00		
2552	15	6	83	CU10	23	5	83	25	00		3
2557	30	7	83	CU10	30	6	83	25	00		3
2558	17	9	83	SP30	15	6	83	30	00		3

Convictions before 1 November 1982 when section 19 of the Transport Act 1982 came into force count as 3 points even though after that date they may carry a greater number, eg no insurance carries 3 points if the defendant was convicted before 1 November 1982 and 4–8 points if convicted after that date. If all the points were added together they would total 15, but this is not permissible because there are more than 3 years between the first and last offence, but if the first offence is omitted there will be 12 points covering the four offences which were all committed in a three-year period.

There are three further matters to be remembered. First, it is the date of the commission of the offence that is relevant for these purposes, not the date of conviction. Second, there is no requirement for *two previous* convictions as there was under the old law, so a defendant can become a totter if he has amassed 12 points from two convictions; and third, there is no requirement for the dates of the offences to be in a strict chronological sequence provided they all took place within a three-year period (and it is arguable that this applies even if that period does not end at the date of the present hearing, but was a period in the past where the endorsements are still relevant).

An exception to the rule of searching back through the licence to add up points is that a disqualification obliterates all the points on the licence before the disqualification was imposed.

Example:

3 *Johnson v Finbow* [1983] 1 WLR 879 – failing to stop and failing to report an accident should be treated as having been committed on the same occasion even though the latter offence may have been committed 24 hours later.

ENDORSEMENTS

Court code	Date of conviction DD	M	YY	Offence code	Date of offence DD	M	YY	Fine ££££	pp	Disqual. period	Penalty points
2558	02	11	82	SP30	09	9	82	30	00		3
2643	03	3	83	IN10	04	2	83	70	00		5
2431	10	5	83	SP30	05	4	83	100	00	3mth	
2558	09	8	83	IN10	06	6	83	60	00		4

In this example the defendant has 4 current penalty points only, as the other points are disregarded because of the subsequent disqualification. As well as wiping out any previous points on the licence a disqualification also serves to prevent any points being awarded on the occasion when it is imposed. If a disqualification is imposed either because it is mandatory or, as here, the magistrates have exercised their discretion to disqualify, the question of awarding penalty points does not arise. But if the bench do not disqualify on these grounds and endorse the licence, awarding penalty points as well, they will then add up the points and if they come to 12 they will announce this and ask whether there are any representations to be made concerning disqualification under the totting provisions. If the defendant is then disqualified under the totting provisions, the points which the bench have already awarded will not be endorsed on the licence.

The period of the totting disqualification

If the defendant is a 'totter', he is liable to a mandatory disqualification for a minimum of six months. However, this period will be increased to a minimum of one year if he has previously been 'totted' within the three years preceding the date of the *commission* of the latest offence whose points are taken into account in deciding whether the offender is liable to this disqualification, and further increased to two years if he has twice been totted in this period.

Mitigating the effects of totting

Although totting is a mandatory disqualification, the period of disqualification may be reduced or even avoided altogether if the magistrates find there are *mitigating circumstances* which make this desirable. Mitigating circumstances is a wholly different concept from special reasons and it is not so technical. Mitigating circumstances generally relate to the circumstances of the offender, for example the hardship suffered by the loss of employment if the offender is disqualified. (But note mitigating circumstances can never affect the imposition of an obligatory disqualification.) However, although mitigating circumstances are not so rigidly defined as special reasons, there are certain statutory limitations on their scope:

Section 19(6) of the Transport Act 1981 provides

> No account is to be taken under subsection (2) (ie mitigating circumstances) of –
>
> (a) any circumstances that are alleged to make the offence or any of the offences not a serious one:
>
> (b) hardship, other than exceptional hardship; or
>
> (c) any circumstances which, within the three years immediately preceding the conviction, have been taken into account under that subsection in ordering the offender to be disqualified for a shorter period or not ordering him to be disqualified.

Paragraph (c) is of particular relevance to defendants such as sales representatives. They will not be able to use the mitigation that they will lose their job as an argument for not being disqualified under the totting provisions if they have already used this mitigation within three years immediately preceding the current conviction.

THE IMPOSITION OF A DISQUALIFICATION

If the magistrates order the accused to be disqualified, the disqualification takes effect immediately. Only one disqualification is imposed, so that if, for example, the defendant is convicted of an offence involving obligatory disqualification for one year and several offences which carry six months disqualification under the totting provisions, he will be disqualified for one year. There is now, since the Transport Act 1981, no such thing as consecutive or concurrent disqualifications, although of course where disqualifications are imposed on separate occasions there may be periods when the disqualification orders overlap.

In theory there is no limit on the period of a disqualification except the provisions already described which set a mimimum period in prescribed circumstances. In practice, the period of disqualification must bear some relation to the gravity of the offence and magistrates are warned not to impose lengthy periods of disqualification on young offenders who are 'car mad' as this is only an invitation for them to commit offences of driving whilst disqualified.[4] If the defendant faces disqualification on several offences under the totting provisions, the magistrates now only impose one period of disqualification in respect of all of them, although they are entitled when fixing that period, to take account of the number of offences concerned.

OTHER FORMS OF DISQUALIFICATION

Disqualification until a driving test is passed[5]

The magistrates may, whether or not they impose the more usual form

4 *R v Farnes* (1982) Times, 12 October.

5 Road Traffic Act 1972, s 93(7).

of disqualification, disqualify a person until such time as he passes a driving test if the offence carried obligatory or discretionary disqualification. This form of disqualification may be imposed even if the defendant has already passed a driving test (ie at the time of the disqualification he is a full-licence holder). Its effect is that the defendant may only drive vehicles under the same conditions as if he were a provisional licence holder, eg displaying 'L' plates and being supervised, until he takes and passes a driving test. If he fails to comply with these requirements, then he is probably committing the offence of driving whilst disqualified.[6]

The purpose of this form of disqualification is not so much to punish the offender as to ensure the safety of the public. It is mainly used where the defendant is very old or infirm or where in committing the offence he has shown marked incompetence so that the court can be sure of his ability to drive before he is allowed on the road again as a full licence holder.[7]

Disqualification on a committal for sentence

The general rule when sentencing is that the sentence should not be split, eg the fine imposed on one day and the disqualification imposed at an adjourned hearing.[8] However, when the accused is convicted for sentence (not committed *for trial* of course), the magistrates may disqualify him until he is dealt with by the Crown Court.

Summary of the procedure following a plea of guilty to an endorseable offence

(a) After the defendant has pleaded guilty the prosecution will outline the facts of the case (and may apply for costs).
(b) The defence solicitor will hand the licence to the court.
(c) If he wishes to argue special reasons why his client should not be disqualified and have his licence endorsed, he should do so at this stage. Normally, the client would be called to give evidence.
(d) If special reasons are not argued or are rejected, the appropriate number of points will be announced after any general mitigation has been given (note the bench must determine the appropriate points for certain offences from the range available).
(e) If the defendant is now liable to be totted, mitigating circumstances may be put forward as to why the period should be

6 *Hunter v Coombs* [1962] 1 All ER 904, [1962] 1 WLR 573.
7 *Scott v Jelf* [1974] RTR 256, [1974] Crim LR 191, DC; *Ashworth v Johnson* [1959] Crim LR 735.
8 *R v Talgarth Justices, ex p Bithell* [1973] 2 All ER 717, [1973] 1 WLR 1327.

reduced, or no disqualification imposed, in a similar way to that of putting forward special reasons (including calling the client to give evidence).

Not all these procedures will be necessary for each case. It is not as common to put forward special reasons as it is to offer mitigating circumstances, and it is a good idea to keep these two processes separate as they depend on wholly different principles. However, mitigating circumstances, and mitigation generally are closely connected and where it is clear that the defendant must be totted because the offence concerned carries a fixed number of points, the defence evidence should be given at the same time.

It is suggested that the advocate dealing with an endorseable offence should think along these lines:

(a) Are there special reasons for not endorsing the licence? If there are and they are accepted, then no question of disqualification or endorsement arises.
(b) If there are no special reasons, does the offence carry a fixed or variable number of points? If the points are variable, are there any mitigating grounds for the magistrates ordering the minimum number of points?
(c) If the licence is endorsed and the appropriate number of points is awarded, does the defendant become liable for disqualification under the totting procedure? If he does, are there any mitigating circumstances in favour of reducing the disqualification or imposing no disqualification at all?

Pleading guilty by letter – the 'MCA' procedure

The general rule of procedure is that a person cannot plead guilty in his absence (although he may plead guilty through an advocate). For minor offences where the likely penalty would be a fine, a defendant would rather have his case dealt with in his absence (imagine for example having to travel from Portsmouth to Carlisle to enter a plea of guilty to a parking offence and to receive a fine of say £12). An alternative to this would be the prosecution proving the case in the defendant's absence, but this would entail prosecution witnesses having to be called to prove what is not in dispute, or statements under section 9 of the Criminal Justice Act 1967 being prepared. Until the Magistrates' Courts Act 1957 was enacted, magistrates' courts used to have to hear evidence in every case where the defendant did not appear to plead guilty in person. The 1957 Act (which gave rise to the colloquial term 'MCA' procedure) is now contained in section 12 of the Magistrates' Courts Act 1980, which provides that where:

(a) the offence concerned does not carry more than three months imprisonment; and

(b) the summons is for the accused to appear before the normal magistrates' court (ie not the juvenile court); and

(c) a notice has been served on the defendant explaining the provisions of section 12 of the Act together with a statement of the prosecution's allegations;

the accused may write to the court and plead guilty and put forward in writing any mitigation he wishes to place before the bench. The accused may at any time before the hearing withdraw his plea in writing. If the offence is endorseable, the summons will have a notice on it advising the defendant to forward his licence with the guilty plea.

This 'MCA' procedure is most commonly used for road traffic cases but it may be used, and often is, for all summary offences which meet the prescribed criteria, for example prosecutions for having no TV licence or offences under local byelaws.

At the hearing, if the accused does not appear, the prosecutor will read out the statement of facts that was served on the accused. The prosecutor cannot include material not contained in this statement as the whole basis of the MCA procedure is that the accused knows precisely the allegations he has to face.

The clerk will then read out the mitigation and produce the driving licence where appropriate. The bench will then announce sentence. The defendant will be informed of the penalty by a notice of fine and his licence will usually be sent to Swansea for endorsement and returned to him from there.

PROBLEMS WITH THE MCA PROCEDURE

The plea of guilty by letter procedure is extremely useful in road traffic cases (and of course for other minor summary offences) but there are restrictions on its use. It cannot be used for either way offences because the mode of trial procedure has to be determined in the presence of the accused. Unfortunately, the offence of fraudulent use of a vehicle excise licence (Vehicles (Excise) Act 1971, s 26(1)) is an either way offence. This offence is often committed by a defendant exchanging a tax disc from one vehicle to another and is combined with offences of having no current excise licence and failing to display a current licence. Accordingly, a case involving such an offence cannot be dealt with under the MCA procedure even though the usual penalty is a fine.

When it comes to the question of sentencing, the MCA procedure is really appopriate only where the penalty envisaged is a fine or absolute discharge as other penalties such as conditional discharge, probation, community service and imprisonment, require the attendance of the defendant. In practice, the usual penalties imposed for traffic offences are a fine or an absolute discharge, but there is another common penalty which requires the presence of the offender in certain circumstances, namely disqualification.[9]

9 MCA 1980, s 11(4).

Where an absent defendant has pleaded guilty and the magistrates are considering disqualifying him either in the exercise of their mandatory[10] or discretionary powers, or under section 19 of the Transport Act 1981, they must adjourn the case and inform him of the reason for the adjournment.[11] If the defendant appears at the adjourned hearing, they may hear the mitigation in the usual way and disqualify him if necessary. If he does not appear, the bench may disqualify him in his absence if they are satisfied that he has received the notice of adjournment in due time for the hearing. Alternatively, the magistrates may wish to have the accused present when they deal with him. Where he has been convicted under the MCA procedure for example and the magistrates are considering disqualification, they may issue a warrant but this power is restricted in several ways.[12] First, there must be an adjournment during which a notice must be sent to him informing him to attend court, and only if he does not appear at the adjourned hearing can the bench then consider a warrant. A warrant may then only be issued if either the offence is imprisonable or disqualification is being considered, and even so this power can only be exercised where they consider it undesirable by reason of the gravity of the offence to continue the proceedings in his absence.

WHERE THE ACCUSED DOES NOT CO-OPERATE WITH THE MCA PROCEDURE

The prosecution and the court may send out a summons and the requisite notices, but at the first hearing, although the summons has been served, the defendant has made no reply. The prosecution will then wish to proceed in the defendant's absence but they cannot usually have their witnesses present at this hearing and so the case will be adjourned and the defendant informed of the purpose of the adjournment. On the next occasion the prosecution will either have their witnesses present or they will have served the evidence on the accused under section 9 of the Criminal Justice Act 1967.

If the accused is not present and the adjournment notice has been served, he will be convicted in his absence. If there are several offences they may be proved together as the defendant does not have to be there to make representations for separate trials.[13]

After conviction there remains the problem of endorsing the licence. The court may order the defendant to produce his licence and the licence will be suspended until it is produced. If the defendant fails to produce his licence he will be guilty of an offence, although prosecu-

10 If the offence carries mandatory disqualification the police cannot proceed against the accused under the MCA procedure.

11 MCA 1980, s 11(4).

12 Ibid, s 13.

13 *Clayton v Chief Constable of Norfolk* [1983] 1 All ER 984, [1983] 2 WLR 555.

tions are few. The court will request a print out from the Driving and Vehicle Licensing Centre at Swansea which will reveal any previous endorsements, although the court cannot rely on the print-out unless the defendant has had seven days' notice of its intended use.[14]

Appeals

The defendant has the same right of appeal against conviction or sentence as any other defendant in a criminal matter, but there is an added factor where he has been disqualified.[15] If the defendant appeals against his disqualification he may apply to the original magistrates' court or the Crown Court for his disqualification to be suspended pending the outcome of the appeal. Such a suspension does not automatically follow the lodging of an appeal; it must be applied for[16] and even then it may only be granted if the court thinks fit.

Removal of disqualification

Where a person has been disqualified from driving[17] he may, in prescribed circumstances, apply to have the disqualification removed. This procedure should be distinguished from an appeal because the applicant is not disputing the correctness of the original sentence, he is maintaining that because of factors arising since the imposition of the sentence it is right to remove his disqualification.

The procedure is governed by section 95 of the Road Traffic Act 1972. The applicant applies to the original court which imposed the disqualification and he may make his application only after a certain period has elapsed after the order was made. This period is

(a) two years, if the disqualification is for less than four years,
(b) one-half of the period of disqualification, if it is for less than ten years but not less than four years,
(c) five years in any other case.

14 Road Traffic Act 1972, s 182.
15 The defendant may appeal against his disqualification either by appealing against sentence, generally, or by including an appeal against disqualification specifically under the provisions of s 94. The provisions covering the suspension of disqualification pending appeal probably refer only to an appeal against disqualification where s 94 is invoked.
16 *Kidner v Daniels* (1910) 102 LT 132, 74 JP 127.
17 But not where he has merely been disqualified until he passes a test. An application for the removal of a disqualification may be made even though the original disqualification was mandatory if the prescribed conditions are met, although the application is less likely to meet with success: see *Damer v Davison* [1976] RTR 44, [1975] Crim LR 522, DC.

(any period when the disqualification was suspended pending appeal is disregarded).

There was a problem for the defendant disqualified under the old totting provisions in force before section 19 of the Transport Act 1981. Under these former provisions the periods of disqualification were imposed separately for each offence and they were consecutive. Accordingly section 95 was of no effect except on those disqualifications where the defendant was disqualified for a period exceeding two years on any particular offence. Thus a defendant who was disqualified for six months on each of six offences so that the total disqualification was three years, could not apply for the removal of the disqualification because no single disqualification exceeded two years. Now, however, by virtue of section 20 of the Transport Act 1981 all periods of totting disqualification (even those imposed before the commencement of the Act) are, for the purpose of applying to remove a disqualification, treated as one continous period.

For the hearing in the magistrates' court the chief constable should be summoned to show cause why the order should not be made, and the police will produce the evidence of the applicant's previous endorsements and the circumstances of the original offence.

The court when deciding whether to remove the disqualification may have regard to:

(a) the character of the person making the application;
(b) his conduct subsequent to the making of the order of disqualification;
(c) the nature of the offence; and
(d) any other circumstances of the case.

If the court decides to remove the disqualification, it may do so either forthwith or from a specified date in the future. Where the application has not been successful the application may be renewed after an interval of three months.

Chapter 14

The mentally disordered defendant[1]

The mental condition of a defendant can affect the course of criminal proceedings at three stages: (a) when the defendant is called on to enter a plea to the information, (b) when the court in the course of a trial has to decide whether the defendant had the mens rea to commit the offence, and (c) when the court passes sentence.

Entering a plea

The Magistrates' Courts Act contemplates that a defendant will answer guilty or not guilty.

> On the summary trial of an information, the court shall, if the accused appears, state to him the substance of the information and ask him whether he pleads guilty or not guilty.[2]

At this stage three things might happen. The defendant might remain absolutely silent, or he might plead guilty or not guilty as the case may be, or he might reply incoherently, irrelevantly or abusively. If the defendant remains silent either through malice or ill will, or because he is physically incapable of speaking, or if the defendant does not answer directly because he is abusive or irrational then a plea of not guilty is entered for him and the trial proceeds in the usual way.[3]

However, in the adversarial system of English law it is necessary for each side to be able to prepare and conduct its case properly. This would not be so where the defendant was mentally ill and did not know what he was pleading to and could not adequately give instructions to his lawyer to defend him. If the defendant failed to make any reply to the information being put to him the court would first have to decide whether he was silent, or mute, by way of malice or by some form of incapacity (by visitation of God). If he is mute by malice there is little

1 For the substantive law on insanity see *Smith and Hogan* pp 159–176 and *Glanville Williams* pp 589–607, and for sentencing see Thomas *Principles of Sentencing* (2nd edn) pp 291–308. The bulk of the law concerning the sentencing of a mentally disordered defendant is contained in the Mental Health Act 1983.

2 MCA 1980 s 9(1).

3 Common law (mute by visitation), Criminal Law Act 1827 (mute by malice). See also A. R. Poole 'Standing Mute and Fitness to Plead' [1968] Crim LR 6.

problem and the trial proceeds. If he is mute by visitation then a suspicion should immediately arise in the mind of the court whether the defendant can properly understand the proceedings and can properly conduct his defence. If, after due inquiry[4] by the court, it is clear that he does understand the proceedings, a plea of not guilty can be entered for him and the trial proceed. Similarly in the case of a defendant who makes his reply incoherently or abusively, the court should ascertain whether he understands the proceedings and can conduct his defence.

Where a defendant is not capable of entering a plea and conducting his own defence he is said, in common parlance, to be 'unfit to plead' and no trial will take place.[5] However, if the defendant is found unfit to plead he is liable to be detained indefinitely in a special hospital.[6] The procedure for deciding whether a defendant is unfit to plead is subject to several limitations. Whereas the procedure governing the power of the court to enter a plea of not guilty where the defendant remains mute is applicable to the summary trial of an information, the procedure for determining whether a defendant is fit to plead is governed by the Criminal Procedure (Insanity) Act 1964 and is only applicable to trial on indictment. Accordingly magistrates have no power to determine whether a defendant is fit to plead, this power is reserved to the Crown Court. Furthermore, even in the Crown Court this plea is used rarely in view of its drastic consequences for the defendant now that it is no longer an alternative to the death sentence.

PROCEDURE

The course of action open to the magistrates when faced with a mentally ill defendant depends to some extent on the status of the offence with which he is charged: whether it is purely indictable, either way, or purely summary and whether it is punishable with imprisonment.

4 In the Crown Court a special jury would be empanelled to decide this issue. The matters that a jury has to decide are contained in the judgment of Alderson B in *R v Pritchard* (1836) 7 C & P 303 referred to in *R v Robertson* [1968] 3 All ER 557 at 560, [1968] 1 WLR 1767 at 1772 'There are three points to be inquired into: *First* whether the prisoner is mute of malice or not; *secondly*, whether he can plead to the indictment or not; *thirdly*, whether he is of sufficient intellect to comprehend the course of the proceedings on the trial, so as to make a proper defence – to know that he might challenge any of (the jury) to whom he may object – and to comprehend the details of the evidence, which in a case of this nature must constitute a minute investigation.' In these circumstances, it can happen that a deaf mute may be unfit to plead, being unable to conduct his defence properly.

5 The terminology adopted in the Criminal Procedure (Insanity) Act 1964 which now governs this procedure is 'under a disability which constitutes a bar to his being tried.'

6 Criminal Procedure (Insanity) Act 1964, s 5(1) and Sch I.

Purely indictable offences

In this case the magistrates would proceed to inquire into the charge as examining justices.[7] If a prima facie case is made out, they would commit for trial at the Crown Court, which could then determine fitness to plead if that were raised as an issue at the trial.

Either way offences

Here the magistrates have a choice. They could decline jurisdiction on the principles outlined in chapter 4 ie that the offence is too serious to be heard by a magistrates' court. In this event the matter would be committed for trial at the Crown Court where the procedure would follow that for trial of a purely indictable offence. But where, as is commonly the case, the offence is not serious, the justices may accept jurisdiction. The next stage of the mode of trial proceedings would normally be that the accused is warned of the justices' power to commit for sentence and asked whether he consents to be tried summarily. If the accused is under a disability he will not be able to give that consent. When consent to summary trial is not forthcoming, the bench could then simply proceed to commit the accused for trial at the Crown Court. However, in many cases this would be wholly inappropriate because the case would not merit detention under a restriction order, and where the court has the benefit of medical reports on the defendant's mental condition and is satisfied that the accused did the act complained of, it may in prescribed circumstances make a hospital order on him without proceeding to a trial of the information or convicting him. This unusual procedure would normally only be done with the consent of the person representing the accused.[8] The purpose of this procedure is to spare the defendant the indignity of prolonging the trial in view of his incapacity, and also to avoid the unedifying spectacle of a criminal trial involving a mentally disordered defendant.

Purely summary offences

Where the offence is purely summary, then of course the magistrates cannot commit the defendant for trial at the Crown Court, and so the question of fitness to plead does not arise. Where the offence is punishable on summary conviction with imprisonment, the court may adopt the procedure outlined above for making a hospital order without convicting the defendant. In the case of a non-imprisonable offence the court would have no alternative but to proceed to a trial of

7 Although it has been argued that if the defendant is unfit to plead there should be no committal proceedings see B. Strachan (1969) 133 J P 338. For the contrary, orthodox view, see (1971) 135 J P 532.

8 See generally *R v Lincoln (Kesteven) Justices, ex p O'Connor* [1983] 1 All ER 901, [1983] 1 WLR 335.

the information. In practice, the prosecution will usually be prepared to withdraw proceedings in this situation against an obviously mentally ill defendant.[9]

Proceedings at the trial

The question of 'fitness to plead' revolves around the defendant's state of mind at the time of his trial. However, a defendant might be quite normal at the time of trial but he might allege that at the time he committed the offence he was suffering from a mental illness which made him not responsible for his action.

The defendant's illness might give rise to two possible situations: (a) that he did not even appreciate what he was doing, eg the defendant strangles his wife believing that he is wringing out some washing; or (b) knowing what he was doing he acted for motives caused by his insanity, eg he strangles his wife under the delusion she is putting arsenic in his tea. On the ordinary principles of mens rea and in accordance with the McNaghten Rules he would be not guilty in situation (a) because he did not intend to kill his wife or indeed anybody; in situation (b) he would be guilty of an offence because he intended to kill the person he in fact killed although his act was occasioned by motives arising from his illness.[10]

Acquittals in situation (a) where the defendant is insane would cause considerable public disquiet and therefore the Crown Court is empowered to accept a verdict of not guilty by reason of insanity. The consequence of this verdict is that the defendant is detained indefinitely in a hospital (usually a special hospital) in the same way as if he had been found unfit to plead.[11] Such a conviction is a halfway house between a conviction where mens rea and actus reus are proved and an acquittal, as in this case the actus reus is proved but not mens rea.

The verdict of not guilty by reason of insanity is not available in the magistrates' court. If a defendant who is sane at the time of trial alleges that he was suffering from mental illness at the time he committed the offence, the trial must continue. If the magistrates find that the defendant did the act alleged with the required mens rea (as in situation (b) above), they may convict him. If they find that he did the act but did not have the mens rea (as in situation (a) above), he must

9 See the description of proceedings in the magistrates' court in the report of the Committee on Mentally Abnormal Offenders (the Butler Committee) (Cmnd 6244), summarised in (1975) 139 J P 631 and also see [1975] Crim L R 673 et seq.

10 Subject of course to any defence he may have such as diminished responsibility.

11 Criminal Procedure (Insanity) Act 1964, s 5(1) and see '1883 and all that' (Criminal Procedure (Insanity) Act 1964), N. Walker [1966] Crim L R 17 for a historical summary of the verdict 'Guilty but insane'.

be acquitted, but if he is still suffering a prescribed mental illness at the time of the trial then if (a) the offence is punishable with imprisonment and (b) there are suitable medical reports, they may make a hospital order or guardianship order without convicting the defendant.[12] Where the offence is not punishable by imprisonment, or the reports do not recommend a hospital order, then the defendant must be discharged without making a hospital order.

Sentencing the mentally abnormal defendant[13]

What will be discussed here are those sentences which are particularly relevant to mentally abnormal offenders. It must be borne in mind that the normal forms of sentence described in chapter 7 are also available.

For the defendant who is mentally disordered certain special forms of sentence may be considered: a hospital or a guardianship order, a hospital order coupled with an order restricting the defendant's discharge from hospital and a probation order with a condition of treatment for a mental condition.

TERMINOLOGY

Mental illness is divided by the medical profession into certain categories. It is not possible always to place a particular case into a defined category as the defendant may exhibit symptoms reflecting two or more forms of illness. However, it is important to make some attempt to make some analysis of the defendant's condition as this may have defined legal consequences. A disposal intended for treatment of the defendant's condition, such as a hospital order, would be clearly inappropriate where the defendant's state of mind was categorised as being untreatable. Furthermore, a hospital order or guardianship order made on the defendant's conviction for an offence may be made where he is diagnosed as suffering from mental illness, psychopathic disorder, mental impairment or severe mental impairment whereas where it has been found that the defendant did the act complained of but he has not been convicted, such an order can only be made where the defendant is suffering from mental illness or severe mental impairment.

The Mental Health Act 1983 draws four broad categories of mental disorder – mental illness, severe mental impairment, mental impairment and psychopathic disorder.[14]

12 Mental Health Act 1983, s 37(3).
13 See *The Sentence of the Court* paras 241–279.
14 Before the amendments made by the Mental Health (Amendment) Act 1982 the categories were mental illness, severe subnormality, subnormality and psychopathic disorder.

Mental illness
This category is not defined but usually embraces psychoses (minor mental abnormalities).

Section 1(2) of the Mental Health Act 1983 defines the other three categories:

> . . . *'severe mental impairment'* means a state of arrested or incomplete development of mind which includes severe impairment of intelligence and social functioning and is associated with abnormally aggressive or seriously irresponsible conduct on the part of the person concerned.
> . . . *'mental impairment'* means a state of arrested or incomplete development of mind (not amounting to severe mental impairment) which includes significant impairment of intelligence and social functioning and is associated with abnormally aggressive or seriously irresponsible conduct on the part of the person concerned.
> . . . *'psychopathic disorder'* means a persistent disorder or disability of mind (whether or not including significant impairment of intelligence) which results in abnormally aggressive or seriously irresponsible conduct on the part of the person concerned.
> (3) Nothing in subsection (2) above shall be construed as implying that a person may be dealt with under this Act as suffering from mental disorder, or from any form of mental disorder described in this section, by reason only of promiscuity or other immoral conduct, sexual deviancy or dependence on alcohol or drugs.

Hospital and guardianship orders[15]

The hospital order
This is an order made by the court under which the defendant is conveyed to and detained in a hospital for the treatment of his medical condition. Once the court has made the order, responsibility for the defendant is handed over to the doctors and it is not therefore a punitive order. It cannot, therefore, be combined with other normal forms of sentence such as imprisonment or probation, although it can be coupled with such orders as are ancillary to a sentence such as orders for costs, compensation, disqualification, etc.

The guardianship order
This is an alternative order which places the defendant under the guardianship of the social service department of a local authority or an approved person. The guardian has then all the powers exercisable by a father over his child.

REQUIREMENTS FOR MAKING A HOSPITAL OR GUARDIANSHIP ORDER

In the magistrates' court such orders can be made where the offender has been convicted of an offence punishable on summary conviction

15 Mental Health Act 1983, ss 37 and 40.

with imprisonment, or if he is suffering from mental illness or severe mental impairment, the court may make either of these orders without convicting him.

The medical requirements are reports from two registered medical practitioners (one of whom must have been approved under section 12 of the Mental Health Act 1983 as having special experience in the diagnosis or treatment of mental disorders) which reveal that the offender is suffering from mental illness, psychopathic disorder, mental impairment or severe mental impairment, and that the mental condition is of such a nature or degree that it warrants his detention in a hospital or his reception into guardianship. The doctors must concur on at least one of the mental conditions described although they may each diagnose further, differing, grounds for the order.

The court must be satisfied on the evidence of the practitioner who would have charge of the patient or the hospital managers that suitable arrangements have been made to provide the treatment about to be ordered and that in all the circumstances such an order would be the most suitable method of dealing with the offender.

THE EFFECTS OF A HOSPITAL ORDER

Once a hospital order is made, a constable or a mental welfare officer[16] has authority to convey the defendant to the hospital specified in the order within 28 days, and then the hospital may detain the defendant. He will be detained for up to six months initially, but before then the doctor must review the case and may apply for authority to detain for a further six months. After that the detention may be, subject to any review by the doctor, renewed for periods of one year at a time. However, whenever authority is required to extend the period of detention in hospital the patient may apply to a Mental Health Review Tribunal for his discharge by virtue of section 66 of the Mental Health Act 1983 and his nearest relative may periodically apply for his discharge (section 69).

Surprisingly, if the patient absconds and evades capture for 28 days, he ceases to be liable to be detained although he could be readmitted under the non-criminal procedure for admission to hospital under Part II of the Act.

A hospital order with a condition restricting discharge[17]

This is an order which can only be made by the Crown Court. The Crown Court may, if it is satisfied that, having regard to the nature of

16 Replaced by 'approved social workers' from 28 October 1984.
17 Mental Health Act 1983, s 41.

the offence, the antecedents of the offender and the risk of his committing further offences if set at large, and the necessity to protect the public from serious harm, add to the hospital order a further order that the offender shall be subject to a special restriction on his discharge either without limit of time or for a specified period. The Crown Court cannot order this without hearing one of the doctors give oral evidence.

Where a restriction order is made the normal provisions about the need for periodic extensions to be made to the hospital order do not apply. Therefore the patient does not get his right to apply to the Mental Health Review Tribunal for his discharge on the renewal of the term of the order, nor can his nearest relative apply for his discharge. However, once a restriction order is in force, either the Home Secretary may order the offender's discharge or the offender himself may apply to the Mental Health Tribunal for his discharge under the procedure set out in sections 70 et seq of the Mental Health Act 1983.

A restriction order should be made in crimes of violence and the more serious cases of sexual offences particularly where the defendant has a history of such cases, unless there are compelling reasons for not adopting this course. Furthermore, a restriction order should be made where a defendant is to be detained in conditions of special security in one of the special hospitals. The restriction order should be used whenever the protection of the public is necessary.[18]

Although a magistrates' court cannot impose a restriction order, if it is satisfied that the conditions set out above are satisfied, it may commit the defendant to the Crown Court with a view to a restriction order being made.[19] Such a committal must be in custody except that if suitable arrangements have been made, he may be committed to a hospital in the interim period and such a committal has the effect of a hospital order with a restriction on discharge unlimited in duration until he appears before the Crown Court.[20]

The probation order with a condition of medical treatment[1]

A probation order with a condition of medical treatment may be made if the court has received a report from a doctor approved under

18 See the guidelines for the use of such an order set out in *R v Gardiner* [1967] 1 All ER 895, [1967] 1 WLR 464.

19 Mental Health Act 1983, s 43.

20 Ibid, s 44.

1 Powers of Criminal Courts Act 1973, s 3. A probation order with a condition of medical treatment can only be made under this section and cannot be made as an ordinary probation order with conditions attached thus circumventing the provisions of s 3.

section 12 which states that the defendant's mental condition is (a) susceptible to treatment but (b) does not warrant detention in a hospital under a hospital order.

Such a probation order would include in it a requirement that the offender should submit to medical treatment for the whole period of the order or for a defined part of it, and the treatment would take one of three forms:

(a) treatment as a resident patient in a hospital or mental nursing home; or
(b) treatment as an outpatient at such an establishment; or
(c) treatment by or under the direction of, a duly qualified medical practitioner.

Naturally, before the court makes such an order it must be satisfied that arrangements have been made for the treatment specified in the order. It should be made clear in the report that such facilities are available.

Once the order has been made, the medical practitioner will have a certain flexibility to amend, with the consent of the probationer, the institution at which the treatment is to be given. The practitioner may also apply, through a probation officer, to the court to extend, amend or revoke the medical treatment.[2]

A condition of medical treatment can only be attached to a probation order if it complies with these requirements.

Obtaining medical reports

Before a hospital or guardianship order can be made the court must have considered the evidence of two doctors, one of whom must be approved under section 12 of the Mental Health Act 1983. Similarly there must be evidence from one doctor, who must be approved under section 12 for a probation order with a condition of treatment for a mental condition.

The evidence of the doctors is usually presented to the court in the form of written reports and for the purposes of obtaining a report the proceedings often require to be adjourned. Section 30 of the Magistrates' Courts Act 1980 gives the court power to adjourn for up to three weeks if the defendant is in custody and four weeks where he is on bail. The court must remand the defendant on an adjournment, and if the remand is on bail there must be conditions attached to that bail to ensure that he makes himself available for inquiries for a report to be made to assist the court when sentencing him. Those conditions should include requirements that he undergoes an examination by one or two

2 Powers of Criminal Courts Act 1973, s 3.

medical practitioners, as the court may direct, and that he shall attend such an institution or such a practitioner as the court shall specify and further that he shall comply with any other directions given to him by a person specified by the court or by any person of a class specified by the court for the purpose of facilitating the preparation of the report.

When an offender is remanded in this way for medical reports the court must send its reasons for concluding that an inquiry should be made into the defendant's medical condition, and any information it has about his condition, to the institution where he is committed or has to attend. Therefore for a remand under this section, it is the court which will arrange for the medical inquiry to be made, usually through the probation service, although the defence may obtain reports instead.

RESTRICTIONS ON THE USE OF SECTION 30 OF THE MAGISTRATES' COURTS ACT 1980

This section can only be used in the case of an offence punishable on summary conviction with imprisonment and an adjournment must be by way of remand with the compulsory addition of certain conditions attached to any bail. However, a remand under this section can be made even though the defendant has not been convicted if the court is satisfied that the defendant did the act complained of. This provision avoids the usual restriction of a remand in custody being for not more than eight clear days where the defendant has not been convicted.

SECTION 10 OF THE MAGISTRATES' COURTS ACT 1980

The more usual method of adjourning criminal proceedings in a magistrates' court is to exercise the power under section 10. This section is the one used when adjourning for the preparation of a normal social inquiry report and it may be used when section 30 is not available, eg when the offence concerned is not punishable with imprisonment.[3] The court may attach conditions to any bail in the usual way and the accused may be remanded for up to four weeks on bail, three weeks in custody.

The distinction between section 10 and section 30

The provisions of section 30 make it imperative for the magistrates to adjourn for an inquiry into the defendant's medical condition whenever they are of the opinion that such an inquiry ought to be made. In this case the procedure described above will follow.

Section 10 on the other hand is the magistrates' general power to adjourn which they would use when they wanted, for example, to inquire into the social background of the defendant as opposed to his

3 *Boaks v Reece* [1957] 1 QB 219, [1956] 3 All ER 986.

medical condition. Section 10 could be used for a medical inquiry where the use of section 30 was precluded, eg where the offence was not punishable with imprisonment.[4]

THE RECEPTION OF MEDICAL EVIDENCE[5]

The medical evidence of the doctors may be admitted either by a written report from each of them or the court may require a practitioner to attend and give oral evidence.[6] When a report is submitted, then unless the report has been submitted on behalf of the accused a copy shall be given to his advocate, or where he is not represented the substance of the report should be disclosed to him.

TRANSFER DIRECTIONS BY THE HOME SECRETARY[7]

When a defendant has been sentenced to imprisonment by the criminal courts, or where he has been remanded or committed to custody for varying purposes, eg remand before trial in the magistrates' court or remand before trial at the Crown Court, the Home Secretary has the power to transfer the defendant from the prison where he is detained to hospital. Before a transfer can be directed, the Home Secretary must be satisfied on the evidence of two doctors (one approved under section 12 of the Mental Health Act 1983) that the accused is suffering from one of several specified mental conditions and that his condition warrants detention in a hospital. Furthermore, a restriction may be placed on the accused's discharge as under section 41 of the Mental Health Act 1983 and where the accused is detained in custody on remand a restriction order must be made.

Where a transfer order has been made on an accused who is in custody as a result of his sentence, then where the Home Secretary has been informed by the appropriate medical officer that hospital treatment is no longer necessary the accused may be transferred back to prison. It should be noted however that transfer directions are only available where the defendant has originally been detained in prison. It

4 By virtue of s 35 of the Mental Health Act 1983 (not in force as at 30 September 1983) the court will have power to remand an accused to *hospital* for the preparation of reports. At the present time a remand must either be in custody or on bail.

S 36 (when in force) will allow the Crown Court to remand an accused awaiting trial at the Crown Court or awaiting sentence after such a trial, to a hospital.

S 38 (when in force) will allow the magistrates to make an interim hospital order before making a final order.

5 Mental Health Act 1983, s 54.

6 Where a doctor gives oral evidence pursuant to an adjournment for an inquiry under s 30 of the MCA 1980, his costs may be ordered from central funds even though the offence might be purely summary (s 30(3) of the MCA 1980).

7 Mental Health Act 1983, ss 47–53.

is not possible to transfer a defendant originally made the subject of a hospital order to a prison. In these circumstances once his detention in a hospital is no longer medically necessary he must be released without further ado unless there is a restriction order in force.

Which form of disposal is more appropriate?[8]

It should always be borne in mind that the forms of disposal discussed in this chapter are in addition to the normal options open to the court and whilst they are aimed essentially at the treatment of the offender rather than as a punishment, the final decision in each case depends on the decision of the court, not the opinions of the doctors.

As the orders mentioned here are designed for the treatment of the offender the first prerequisite for their use is that any mental condition should be susceptible to treatment. Second, a hospital order involves the detention of the accused in a hospital or other such institution and any order depriving a person of his liberty should be warranted by the circumstances of the case. This is even more so when the Crown Court is contemplating a restriction order which should be based on the requirement of protection of the public.

The factors which influence doctors in preparing their reports may be revealed by an extract from a memorandum prepared jointly by the Home Office and the Department of Health and Social Security.[9]

> Uncertainties or differences of opinion about the value of hospital treatment in a particular case are probably the main reasons for difficulties over the placement of an offender. Such doubts are intensified when admission to hospital also entails the provision of a fairly high level of security for an unspecified length of time. The following considerations may help to resolve such difficulties.
>
> *Persons suffering from severe mental impairment*
> Prison is not a suitable place for persons suffering from severe mental impairment. Facilities for their care and treatment are provided, according to the requirements of the individual, by local authorities, hospitals in the National Health Service and the special hospitals.
>
> *Persons suffering from acute psychosis*
> Offenders exhibiting acute psychosis ordinarily require treatment in a psychiatric hospital or unit, where the majority respond well and quickly to the treatments now available. Arrangements for these are usually easily made.
>
> *Persons suffering from chronic psychiatric conditions*
> Persons with chronic schizophrenia and certain other chronic psychiatric

8 *Sentence of the Court* paras 259–273.

9 Reproduced from *Sentence of the Court* para 262 with modifications to take account of the different terminology substituted by the Mental Health Act 1983.

conditions sometimes commit repeated offences of a comparatively minor nature because of their social incompetence. The disposal of such a person who appears before a court may present difficulty because even though the offender is mentally ill, admission to hospital may not be appropriate unless special treatment or nursing is required; on the other hand committal to prison may be neither helpful nor humane. Recent advances in treatment now offer improved prospects for the management of chronic mental illness in the community, and if this is considered the appropriate course, the courts have power to require the offender to undergo treatment of this nature as a condition of a probation order.

Persons suffering from mental impairment

Some offenders suffering from mental impairment uncomplicated by other forms of mental disorder may require social training which can be given in the penal system or under care from the local authority. Hospital treatment may be indicated for those who would be unable to cope with training within the penal system, and for those whose behaviour is too disturbed to be managed in the community.

Persons suffering from pyschopathic disorder

Severely disturbed young psychopathic offenders and disturbed young mentally impaired offenders may be susceptible to treatment in hospital. The prospects of success are greatest if treatment can be given before aggressive or inadequate behaviour becomes ingrained.

An offender of any age suffering from pyschopathic disorder may be treated in hospital provided the hospital is prepared to receive him on the ground that there are reasonable prospects that the disorder will respond to treatment or nursing care and attention, but the development of treatment for psychopathic disorder is still at a very early stage and there are at present differences of opinion about the value of treatment. These are likely to be resolved only in the light of experience of attempts to deal with the condition in varied settings. Susceptibility to treatment can often be determined only after a period of observation under controlled conditions.

There is no alternative means of disposal available if a psychopathic offender admitted under a hospital order is then found to be untreatable. In this situation the combination of lack of motivation towards treatment and resentment at being regarded as mentally disordered often produces highly disruptive behaviour in the patient, and for those reasons many psychiatrists are reluctant to accept adult psychopathic offenders for treatment. Nevertheless those hospitals or units which are prepared to receive such patients are encouraged to do so. The difficulties may be mitigated if the offender is given a prison sentence by the court with a view to assessment and the possibility of transfer to hospital under section 47 of the Mental Health Act if this is found suitable after such assessment. Experience has shown that some unstable psychopaths who have been sentenced to imprisonment have benefited from transfer to hospital under section 47, and if a patient so transferred no longer requires treatment once the more overtly unstable phase has passed, or is found after observation in hospital not to be susceptible to treatment, he can be returned to prison to complete his sentence, or discharged if the date on which he would have been released from prison has passed.

Where in the light of these considerations hospital treatment is indicated for persons suffering from pyschopathic disorder, those who are grossly unstable, aggressive and paranoid, and are subject to uncontrolled outbursts in which they are dangerous to society, may be considered for admission to special hospitals: while those whose behaviour is not dangerous to society, even though they repeatedly and seriously endanger themselves, may be suitable for treatment in National Health Service hospitals. Offenders suffering from forms of psychopathy in which delinquency rather than disturbed behaviour is the more prominent characteristic can generally be dealt with in prison.

Security in National Health Service hospitals

When a hospital doctor offers to accept, as responsible medical officer, offenders for treatment in accordance with the criteria described above he (acting for the hospital authority) undertakes responsibility for exercising reasonable care in detaining them. Hospitals vary as to the type of patient normally catered for and as to the security facilities at their disposal. When an offender is being considered for admission in pursuance of a hospital order or a transfer direction (whether or not the special restrictions under section 41 of the Mental Health Act are likely to be applied) the reporting doctors and the court, or the Home Secretary in the case of a transfer direction, will wish to be satisfied that the existing security arrangements at the hospital will permit this responsibility to be adequately discharged. The degree of care required in a particular case will depend upon the degree of risk which an offender might present to the public should he abscond.

Chapter 15

Enforcement of court orders

Introductory

In previous chapters mention was made of the various orders which the court could make being either substantive sentences such as imprisonment, probation and fines, or ancillary orders such as costs, compensation and restitution. When the court makes any one of these orders the decision is announced, the entry made in the court register and, where appropriate, an order is drafted and signed by the clerk or a magistrate. However, the matter does not end there, because a decision announced in court has to be put into effect. If a probation order is made, the defendant has to comply with the instructions of the probation officer for the period specified in the order. If a fine has been ordered, the defendant should hand over the appropriate sum of money to the court. This chapter is concerned with the enforcing of court orders against reluctant defendants to ensure that the will of the court is carried out.

For the purpose of explaining the methods available of enforcing court orders, it is convenient to divide up these orders into three categories. First, there are those orders which have their own method of enforcement contained in the statute which created them. Examples of these are Probation and Community Service Orders, conditional discharges and suspended sentences. The powers to deal with breaches of these orders are found in the Powers of Criminal Courts Act 1973 and are discussed in chapter 7.

The second category consists of those orders which are made by the court which require the doing of something other than the payment of money or which prohibit the doing of something. An example of such an order might be an order for the restitution of goods by a person having possession of them to a person entitled to recover them, made under section 28 of the Theft Act 1968.

The third category contains those orders which specify the payment of money, and such orders include: fines, costs, compensation and legal aid contribution orders.

Orders other than for the payment of money

The method of enforcing such an order is to be found in section 63 of the Magistrates' Courts Act 1980. This section applies to the enforcement of all orders except those whose enforcement is provided for by other enactments.[1] The section also provides authority for the court to specify further matters in the original order making provisions for the way in which the order is to be carried out and for generally giving effect to the order.[2]

The section goes on to say that anyone disobeying an order of the court which is within the terms of section 63 may be ordered to pay a fine of up to £50 for every day in which he is in default, or up to £1,000 (whichever is the greater), or the court may commit him to prison forthwith either until he remedies his default or for up to two months (whichever is the lesser term). Once he has suffered the maximum penalty, there is no further power to enforce the order for the *same* default.

The provisions of section 63 are exercised by either the court acting of its own motion and issuing a summons (although there is in fact no complaint) or by a complaint being made by an aggrieved party and a summons being issued. A hearing would take place in either event.[3]

Orders for the payment of money[4]

The procedure outlined above for the enforcement of orders other than for the payment of money is a procedure which is not commonly used and, when it is, the main use is to enforce orders made under the magistrates' domestic jurisdiction. On the other hand, enforcement proceedings for orders for the payment of money are very common.

The important point to remember here is that there are four categories of money payment orders: orders enforceable as

(a) a civil debt,
(b) an affiliation order,
(c) an order for a sum adjudged to be paid on a conviction: such as a fine, costs or compensation, and
(d) a legal aid contribution order.

Although the methods employed for enforcing these orders is the same in principle, there are restrictions placed on the procedure in the case of certain money payment orders.

1 Eg breach of a probation order: Powers of Criminal Courts Act 1973, s 6.
2 MCA 1980, s 63(1).
3 Contempt of Court Act 1981, s 17 and Sch 3.
4 The main provisions concerning the enforcement of money orders are to be found in the MCA 1980, ss 58 and 75–96.

General provisions

Any sum of money ordered to be paid by a magistrates' court is enforceable as a civil debt unless it is expressed to be enforceable by any of the other three methods.[5] In practice, civil debt proceedings are not very common and so a description will be given of how orders for sums adjudged to be paid by a conviction are enforced. Then the differences will be explained concerning the remaining three categories.

THE ENFORCEMENT OF SUMS ADJUDGED TO BE PAID BY A CONVICTION

These sums include fines, costs payable by a defendant and compensation.[6] When the court announces a fine, etc, the whole of the amount ordered should be paid over by the defendant before he leaves the court. Where the defendant cannot pay the whole amount forthwith, the court has the power to dispense with immediate payment.[7] It may allow the defendant time to pay the amount (that is, to pay the amount within a specified time) or it may fix repayment by instalments. If the defendant has been given time to pay, he may write to the court and ask for further time to pay or ask for payment by instalments which may be granted without a court hearing, or his attendance at court may be required so that he can explain his situation more fully. Similarly, if he has been allowed to pay by instalments, he may ask for those instalments to be varied.[8] It should be noted that where a defendant has been given time to pay he is only in default if payment is not received by the last day of the period, and if he is allowed to pay by instalments he is not in default if he pays the instalments as ordered, but if he defaults in any one instalment the whole amount owing becomes due.

Accordingly, there is a drawback to each method of enforcement. Enforcement of the time to pay method has to wait until the last day of the allowed period for payment. The enforcement of payments by instalments is only permissible where the defendant makes a default in payment. It is not unknown for a large fine to be ordered to be paid back at a low rate each week and this may extend over a long period. If the defendant complies with the order, the court cannot bring back the defendant to increase the rate of payment or order the balance to be paid forthwith. The rate of payments cannot be varied in this situation.[9]

5 MCA 1980, s 58(2).
6 Ibid, s 150(3).
7 Ibid, s 75.
8 Ibid, s 85A.
9 The only situation in which this can be done is where a means inquiry has been adjourned on terms, but this of course will be inapplicable unless there has been a default; or where the defendant has requested a variation in the amount of the instalments.

Where default is made in payment

WHERE THE DEFENDANT IS ORDERED TO PAY FORTHWITH

If the defendant is present in court and is fined or ordered to pay costs or compensation, the court may take one of three courses of action:
(a) impose imprisonment in default of payment to take effect immediately (eg fined £50 or 14 days in default. If the money is not handed over the defendant goes to prison for 14 days or until he does pay, whichever is the sooner);
(b) suspend the term of imprisonment by the issue of the warrant of commitment being postponed on terms as to the payment of the money; or
(c) issue a distress warrant.

The fixing of a term of imprisonment at the hearing which imposes the financial penalty (ie the original sentencing court), whether the imprisonment is immediate or postponed, is restricted to three situations:
(a) where the offence is punishable by imprisonment and the defendant has the means to pay forthwith;
(b) where he is of no fixed abode and so other methods of enforcement are unlikely to be successful or he is likely to leave the country, eg a foreign lorry driver; and
(c) where the defendant is already serving a custodial sentence and so it is expedient that he serve the imprisonment in default instead of paying the order.[10]

An example of this is where the defendant has a number of offences, some imprisonable and some not. On the imprisonable offences he receives a custodial sentence and on the non-imprisonable offences he is fined and given imprisonment forthwith in default to be served concurrent with the substantive sentence.[11]

There are other restrictions and enactments affecting the imposing of prison sentences in default of payment but these are discussed in relation to the means inquiry.

To help the court to find out whether the defendant has the means to pay the fine forthwith the court may order him to be searched and may order any money found on him to be paid towards the liabilities he has incurred. But the court cannot take the money if it is satisfied that the money does not belong to him or that the loss of the money would be more injurious to his family than would his detention.[12] It should be noted that this power may be exercised at the original sentencing court as well as at any subsequent enforcement proceedings.

10 MCA 1980, s 82.
11 For the question of whether the terms should be concurrent or consecutive see G. S Chambers (1975) 139 JP 118.
12 MCA 1980, s 80.

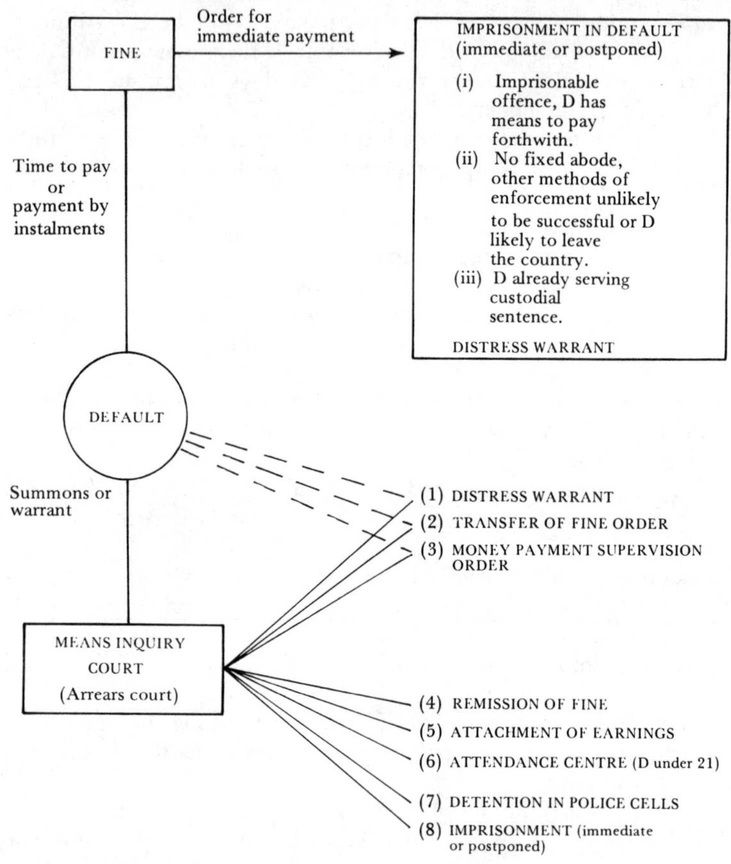
SUMMARY OF ENFORCEMENT PROCEDURE
FINE
Order for immediate payment
IMPRISONMENT IN DEFAULT
(immediate or postponed)
(i) Imprisonable offence, D has means to pay forthwith.
(ii) No fixed abode, other methods of enforcement unlikely to be successful or D likely to leave the country.
(iii) D already serving custodial sentence.
DISTRESS WARRANT
Time to pay or payment by instalments
DEFAULT
Summons or warrant
MEANS INQUIRY COURT (Arrears court)
(1) DISTRESS WARRANT
(2) TRANSFER OF FINE ORDER
(3) MONEY PAYMENT SUPERVISION ORDER
(4) REMISSION OF FINE
(5) ATTACHMENT OF EARNINGS
(6) ATTENDANCE CENTRE (D under 21)
(7) DETENTION IN POLICE CELLS
(8) IMPRISONMENT (immediate or postponed)

WHERE THE DEFENDANT IS GIVEN TIME TO PAY OR ALLOWED TO PAY BY INSTALMENTS

In either of these situations, the default in payment will not become apparent until some time after the initial hearing. After the original hearing the defendant must be sent a fine notice from the court setting out the details of the various monetary orders made against him and what instructions have been given about payment.[13] No enforcement proceedings may be taken in these circumstances unless the notice has been served on the defendant. A record of any payments received and owing will be kept in the justices' clerk's office either on a card index or a computer.

Where the records show the defendant is in default the magistrates may have the following courses of action open to them:

(a) supervision (usually by a probation officer) to help the defendant to meet his financial obligations;
(b) transferring the enforcement of the fine to the area where the defendant lives;
(c) commencing proceedings for an attachment of earnings order;
(d) issuing a distress warrant;
(e) imposing imprisonment either immediately or with a postponed warrant of commitment.

A money payments supervision order, a transfer of fine order and a distress warrant may be issued by the court merely on proof that a default has been made and with no hearing at which the defendant is present, and it is not unusual for a transfer of fine order to be made in this way. An attachment of earnings order will be made after proceedings for such an order have been started by way of a complaint and a summons issued for a hearing at which the defendant would be present. On the other hand, imprisonment in default of payment cannot be imposed after the original hearing in these circumstances unless there is an inquiry into the defendant's means at which he is present, or where he is already serving a term of imprisonment or detention in a detention centre.

If the defaulter is serving a custodial sentence, however, he may not have the outstanding fines commuted to terms of imprisonment in default unless he is given notice of the court's intention and is allowed to make representations either in writing, or orally to the court.[14]

In the case of a default in payment, the usual practice in the great majority of cases is for the court to start proceedings for a means inquiry to secure the defendant's presence at court. On this occasion the defendant will be present and the court may then take any of the

13 Magistrates' Courts Rules 1981, r 46 and this rule is mandatory; *R v Farnham Justices, ex p Hunt* (1976) 140 JP 453.

14 *Re Hamilton, Re Forrest* [1981] AC 1038, [1981] 2 All ER 711.

options already briefly described. It is important to remember that unless the court fixes imprisonment at the original sentencing court in the circumstances already outlined either being an immediate issue of a commitment warrant or a postponed issue of a warrant, there must be a means inquiry in the defendant's presence before either sort of warrant of commitment can be issued.[15] If imprisonment is not fixed at the means inquiry, the defaulter must again be brought to court before imprisonment can be imposed.[16]

The basic position then, is that a warrant of commitment for default in paying a fine cannot be issued unless when the term of imprisonment was fixed the defendant was present before the court.

The means inquiry

When a defendant is in default in making his payments as ordered by the court, a summons or warrant may be issued to secure the attendance of the defaulter at a means inquiry.[17] There are four points to note about this procedure:

(a) there is no requirement for a complaint or information to be laid;
(b) the court may choose either a summons or a warrant;
(c) these are civil proceedings and so the Bail Act 1976 does not apply. Therefore where a warrant with bail is issued, the court will fix an amount of money (recognizances) which the defendant will forfeit if he fails to comply with the terms of the bail; and
(d) if the defaulter pays up the whole amount of money owing (not merely the amount by which he is in arrears) to the court or to the police officer holding the warrant, the proceedings are at an end because the terms of the magistrates' original order have been complied with.[18] This is the reason why it is necessary for the police officer holding a means inquiry warrant to have it in his possession when arresting a defaulter, because the warrant must bear on the face of it the amount of money owing. In this way the defaulter may buy his way out of the proceedings against him.[19]

The means inquiry is what its name implies, an inquiry into the means of the defaulter and into his reasons for not paying as ordered. It takes the form of an examination before a bench of magistrates and the

15 MCA 1980, s 82(3).
16 Ibid, s 82(5).
17 There is also a procedure under s 86 of the MCA 1980 for the court itself, when allowing time to pay, or payment by instalments, to fix a day for a means inquiry at which the defendant must appear if he is in default.
18 MCA 1980, s 83(4).
19 See *R v Purdy* [1975] QB 288, [1974] 3 All ER 465 for the meaning of 'possession' of a warrant.

questioning is usually conducted by the clerk. The defaulter will be sworn and will be asked questions about his income and expenditure, why he has not paid in the past and his proposals for payment of the sums due. Unless the case presents some unusual complications the hearing will be quite short. In fact, there is a procedure for ordering the defaulter to bring with him to court a prepared statement of his means, or to send it in advance.[20]

However, although the means inquiry is usually a brief hearing and may involve stereotyped questioning by the clerk who may himself be following a prepared form, the hearing is not a formality, for the bench may not commit the defaulter to prison in the face of evidence that he has no means to pay.[1]

It is quite common for there to be a court entirely devoted to the holding of these means inquiries, and such a court may be called an 'arrears' court. It is at this hearing, having regard to the evidence given by the defaulter, that the magistrates decide which method of dealing with the case is the most appropriate. To help the court decide on its course of action it may exercise its power to have the defaulter searched or it may ask a probation officer to prepare a report on the defaulter's means.[2]

At the means inquiry the options open to the court are as follows.

ADJOURNMENT

The court may adjourn the means inquiry on terms as to the payment of the sum outstanding or to a definite date (eg proceedings adjourned sine die provided the defaulter pays £10 per week).

TRANSFER OF FINE ORDER[3]

Where it appears to the court dealing with the enforcement of one of its fines, that the defendant now lives in another petty sessional area, the court may transfer the fine to the court for that other area. Once the order is made, the original court ceases to enforce the fine, transferring this responsibility to the second court. This latter court can then proceed in the same way as if it had imposed the fine and was seeking to enforce the fine after the initial hearing.

20 MCA 1980, s 84. Failure to comply with the order carries a maximum penalty of £50, and a false statement made knowingly or recklessly carries a maximum penalty of four months' imprisonment and a fine of £100.

1 *R v Woking Justices, ex p Johnstone* [1942] 2KB 248, [1942] 2 All ER 179. See *R v Liverpool City Justices, ex p Lanckriet* [1977] Crim LR 299, DC for an example of a means inquiry that was too brief.

2 MCA 1980, s 80, although in fact there is no statutory authority to require the preparation of a means inquiry report for a fine (see also Magistrates' Courts Act 1980, s 72).

3 MCA 1980, s 89.

MONEY PAYMENT SUPERVISION ORDER[4]

The court may place the defaulter under the supervision of a person appointed by the court (usually a probation officer) to assist and encourage the defaulter to comply with the order of the court for payment. Such an order would last until the whole of the sum owing has been paid.

REMISSION OF THE FINE[5]

At the means inquiry the court may if it thinks it is just to do so, having regard to any change in circumstances since the fine was imposed, remit all or part of the fine. However, two points should be noted:

(a) remission can only take place in the presence of the defendant at a means inquiry;
(b) remission applies only to a fine. Although throughout this chapter the term fine has been used to include costs and compensation and any sum adjudged to have been paid on a conviction, remission applies only to a fine. The court cannot remit costs or compensation (in practice the court may have an arrangement with the police prosecutions department which allows the court to write off costs, and in the case of compensation the aggrieved parties may be written to in order to inquire whether they will agree to forego any compensation due to them).[6]

ATTACHMENT OF EARNINGS

There is a procedure for ordering that sums payable to the court be deducted from the debtor's wages and be paid direct to the court by the debtor's employer. This is a self-contained code of procedure set out in the Attachment of Earnings Act 1971. The Act provides for proceedings to be started by way of complaint for an attachment order, with a summons issued followed by a court hearing.[7] The court would wish to know sufficient details to identify the debtor to his employer, eg the name of his employer, his place of work and his works number. If it decides to make such an order, the court would fix the normal deduction rate, which is the amount actually deducted from the debtor's wages to satisfy the court order, and a protected earnings rate which is an amount which the debtor must receive in his wage packet each week or month as appropriate after all deductions have been made. The protected earnings rate should be sufficient to cover all the debtor's needs which the court thinks are reasonable.[8]

4 Ibid, s 88.
5 Ibid, s 85.
6 Ibid, s 85 (2).
7 Attachment of Earnings Act 1971, s 19.
8 Ibid, s 6.

Although there is a distinct code of procedure set out in the Attachment of Earnings Act, it is clear that in practice means inquiry courts make such orders at a means inquiry without the formal step of issuing attachment proceedings.[9]

An attachment order is useful where

(a) the debtor has a steady job and work record,
(b) the debtor has an employer large enough not to be unduly inconvenienced by such an order and consequently where the debtor's job will not be jeopardised by any ill will from the employer, and
(c) the amount imposed is sufficiently large to make the use of the machinery of an attachment order worthwhile.

DISTRESS[10]

A warrant of distress authorises the person named on the warrant to seize the goods of the debtor and to sell them. The proceeds of the sale are then employed to pay the debt due to the court and the costs of the distraint. The particular restrictions on the use of distress are set out in rule 54 of the Magistrates' Courts Rules 1981 and need not be set out here. However, it may be said that the distress warrant is not as useful as it may seem. The difficulties may be summarised as follows:

(a) the court has to have a person prepared to carry out the distraint; the police are not usually interested, although some larger courts may have their own enforcement officer or employ bailiffs;[11]
(b) very often the debtor is not the sort of person who would have many assets, and those he has are on hire purchase and thus not owned by him and not subject to distraint.

The most effective use for distraint is for enforcing the payment of debts by limited companies where the next sanctions to be mentioned, attendance centre and imprisonment, are not available.

ATTENDANCE CENTRE

Where the defendant is under 21 he may be sent to an attendance centre for the number of hours specified by the court. But as in the case of imprisonment the number of hours to be served will be reduced in proportion to the amount of the fine that has been paid.[12] When the court fixes the original number of hours, however, it is not bound by a schedule of hours related to the amount owing but may choose any number of hours between 12 and 24 or 36.

9 For a discussion of this problem see (1971) 135 JP 671 and, contra, at p 814.
10 Magistrates' Courts Rules 1981, r 54.
11 See C. T. Latham 'The Enforcement of Fines' [1973] Crim LR 552.
12 Criminal Justice Act 1982, s 17.

IMPRISONMENT

The final sanction for non-payment is that of imprisonment or other forms of detention. At the original hearing which imposed the financial penalty or order where the court has that power,[13] or at the means inquiry where the court is satisfied that

(a) in the case of an offence punishable with imprisonment the defendant has the means to pay forthwith or,
(b) (not limited to offences punishable with imprisonment) the default is due to the offender's wilful refusal or culpable neglect and it has considered or tried all other methods of enforcing payment and it appears that they are inappropriate or unsuccessful,[14] the court may send the defaulter to prison.

Where the defaulter is aged 17 and under 21 he may not be committed to prison, but he may be committed in a similar manner under section 9 of the Criminal Justice Act 1982. Before such a person can be committed to custody the court shall obtain information about the circumstances and shall take into account any information before the court which is relevant to his character and physical and mental condition, and shall state why no other method of dealing with him is appropriate.[15]

The defaulter may be sent to prison forthwith at the original hearing or at the means inquiry, or the court may postpone the issue of the commitment warrant until such time and on such conditions as it thinks just.[16]

The maximum amounts of imprisonment that may be imposed for each fine or order are set out in Schedule 4 to the Magistrates' Courts Act 1980:

An amount not exceeding £25	7 days
An amount exceeding £25 but not exceeding £50	14 days
An amount exceeding £50 but not exceeding £200	30 days
An amount exceeding £200 but not exceeding £500	60 days
An amount exceeding £500 but not exceeding £1,000	90 days
An amount exceeding £1,000 but not exceeding £2,500	6 months
An amount exceeding £2,500 but not exceeding £5,000	9 months
An amount exceeding £5,000	12 months

However, should the defendant have made a part payment then the number of days of imprisonment will be reduced in proportion. Any period for default of payment of any sum can be made consecutive to

13 MCA 1980, s 82(1).
14 Ibid, s 82(4). Note that the magistrates need not state in open court the reasons for their decision though the warrant of commitment must include a statement of the reason.
15 Criminal Justice Act 1982, s 2(1) (but it is not *obligatory* to have a report from the probation service).
16 MCA 1980, s 77.

that for another sum[17] but consecutive terms of imprisonment imposed in default on the same occasion cannot exceed the normal limits for imprisonment, ie six months for purely summary offences and 12 months for either way offences.[18] These limits do not apply to a fine and a substantive period of imprisonment imposed for the same offence (note that imprisonment imposed by the court at different hearings on different days will not count as imprisonment on the same occasion).[19]

Second, the term of imprisonment cannot be reduced by part payment to below five days, therefore no matter how much is paid off a fine the defendant will have to serve five days unless he completely clears the amount outstanding.[20]

Third, it is the practice to attach any costs to a particular fine and compensation to the fines for the particular offences for which compensation is claimed, for enforcement purposes.[1]

Finally, when determining the amount of imprisonment to be imposed, the court should apply general sentencing principles to decide whether the amounts should be concurrent or consecutive. Perhaps a simple example might make the position clear.

Consider a defendant who on 1 March was fined £50 for an offence of criminal damage committed on 1 February with £30 costs and £40 compensation. The same defendant is fined again on 1 June for road traffic offences committed on 1 April. On this second occasion he is fined £10 for having a defective indicator with £10 costs, £10 for no test certificate and £5 for failing to display a current vehicle excise licence. The defendant makes no payment, and is brought before the means inquiry court on 1 August. The court decides to impose imprisonment in accordance with Schedule 4 of 30 days for the total of £120 for the fine, costs and compensation ordered on 1 March. For the subsequent offences dealt with on 1 June, the court decides the days in default shall be concurrent, ie seven days in all. However, these may be made consecutive to the 30 days making 37 days in all. But there is one final check: the warrant actually committing the defaulter to prison would be for a total of £155. The maximum imprisonment for this sum according to Schedule 4 is 30 days. Therefore, if the court desires the defendant to serve 37 days, two separate warrants will have to be drafted.[2]

17 Ibid, s 133.

18 Ibid, s 133 and see *R v Metropolitan Stipendiary Magistrate for South Westminster, ex p Green* [1977] 1 All ER 353. Note: this does not prevent a term in excess of six months for a single offence imposed in accordance with MCA 1980, Sch 4 (s 31(3) and s 133(3)).

19 MCA 1980, s 133(4).

20 Ibid, Sch 4 para 2(2).

1 This practice was mentioned, without comment, in *R v Southampton Justices, ex p Davies* [1981] 1 All ER 722, [1981] 1 WLR 374.

2 For this, and the whole question of fixing days in default see the *Southampton Justices'* case, above.

Having fixed the days in default, the court may either send the defaulter to prison forthwith, or postpone the issue of the warrant on such terms as it thinks just, eg the issue of the warrant postponed on payment of £5 per week. If the defendant fails to keep up the instalments, the court may issue the warrant without any further hearing.[3] Once the court has fixed the terms for the postponement, it may not vary them,[4] although in practice courts will sometimes take account of a calamitous change in the defaulter's circumstances making it impossible for him to comply with the terms of the postponed commitment.[5] Where the warrant has been issued there is no power to withdraw the warrant.

OTHER FORMS OF CUSTODY

As well as imposing imprisonment, the court has the option of ordering a defaulter over 17 to be detained in police cells for up to four days, or within the precincts of the court or at a police station until 8 o'clock on the evening of the day on which the order is made, or it may order the detention of a defaulter over 17 overnight at a police station.[6]

REDUCTION BY PART PAYMENT

Once the defaulter has actually arrived in prison he may buy his release by paying off the sum owing. If he makes only a part payment, then the term is reduced in proportion by a formula which differs slightly from that used for taking account of payments made before the defaulter is received into custody.[7]

Penalties imposed by the crown court[8]

Where the Crown Court imposes a financial order or penalty, then unless the defendant is committed to prison forthwith in respect of a default, the enforcement of those sums is undertaken by the magistrates' court. The Crown Court fixes the amount of imprisonment in default of the payment of the sum up to a maximum of 12 months according to the same scale as that of the magistrates' court. The order is enforced by the particular magistrates' court specified by the Crown

3 *R v Chichester Justices, ex p Collins* [1982] 1 All ER 1000, [1982] 1 WLR 334, HL.
4 *R v Clerkenwell Stipendiary Magistrate, ex p Mays* [1975] 1 All ER 65, [1975] 1 WLR 52.
5 See the argument at (1964) 128 JP 463.
6 MCA 1980, ss 134–136. There is no requirement for a means inquiry in these circumstances.
7 MCA 1980, s 79.
8 Powers of Criminal Courts Act 1973, ss 31–34.

Court. Credit is given for any part payment made by a reduction in the term originally fixed but the magistrates cannot remit any fine without the express authority of the Crown Court. If the defendant defaults in payment he may be committed to prison, after a means inquiry, for the period fixed by the Crown Court.[9]

Sums enforceable as affiliation orders, civil debt and legal aid contribution orders[10]

There are some financial orders which cannot be enforced as if they were sums adjudged to be paid by way of a conviction. The two orders which concern the criminal lawyer are costs ordered to be paid by a prosecutor, which are enforceable as a civil debt, and a legal aid contribution order, which is basically a civil debt but is enforced in much the same way as an affiliation order. (The main orders enforceable as affiliation orders are financial orders made in the magistrates' domestic jurisdiction.)

An affiliation order is enforced by a complaint being laid and the defaulter being summoned to court or a warrant being issued. The court may then enforce the order in a similar way to a fine although the imprisonment is limited to six weeks maximum and unlike a fine there is the power to review a postponed committal. A civil debt order is enforced in a similar way but there is no imprisonment for a civil debt (except for the enforcement of certain debts owed to the government such as income tax). Furthermore, a defaulter cannot be searched in civil debt proceedings nor can the magistrates (in contrast to the county court) make an attachment of earnings order. Finally, the complaint for a civil debt employs the usual provisions for civil procedure in the Magistrates' Courts Act 1980, Part II which makes it more difficult to issue a warrant in the first instance.

The bankrupt defaulter

During enforcement proceedings it may become apparent that the defaulter is, or is about to become, bankrupt. The court has two options. A fine (or costs and compensation) is provable in the debtor's bankruptcy. Therefore the court may take its chance in the bankruptcy and receive a payment from the bankruptcy proceedings. Although this procedure is available, it is not obligatory and instead the court may enforce the order in the usual way taking into account the debtor's financial circumstances after the bankruptcy.[11]

9 See (1982) 146 JP 762 (Practical Point).
10 See particularly MCA 1980, ss 92–96.
11 *Re Savundra* [1973] 3 All ER 406, [1974] 1 WLR 1147.

The lodging of fines

This refers to the case of a defaulter already in custody on other matters where the court commutes the payment of a fine into imprisonment to be served concurrent or consecutive to the existing sentence. Lodging may take place either because the defaulter invites the court to take this action, or the court may act of its own motion. However, the court cannot act without giving the defendant the right to make written or oral representations to the court.[12] The court has to decide, if it does lodge the fines (and the defaulter has no automatic right to have them lodged),[13] whether to make the term in default concurrent or consecutive to the existing sentence. It would be influenced in its decision by such factors as whether it would be fair to impose an extra custodial term for trivial matters, or whether it would be fair to extend an existing long custodial sentence.

Juveniles

In chapter 12 it is mentioned that the convicting court has the obligation in certain prescribed situations to make the parent or guardian responsible for the payment of a financial penalty which has been imposed on a juvenile. If the parent or guardian is made responsible, enforcement proceedings can be taken against the defaulting adult in the same way as against any other defaulter.

Where payment of the fine has been ordered against a juvenile, the court may enforce it against the juvenile directly, or against his parent or guardian. The methods of enforcement previously described are available against a juvenile with the exception of imprisonment. An attendance centre order can be made for a default but only after a means inquiry has been held.[14]

However, a juvenile usually has limited means and in these circumstances the court, after a means inquiry with the juvenile, can order the parent either to enter into a recognizance to ensure that the defaulter pays, or it can transfer the obligation to pay the sum due onto the adult. The court cannot make such an order for its own convenience, it must be first satisfied that the juvenile has had the means to pay and has refused or neglected to pay.[15]

Enforcement by the High Court

For the sake of completeness it should be mentioned that at a means inquiry the court may instruct the clerk to commence enforcement proceedings in the

12 *Re Hamilton, Re Forrest* [1981] AC 1038, [1981] 2 All ER 711.
13 *R v Leeds Prison Governor, ex p Huntley* [1972] 2 All ER 783, [1972] 1 WLR 1016.
14 Criminal Law Act 1977, s 36; MCA 1980, s 81(3).
15 MCA 1980, s 81.

county court or High Court. This action may be appropriate where certain enforcement procedures are not available to the magistrates. Such procedures are, for example, an attachment of earnings order for a civil debt, or garnishee proceedings.

Conclusions

The law of enforcement is complex and in the author's view unnecessarily so. The role of the advocate is necessarily limited by the unavailability of legal aid. Nevertheless it is important for a solicitor to have some knowledge of the subject in order to provide a complete service for his client. It is useful, to say the least, for a defendant to know whether he can have his fines lodged, whether he can seek relief from an overburdensome order to pay a fine within a specified number of days and what alternatives he may offer the court for repayment of a sum due.

Chapter 16

Civil proceedings

Magistrates' civil jurisdiction

The civil jurisdiction of a magistrates' court can conveniently be divided up into the following categories:

(1) Domestic proceedings.
(2) Powers of binding over.
(3) Enforcement of court orders.
(4) Licensing.
(5) Appeals from executive decisions.
(6) Orders requiring dogs to be kept under proper control or destroyed.
(7) Applications under the Police (Property) Act 1897.

The work of the magistrates' court in domestic proceedings is outside the scope of this book and the court's power of binding over and enforcement of court orders are dealt with in chapters 11 and 15 respectively.

The magistrates' court has a considerable jurisdiction in licensing matters covering the sale and consumption of alcohol and the regulation of betting and gaming and these matters are specialist subjects requiring separate consideration.[1] The justices do have a role as an appellate tribunal against decisions made by non-judicial bodies such as local authorities and the Driver and Vehicle Licensing Centre at Swansea.[2] Where an appeal may lie to the magistrates against a decision made by such a body such an appeal is a civil proceeding generally started by way of a complaint.[3]

This chapter is mainly concerned with those civil matters which would be of interest to a criminal lawyer namely orders requiring a dog to be kept under proper control, and applications under the Police (Property) Act.

1 See *Paterson's Licensing Acts* (editions produced annually).

2 Eg the right to appeal to a magistrates' court against the refusal of the grant of a licence to drive private hire vehicles (s 52 of the Local Government (Miscellaneous Provisions) Act 1976 or the right of appeal against the Secretary of State's refusal to grant a driving licence under s 87 of the Road Traffic Act 1972 (s 90 of the Road Traffic Act 1972)).

3 Magistrates' Courts Rules 1982, r 34 and see the Public Health Act 1936, s 300.

An outline of civil procedure

The provisions governing civil proceedings are contained in Part II of the Magistrates' Courts Act 1980 (ie ss 51–74), which deals inter alia with the commencing of proceedings, the hearing of a complaint and adjournment of a hearing. It is a separate code from Part I of the Act (ss 1–50) which deals with the commencement and hearing of criminal cases. Although separate parts of the Magistrates' Courts Act 1980 deal with the hearing of criminal and civil matters, the two jurisdictions share the remaining parts of the Act (Part III satisfaction and enforcement; Part IV witnesses and evidence; Part V appeal and case stated; Part VI recognizances; Part VII miscellaneous and supplementary) with any necessary modifications spelled out in the relevant statutory provisions.

Apart from domestic proceedings, it is not very common for the advocate to be involved in any civil proceedings in the magistrates' court and consequently it is very easy to forget that one is not dealing with criminal matters, so that for example, the Bail Act 1976 does not apply nor are there 'section 9' statements, nor does the defendant plead 'guilty' or 'not guilty'. A few of the more important distinctions between civil and criminal proceedings are sketched below.

COMMENCING PROCEEDINGS

Civil proceedings are started by the laying of a complaint, which is the same as an information in criminal matters. It is important, however, to make sure that the document has the correct title as civil proceedings incorrectly started by way of an information and criminal proceedings started by the laying of a complaint, will be invalid.[4]

The fact that the proceedings have been started by way of a complaint serves to show that the civil code of procedure must be followed. This means that, after due consideration of the complaint by a justice a summons may be issued to the defendant.[5] There is no power to issue a warrant directly after the laying of a complaint. The complaint must be laid before a justice for the commission area in which the matter complained of has taken place.[6]

If the summons has been duly served (proof of service being established in the same way as for a summons in criminal proceedings), but the defendant does not appear at the hearing, the court may at this stage issue a warrant for his arrest if the complaint has been substantiated on oath.[7] A warrant may be issued either with or without bail. As the Bail Act 1976 only applies to criminal proceedings, any bail

4 *R v Nottingham Justices, ex p Brown* [1960] 3 All ER 625, [1960] 1 WLR 1315.
5 MCA 1980, s 51.
6 Ibid, s 52.
7 Ibid, s 55.

in civil proceedings is still based on the concept of the defendant being released on his own recognizances, which means that he might be released (for example) on bail of £100. If he fails to surrender to his bail, he may be liable to forfeit all or part of the £100.

THE HEARING OF THE COMPLAINT

At the hearing of the complaint the court may proceed in the absence of the defendant provided it is satisfied that he was aware of the hearing date, or it may issue a warrant as described above, but if the defendant has given evidence, a warrant may not be issued thereafter.[7a] If the complainant fails to appear the court may dismiss the complaint or proceed in his absence if his evidence has already been received.[8]

Proceedings may of course be adjourned either generally (ie without fixing a date) or to a specified day. If, however, the defendant has been brought to court on a warrant the magistrates may wish to remand him, and if they do they must fix a date for the adjourned hearing. The usual rules about the length of an adjournment on a remand apply equally to civil proceedings.[9]

The procedure at the hearing is partly governed by section 53 of the Magistrates' Court Act 1980:

> (1) On the hearing of a complaint, the court shall, if the defendant appears, state to him the substance of the complaint.
> (2) The court, after hearing the evidence and the parties, shall make the order for which the complaint is made or dismiss the complaint.
> (3) . . .

Although the defendant does not plead guilty or not guilty and although it might appear that evidence has to be called in all cases, if the defendant does specifically admit the facts on which the complaint is based, the court may proceed without hearing evidence.[10]

The order of speeches is the same as in a criminal case with the complainant calling his evidence first.[11] In calling evidence the parties must bear in mind that the statutes on evidence and procedure which they are familiar with in criminal proceedings do not apply. Accordingly, statements admitted in evidence under section 9 of the Criminal Justice Act 1967 are not admissible. However, in civil proceedings matters not in dispute may be admitted in evidence with the agreement of the parties.[12]

7a Ibid, s 55.
8 Ibid, s 56.
9 Ibid, ss 128 and 129.
10 *Berkhamstead R.D.C. v Duerdin-Dutton* [1964] Crim LR 307, DC and p 396, (1964) 108 Sol Jo 157.
11 Magistrates' Courts Rules 1981, r 14.
12 Note also the provisions of the Civil Evidence Act 1938 concerning the admissibility of documentary evidence. (At the time of writing the provisions of ss 1–10 of the Civil Evidence Act 1968 have not been brought into force in relation to magistrates' courts).

Submission of no case to answer

At the conclusion of the complainant's case the defendant may make a submission of no case to answer. The submission is similar to that which can be made in criminal proceedings with the exception that the burden of proof is different and also that if a submission is made and is unsuccessful, the defendant may not thereafter call any further evidence. The court should put the defence solicitor to an election whether to make a submission of no case or call evidence.[13]

The magistrates' decision

The burden of proof in civil proceedings is on the balance of probabilities and not beyond reasonable doubt as in a criminal case. If the magistrates are satisfied by the complainant's evidence, they will announce that the complaint is proved, otherwise they will announce that the complaint is dismissed.

Costs

Central funds are only available for indictable matters in criminal proceedings and therefore a complainant or defendant seeking his costs may only obtain them against the other party.

The power to award costs is set out in section 64 of the Magistrates' Courts Act 1980:

> (1) On the hearing of a complaint, a magistrates' court shall have power in its discretion to make such order as to costs –
>
> (a) on making the order for which the complaint is made, to be paid by the defendant to the complainant;
>
> (b) on dismissing the complaint, to be paid by the complainant to the defendant,
>
> as it thinks just and reasonable; . . . .

Just as in the case of the award of costs in a purely summary case in criminal proceedings, the court must fix the amount of costs to be paid at the hearing; costs cannot be assessed afterwards by the clerk.

Correcting mistakes

There is no equivalent provision to section 142 of the Magistrates' Courts Act 1980 which allows the court to recall the case and correct any mistake after the court is functus officio.

Legal Aid

Apart from a complaint for a bind over, the magistrates' court cannot itself grant legal aid for a civil matter. Application has to be made to the Law Society.

Appeal

There is a right to appeal to the Crown Court by a person who has been

13 *Alexander v Rayson* [1936] 1 KB 169.

bound over or in certain proceedings involving appeals from decisions of local authorities,[14] but otherwise unless there is a specific right of appeal a person aggrieved by a decision of a magistrates' court in (non-domestic) civil proceedings may only appeal to the High Court by way of case stated, or apply to the High Court for judicial review of the decision.

Dangerous dogs

Section 2 of the Dogs Act 1871 provides:

> Any court of summary jurisdiction may take cognisance of any complaint that a dog is dangerous and not kept under proper control, and, if it appears that the dog is dangerous, may make an order for the dog to be kept by the owner under proper control or destroyed. . . .

This provision is commonly used where, for example, a domestic pet has escaped from his home and has bitten the nextdoor neighbour.[15] A complaint will be laid by the police who must allege that the dog *is* dangerous and *is* not under proper control, also that the defendant *is* the owner. The problems arise with the use of the word 'is'. Sometimes the dog changes ownership before the case arrives at court, in which case the new owner must be summoned. Then the police must establish the dog is currently dangerous, although this may be proved by his having bitten on the earlier occasion, also the dog's 'previous convictions' may be cited.[16] Finally it must establish that the dog is currently not under proper control; if it is dangerous but is under proper control no order can be made.

If the justices are satisfied with the complaint, they may make an order for the dog to be kept under proper control or destroyed. The magistrates have a discretion which order to make. The court could order the dog to be destroyed on its first 'conviction' although this would be extremely unusual. If a destruction order is made the owner may appeal to the Crown Court.[17]

It can happen that these proceedings are associated with criminal proceedings. Strictly, these proceedings should be kept separate from the criminal proceedings.[18] Problems could arise with the hearing of civil and criminal proceedings together, eg admissibility of evidence

14 Magistrates' Courts (Appeals from Binding Over Orders) Act 1956 and see ch 11 and, for example, Public Health Act 1936, s 301.

15 Eating the neighbour's pet rabbit may not be sufficient as it is in the nature of dogs to chase, wound and kill other small animals: *Sansom v Chief Constable of Kent* [1981] Crim LR 617.

16 *Maile v Lenton* (1982) Times, 9 February.

17 Dogs Amendment Act 1938, s 1.

18 *R v Dunmow Justices, ex p Anderson* [1964] 2 All ER 943, [1964] 1 WLR 1039.

and the differing burden of proof, but often where there is nothing in dispute the matters are dealt with at the same time.

Applications under the Police (Property) Act 1897

In the course of their work, the police may receive property into their possession and then have the problem of deciding how to dispose of it. For example, the trial court may have made a forfeiture order under section 43 of the Powers of Criminal Courts Act 1973 (forfeiture of articles used in the course of crime), or the police might be investigating an allegation of theft or receiving stolen goods. After the case has been concluded and the defendant convicted, the owners of the goods might remain unidentified. Before the police could dispose of the property they would wish to have protection against the true owner appearing and suing them for damages for disposing of his property. Conversely a person might lay claim to property in the possession of the police and wish to have an order requiring the goods to be handed over to him.

A dispute over property rights could always be resolved by litigation in the civil courts, but in a similar manner to the awarding of compensation in criminal cases, expensive litigation can be avoided in simple, straightforward cases by the magistrates making an order under the Police (Property) Act 1897. This provides:

> 1(1) Where any property has come into the possession of the police in connection with their investigation of a suspected offence . . . a court of summary jurisdiction may, on application either by an officer of the police or by a claimant of the property, make an order for the delivery of the property to the person appearing to the . . . court to be the owner thereof, or, if the owner cannot be ascertained, make such order with respect to the property as to the . . . court may seem meet.

The 'application' can be made by a complaint followed by summons or by way of an application with notices served on any interested parties.[19] The difference between the two procedures is that there is no power at all to award costs on the hearing of an *application* as the proceedings are not covered by section 64 of the Magistrates' Courts Act 1980.

If proceedings are started by way of complaint, for example by a claimant to the property in question, and the police appear as defendants and do not oppose the complaint, then it is improper to make any order for costs against the police. Even where the police do oppose the complaint but the court is satisfied that it was reasonable for them to do so to assist the court to assess the validity of the claim, it

19 *R v Uxbridge Justices, ex p Metropolitan Police Comr* [1981] 3 All ER 129, [1981] 3 WLR 410.

would be proper for no order for costs to be made against the police, even if the order for the delivery of the property sought by a claimant were made.

DISPOSAL OF PROPERTY[20]

Where no successful claim is made on the property in the possession of the police, they may sell the property, or if it is not in the public interest that it should be sold, it will be destroyed after the period for making a claim has expired or, in some circumstances, after a period of a year. Any moneys received by the police are used to defray expenses and the excess placed in a Police Property Act Fund out of which charitable donations may be made.

20 Police (Disposal of Property) Regulations 1975.

Appendix

The Legal Aid Act 1982

The Legal Aid Act 1982, which is being brought into force in stages, makes several fundamental amendments to the existing scheme of legal aid.

Section 1 makes provision for the setting up of Duty Solicitor Schemes on a national basis. Previously such schemes were arranged locally and the scope of the service provided would vary from area to area. A Duty Solicitor Scheme will be administered by a committee set up under section 15 of the Legal Aid Act 1974 and the committee may include a justices' clerk, a justice of the peace and such other additional members as the Lord Chancellor may direct.

Section 2 enables examining justices to grant legal aid both for the proceedings in the magistrates' court and, in the event of the defendant being committed, for proceedings in the Crown Court, thus making one continuous legal aid order.

Section 4 makes legal aid available for a defendant who is being dealt with for breach of a partly suspended sentence.

The most substantial changes to the present system for granting legal aid are, however, contained in sections 5–10.

It will have been apparent from chapter 4 that the present scheme for legal aid is not satisfactory. Criticism may be directed at two aspects in particular: the inconsistency in granting or refusing legal aid and the haphazard method of calculating the amount of contributions required when legal aid is granted in an individual case.

The Act, and the regulations to be made thereunder, propose to deal with these deficiencies by reforming the method of calculating contributions and by transferring some of the functions presently exercised by the magistrates' court to 'Legal Aid Committees'.

Contributions

It is proposed that the Legal Aid in Criminal Proceedings (General) Regulations 1968 be amended by regulations made under section 7 of the Act. If what is proposed is put into effect, the new scheme would make provision for an applicant's contribution to be calculated as follows:

His disposable income would be calculated by deducting from the income he actually receives (ie his net pay) allowances for his housing costs, the cost of his travel to work and allowances for his dependants. The allowances for dependants would be based on a figure 50% above the corresponding allowances for supplementary benefit.

The resulting figure will be the disposable income. The applicant will be entitled to have a 'free limit' of £40 per week before being called upon to make a contribution to his legal aid costs. This is a slightly higher limit than the equivalent rate for civil legal aid because the scheme will not include some of the discretionary allowances which are available in the civil scheme. One-quarter of the income above the free limit will be deemed to be available for a legal aid contribution. The full amount of any capital in excess of £2,500 (excluding the main dwelling house, personal and household effects and tools of his trade) will be available for a contribution.

If income rises or falls beyond certain limits, the assessment of the contribution will be subject to reassessment.

If legal aid is granted and the applicant is liable to make a contribution, he will have to pay either in full forthwith if his means are such that this is possible, or by weekly instalments. These instalments would start seven days from the date of the grant of legal aid (ie in most cases before the actual court hearing). It is felt that these instalments should not extend beyond a specified maximum period (one proposal is for a maximum period of 12 months). The amount of each instalment is to be fixed according to a predetermined scale, eg where the disposable income is £40–£46 per week the contribution would be payable at £1 per week, £46–50 per week at £2 per week and so on. Should an applicant fail to pay these instalments, he would be invited to give an explanation for his failure and in the absence of a satisfactory explanation his legal aid would be revoked forthwith.

The grant and refusal of legal aid

In chapter 4 it was explained that the grant of legal aid depended on the application satisfying two criteria: that the applicant's means are such that he requires assistance and that the interests of justice require that he be represented. The new provisions would not alter these requirements, but they would amend the way in which an application is considered.

The new proposals envisage that an application would be made to the justices' clerk in the usual way. He would have power to grant the application, but not, in the case of purely summary offences, refuse it. If the clerk were not inclined to grant the application, it would be referred to a magistrate who would make the final decision whether to grant or refuse legal aid. However, in the case of a specified category of offences (such as indictable and either way offences), the clerk would have the power to refuse the application. In situations where the clerk has refused the application, the applicant could re-apply to the legal aid committee, but only where the application was refused on the 'interests of justice' criterion. In any event, the court would have a final discretion whether to grant legal aid in a particular case.

Other functions of the legal aid committee

Section 5 of the Legal Aid Act 1982 provides for the legal aid committees to exercise further functions in respect of legal aid, namely the power to allow representation by solicitor and counsel in the magistrates' courts (section 30 of the Legal Aid Act 1974) and the amendment and revocation of legal aid orders (section 31 of the Legal Aid Act 1974).

In addition, the committee would have the power to authorise expenditure in advance in a similar way to that in civil legal aid (rule 62 of the Legal Aid (General) Regulations 1980).

Initially the application for representation by counsel would be made to the justice's clerk. If it were refused, application could then be made to the legal aid committee. Even if the committee refused the application, the court might still grant the application, after, for example, hearing further information or being made aware of a change of circumstances.

General comments

The new proposals seek to ensure a greater consistency in the consideration of legal aid applications. The proposals for the assessment of contributions will, at last, provide a coherent framework for these calculations and provide some conformity of practice.

As regards the proposals for the granting or refusing or legal aid, these will ensure that the decision to grant in straightforward cases will continue to be made expeditiously by the justices' clerk and those cases where the decision is not clear cut and where perhaps fuller consideration is necessary, will be decided more consistently by legal aid committees rather than by individual justices or magistrates' courts. However, it remains to be seen whether recourse to a committee can be made in sufficient time not to cause delay to the criminal process.

Index